FRAUDS, MYTHS, AND MYSTERIES

Science and Pseudoscience in Archaeology

EIGHTH EDITION

KENNETH L. FEDER

Central Connecticut State University

FRAUDS, MYTHS, AND MYSTERIES: SCIENCE AND PSEUDOSCIENCE IN ARCHAEOLOGY, EIGHTH EDITION

Published by McGraw-Hill, a business unit of The McGraw-Hill Companies, Inc., 1221 Avenue of the Americas, New York, NY, 10020. Copyright © 2014 by The McGraw-Hill Companies, Inc. All rights reserved. Printed in the United States of America. Previous editions © 2011, 2008, and 2006. No part of this publication may be reproduced or distributed in any form or by any means, or stored in a database or retrieval system, without the prior written consent of The McGraw-Hill Companies, Inc., including, but not limited to, in any network or other electronic storage or transmission, or broadcast for distance learning.

Some ancillaries, including electronic and print components, may not be available to customers outside the United States.

This book is printed on acid-free paper.

1 2 3 4 5 6 7 8 9 0 DOC/DOC 1 0 9 8 7 6 5 4 3

ISBN 978-0-07-803507-4
MHID 0-07-803507-4

Senior Vice President, Products & Markets: *Kurt L. Strand*
Vice President, General Manager, Products & Markets: *Michael Ryan*
Vice President, Content Production & Technology Services: *Kimberly Meriwether David*
Executive Director of Development: *Lisa Pinto*
Managing Director: *Gina Boedeker*
Brand Manager: *Courtney Austermehle*
Editorial Coordinator: *Adina Lonn*
Marketing Specialist: *Alexandra Schultz*
Managing Development Editor: *Penina Braffman*
Director, Content Production: *Terri Schiesl*
Project Manager: *Erin Melloy*
Buyer: *Jennifer Pickel*
Cover Image: *Kenneth Feder*
Typeface: *10/12.5, Palatino LT*
Compositor: *Laserwords Private Limited*
Printer: *R. R. Donnelley*

All credits appearing on page or at the end of the book are considered to be an extension of the copyright page.

Library of Congress Cataloging-in-Publication Data
Feder, Kenneth L.
  Frauds, myths, and mysteries : science and pseudoscience in archaeology /
Kenneth L. Feder, Central Connecticut State University.—Eighth edition.
    pages cm
  ISBN 978-0-07-803507-4 (alk. paper)
  1. Forgery of antiquities. 2. Archaeology. I. Title.
  CC140.F43 2014
  930.1—dc23
      2012051771

The Internet addresses listed in the text were accurate at the time of publication. The inclusion of a website does not indicate an endorsement by the authors or McGraw-Hill, and McGraw-Hill does not guarantee the accuracy of the information presented at these sites.

www.mhhe.com

For Murray H. Feder, Ph.D.
February 23, 1925- August 3, 2012
My teacher. My mentor. My father.

Brief Contents

Contents

5   **Who Discovered America? 97**

6   **Who's Next? After the Indians, Before Columbus 119**

Preface

Frauds, Myths, and Mysteries: The Book That Almost Never Was

If anyone predicted, back in 1986 when I first began circulating the manuscript for this book, that in 2013 I'd be working on its eighth edition, that the book would be used in college courses all across the United States and Canada, and that cable television documentarians would regularly invite me to be a talking head concerning topics dealt with in the book, I would have thought they were crazy. I no longer remember the precise number of rejection letters my unsolicited manuscript initially produced; I stopped counting at sixteen. Those letters were dreary in their sameness—metaphorical pats on the head for producing an "unusual manuscript" that seemed very interesting, but not one that might lead to a book that archaeologists would be willing to consider for adoption in their courses. After all, the rejection letters maintained, a semester is already too short a period of time to cover all the methodology that should be covered in an introductory archaeology course. That same semester framework, I was told, hardly allowed sufficient time in a world prehistory survey course to cover the breadth of genuine human antiquity, let alone the deadends of frauds and myths. There just wouldn't be enough time in standard archaeology and prehistory courses, or so the rejection letters maintained, to include a deconstruction of preexisting misapprehensions students might harbor about the archaeological record and its study. And while the book seemed well suited to a course dedicated to the discussion of popular misconceptions about antiquity—the discussion, in fact, of "frauds, myths, and mysteries" about the human past—the unanimous opinion of the rejection letter writers was that there couldn't be very many such courses in the first place.

All that changed when I approached Jan Beatty, then an editor at Mayfield Publishing. I knew Jan from another book of mine and I passed the *Frauds* manuscript along to her hoping she could suggest the name of a small publisher who might be willing to take a chance on my *Frauds* book, never really thinking that Mayfield would be interested. Jan read through it, called, and, to my surprise, suggested that before I sent it to anyone else she would send it out for review for Mayfield's consideration. At the time, I thought that she and the Mayfield crew did this merely as a favor to me. I was wrong. Jan is a terrific editor with a great track record for signing successful anthropology texts and saw potential in the *Frauds* book where others didn't. Mayfield published the book and when McGraw-Hill bought out Mayfield it continued publishing it. The fact that this book has been in print now for more than twenty years and is going into its eighth edition is a direct reflection of its success, a success made possible by Jan's vision. She must have been psychic or something. Kidding. I am forever grateful for her support.

What's in the Eighth Edition?

I guess I should almost be thankful for the ever-busy purveyors of nonsense about the human past. Almost. Without their diligent efforts to concoct new scenarios about human antiquity wholly unsupported by archaeological data, it wouldn't be necessary for me to constantly update *Frauds*; students would be able to rely on old, recycled, and less expensive versions of the book; and "poof," there would go my royalties. So here's a big shout out of thanks to the tellers of tall tales about lost continents, ancient astronauts, wayfaring Celts, doomsaying Maya, and all the rest. I couldn't do it without you. Or, at least, I wouldn't need to.

There's a lot of new material in this eighth edition of *Frauds*, and I've cycled out some stuff that's no longer current. All of the chapters are updated. Some of the most important specific additions are:

- Chapter 1: I'm including the responses to a new survey question I have been posing to my students concerning the alleged 2012 Maya apocalypse. I've also added more detail about the Nazi misuse of archaeology.

- Chapter 2: In my discussion of Occam's razor, I now apply it to the seventeenth-century explanation of deeply buried stone tools in Europe.

- Chapter 4: I have updated, as I must in each edition, my discussion of the evidence for human evolution.

- Chapter 5: I've made substantial and significant changes to the sections focused on the archaeology of the first settlers of the New World. There's new stuff on the molecular archaeology of the first Americans and a greatly expanded and revised section on pre-Clovis, focused on the Manis and Debra L. Friedkin sites.

- Chapter 6: I have made an effort to tighten up, and make more succinct, my presentation of the evidence for pre-Columbian human visitation to the New World within a general context of how the historical sciences can test hypotheses through a "convergence of evidence" (Sherman and Grobman 2000). My focus has shifted from a highly detailed debunking of specific claims, to a tighter focus on how historians and archaeologists can assess them.

- Chapter 8: I've included a statistical comparison between Plato's description of Atlantis and the actual archaeological record of Minoan Crete. The two turn out to be wholly unalike. Who knew?

- Chapter 9: On the topic of ancient aliens, I have included the insightful perspectives of researchers Cartman, Marsh, McCormick, and Broflovski.

- Chapter 10: I've expanded my discussion of Egyptian pyramid building and added an FAQ about Egyptian tomb curses; they did exist, but there wasn't one on Tut's tomb.

- Chapter 11: I've updated the section on how archaeologists really find and excavate sites, focusing on my 2011 field school at an ancient soapstone quarry in Connecticut. I've thoroughly updated the Current Perspectives section, discussing how the real technology of remote sensing is far cooler than psychic archaeology. It also has a distinct advantage over psychic power; it actually works.

- Chapter 12: Because the supporters of these perspectives are always working, as I have done in each edition of *Frauds*, I've had to dramatically update my discussion of scientific creationism and intelligent design and the impacts these are having on science education in the United States.

- Chapter 13: I have reorganized and revamped the section on the Maya and, especially, the Maya apocalypse; if it did actually occur on December 21, 2012, you wouldn't be reading this anyway, so the addition of all this new stuff would be moot.

Special Features of *Frauds*

- A Quick Start Guide follows this Preface. Like the quick start guides you may sometimes receive with new software, the Quick Start Guide for *Frauds* provides a quick summary, in this case, of how to assess claims made in the name of science in general, and the study of the human past, in particular.

- Each chapter has an associated **Frequently Asked Questions** section. These questions represent a sample of queries from my students over the years that relate specifically to the issues and controversies addressed in the chapter.

- The informal, uncontrolled, unfiltered, and freewheeling context of the web continues to have exciting implications for disseminating information about the human past. These same qualities of the Internet, however, also mean that more misinformation about the past can be spread to a far greater number of people far more quickly. Tall tales about the human past no longer need rely on word of mouth to be spread; anyone with a computer and an Internet provider can shout such nonsense to the world. The good news here is that archaeologists can shout back. There are many fine websites presenting genuine archaeological discoveries and some that respond explicitly to the nonsense that dogs our discipline. Each chapter includes an annotated list under the title **Best of the Web** with a selection of websites (and their Internet addresses) put up by museums, individual archaeologists (amateur and professional), anthropology departments, and others. A brief description of what each of these sites presents is also given. Don't look for the bizarre, absurd, extreme, or nonsensical on my lists. These sites are produced by people who conduct field research, analyze artifacts and sites, and are committed to the scientific interpretation of the human past.

- To make it easier to locate and scan the Best of the Web sites, the *Frauds* home page is available at www.mhhe.com/frauds8e. Every website listed in the Best of the Web sections of *Frauds* is linked to and accessible through the *Frauds* page. Instead of typing in the URLs, you need only get onto the *Frauds* page. From there, click on the Student Edition link. Then click on the Best of the Web link. This brings up a chapter-by-chapter listing of links to the websites listed under Best of the Web in the book. Simply click on any of the URLs and you will be taken to that site.

- Each chapter presents **Critical Thinking Exercises.** In these I attempt to challenge the reader to apply the scientific method and scientific reasoning to the general issues raised in the specific archaeological examples that are at the core of each chapter. In answering the questions posed or in carrying out the specific exercise, the reader must be able to synthesize and apply the most important messages of the chapter.

- The Video Companion Guide can be found on the *Frauds* website. The purpose of this guide is twofold: (1) to direct readers to helpful video documentaries of the topics covered in each of the chapters of this book and (2) to assist the professor who is looking for audiovisual material to accompany this book in a university course.

Acknowledgments

A published book is always a collaborative effort and I am truly grateful for all of the work done by the usual group of suspects at McGraw-Hill. It has been especially terrific working with the usual gang of suspects at the McGraw-Hill mothership, especially Craig Leonard who has been fantastic in shepherdeing me through the entire process. Also, thanks are due to managing editor Penina Braffman whose managing has been tip-top, and Managing Director Gina Boedeker whose, um, management has been so well directed. Thanks as well to Project Manager Erin Melloy, my truly fabulous copyeditor Susan Nodine and a special shout out to the folks at Laserwords. Ligo; though you are half a world away, we were always on the same page.

Friends, colleagues, and critics as well contributed in various ways to the successful completion of this edition of *Frauds*. For their always thoughtful corrections and probing, for the role some served as a sounding board, for their generosity with their photographs, reprints, and expertise I would like to thank Terry Barnhart, Nick Bellantoni, Richard Boisvert, Deborah Bolnick, Bob Brier, Jarrod Burks, Jon Erlandson, John Gifford, Jean-Pierre Houdin, Brad Lepper, Kevin McBride, David Mills, Brona Simon, Charlotte C. W. Taylor, and Michael Waters. I would also like to give a special thanks to Jenn Davis whose illustrations are amazing and for being generally amazing herself.

Reviewers make a crucial contribution to a new edition of a book. Usually, these folks are using the current version in the classroom and are acutely aware of what works and what doesn't and, especially in the case of *Frauds,* what misconceptions are currently bedeviling those who teach archaeology. Many grateful thanks to the reviewers of this edition: Lisa Becker, *Anoka-Ramsey Community College*; Ricardo Fernandez, *Ball State University*; Linda Jencson, *Appalachian State University*; Marc Levine, *University of Colorado*; Kenneth Lewis, *Michigan State University*; Ben Marwick, *University of Washington*; Heather McKillop, *Louisiana State University*; Sean Rafferty, *University of Albany*; and Curtis Runnels, *Boston University*.

Thanks as always to my father, Dr. Murray H. Feder, for his historical insights, splendid photographs, and late-night phone calls. Thanks as well to my mother, who complained that she didn't get appropriate acknowledgment in a previous edition of this book. It was an oversight, Mom. This book has grown up with Josh, my now twenty-six-year-old son. In fact, one of Josh's first intelligible sequences of words referred to my disappearing into my office every afternoon to work on the first edition: "Dada work, book." More than twenty years later it's nice to know that he still finds its content interesting enough to want to occasionally chat with his old man about it, though I don't think he's that impressed that I apparently have a "fan club" in Holland. My nineteen-year-old son, Jacob, continues to be amused when he sees his dad on the television being interviewed about Atlantis, the Cardiff Giant, or human sacrifice in ancient New Hampshire. After one of the supporters of the ancient astronaut hypothesis had his say in a recently broadcast documentary about ancient astronauts in which I participated, Jacob turned to me and asked, "What is that guy smoking?" It made me so proud. Well, sort of.

Quick Start Guide

I have just purchased a digital camera. There is a thick manual that I understand I will need to read to be able to use the camera to its fullest capability, but I want to get started—I want to jump ahead a bit and take the thing out for a spin. Fortunately, the camera came with a highly condensed version of the key information contained in the manual. It's called the *Quick Start Guide*, and it provides a very brief, succinct summary of the information needed to begin using the camera.

It occurs to me that this book is, in fact, a thick manual focusing on how to think about the human past. Certainly, you need to read the entire "manual" to understand what you need to know to assess claims made about human antiquity, but the equivalent of a quick start guide would be a useful prelude to the book. My version of a quick start guide follows.

During the time it takes you to read this book, you will likely encounter—in newspapers and magazines, on television shows, in books, and on websites—assertions about the human past that contradict views widely accepted by archaeologists. Some of these claims can easily be proven false, but some may be accurate. How can you assess the validity of an extraordinary claim or revolutionary interpretation about the human past that appears in popular media? Though there is no simple way to determine accuracy absolutely, you can make a good start in your assessment by answering the following questions:

◈ Where is the particular claim or discovery presented? Is it in an article in a peer-reviewed journal, where other scientists in the same field have had an opportunity to appraise its validity and comment on it? Does the story appear in a widely respected magazine with science advisors on its staff, in a newspaper article written by an experienced science writer, or in a television news report or special series produced by a national network or a science-based organization? These are all sources that we can feel confident in. Of course, they are not perfect, mistakes are made, and some claims or hypotheses may turn out to be false, but they usually check their facts and apply the scientific method (see Chapter 2). On the other hand, is the report about the human past found on an anonymous website with no attributed source, in the informal discussions of an Internet chat group, or in an audiovisual presentation prepared by an individual affiliated with a political or religious organization with a particular axe to grind? In these cases, it is wise to be skeptical about the objectivity of the source and the accuracy of the claim.

◈ Who is making the claim? Is it a trained scientist? Just as important, is it a researcher trained in archaeology, anthropology, or history? Remember, a scientist skilled in an unrelated field may be no better prepared than a nonscientist to assess an archaeological discovery or interpretation. Certainly, researchers with Ph.D.s in archaeology, anthropology, or history make mistakes in their chosen fields, but they are less likely to make mistakes on issues related to the human past than are people with little experience or study in those fields.

◈ In assessing the validity of any assertion about the human past that appears in popular media, you need to ask yourself the following:

How does the person announcing the discovery, making the claim, or interpreting the results of a study "know"? Does the discussion or claim seem to follow standard scientific thinking as presented in this and other books that explain how science works (see Table 2.4)? Are hypotheses based on observations? Are hypotheses tested with independent data? Among a series of explanations offered for some phenomenon, is the simplest one (with no other unsupported assumptions) presented as the most probable? Or does the claimant instead assert that his or her knowledge is simply the result of revelation, intuition, or faith and that no proof is needed?

◈ Are other experts consulted, and how do they respond to the claims being made? Are other scientists convinced? Are other scientists uncertain, skeptical, but intrigued? Are other scientists quite certain the claims are unfounded, and on what basis are they so skeptical? Are alternate points of view offered; are other interpretations presented? Accepting the authority of scientists just because they have diplomas or teach at prestigious universities is a mistake, but when experienced researchers working in the same field are universally skeptical, it's a pretty good idea for you to be skeptical too—unless and until supporting data are forthcoming.

◈ Are confirming data presented? Are the "petrified giant," the humanlike cranium with the apelike jaw, the Hebrew tablet in the ancient archaeological site in Ohio, and other archaeological "mysteries" unique, one-of-a-kind objects, or are scientists able to confirm the validity of these by finding additional examples?

◈ Is enough information presented for you to make an informed decision concerning the legitimacy of what is being asserted? Or, instead, are you left with important questions that the report simply does not address?

Analyze new ideas about the human past with the same careful approach you would apply when purchasing a used car. Have an open mind, of course, but be skeptical of claims that can't be backed up with hard facts.

 **1**

Science and Pseudoscience

Extrasensory perception. Astrology. Faith healing. Alien abductions. Psychic cats. Ancient astronauts. Crop circles. If all of the claims related to these and other supposed phenomena were true, this world would be an extraordinarily strange place, far different from what orthodox science would suppose.

For example, aliens from outer space would regularly fly over the earth, kidnap people, and perform medical exams on them, with a particular emphasis on a best left unmentioned bodily orifice. Along with their medical research, the aliens would flatten farmers' wheat crops, leaving monumentally scaled, perplexing, but beautiful designs in their fields. Oh, and no fewer than a dozen such "space aliens" would have served in the U.S. Senate (which, come to think of it, would explain a lot of what goes on there).

People could read minds, and your future could be predicted by shuffling and dealing a special deck of playing cards (called Tarot). A sixteenth-century physician could have predicted the September 11 attack on the United States with chilling accuracy. Wearing a quartz crystal suspended on a chain around your neck would make you more energetic. The exact location and positioning of your furniture and the orientation of the stairway leading to the second floor of your house would play a substantial role in determining your health as well as your economic and psychological well-being. The same rules would apply to other animals and, as a result, it would be entirely reasonable that in February 2007 the Los Angeles Zoo paid $4,500 to a feng shui consultant to make sure that the physical design of the new enclosure being built for three golden monkeys would afford them a strong life force. Lucky monkeys.

Furthermore, the precise locations of enormously distant celestial bodies at the instant of your birth would determine your personality as well as your future. And, of course, the ancient Maya of Central America predicted that the world would come to an end on December 21, 2012. Because you are still alive and reading this, I guess that particular "prediction" wasn't so accurate after all. Maybe next year.

There's more. Plants would think and have feelings and dolphins would write poetry. Autism could be cured through exorcism (though, to be honest, in the one cited case, the child died during the procedure), which begs the question, how did they know the kid was cured or, chillingly, how exactly did they define "cure"? Some people would spontaneously burst into flames for no apparent reason; and tiny ridges on your hands, bumps on your head, and even the shape of your behind could be used to understand your personality.

In this extraordinary version of the world, it might not be a bad idea to insure yourself against the possibility of being abducted by extraterrestrials. I am not making this up: I personally am covered for $10 million (for the low, low price of $19.95, as offered by an insurance agency in Florida). My heirs can double this payment to $20 million if they are able to prove that the aliens ate me! Finally, in this most peculiar world, human prehistory could best be understood as the result of supernatural occurrences, enormous cataclysms, and the interference of extraterrestrial space aliens.

It would be a strange world indeed, and the list of extreme, mysterious, and occult claims goes on and on (Figure 1.1). For many of you, some of these claims—all of which have actually been published—might at least seem to be interesting to think about. Some of you might believe them.

Belief in the Unbelievable

Well if you find yourself in agreement with at least some of these claims, rest assured you are not alone. In 2007, the Associated Press in conjunction with the Ipsos News Center research organization polled more than 1,000 adults on paranormal phenomena, with the results shown in Table 1.1.

Table 1.1 *Ipsos News Center 2007 Opinion Survey*

Believe in ghosts	34%
Have seen a ghost	23
Believe in extrasensory perception	48
Believe that UFOs are extraterrestrial spacecraft	43
Have seen a UFO	14
Believe in the efficacy of spells and witchcraft	19
Admit to being superstitious	20

Source: USA Today, October 26, 2007.

Noah's Ark Found in Iran

Mayans Had Contact with Aliens

Railway Station Found on Mars

Alien Mummy Goes on Rampage

Scientists Create Alligator-Chickens (save money on feeding; they can eat themselves)

Scientists Capture Leprechaun

Obama Releases Chupacabra into Arizona (to force them to change state immigration policy)

Alien Spaceships to Attack in November (2011)

Mystery Panties in Ohio (3,000 pairs found scattered in Fairfield County)

Zombies Join Occupy Wall Street Protest

Figure 1.1 Actual headlines as they appeared in issues of tabloid, or "supermarket," newspapers.

So essentially, more than one-third of the sample believed in ghosts and nearly one-quarter had seen one. At the same time, nearly half believed in ESP and just a little shy of that believed that UFOs are extraterrestrial aircraft.

In a AP-GfK poll conducted late in 2011, about 77 percent of the 1,000 people surveyed expressed some belief in angels. More recently, the National
Geographic Society conducted a poll in conjunction with the launch of its
new show called *UFO Chasers*. From the results, it concluded that 36 percent
of Americans now believe that UFOs exist, only 17 percent are skeptics, and
2 percent, apparently, would shoot an extraterrestrial if they saw one
(DiBliaso 2012).

High levels of belief in things like ESP, UFOs, and angels are not
restricted to the United States. In a 2007 poll conducted in Great Britain,
38 percent of the people questioned believed in ghosts (36 percent of those
believers claim to actually have seen one), 41 percent accepted the reality of
telepathy (the ability to read another person's mind), and 31 percent thought
that world governments are currently concealing evidence of the existence of
extraterrestrial aliens.

Perhaps the public is generally accepting of such claims, unaware that
there isn't very much scientific evidence for any of them. One might hope, however, that bright, highly educated college students would be more skeptical—
open-minded, of course, but understanding that without clear scientific evidence ghosts, telepathy, astrology, angels, and the like remain unverified, wor-
thy, perhaps, of further study, but certainly not proven phenomena.

Poll results show, however, that this isn't necessarily the case.

For example, I have taken several surveys of college students at various
institutions (Feder 1984, 1987, 1995b, 1998), and there is a depressingly high
level of belief in unsubstantiated claims about the human past even among
university students. Check out the graphs (Figure 1.2) for the opinions of
my students over the past nineteen years on two of the topics I ask about:
the Lost Continent of Atlantis (see Chapter 8) and the assertion that extraterrestrial aliens visited earth in antiquity (see Chapter 10). Both of these topics
are current favorites of cable documentaries, with the latter even being the
focus of its own series (*Ancient Aliens*) on the History Channel. You can see
from the graphs that student opinion about these claims has varied over the
years since my first survey in 1983. Right now, I think largely as a result of
those aforementioned cable documentaries and the *Ancient Aliens* series, a
substantial group (a little more than 31 percent) of the students entering my
introductory course in archaeology agree, either strongly or mildly, with the
statement: "There is good evidence for the existence of the Lost Continent of
Atlantis." In that same sample, 30 percent agree with the statement: "Aliens
from other worlds visited the earth in the prehistoric past." Both of these
claims are demonstrably wrong, as we will see later in this book.

It is early in 2012 as I am writing this and, as you likely are aware,
there is a common conception (a misconception, but more about that in
Chapter 13) that the ancient Maya people of Central America predicted the
end of the world for December of this year (i.e., 2012). I asked students in

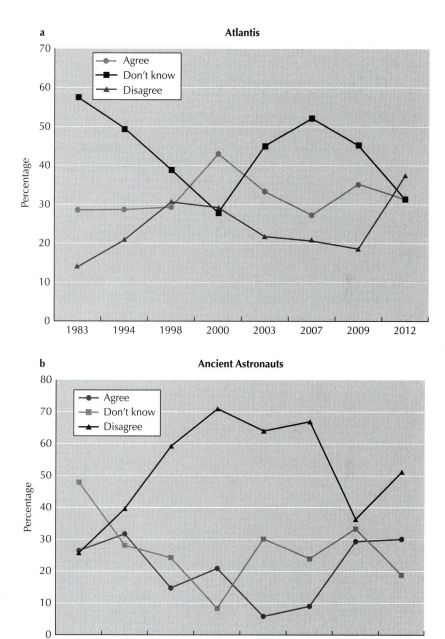

Figure 1.2 Percentage of my students in 1983, 1994, 1998, 2000, 2003, 2007, 2009, and 2012 who agreed with, were not sure about (didn't know), or disagreed with the statements: (a) "There is good evidence for the existence of the Lost Continent of Atlantis" (b) "Aliens from other worlds visited the earth in the prehistoric past."

my current survey if they agreed with the statement: "The ancient Maya people predicted the world would end on December 21, 2012." Figure 1.3 shows the results. Though a healthy percentage (35 percent) of my students strongly disagreed with that assertion, 13.75 percent strongly agreed and another 18.75 percent mildly agreed. Adding those figures up produces a statistic of 32.5 percent, just about one-third, who agreed to some extent that the Maya predicted that the end time would occur at the end of 2012. I guess I should have asked how many were planning to exchange Christmas presents early that year, you know, just in case the Maya were right.

Okay, clearly I'm skeptical about this stuff, but it is certainly fair to ask if the kinds of beliefs or claims mentioned in the surveys discussed here can be dismissed so easily. "Science," after all, is merely a process of understanding the world around us through the application of logical thought (see Chapter 2). Most of us like to think of ourselves as scientific-minded, but is science perfect? Do scientists know everything? Are they always right? Of course not. Science has scoffed at things in the past that eventually turned out to be true (see the discussion of meteors in Chapter 2). Maybe scientists are wrong to dismiss a lot of other interesting claims. Maybe there is more to some of them than closed-minded scientists are willing to admit. There could be something to UFOs, ESP, astrology, reincarnation, dowsing, the Chupacabra, Bigfoot, the Loch Ness Monster, ancient aliens, faith healing,

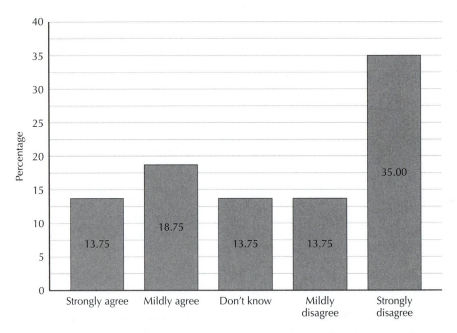

Figure 1.3   The ancient Maya people predicted the world would end on December 21, 2012

and so on; magazines, television, and movies flaunt these topics frequently. They can't all be fake, can they?

I have a confession to make. I used to read books on flying saucers and psychic power. I owned a Ouija board and a pendulum, and I analyzed handwriting and conducted ESP tests. I felt that there had to be some truth to these interesting ideas.

But it bothered me that the results of my ESP tests never really deviated from chance expectations, and my Ouija board didn't work at all. I owned a small telescope and spent a lot of time looking at the nighttime sky, but I never saw anything that did not have some natural or ordinary explanation (an airplane, helicopter, blimp, bird, satellite, star, planet, or whatever). Yet I kept searching. Like most people, I was fascinated by these possibilities rejected by orthodox science. In truth, I wanted to believe.

In the late 1960s, lured by the promise of four books for a dollar in the introductory offer, I signed up for a book club catering to occult tastes. In return, I received *The Complete, Illustrated Book of the Psychic Sciences; Yoga, Youth, and Reincarnation; The Black Arts;* and *The Morning of the Magicians.* The first three contained interesting little tidbits that seemed perfectly reasonable to me at the time: evidence of "real" hauntings and prophetic dreams, the usefulness of astrology, testimony about people's subconscious memories of past lives, and so on. The yoga book, along with some strange claims about reincarnation, actually taught some healthy exercises.

It was the fourth book, though, that really opened my eyes. Without their knowing it, the authors of this marvelous collection of outrageous claims, Louis Pauwels and Jacques Bergier (1960), played an important role in converting me from a completely credulous individual, open to all sorts of absolutely absurd ideas, to a scientific rationalist, still open to the possibility of all sorts of absolutely absurd ideas, but demanding substantial evidence that, unfortunately, their claims all seemed to lack.

The Morning of the Magicians

Remarkable claims about things scientists were trying to hide from the public filled *The Morning of the Magicians*—evidence for reincarnation, levitation, ghosts, and so on. As always when I read most of these books, the first claim left me excited and fascinated. The second claim provided almost the same sense of intellectual exhilaration. But the third, fourth, fifth, and sixth were just more of the same. I slowly began to lose the ability to be surprised by the authors' claims of effective magical incantations, telepathy, the mystically engineered transformation of lead to gold, and the like. As exciting as any one of these claims might have been, the cumulative effect was simply a buildup of an intellectual resistance to surprise. I became immune to the claims. I was bored.

In skimming through the book, I found a section on remarkable discoveries in prehistoric archaeology related to the occult. It surprised me that there was any archaeology in the book at all; I had never considered connections between the paranormal and archaeology. Fascinated by the possibilities, I immediately began to read that section.

The authors' extraordinarily strange view of the past is best summed up in their own words:

> It is possible that our civilization is the result of a long struggle to obtain
> from machines the powers that primitive man possessed, enabling
> him to communicate from a distance, to rise into the air, to liberate the
> energy of matter, abolish gravitation, etc. (Pauwels and Bergier 1960:109)

In other words, according to the authors of *The Morning of the Magicians*, today we are simply rediscovering abilities that prehistoric people had—the ability to fly, to harness the energy of the atom, and to communicate electronically, for example. Although today we do so with machines, prehistoric people apparently could do it with their minds. Pauwels and Bergier were honest enough; they had entirely, openly, and unabashedly abandoned a skeptical approach: "No hypothesis is excluded: an atomic civilization long before what we call the prehistoric era; enlightenment received from the inhabitants of Another World, etc." (p. 105).

On simple facts, they were consistently wrong. These were things that might not be noticed by a nonarchaeologist. For example, they stated that the Toltecs built the Pyramid of the Sun at the Mexican site of Teotihuacán (p. 115). That's like saying that billionaire real estate developer Donald Trump built the White House. Teotihuacán was at its peak more than 700 years before the Toltecs rose to power.

They stated that the Maya civilization of Mesoamerica is "far older than that of Greece" (p. 115). Yet classical Greece dates to well over 2,500 years ago, whereas the Maya civilization was at its peak more than 1,000 years later, barely 1,500 years ago.

How, I wondered, could authors who seemed so well informed about physics, psychology, chemistry, biology, and history be so confused when it came to my own field of archaeology? How could they so eloquently "prove" the existence of all sorts of occult things related to these other fields of science and be so lacking in their knowledge of the human past?

Then it struck me. Of all the disciplines discussed in *The Morning of the Magicians*, archaeology was the only one with which I had more than just a passing familiarity. The more I thought about it, the clearer it became. The often bizarre claims in *The Morning of the Magicians* that were related to physics, chemistry, biology, psychology, and history seemed plausible to me primarily because I did not have the knowledge necessary to assess them intelligently.

It was a valuable lesson indeed. The authors had not mysteriously abandoned scholarly research and the scientific method (see Chapter 2 of this book) only in the one field in which I was well versed. As I looked further into their claims, it became obvious that they had ignored the truth in just about every phenomenon they had described.

I began to read a number of books written by scientists in various fields who had been similarly appalled by the extreme claims made by occultists like Pauwels and Bergier. Again and again, I saw reactions and arguments that mirrored mine after reading the prehistory section of *The Morning of the Magicians*. When astronomers analyzed claims about extraterrestrial life, astrology, and UFOs; when psychologists examined telepathy and clairvoyance; when physicists and chemists investigated alleged evidence for perpetual motion machines or alchemy, they were nearly unanimous in their skepticism. In other words, claims that may have sounded good to me could easily be discounted, disproven, and disposed of by people who knew more than just a little bit about them. All those interesting occult claims that had fascinated me could be shown to be, at best, highly speculative and unproven or, at worst, complete nonsense.

Pseudoscience and Archaeology

I then began to search out more of the unsubstantiated, occult, and speculative claims that were being made about the prehistoric past by people who, it seemed, were wholly ignorant of modern archaeology. I have been doing this ever since, and it has been a surprisingly fruitful, sometimes hilarious, often depressing search. Little did I realize when I began to read *The Morning of the Magicians* how popular archaeological occultism and fraud are.

No one can deny that archaeology generates a great deal of public interest. People are fascinated by subjects like pyramids, cave paintings, human evolution, Stonehenge, and the Maya. Archaeology survives because people are interested enough in it to take courses, go to museums, visit sites, and buy books about it—including this book.

Sadly, some attempt to exploit this interest by making unsubstantiated claims about the discoveries made in this fascinating field. *The Morning of the Magicians* was not the first, and it certainly will not be the last, of the published, printed, spoken, filmed, or televised attempts to twist and pervert the discoveries made in archaeology.

Because professional archaeologists spend the bulk of their time writing and talking to each other about their discoveries, the public often learns about archaeology from books and cable documentaries written and produced by those whose major motivation may be not to educate people but rather to prove some pet theory or make a lot of money. The result is a public interested in the human past but often grossly misinformed about it.

In other words, archaeology is a fascinating field that has, ironically, suffered because of its popularity. There are lots of interesting, often quite funny,
examples of the misuse of archaeology. Book publishers, cable TV documentary producers, websites, magazines, and tabloid newspapers have fed us a
steady diet of ancient astronauts, psychic archaeology, Bigfoot, Atlantisology,
and so on. And there is nothing new about it.

An important question to ask is, Why? From the tales related in this
book, seven basic motives or explanations are revealed:

1. Money, undeniably, can be a major motivating factor. The public's
   interest in archaeology is so great that many people willingly pay to
   see artifacts or read about sites. The opportunities for charlatans to
   take advantage of an interested audience through book deals, lecture
   tours, T-shirts, commemorative mugs, and assorted other bric-a-brac
   are virtually limitless. Quite a bit of money has been and will continue
   to be made from people's great curiosity about human antiquity (see
   Chapter 3, for instance).

2. Fame is another consideration. The desire to find the oldest site or
   the one that shows everybody else to be wrong has motivated many,
   including some professional archaeologists. This desire for fame and
   notoriety has unfortunately led more than a few to alter or exaggerate
   their data.

3. Nationalism is a broader sort of fame that has also served as a motive
   for extreme or unsubstantiated archaeological claims. The desire to
   prove some sort of nationalistic claim through archaeology has been
   common. Wanting to show that "we" were here first or that "we" were
   civilized before "you" has led some to play fast and loose with the
   archaeological facts. The Nazis provide a particularly odious example
   of this. In the 1930s and 1940s they went so far as to publish maps
   showing the claimed geographical extent of their Aryan ancestors during the Neolithic, a time dated to 5,000 years ago, all based on their
   interpretation of artifacts found at ancient archaeological sites excavated in Europe. The presence of these ostensible "Germanic" artifacts
   was viewed as evidence of previous German ownership of these other
   territories, providing at least a partial rationale for evicting or even
   slaughtering the non-Germans living there. It was all nonsense, but
   it was scary and deadly nonsense nonetheless. An informative article
   by Bettina Arnold (1992) chronicles this appropriation of archaeology
   by the Nazis. As Arnold (1992:33) points out, the Nazis were perfectly
   upfront about their lies. She quotes Heinrich Himmler, the Nazi also
   charged with running the death camps, concerning his opinion of the
   purpose of archaeological research: "In all this troublesome business
   we are only interested in one thing—to project into the dim past the

picture of our nation as we envisage it for the future . . . Our teaching of German origins has depended for centuries on falsification. We are entitled to impose one of our own at any time." Amazing and grotesque; a frightening and extreme example of the misuse of archaeology.

4. Racism comes in many guises, some obvious, some implicit, some overtly hateful, and some simply based on misconceptions about other people. An inability to recognize the intelligence and capability of the ancestors of a group of people other than your own, a group of people whose continent of origin, skin color, or hair texture is different from your own, is fundamentally based on the scientifically baseless assumption that some groups of people are biologically or genetically further along on some intelligence and ability scale than are others. The historical rejection of the likelihood that the ancestors of modern American Indians were capable of producing monumentally scaled earthworks or fine works of art (see Chapter 7); the belief that ancient Egyptians necessarily required outside help (from Atlantis or even outer space) in crafting their spectacular civilization (see Chapters 8, 9, and 10); or the notion that the ancient civilizations of Mesoamerica must have been inspired by contact with more civilized or more "advanced" cultures (see Chapters 8, 9, and 13) are predicated on an assumption of incapability on the part of those particular groups and the superiority of others. Such an assumption about people other than your own is, in fact, a primary element of racism but unfortunately may explain why some archaeological pseudoscience is so popular. Among a number of other ways we can characterize it, racism is based on pseudoscience; the archaeological record shows that any claim of racial superiority is baseless.

5. Unfortunately, religion has also played a significant role in archaeological fraud. Many religions have their roots in remote antiquity. Some of their adherents dabble in archaeology, trying to prove the validity of their religious beliefs or claims through the discovery of archaeological evidence. Martin Luther, leader of the Protestant Reformation in the sixteenth century, asked, "What harm would it do if a man told a good strong lie for the sake of the good and for the Christian Church . . . a useful lie, a helpful lie, such lies would not be against God; he would accept them" (cited in Arthur 1996:88). Perhaps for some, an archaeological fraud that led people to the Church might be just such a "useful lie."

6. The desire for a more "romantic" past also plays a role. For some, lost continents, ancient astronauts, and psychic archaeologists seem more interesting than the discoveries of genuine archaeology. The quest for a more romantic past is the cause of at least some of the public's desire

and willingness to believe claims that, if given some thought, could be easily disposed of.

7. Finally, and put bluntly, some of the extreme, unproven, bizarre, silly, and crazy claims made about the human past can be traced to the mental instability of their proponents. In other words, crazy claims may sometimes originate in crazy minds.

Why I Wrote This Book

My purpose is simple. I am passionately curious about human antiquity, and I enjoy few things as much as sharing that passion through my teaching and publications, including this book. I find the misrepresentation of what we actually know about that past to be troubling and, in truth, genuinely aggravating and attempt in these pages to respond to some of the more egregious examples. Simply stated, my purpose here is to provide the perspective of a professional archaeologist on unsubstantiated claims made about the human past, as well as on extreme claims made concerning how we can learn about that past.

The nonarchaeological topics I mentioned earlier in this chapter (UFOs, ESP, etc.) have been discussed at length by experts in the relevant scientific fields. They will not be the focus here. Two excellent journals present articles where paranormal or extreme claims made in the name of science are skeptically assessed (*The Skeptical Inquirer* and *Skeptic*). In addition, I have provided a brief list of books focusing on these nonarchaeological topics (Table 1.2).

Table 1.2   *Skeptical Publications on Extreme Claims Not Directly Related to Archaeology*

Topic	Author	Book title	Year	Publisher
Assorted and General	Robert Todd Carroll	*The Skeptic's Dictionary*	2003	John Wiley & Sonsa
	Melvin Harris	*Investigating the Unexplained*	2003	Prometheus Books
	Lynne Kelly	*The Skeptic's Guide to the Paranormal*	2005	Thunder's Mouth Press
	Guy P. Harrison	*50 Popular Beliefs That People Think Are True*	2012	Prometheus Books
Astrology	J.V. Stewart	*Astrology: What's Really in the Stars*	1997	Prometheus Books

Topic	Author	Book title	Year	Publisher
Astronomy	Philip Plait	*Bad Astronomy*	2002	John Wiley & Sons
Bermuda Triangle	Larry Kusche	*The Bermuda Triangle Mystery Solved*	1995	Prometheus Books
	Brian Hicks	*Ghost Ship*	2004	Ballantine Books
Bigfoot/ Sasquatch	David J. Daegling	*Bigfoot Exposed*	2004	AltaMira Press
	Greg Long	*The Making of Bigfoot*	2004	Prometheus Books
	Joe Nickell	*Tracking the Man-Beasts*	2011	Prometheus Books
Chupacabra	Benjamin Radford	*Tracking the Chupacabra*	2011	University of New Mexico Press
ESP	Massimo Polidoro	*Secrets of the Psychics*	2003	Prometheus Books
	Georges Charpak and Henri Broch	*Debunked: ESP, Telekenesis and Other Pseudoscience*	2004	Johns Hopkins
Faith Healing and Miracles	James Randi	*The Faith Healers*	1989	Prometheus Books
	Joe Nickell	*Looking for a Miracle*	1993	Prometheus Books
Hollow Earth	David Standish	*Hollow Earth*	2006	Da Capo Press
Holocaust Denial	Michael Sheremer and Alex Grobman	*Denying History: Who Says the Holocaust Never Happened and Why Do They Say It?*	2000	University of California Press
Lake Monsters	Ronald Binns	*The Loch Ness Mystery Solved*	1984	Prometheus Books
	Steuart Campbell	*The Loch Ness Monster: The Evidence*	1995	Prometheus Books
	Benjamin Radford and Joe Nickell	*Lake Monster Mysteries: Investigating the World's Most Elusive Creatures*	2006	Univeristy Press of Kentucky
Medical Quackery	James Harvey Young	*American Health Quackery*	1992	Princeton University Press

Continued

Table 1.2 *continued*

Topic	Author	Book title	Year	Publisher
Pareidolia	Christopher Cihlar	*Grilled Cheese Madonna*	2006	Broadway Books
	Buzz Poole	*Madonna of the Toast*	2007	Mark Batty Publisher
Psychic Detectives	Joe Nickell	*Psychic Sleuths*	1994	Prometheus Books
Satanic Cults	Mike Hertenstein and Jon Trott	*Selling Satan: The Tragic History of Mike Warneke*	1993	Cornerstone Press
	Robert Hicks	*In Pursuit of Satan: The Police and the Occult*	1991	Prometheus Books
UFOs	Curtiss Peebles	*Watch the Skies: A Chronicle of the Flying Saucer Myth*	1994	Smithsonian Institution Press
	Kal K. Korff	*The Roswell UFO Crash*	1997	Prometheus Books
	Joel Achenbach	*Captured by Aliens*	1999	Simon and Schuster
	Karl T. Pflock	*Roswell: Inconvenient Facts and the Will to Believe*	2001	Prometheus Books
	Susan A. Clancy	*Abducted: How People Come to Believe They Were Kidnapped by Aliens*	2005	Harvard University Press
Urban Legends	Jan Harold Brunvand	*Too Good to Be True: The Colossal Book of Urban Legends*	2001	Norton
	Jan Harold Brunvand	*Encyclopedia of Urban Legends*	2002	Norton
	Jan Harold Brunvand	*The Choking Doberman: And Other Urban Legends*	2003	Norton
	Jan Harold Brunvand	*Be Very Afraid: The Book of Scary Urban Legends*	2004	Norton

In this book, I present a discussion of the scientific method (Chapter 2) and then go on to detail popular frauds in the field of prehistoric archaeology—the Cardiff Giant (Chapter 3) and Piltdown Man (Chapter 4). Next, I explore the controversy concerning the origin of the American Indians (Chapter 5) and the debate over who discovered the Americas after the Indians (Chapter 6), and the historical argument over the source of the so-called Moundbuilder culture of North America (Chapter 7). Next, I delve into some unsubstantiated claims about the prehistoric archaeological record—the Lost Continent of Atlantis (Chapter 8), the ancient astronaut hypothesis (Chapter 9), the mysteries swirling around the civilization of ancient Egypt (Chapter 10), the efficacy of psychic archaeology (Chapter 11), and alleged archaeological evidence for particular religious beliefs (Chapter 12). Finally, some genuine archaeological mysteries are assessed in Chapter 13. Throughout, the theme will be how the methodology of science allows us to assess claims made in the name of the science of archaeology.

There is a reason for focusing on the history of the misuse and misinterpretation of the archaeological record as well as on individual misadventures. Only, for example, by seeing the contemporary claims of the Swiss author Erich von Däniken (see Chapter 9) as what amounts to our modern version of the Cardiff Giant (Chapter 3), only by realizing that the claims of the advocates of "intelligent design" (Chapter 12) have been around for close to two hundred years and discredited for almost that long, and only by seeing that the public has been pretty gullible about archaeology almost from its inception can we hope to understand the entire phenomenon in its proper context. And only by understanding it can those of us dedicated to the study of the human past hope to deal with it.

◈ ◈ ◈ FREQUENTLY ASKED QUESTIONS ◈ ◈ ◈

1. *What's the harm in believing pseudoscientific or nonscientific claims about the world?*

It must be admitted that the impact of belief in at least some unsubstantiated claims may be minor. For example, you might buy a new weight-loss product based on the manufacturer's claim that the all-natural elixir was discovered while studying a colony of wild gorillas living in "Surinam" (Selling It 2000). The company's brochure offered the claim that after ingesting the material now incorporated into their product, the gorillas became eerily skinny. Interestingly, Suriname is a country in South America, and there are no colonies of wild gorillas there, chubby or slim. Gorillas live in Africa, not South America! You certainly should feel foolish if you purchased a product based on testimonials about skinny gorillas from a company that doesn't even know on which continent gorillas actually live—but what's the harm?

There is great harm when people do not obtain appropriate medical intervention for serious illnesses—opting for unproven remedies and dying prematurely as a result. In extreme cases, charismatic leaders have led their gullible followers—some of whom believed in the psychic powers of the leader (the Reverend Jim Jones of the People's Temple) or the extraterrestrial connections of the leader (Marshall Applewhite of Heaven's Gate)—to their deaths. Belief in nonsense often is just foolish, but it sometimes is tragic.

2. Hasn't ESP already been proven in the lab?

In fact, the existence of the many different manifestations of ESP, including telepathy (the ability to know what is in another person's mind) and clairvoyance (the ability to "see clearly" and know the future), has never been satisfactorily proven under controlled conditions. And how about this: Magician James Randi has, through his James Randi Educational Foundation, offered a $1 million prize to anyone who can, under a set of established and mutually agreed upon controls (to prevent cheating or "sensory leakage"), prove the existence of such a power (http://www .randi.org/research/index.html). Randi provides a list of people who have agreed to be tested (http://forums.randi.org/forumdisplay.php?f=43). So far, no one has won a penny.

3. Will science ever eliminate superstition and pseudoscience?

No, it likely never will. We human beings have an enormous capacity to understand the world around us, but that understanding brings with it a heavy burden. Comfortable fables may not reflect the way things actually work, but they may help us all—even the scientists among us—to deal with the more terrible and frightening things that afflict our lives. In Stephen Sondheim's musical *Into the Woods*, Little Red Riding Hood sings, "Maybe it's nice to know a lot. . . . And a little bit not." Or, as writer Joel Achenbach (1999:78) puts it in his terrific book *Captured by Aliens*, "The nightmare of science is that sometimes you learn things that you do not want to know." Science can only show what works and what does not. Ultimately, it is up to each of us to accept or ignore what science reveals.

 BEST OF THE WEB

http://www.csicop.org/

Website for the Committee for Skeptical Inquiry (CSI) and its journal, the *Skeptical Inquirer*. Online articles from the magazine, a newsletter, and an annotated bibliography are all useful elements of this site.

http://www.skeptic.com/

Website for the Skeptic Society and *Skeptic* magazine.

http://skepdic.com/

Voluminous dictionary of terms, concepts, and claims defined and explained with a skeptical perspective, from acupuncture to zombies. Includes many of the claims discussed in this book.

http://www.badarchaeology.net

Produced by self-avowed "angry archaeologists" Keith Fitzpatrick-Matthews and James Doeser. This website presents unapologetically strong refutations of, well, bad archaelogy. Lots of fun, the site focuses on bad archaeology in Europe.

 CRITICAL THINKING EXERCISES

1. What are the differences between a supermarket weekly and a regular newspaper? Are they always different?

2. Which of the topics listed in Table 1.2 (UFOs, ESP, and the rest) do you accept as genuine phenomena? On what basis do you accept those claims?

Epistemology:
How You Know What You Know

Knowing Things

The word *epistemology* means the study of knowledge—how you know what
you know. Think about it. How does anybody know anything to be actual,
truthful, or real? How do we differentiate fact from fantasy in archaeology or
in any other field of knowledge? Everybody knows things, but how do we
really know these things?

For example, suppose I were to ask you to name the "tallest mountain
in the world." Most of you, I am pretty sure, would respond confidently with
the answer "Mount Everest," giving the Western name for the mountain that
the native people of Tibet call Chomolungma (Goddess of the Universe). Most
people know that Everest is "the tallest mountain in the world," and some of
you might even know that its height is about 29,035 feet (8,850 meters) above
sea level (Figure 2.1). Did you also know, however, that though the peak of
Everest represents the highest point on earth, it isn't really our planet's tallest
mountain if, instead of "above sea level" you define a mountain's height as the
distance from base to summit? That distinction belongs to Mauna Kea, a mountain in Hawaii whose summit is 33,476 feet (10,203 meters) higher than its base,
which is located deep under water and, therefore, far below sea level. Mauna
Kea is, in fact, an astonishing 4,441 feet (1,354 meters) taller than Everest.

However you define "tallest mountain," the truth is that I have never
been to Tibet or even Hawaii. I certainly haven't measured Everest; I haven't
climbed to its summit to confirm that, in fact, I am above every other mountain I can see. For that matter, I haven't measured any of the other tall peaks
to compare them to Everest or Mauna Kea. So how do I know anything about
mountains in the first place, much less which is tallest?

On the subject of mountains, there is a run-down stone monument on
the top of Bear Mountain in the northwestern corner of Connecticut. The

Figure 2.1 If asked to name the tallest mountain in the world, most people would respond "Mount Everest," and some might even know that it peaks at about 29,035 feet (8,850 meters) above sea level. But how many know that, if you measure the height of a mountain from base to summit, Mauna Kea, in Hawaii, is taller (33,476 feet [10,203 meters])? And how do we know this anyway? (© Royalty-Free/Corbis)

monument was built toward the end of the nineteenth century and marks the "highest ground" in the state (Figure 2.2). When the monument was built to memorialize this most lofty and auspicious of peaks—the mountain is all of 2,316 feet (706 meters) above sea level—people knew that it was the highest point in the state and wanted to recognize this fact with the monument.

Figure 2.2 Plaque adorning a stone monument perched atop Bear Mountain in the northwestern corner of Connecticut. Note that the height of the mountain is given as 2,354 feet [it actually is only 2,316 feet (706 meters)] and, in either case, though memorialized as "the highest ground" in the state, it is not. (K. Feder)

There is only one problem. In recent times, with more accurate, sophisticated measuring equipment, it has been determined that Bear Mountain is not the highest point in Connecticut. The slope of Frissell Mountain, which actually peaks in Massachusetts, reaches a height of 2,380 feet (725 meters) on the Connecticut side of the border, eclipsing Bear Mountain by about 64 feet (20 meters).

So, people in the late 1800s and early 1900s "knew" that Bear Mountain was the highest point in Connecticut. Today we *know* that they really did not "know" that, because it was not true—even though they thought it was and built a monument saying so.

Remember my statement that the height of Everest is 29,035 feet (8,850 meters)? You will find that number in books on world geography or geology, in encyclopedias, and, in fact, in almost every published reference to the great peak—but only after November 1999. Until late in 1999, it was believed that the peak of Everest was "only" 29,028 feet (8,848 meters) above sea level. That figure was determined in 1954 using the best technology available at the time. Our technology for doing such things as measuring elevations has improved radically in the intervening years. In a project sponsored by the National Geographic Society, a team of climbers ascended Everest in March 1999 to remeasure the "roof of the world." Using information gleaned from Global Positioning System satellites, it was determined that Everest is actually 7 feet higher, 29,035 feet high, and may be growing, if only by a small fraction of an inch each year, as a result of geological forces (Roach 1999).

One of the defining characteristics of science is its pursuit of modification and refinement of what we know and how we explain things. Scientists realize they have to be ever vigilant and, contrary to what some people seem to think, ever open to new information that enables us to tweak, polish, overhaul, or even overturn what we think we know. Science does not grudgingly admit the need for such refinement or reassessment but rather embraces it as a fundamental part of the scientific method.

But now back to epistemology. You and I have likely never personally assessed or verified the measurements of Everest, Mauna Kea, or any other mountain. So what criteria can we use to determine if any of what we think we know about these peaks is true or accurate? It all comes back to epistemology. How, indeed, do we know what we think we know?

Collecting Information: Seeing Isn't Necessarily Believing

In general, people collect information in two ways:

1. Directly through their own experiences
2. Indirectly through specific information sources such as friends, teachers, parents, books, TV, the Internet, and so forth

People tend to think that obtaining information directly and personally by seeing it or experiencing it for themselves is always the best way. Think of the old expression, "Seeing is believing." In other words, you can believe something as long as you see it with your own eyes. But there's a problem here; our eyes aren't all that reliable. In fact, most people are pretty poor observers.

For example, the list of animals that people claim to have observed—and that turn out to be figments of their imagination—is staggering. It is fascinating to read Pliny, a first-century thinker, or Topsell, who wrote in the seventeenth century, and see detailed accounts of the nature and habits of dragons, griffins, unicorns, mermaids, and so on (Byrne 1979). People claimed to have seen these animals, gave detailed descriptions, and even drew pictures of them (Figure 2.3). Many folks read their books and believed them.

Nor are untrained observers very good at identifying known, living animals. A red or "lesser" panda escaped from the zoo in Rotterdam, Holland, in December 1978. Red pandas are very rare animals indigenous to China, Tibet, Nepal, and Burma, not Holland. They are distinctive in appearance and cannot be readily mistaken for any other sort of animal (Figure 2.4). The zoo informed the press that the panda was missing, hoping the publicity would alert people in the area of the zoo and aid in the

Figure 2.3 The "Lamia," depicted here in a seventeenth-century woodcut, was supposed to be a real creature, a hideous combination of mammal and fish and, apparently, male and female. People actually claimed to have seen the Lamia. They didn't: it's imaginary.

Figure 2.4   Red pandas are distinctive looking animals and not readily mistaken for any other kind of creature. Nevertheless, the case of the missing red panda in Holland, and the many false sightings of it long after it had been killed, is a cautionary tale indicating we should be skeptical about accepting eyewitness accounts too literally. (Jennifer Davis)

panda's return. Just when the newspapers came out with the panda story, it was found, quite dead, along some railroad tracks adjacent to the zoo. Nevertheless, more than one hundred sightings of the panda *alive* were reported to the zoo from all over the Netherlands *after* the animal was obviously already dead. These reports did not stop until several days after the newspapers announced the discovery of the dead panda (van Kampen 1979). So much for the absolute reliability of firsthand observation. Think about that the next time you read an eyewitness account of the sighting of a Bigfoot, a Sasquatch, the Loch Ness Monster, or a Chupacabra. Have you seen the show, *Finding Bigfoot*, where a group of researchers follows up on eyewitness accounts of the creature? It turns out the show ought to be called *Not Finding Bigfoot*. They never find it. The eyewitness accounts that inspire their search just aren't that reliable.

Collecting Information: Relying on Others

In exploring the problems of secondhand information, we run into even more complications. When we are not in place to observe something firsthand, we are forced to rely on the quality of someone else's observations, interpretations, and reports—as with the reported heights of Mount Everest and Mauna Kea.

In assessing a report made by others, you need to ask yourself several questions: How did they obtain the information in the first place—revelation, intuition, science? What are their motives for providing this information? What agenda—religious, philosophical, nationalistic, or otherwise—do they have? What is their source of information, and how expert are they in the topic?

Most people obtain information about the world and current events from established sources such as television news, books, or newspapers. Let's look at the last of these.

Not all newspapers are equally accurate and believable. The *New York Times* has a reputation for factual reporting and carries the following promise in its masthead: "All the News That's Fit to Print." No one, not even their publishers, would characterize tabloid papers like the *Enquirer,* the *Star,* the *Examiner,* the *Sun* (all ordinarily found in supermarket checkout lines), or the *Weekly World News* (now available only in an online edition) in those same terms. When asked about the accuracy of some of the more bizarre stories that appear in his paper, the editor of the *Weekly World News* responded, "For heaven's sake, we entertain people. We make people feel better" (Johnson 1994:27). Notice there is nothing in that response that defends or maintains the accuracy of the stories.

Granted, not everything in the tabloids is utter crap. In fact, the story that presidential aspirant John Edwards had an affair that resulted in the birth of a child while his wife was enduring treatment for breast cancer (from which she ultimately died) was broken in 2007 by none other than the *National Enquirer.* Certainly, however, notions of objectivity and mutually confirming sources is not the standard operating procedure for the tabloids.

Tabloid stories often are absurd, and few of the writers or even the readers believe them (Bird 1992). This still leaves us with a broader issue: How do we know what to believe? This is a crucial question that all rational people must ask themselves, whether talking about medicine, religion, archaeology, or anything else. Again, it comes back around to epistemology; how do we know what we think we know, and how do we know what or whom to believe?

Science: Playing by the Rules

There are ways to knowledge that are both dependable and reliable. We might not be able to get to absolute truths about the meaning of existence, but we can figure out quite a bit about our world—about chemistry and biology, psychology and sociology, physics and history, and even prehistory. The techniques used to get at knowledge we can feel confident in—knowledge that is reliable, truthful, and factual—are referred to as *science*.

In large part, science is a series of techniques used to maximize the probability that what we think we know really reflects the way things are, were, or will be. Science makes no claim to have all the answers or even to be right all the time. On the contrary, during the process of the growth of knowledge and understanding, science is often wrong. Remember that even as seemingly fundamental a fact as the height of the tallest mountain on earth is subject to interpretation (how do you define "tallest"), reassessment, and correction. The only claim that we do make in science is that if we honestly, consistently, explicitly, and vigorously pursue knowledge using some basic techniques and principles, the truth will eventually surface and we can truly know things about the nature of the world in which we find ourselves.

The question then is, What exactly is science? Hollywood certainly has a number of different stereotypes of scientists (Frayling 2005). The classic Doctor Frankenstein (Figure 2.5) comes immediately to mind. Author Christopher Frayling (2005) maintains that movie stereotypes have, in essence, defined the public perception of science and scientists.

So much for Hollywood. Scientists are not misfits or megalomaniacs. We are just people trying to figure out how the world and the universe work. Although the application of science can be a slow, frustrating, all-consuming enterprise, the basic assumptions we scientists hold are very simple. Whether

Figure 2.5   Gene Wilder depicted a stereotypical—and quite hilarious—mad scientist in the movie *Young Frankenstein*. As funny as his character was, it reflects a common, though quite mistaken, view of what real scientists are like and how they go about their research. (© Motion Picture & TV Photo Archive)

we are physicists, biologists, or archaeologists, we all work from four underlying principles. These principles are quite straightforward, but equally quite crucial.

1. There is a real and knowable universe.

2. The universe (which includes stars, planets, animals, and rocks, as well as people, their cultures, and their histories) operates according to certain understandable rules or laws.

3. These laws are immutable—that means they do not, in general, change depending on where you are or "when" you are.

4. These laws can be discerned, studied, and understood by people through careful observation, experimentation, and research.

Let's look at these assumptions one at a time.

There Is a Real and Knowable Universe

In science we have to agree that there is a real universe out there for us to study—a universe full of stars, animals, human history, and prehistory that exists whether we are happy with that reality or not.

Recently, it has become fashionable to deny this fundamental underpinning of science. A group of thinkers called deconstructionists, for example, insists that all science and history are merely artificial constructs, devoid of any objective reality or truth. As scientists Kurt Gottfried and Kenneth Wilson (1997:545) state, the deconstructionists claim that "scientific knowledge is only a communal belief system with a dubious grip on reality." Deconstructionists try to take apart common beliefs in an attempt to show that much of what we think we know is purely subjective and culturally based. On some issues, they are probably right.

Some deconstructionists go futher and describe science itself as a purely Western mode of thought, a mechanistic approach based on inequality, capitalist exploitation, and patriarchy. Science, to the deconstructionists, is merely the Western "myth"; it is no more objective and no more "real" than nonscientific myths.

As Theodore Schick and Lewis Vaughn (2010) point out, however, if there is no such thing as objective truth, then no statements, including this one—or any of those made by the deconstructionists themselves—are objectively true. We could know nothing because there would be nothing to know. This is not a useful approach for human beings. Science simply is not the same as myth. Science demands rigorous testing and retesting, and it commonly rejects and discards previous conclusions about the world as a result of such testing. The same cannot be said for nonscientific explanations about how things work.

The Universe Operates According to Understandable Laws

In essence, what this means is that there are rules by which the universe works: Stars produce heat and light according to the laws of nuclear physics; nothing can go faster than the speed of light; all matter in the universe is attracted to all other matter (the law of gravity).

Though human societies are extremely complex systems and people do not operate according to rigid or unchanging rules of behavior, social scientists can nevertheless perceive patterns and regularities in how human groups react to changes in their environment and how their cultures evolve through time. For example, development of complex civilizations in Egypt, China, India/Pakistan, Mesopotamia, Mexico, and Peru was not based on random processes (Chang 2002; Demarest 2004; Diehl 2004; Headrick 2007; Lamberg-Karlovsky and Sabloff 1995; Martin 2008). Their evolution seems to reflect similar general patterns. This is not to say that all of these civilizations were identical, any more than we would say that all stars are identical. On the contrary, they existed in different physical and cultural environments, and so we should expect that they would be different. However, in each case the rise to civilization was preceded by development of an agricultural economy and socially stratified societies. In each case, civilization was also preceded by some degree of overall population increase as well as increased population density in some areas (in other words, the development of cities). Again, in each case we find monumental works (pyramids, temples), evidence of long-distance trade, and development of mathematics, astronomy, and methods of record keeping (usually, but not always, in the form of writing). The cultures in which civilization developed, though some were unrelated and independent, shared these factors because of the nonrandom patterns of cultural evolution.

The point is that everything operates according to rules. In science we believe that by understanding these rules or laws we can understand stars, organisms, and even ourselves.

The Laws Are Immutable

That the laws do not change under ordinary conditions is a crucial concept in science. A law that works here works there. A law that worked in the past will work today and will work in the future.

For example, if I go to the top of the Leaning Tower of Pisa today and simultaneously drop two balls of unequal mass, they will fall at the same rate and reach the ground at the same time, just as they did when Galileo performed a similar experiment in the seventeenth century. If I perform the same experiment countless times, the same thing will occur because the laws of the universe (in this case, the law of gravity) do not change through time.

They also do not change depending on where you are. Go anywhere on the earth and perform the same experiment—you will get the same results (try not to hit any pedestrians or you will see some other "laws" in operation). This experiment was even performed by U.S. astronauts on the moon during the *Apollo 15* mission. A hammer and a feather were dropped from the same height, and they hit the surface at precisely the same instant (the only reason this will not work on earth is because the feather is caught by the air and the hammer, obviously, is not). Check it out on YouTube at: http://www .youtube.com/watch?v=5C5_dOEyAfk&feature=youtube_gdata_player. We have no reason to believe that the results would be different anywhere or "anywhen" else.

If this assumption of science, that the laws do not change through time, were false, many of the so-called historical sciences, including prehistoric archaeology, could not exist.

For example, historical geologists are interested in knowing how the various landforms we see today came into being. They recognize that they cannot go back in time to see how, for example, Bryce Canyon, in Utah was formed (Figure 2.6). However, because the laws of geology that governed the development of Bryce Canyon have not changed through time and because these laws are still in operation, historical geologists can study the formation of geological features today and apply what they learn to the past. The same laws they can directly study operating in the present were operating in the past when geological features that interest them first formed.

In the words of nineteenth-century geologist Charles Lyell, the "present" we can observe is the "key" to understanding the past that we cannot. This is true because the laws, or rules, that govern the universe are constant—those that operate today operated in the past. This is why science does not limit itself to the present but makes inferences about the past and even predictions about the future (listen to the weather report for an example of this). We can do so because we can study modern, ongoing phenomena that work under the same laws that existed in the past and will exist in the future.

The Laws Can Be Understood

This may be the single most important principle in science. The universe is, theoretically at least, knowable. It may be complicated, and it may take many years to understand even apparently simple phenomena. Each attempt at understanding leads us to collect more data and to test, reevaluate, and refine our proposed explanations—for how planets formed; why a group of animals became extinct while another thrived; or how a group of ancient people responded to a change in their natural environment, contact with a group of foreigners, or adoption of a new technology. We rarely get it right the first time and are continually collecting new information, abandoning

Figure 2.6   By projecting back in time the physical, geological processes they can investigate operating in the present, geologists can reconstruct how ancient landforms, like the spectacular spires of Bryce Canyon, developed through time. (K. Feder)

some interpretations while refining others. We constantly rethink our explanations. In this way, little by little, bit by bit, we expand our knowledge and understanding. Through this kind of careful observation and objective research and experimentation, we can indeed know things.

So, our assumptions are simple enough. We accept the existence of a reality independent of our own minds, and we accept that this reality works according to a series of unchanging patterns, rules, or laws. We also claim that we can recognize and understand these laws, or at least recognize the patterns that result from these universal rules. The question remains then: How do we do science—how do we explore the nature of the universe, whether our interest is planets, stars, atoms, or human prehistory?

The Workings of Science

We can know things by employing the rules of logic and rational thought. Scientists—archaeologists or otherwise—usually work through a combination of the logical processes known as *induction* and *deduction*. The dictionary definition of induction is "arguing from specifics to generalities," whereas deduction is defined as the reverse, arguing from generalities to specifics.

What is essential to good science is objective, unbiased observations—of planets, molecules, rock formations, archaeological sites, and so on. Often, on the basis of these specific observations, we induce explanations called *hypotheses* for how these things work.

For example, we may study the planets Mercury, Venus, Earth, and Mars (each one presents specific bits of information). We then induce general rules about how we think these inner planets in our solar system were formed. Or we might study a whole series of different kinds of molecules and then induce general rules about how molecules interact chemically. We may study different rock formations and make general conclusions about their origin. We can study a number of specific prehistoric sites and make generalizations about how cultures evolved.

Notice that we cannot directly observe planets forming, the rules of molecular interaction, rocks being made, or prehistoric cultures evolving. Instead, we are inducing general conclusions and principles concerning our data that follow logically from what we have been able to observe.

This process of induction, though crucial to science, is not enough. We need to go beyond our induced hypotheses by testing them. If our induced hypotheses are indeed valid—that is, if they really represent the actual rules according to which some aspect of the universe (planets, molecules, rocks, ancient societies) works—they should be able to hold up under the rigors of scientific hypothesis testing.

Observation and the suggestion of hypotheses, therefore, are only the first steps in a scientific investigation. In science we always need to go beyond observation and hypothesizing. We need to set up a series of "if . . . then" statements; "if" our hypothesis is true, "then" the following deduced "facts" will also be true. Our results are not always precise and clear-cut, especially in a science like archaeology, but this much should be clear—scientists are not just out there collecting a bunch of interesting facts. Facts are always collected within the context of trying to explain something or of trying to test a hypothesis.

The Case of Childbed Fever

Here's an example of how this process works. In nineteenth-century Europe, the hospital could be a very dangerous place for a woman about to give birth. Death rates in some so-called lying-in wards were horrifically high, the result of what became known as "childbed fever." A seemingly healthy young woman would arrive at the hospital with an unremarkable pregnancy, experience a normal labor, and give birth to a healthy baby. Over the course of the hours and days following birth, however, she might exhibit a rapid pulse, high fever, distended and painful abdomen, foul discharge, and delirium—and then would die.

Table 2.1 *Number of Maternal Deaths Following the Birth of a Child. (Note the incredibly and tragically high maternal death rates in hospitals of the nineteenth century.)*

	Home Birth	Hospital
Modern United States	1 per 10,000	1 per 10,000
London mid-nineteenth century	10 per 10,000	600 per 10,000
Paris mid-nineteenth century	50 per 10,000	547–880 per 10,000
Dresden mid-nineteenth century	unknown	304 per 10,000

Oddly, while childbed fever took a horrible toll in hospital deliveries, it was rare or absent in home births. In fact, as Sherwin Nuland (2003:97), physician and author of a fascinating book on childbed fever, points out, a woman was generally much safer if she gave birth on the street or in an alley on her way to the hospital than if she actually arrived there. The statistics he gathered certainly support his claim. Take a look at Table 2.1. The nineteenth-century hospital death rates (expressed as the number of maternal deaths per every 10,000 births) are astonishingly, frighteningly high—many times higher than home birth death rates in these same cities—and contrary to what many of us might have expected.

The situation was more complicated for Austria's Vienna General Hospital where there were two separate maternity divisions.

Each year between 6,000 and 7,000 women arrived at the gates of the hospital to give birth, and about half ended up in each of the two divisions. In Division 2, in a given year, on average, about 60 women died soon after giving birth, a death rate of about 2 percent (which figures out to 200 per 10,000; see Table 2.2). Astonishingly, in Division 1, in the same hospital, the number of yearly deaths was more than ten times higher, with more than 600 (2,000 per 10,000 births) and as many as 800 dying in a given year, a terrifying death rate as high as 27 percent (Nuland 2003:97).

Physicians were, needless to say, appalled by such statistics and patients were, understandably, terrified. Many doctors performed autopsies

Table 2.2 *Number of Maternal Deaths Following the Birth of a Child in the Vienna General Hospital. (Note the stunning decline in mortality in Division 1 after 1848.)*

	Before 1848: Before Cleaning with Chlorinated Lime	1848: After Cleaning with Chlorinated Lime
Vienna mid-nineteenth-century Division 2	200 per 10,000	130 per 10,000
Vienna mid-nineteenth-century Division 1	2,000 per 10,000	120 per 10,000

Table 2.3 *Hypotheses Proposed to Explain Childbed Fever Before Semmelweis*

Atmospheric disturbances

Tight petticoats

Foul hospital air

Blocked milk ducts

Female modesty

Fear of childbed fever

---

on women who had died of childbed fever and found them ravaged by an aggressive infection and filled with an intensely foul smelling whitish fluid. Many of these physicians were more than willing to propose hypotheses suggesting possible causes of the condition (Table 2.3). Some doctors proposed the ironic and circular explanation that childbed fever had a psychological origin, the result of the great fear many women had of the hospital because of the possibility of contracting childbed fever!

Back in Vienna at the General Hospital, Ignaz Semmelweis, a young Hungarian doctor who had been turned down for a couple of plum assignments, ended up, by default, in obstetrics. Determined to solve the childbed fever riddle, Semmelweis realized that the General Hospital, with its two divisions having very different mortality rates, presented a unique opportunity to experimentally test the various hypotheses proposed to explain childbed fever.

Semmelweis and some of his colleagues at the hospital recognized a handful of potentially important differences between the two obstetrical divisions in the hospital and induced a series of possible explanations for the drastic difference in their mortality rates. They suggested:

1. Division 1 tended to be more crowded than Division 2. The overcrowding in Division 1 was a possible cause of the higher mortality rate there.

2. Women in Division 2 were assisted by midwives who directed the women to deliver on their sides, while those in Division 1 were attended to by physicians and medical students who kept women on their backs during delivery. Birth position was a possible cause of the higher mortality rate.

3. There was a psychological factor involved; the hospital priest had to walk through Division 1 to administer the last rites to dying patients in other wards. Perhaps this sight so upset some women already weakened by the ordeal of childbirth that it contributed to their deaths.

4. Unlike the women in Division 2, who were assisted by experienced midwives using far less invasive techniques, the women in Division 1 were attended to by medical students being trained in obstetrics. Perhaps all of the additional poking and prodding conducted during this training was harmful and contributed to the higher death rate of women in Division 1.

These induced hypotheses all sounded good. Each marked a genuine difference between Divisions 1 and 2 that might have caused the difference in the death rate. Semmelweis was doing what most scientists do in such a situation; he was relying on creativity and imagination in seeking out an explanation.

Creativity and imagination are just as important to science as good observation. But being creative and imaginative was not enough. It did not help the women who were still dying at an alarming rate. Semmelweis had to go beyond producing possible explanations; he had to test each one of them. So, he deduced the necessary implications of each:

1. If hypothesis 1 were correct, then alleviating the crowding in Division 1 should reduce the mortality rate. The result: no change. So the first hypothesis was rejected. It had failed the scientific test; it did not explain the difference in mortality rates and it simply could not be correct.

2. Semmelweis went on to test hypothesis 2 by changing the birth positions of the women in Division 1 to match those of the women in Division 2. Again, there was no change, and another hypothesis was rejected.

3. Next, to test hypothesis 3, the priest was rerouted. Women in Division 1 continued to die of childbed fever at about five times the rate of those in Division 2. This hypothesis was also rejected.

4. To test hypothesis 4, it was decided to limit the number of invasive procedures used on the women to train the students in their examination techniques. The statistics showed that this had no impact on the death rate in Division 1; 10 or 11 percent of the women continued to die even when fewer students were allowed to examine them internally.

Then, as so often happens in science, Semmelweis had a stroke of luck. An acquaintance—also a doctor—died, and the manner of his death provided Semmelweis with another possible explanation for the problem in Division 1. Though Semmelweis's friend was not a woman who had recently given birth, he did have precisely the same symptoms as did the women who were dying of childbed fever. Most important, this doctor had died of a disease similar to childbed fever soon after accidentally cutting himself during an autopsy.

Viruses and bacteria were unknown in the 1840s. Surgical instruments were not sterilized, no special effort was made by doctors to clean their hands, and doctors did not wear gloves during operations and autopsies. Supposing that there was something bad in dead bodies and this something had entered Semmelweis's friend's system through his wound—could the same bad "stuff" (Semmelweis called it "cadaveric material") get onto the hands of the physicians and medical students, who then might, without washing, go on to help a woman give birth? Then, if this cadaveric material were transmitted into the woman's body during the birth of her baby, it might lead to her death.

This possibility inspired Semmelweis's final hypothesis: The presence of physicians and medical students in Division 1 was at the root of the mystery. Students who attended the women in Division 1 regularly conducted autopsies as part of their training and so would be in contact with dead bodies on the same days they were assisting women giving birth. Furthermore, physicians would frequently perform autopsies on the bodies of women who had already died of childbed fever, often going directly from the autopsy room to the birthing rooms to assist other women giving birth. Herein was a grimly ironic twist to this new hypothesis; the attempt by physicians to solve the mystery of childbed fever by performing autopsies on its victims was one of the most important factors in transmitting the disease to additional women.

To test this hypothesis, Semmelweis instituted new policies in Division 1, including the requirement that all attending physicians and students cleanse their hands with chlorinated lime, a bleaching agent, before entering. The result: the death rates in both divisions dropped (see Table 2.2). Division 2, always the safer one, came down from a rate of 200 to a rate of 130 maternal deaths for every 10,000 births. Division 1 declined far more dramatically, from the previously cited maternal death rate of 2,000 to a rate of 120 per 10,000 births. Semmelweis had both solved a mystery and halted an epidemic.

Science and Nonscience: The Essential Differences

Through objective observation and analysis, a scientist, whether a physicist, chemist, biologist, psychologist, or archaeologist, sees things that need explaining. Through creativity and imagination, the scientist suggests possible hypotheses to explain these "mysteries." The scientist then sets up a rigorous method through experimentation or subsequent research to deductively test the validity of a given hypothesis. If the implications of a hypothesis are shown not to be true, the hypothesis must be rejected and then it's back to the drawing board. If the implications are found to be true, we can uphold or support our hypothesis.

A number of other points should be made here. The first is that for a hypothesis, whether it turns out to be upheld or not, to be scientific, it must be testable. In other words, there must be clear, deduced implications that can be drawn from the hypothesis and then tested. Remember, in the methodology of science, we ordinarily need to

1. Observe.

2. Induce general hypotheses or possible explanations for what we have observed.

3. Deduce specific things that must also be true if our hypothesis is true.

4. Test the hypothesis by checking out the deduced implications.

Testing a hypothesis is crucial. If there are no specific implications of a hypothesis that can be analyzed as a test of the validity or usefulness of that hypothesis, then you simply are not doing and cannot do "science."

For example, suppose you observe a person who appears to be able to "guess" the value of a playing card picked from a deck. Next, assume that someone hypothesizes that "psychic" ability is involved. Finally, suppose the claim is made that the psychic ability goes away as soon as you try to test it (actually named the "shyness effect" by some researchers of the paranormal). This assertion renders the claim of psychic power untestable and therefore not scientific.

Beyond the issue of testability, another lesson is involved in determining whether an approach to a problem is scientific. Semmelweis induced four different hypotheses to explain the difference in mortality rates between Divisions 1 and 2. These "competing" explanations are called *multiple working hypotheses.* Notice that Semmelweis did not simply proceed by a process of elimination. He did not, for example, test the first three hypotheses and—after finding them invalid—declare that the fourth was necessarily correct because it was the only one left that he had thought of.

Some people try to work that way. A light is seen in the sky. Someone hypothesizes it was a meteor. We find out that it was not. Someone else hypothesizes that it was a military rocket. Again this turns out to be incorrect. Someone else suggests that it was the Goodyear blimp, but that turns out to have been somewhere else. Finally, someone suggests that it was the spacecraft of beings from another planet. Some will say that this must be correct because none of the other explanations panned out. This is nonsense. There are plenty of other possible explanations. Eliminating all of the explanations *we* have been able to think of except one (which, perhaps, has no testable implications) in no way allows us to uphold that final hypothesis. You will see just such an error in logic with regard to the Shroud of Turin discussed in Chapter 12.

A Rule in Assessing Explanations

Finally, there is another rule to hypothesis making and testing. It is called *Occam's razor* or *Occam's rule*. In thinking, in trying to solve a problem, or in attempting to explain some phenomenon, "Entities are not to be multiplied beyond necessity." In other words, the explanation or hypothesis that explains a series of observations with the fewest other assumptions or leaps—the hypothesis that does not multiply these entities beyond necessity—is the best explanation.

Here's an example. My archaeology class was to begin in about ten minutes, and the previous class was just dispersing from what had obviously been a raucous session. As I entered the room, I noticed the three-dimensional, geometric shapes made of heavy stock paper suspended by string from the seminar room ceiling. I caught the attention of the professor, a truly gentle soul and one of the nicest people I had met in my first year of teaching, and I asked the obvious question: "What's the deal with the shapes?" She smiled and launched into a passionate discourse about the exercise just conducted by the class—an experiment in "psychokinesis," the ostensible ability to move or otherwise affect objects simply by the power of thought. Perhaps my jaw dropped a little too obviously, and my colleague asked, "Would you like to see me do it?" Without waiting for a response, she gazed up at the shape directly above her head and closed her eyes; when she opened them we both looked up to see the suspended object swaying back and forth. "See?" she said.

Before you get too terribly excited about this demonstration, perhaps I should add that it was a rather breezy day and the windows in the seminar room were wide open. The object toward which my colleague had directed her ostensibly paranormal talents indeed was moving, but so were all of the other suspended objects, as were papers on the desk at the front of the class and just about anything else that wasn't nailed down. I pointed out that, just perhaps, the suspended object was moving simply because of the wind. My colleague just smiled broadly, patted me on the shoulder, and said, "Oh Kenny, you're such a skeptic." Indeed I am, and in this story rests the essence of Occam's razor. Could the object have been moving as the result of my colleague's psychokinetic prowess? Well, yes. But it also could have been moving as a result of open windows and wind. Which explanation—psychokinesis or wind—requires the least violence to our understanding of reality? Which requires the fewest logical leaps or as yet unsupported assumptions about how the universe operates? Occam's razor directs the gambler in reality's casino to bet on the sure thing or, at least, the surer thing, until a preponderance of evidence convinces one otherwise. In this particular case, I'm betting on the wind.

Here's another example of the application of Occam's razor. Consider the case of the symmetrical, axe-shaped pieces of chipped stone found in the seventeenth century in apparently ancient soil layers in Europe (Figure 2.7). Today, anyone looking at these objects would immediately conclude that they were artificial, the product of human ingenuity and labor, "Stone Age" artifacts made by our prehistoric ancestors.

This commonsense interpretation that the objects had been made by a past people was problematic for many thinkers in past centuries. Based on a common interpretation of the Bible, there could have been no "Stone Age", no period in antiquity when people made tools of stone, so the objects in question, in this view, could not have been made by ancient human beings. Thinkers who denied that the stone axes had been made by ancient people had to come up with alternate explanations. Some were rather fanciful. Perhaps these "hand axes" were not the handiwork of ancient human beings, but had been made recently by elves or fairies; some went so far as to call the stone tools "fairy stones." Seriously. Other scientists disagreed, suggesting, instead, a more natural—but also implausible—explanation: Perhaps bolts of lightning struck the earth and produced such objects. These thinkers called the stone objects "thunderstones." Of course, there was no evidence that elves or fairies actually existed, much less that they occupied their time making stone axes. Similarly, no researcher had found symmetrically

Figure 2.7 Symmetrical, flaked stone objects like this hand axe were found in Europe at least as far back as the seventeenth century. Though they clearly are the result of human handiwork, abandoning Occam's razor, many thinkers disputed this and suggested that these objects had been made by fairies or bolts of lightning. (K. Feder)

chipped stone objects at the location of lightning strikes. Apply Occam's razor here; chipped stone objects that looked like tools should be assumed to be the product of human labor unless and until substantial evidence in support of an alternative explanation is forthcoming. Other explanations raised more questions—about elves, fairies, and lightning's capacity to make useful tools—than they answered.

The Art of Science

Don't get the impression that science is a mechanical enterprise. Science is at least partially an art. It takes great creativity to recognize a "mystery" in the first place. You've probably heard the story of how Sir Isaac Newton "discovered" gravity by watching an apple fall from a tree. Certainly, countless apples had fallen from countless trees and undoubtedly conked the noggins of multitudes of stunned individuals who never thought much about it. It took a fabulously creative individual to even recognize that herein lay a mystery. As recorded by his friend, William Stukeley, in 1752, Newton wondered "why should the apple always descend perpendicularly to the ground . . . why should it not go sideways, or upwards? but constantly to the earth's centre? assuredly, the reason is that the earth draws it. There must be a drawing power in matter" (Stukeley 1752). It took great imagination to recognize that in this simple observation of an apple falling to the ground rested the eloquence of a fundamental law of the universe.

Where Do Hypotheses Come From?

Coming up with hypotheses is not a simple or mechanical procedure. The scientific process requires creativity. Hypotheses arrive as often in flashes of insight as through plodding, methodical observation. Consider this example.

My field crew and I had just finished excavating the 2,000-year-old Loomis II archaeological site in Connecticut where a broad array of different kinds of stones had been used for making tools. Some of the "lithics" came from sources close to the site. Other sources were located at quite a distance, as much as a few hundred miles away. These nonnative "exotic" lithics were universally superior; tools could be made more easily from the nonlocal materials, and the edges produced were much sharper.

At the time the site was being excavated, I noticed that there seemed to be a pattern in terms of the size of the individual tools we were recovering. Tools made from the locally available and generally inferior materials of quartz and basalt were relatively large, and the pieces of rock that showed no evidence of use—archaeologists call these discarded pieces *debitage*—were also relatively large. In contrast, the tools made from the superior materials—a black flint and two kinds of jasper—that originated at a great distance from the site were much smaller. Even inconsequential flakes of exotic stone—pieces you could barely hold between two fingers—showed evidence of use, and only the tiniest of flakes were discarded without either further modification for use or evidence of use, such as for scraping, cutting, or piercing.

I thought it was an interesting pattern but didn't think much of it until about a year later when I was cleaning up the floor of my lab after a class in experimental archaeology where students were replicating stone tools. We used a number of different raw materials in the class, and just as was the case for the 2,000-year-old site, stone of inferior quality was readily available a few miles away, whereas more desirable material was from more distant sources.

As I cleaned up, I noticed that the discarded stone chips left by the students included perfectly serviceable pieces of the locally available, easy-to-obtain stone, and only the tiniest fragments of flint and obsidian. We obtained flint in New York State from a source about 80 miles from campus, and we received obsidian from Wyoming from a source more than twenty times farther away (more than 1,600 miles). Suddenly it was clear to me that the pattern apparent at the archaeological site was repeating itself nearly two thousand years later among my students. More "valuable" stone—functionally superior and difficult to obtain—was used more efficiently, and there was far less waste than in stone that was easy to obtain and more difficult to work. I could now phrase this insight as a hypothesis and test it using the site data: More valuable lithic materials were used more efficiently at the Loomis II archaeological site (Feder 1981b). In fact, by a number of measurements, this turned out to be precisely the case. The hypothesis itself came to me when I wasn't thinking of anything in particular; I was simply sweeping the floor.

It may take great skill and imagination to invent a hypothesis in the attempt to understand why things seem to work the way they do. Remember, Division 1 at the Vienna General Hospital did not have written over its doors "Overcrowded Division" or "Division with Student Doctors Who Don't Wash Their Hands After Autopsies." It took imagination, first, to recognize that there were differences between the divisions and, second, to hypothesize that some of the differences might logically be at the root of the mystery. After all, there were many differences between the divisions: their compass orientations, the names of the nurses, the precise alignment of the windows, the astrological signs of the doctors who worked in the divisions, and so on. If a scientist were to attempt to test all of these differences as hypothetical causes of a mystery, nothing would ever be solved. Occam's razor must be applied. We need to focus our intellectual energies on those possible explanations that require few other assumptions. Only after all of these have been eliminated can we legitimately consider others. As summarized by that great fictional detective, Sherlock Holmes in the story The Reigate Puzzle:

> It is of the highest importance in the art of detection to be able to recognize, out of a number of facts, which are incidental and which are vital. Otherwise, your energy and attention must be dissipated instead of being concentrated. (Doyle 1891–1902:275)

Semmelweis concentrated his attention on first four, then a fifth possible explanation. Like all good scientists he had to use some amount of what we can call "intuition" to sort out the potentially vital from the probably incidental. Even in the initial sorting we may be wrong. Overcrowding, birth position, and psychological trauma seemed like very plausible explanations to Semmelweis, but they were wrong nonetheless.

Testing Hypotheses

Finally, it takes skill and inventiveness to suggest ways for testing the hypothesis in question. We must, out of our own heads, be able to invent the "then" part of our "if . . . then" statements. We need to be able to suggest those things that must be true if our hypothesis is to be supported. There really is an art to that. Anyone can claim there were giant human beings in antiquity (Chapter 3), a mysterious race of ancient "mound builders" in North America (Chapter 7), or a Lost Continent of Atlantis (Chapter 8), but often it takes a truly inventive mind to suggest precisely what archaeologists must find if the hypothesis of their existence is indeed to be validated.

It might seem obvious that medical researchers, physicists, or chemists working in labs can perform experiments, observe the results, and come to reasonable conclusions about what transpired. But how about the historical disciplines, including historical geology, history, and prehistoric archaeology? Researchers in these fields cannot go back in time to be there when the events they are attempting to describe and explain took place. Can they really know what happened in the past?

Yes, they can, by what historians Michael Shermer and Alex Grobman (2000:32) call a "convergence of evidence." For example, in their book *Denying History: Who Says the Holocaust Never Happened and Why Do They Say It?* they respond to those who deny that the Germans attempted to exterminate the Jewish population of Europe in the 1930s and 1940s. After all, even though that era isn't ancient history, we still can't return to observe it for ourselves, so how do we know what really happened? Shermer and Grobman marshal multiple sources of evidence, including documents like letters, speeches, blueprints, and articles where Germans discussed their plans; eyewitness accounts of individual atrocities; photographs showing the horror of the camps; the physical remains of the camps themselves; inferential evidence like demographic data showing that approximately 6 million European Jews disappeared during this period. Though we cannot travel back in time to the 1940s, these different and independent lines of evidence converge, allowing us to conclude with absolute certainty that a particular historical event—in this case, the Holocaust—actually happened. Indeed, we can know what happened in history—and prehistory.

Ultimately, whether a science is experimentally based or not makes little logical difference in testing hypotheses. Instead of predicting what the results of a given experiment must be if our induced hypothesis is useful or valid, we predict what new data we must be able to find if a given hypothesis is correct.

For instance, we may hypothesize that long-distance trade is a key element in the development of civilization. We deduce that if this is correct—if this is, in fact, a general pattern of cultural evolution—then we expect to find large quantities of trade items in the locations where civilization developed. We might further deduce that these items should be found in contexts that denote their value and importance to the society (for example, in the burials of leaders). We must then determine the validity of our predictions and, indirectly, our hypothesis by going out and conducting more research.

Testing of hypotheses takes a great deal of thought, and we can make mistakes. We must remember: We have a hypothesis, we have the deduced implications, and we have the test. We can make errors at any step in the process—the hypothesis may be incorrect, the implications may be wrong, or the way we test them may be incorrect. Certainty in science is a scarce commodity. There are always new hypotheses, alternative explanations, and more deductive implications to test. Nothing is ever finished, nothing is set in concrete, nothing is ever defined or raised to the level of religious truth.

The Human Enterprise of Science

Science is a human endeavor practiced by imperfect human beings. It can be difficult for a scientist not to "fall in love" with a hypothesis—because it seems interesting or clever, because it's new and exciting, and, mostly, because he or she came up with it—but it's a trap that must be avoided. Unfortunately, scientists do not always succeed in steering clear of this kind of attachment to an idea; in fact, they are sometimes unsuccessful to the point of ignoring contradictory data or even fudging results to better fit a preconceived notion. In a shocking survey of more than 3,200 American scientists, though very few (0.3 percent) admitted that they had actively falsified research data, 6 percent acknowledged omitting in their presentations to colleagues data that contradicted their previous work, and a remarkable 15.3 percent confessed that they had ignored specific pieces of data or observations "based on a gut feeling that they were inaccurate" (Martinson, Anderson, and de Vries 2005:737).

I think those scientists who revealed that they had omitted or ignored data that contradicted their previous work had fallen into the trap of being in love with their own ideas. People fall in love with other people and learn to overlook their imperfections and inconsistencies, and that's probably a good thing. But it's not so good with scientific explanations. We don't want to overlook the imperfections, inadequacies, and errors in a hypothesis; we want to explore them and, in this way, find ways toward better explanations. In essence, and to extend the analogy far beyond where I should, we need always to be ready to file for divorce from those mistakes, blunders, and dead ends, prepared to move on and not look back.

Beyond this, scientists are not isolated from the cultures and times in which they live. They share many of the same prejudices and biases of other members of their societies. Scientists learn from mentors at universities and inherit their perspectives. It often is quite difficult to go against the scientific grain, to question accumulated wisdom, and to suggest a new approach or perspective.

Beyond this, it isn't easy for any scientist to question the validity of claims made by well-respected authorities. For example, today we take it for granted that sometimes quite large, extraterrestrial, natural objects go streaking across the sky and sometimes even strike the ground (then they are called meteorites; see Figure 2.8). You may even be aware that major meteor showers can be seen twice a year: the Perseid shower in August and the Leonid shower in November. Perhaps you have been lucky enough to see a major meteor or "bolide," an awesome example of nature's fireworks. But until about two hundred years ago the notion that solid stone or metallic objects originating in space regularly enter the earth's atmosphere and sometimes strike the ground was controversial and, in fact, rejected by most scientists. In 1704 Sir Isaac Newton categorically rejected the notion that there could be meteors because he did not believe there could be any cosmological source for them.

The quality of an argument and the evidence marshalled in its support should be all that matters in science. The authority or reputation of the scientist should not matter, at least not all that much. Nevertheless, not many scientists were willing to go against the considered opinion of as bright a scientific luminary as Isaac Newton. Even so, a few brave thinkers risked their reputations by concluding that meteors really did originate in outer space. Their work was roundly criticized, at least for a time. But science is "self-corrective." Hypotheses are constantly being refined and retested as new data are collected.

In 1794, over the skies of Siena, Italy, there was a spectacular shower of about three thousand meteors, seen by tens of thousands of people (Cowen 1995). Even then, a nonmeteoric explanation was suggested. By coincidence, Mount Vesuvius had erupted just eighteen hours before the shower, and some tried to blame the volcano for being the source of the objects flaming across the Italian skies.

Figure 2.8   Anyone looking up at night can't help but notice that occasionally, bright streaks of light cross the sky. Many scientific luminaries, including Sir Isaac Newton, rejected the hypothesis that this could be explained by bits of extraterrestrial stone and metal burning up in the earth's atmosphere. Today, we know that this is precisely what these flashes are, and we call them meteors. (© Chad Baker/Photodisc/Getty Images)

Critics did what they could to dispel the "myth" of an extraterrestrial source for the streaks of light over Siena, but they could not succeed. Further investigation of subsequent major meteor falls in the late 1700s and early 1800s, as well as examination of the chemical makeup of some of the objects that had actually fallen from the sky (an iron and nickel alloy not found on earth), convinced most by the early nineteenth century that meteors are what we now know them to be—extraterrestrial chunks of stone or metal that flame brightly when they enter our planet's atmosphere.

Archaeology has had its biases and misconceptions as well. Unlike today where surveys show that about half of the students entering the discipline are women, in the past the vast majority of archaeologists were men who tended to focus on the role of men in past societies. Even until fairly recently, in reconstructions of life in Ice Age Europe, ancient men seemed to be having all the fun: hunting big game animals, making tools, conducting ceremonies, traveling far and wide, even painting the beautiful images seen on cave walls in France and Spain (see Chapter 13). If the role of women in ancient societies was discussed at all, it was in the context of child bearing and rearing and maybe, if they were lucky in this biased reconstruction of prehistory, making clothing (Gifford-Gonzalez 1993). These archaeologists considered themselves to be scientists but were largely unaware of their implicit bias. They simply took it for granted that men's roles, in past and present, were more active and important and that women did the grunt work and were hardly worth mentioning. There is little in the archaeological record to support this assumption, but it was believed nonetheless.

In science we propose, test, tentatively accept, but never prove a hypothesis. We keep only those hypotheses that cannot be disproved. As long as a hypothesis holds up under the scrutiny of additional testing through experiment and is not contradicted by new data, we accept it as the best explanation so far. Some hypotheses sound good, pass the rigors of initial testing, but are later shown to be inadequate or invalid. Others—for example, the hypothesis of biological evolution—have held up so well (all new data either were or could have been deduced from it) that they will probably always be upheld. We usually call these very well supported hypotheses *theories.* However, it is in the nature of science that no matter how well an explanation of some aspect of reality has held up, we must always be prepared to consider new tests and better explanations.

We are interested in knowledge and explanations of the universe that work. As long as these explanations work, we keep them. As soon as they cease being effective because new data and tests show them to be incomplete or misguided, we discard them and seek new ones. See Table 2.4 for a number of works that discuss the scientific method.

Table 2.4 *Books That Explain the Scientific Method*

Author	Book Title	Year	Publisher
Carl Sagan	*The Demon-Haunted World*	1996	Random House
Michael Shermer	*Why People Believe Weird Things*	1997	W.H. Freeman
Robert Park	*Voodoo Science: The Road from Foolishness to Fraud*	2000	Oxford University Press
Charles Wynn and Arthur Wiggins	*Quantum Leaps in the Wrong Direction*	2001	Joseph Henry Press
Stephen Carey	*A Beginner's Guide to Scientific Method*	2003	Wadsworth
Robert Bartholomew and Benjamin Radford	*Hoaxes, Myths, and Manias: Why We Need Critical Thinking*	2003	Prometheus Books
Howard Kahane and Nancy Cavender	*Logic and Contemporary Rhetoric: The Use of Reason in Everyday Life*	2005	Wadsworth

Continued

Table 2.4   *continued*

Author	Book Title	Year	Publisher
Michael Shermer	*Science Friction: Where the Known Meets the Unknown*	2005	Henry Holt
Jamie Whyte	*Crimes Against Logic: Exposing the Bogus Arguments of Politicians, Priests, Journalists, and Other Serial Offenders*	2005	McGraw-Hill
Thomas Kida	*Don't Believe Everything You Think*	2006	Prometheus Books
Susan Haack	*Defending Science—Within Reason*	2007	Prometheus Books
Theodore Schick and Lewis Vaughn	*How to Think About Weird Things: Critical Thinking for a New Age*	2010	McGraw-Hill
Massimo Pigliucci	*Nonsense on Stilts: How to Tell Science from Bunk*	2010	University of Chicago Press
Richard Dawkins	*The Magic of Reality*	2011	Free Press

Science and Archaeology

The study of the human past is a science and relies on the same general logical processes that all sciences do. Unfortunately, perhaps as a result of its popularity, the data of archaeology have often been used by people to attempt to prove some idea or claim. Too often, these attempts have been bereft of science.

Archaeology has attracted frauds and fakes. Myths about the human past have been created and popularized. Misunderstandings of how archaeologists go about their tasks and what we have discovered about the human story have too often been promulgated. As I stated in Chapter 1, my purpose is to describe the misuse of archaeology and the nonscientific application of the data from this field. In the chapters that follow, the perspective of science will be applied to frauds, myths, and mysteries concerning the human past.

❖ ❖ ❖ FREQUENTLY ASKED QUESTIONS ❖ ❖ ❖

1. Can science answer all of our questions?

No, but it never promised to. Science is a process, a way to approach questions about the physical world (including people and their cultures), not the metaphysical world. Scientists endeavor to understand how the universe works. The search for meaning is valuable and we all do it: Why are we here in this universe? What is the point of our existence? How should we behave toward one another? How should we treat the planet on which we live? Though science can provide the framework for a worldview or philosophy, the answers to these philosophical questions are not discovered through science.

2. Doesn't scientific truth change in every generation?

In a sense, this is true. But our understanding of the world is not simply cyclical. We do not build an edifice of knowledge today only to tear it down tomorrow. The knowledge accumulated by each generation of scientists is refined and built upon by each subsequent generation. We really do know more today about how the solar system formed, the constituents of atoms, earth history, the etiology of disease, and the evolution of our species than we knew a century, a decade, or even a year ago.

 BEST OF THE WEB

For an in-depth discussion of the etiology and history of childbed fever, see: **http://www.ncbi.nlm.nih.gov/pmc/articles/PMC1088248/**

Podcasts

There are some terrific podcasts produced by various organizations and individuals in which a skeptical approach is applied to topics such as UFOs, ESP, Atlantis, ancient astronauts, Bigfoot, and other such phenomena on the fringes of science. Some have an extensive backlog of interviews with experts in various related fields of science and they're a wonderful resource. For a detailed listing of them, check out the article "A Skeptic's Guide to Podcasts" by D. J. Groth in the November/December 2009 issue of the journal *Skeptical Inquirer*. Among my favorites are "The Skeptic's Guide to the Universe" (http://www.theskepticsguide.org, produced by the New England Skeptical Society in association with the James Randi Educational Foundation and hosted by Steve, Bob, and Jay Novella), "Monstertalk" (http://www.skeptic.com/podcasts/monstertalk/, hosted by Blake Smith), and "Skepticality" (http://www.skeptic.com/podcasts/skepticality/, hosted by Derek and Swoopy). "Skepticality" and "Monstertalk" are affiliated with Michael Shermer and the Skeptical Society. In the spirit of full disclosure, I've done interviews for the "Skeptic's Guide" and "Monstertalk"; you can check them out online. The podcasts are available through iTunes and directions for accessing them are available on the podcast websites.

CRITICAL THINKING EXERCISES

1. A televised "documentary" called "The Alien Autopsy" purported to depict the genuine autopsy of an extraterrestrial alien killed in a crash, presumably at Roswell, New Mexico, more than sixty years ago. Using Occam's razor, how would you explain such a film? What kind of evidence would be needed before you would accept the claim that the alien autopsy shown in the film represents the genuine examination of the corpse of an extraterrestrial alien? After answering these questions, visit the website http://www.trudang.com/autopsy/autopsy .html for the perspective of a group of Hollywood special effects experts.

2. How do we know that the Holocaust really happened? What is meant by the assertion that we know it happened as the result of a "convergence of evidence"?

3. Now go back and look at the topics listed in Table 1.1 in Chapter 1. How would you test each of these topics scientifically—in other words, how would you test the validity of UFOs as extraterrestrial spacecraft, the reality of ESP, and the rest?

3

Anatomy of an
Archaeological Hoax

It is not certain which was the best part for Shinichi Fujimura before he was found out and relegated to a psychiatric hospital. Perhaps it was being a well-respected, internationally known archaeologist, even though he had no degree or even training in the subject. Maybe it was when the newspapers called him "God's Hand" for his remarkable ability to regularly find archaeological sites more than ten times older than any previously discovered in Japan. It might have been seeing artifacts he had personally unearthed gracing the exhibit cases of the National Museum of his home nation. Or perhaps the most gratifying aspect of the entire affair was having his colleagues joyfully proclaim that his work would lead to rewriting the textbooks of Japanese history—and then their rewriting of those textbooks, gratefully acknowledging Fujimura for his inestimable contribution to the discipline of archaeology.

Well, they are rewriting the textbooks again in response to the accomplishments of Shinichi Fujimura, but this time it is a result of the revelation—and admission—that he was a fraud. Before Fujimura, an amateur prehistorian with little scientific training, Japanese prehistory was a mere 35,000-year tip on the more than 600,000-year iceberg that is northeast Asian prehistory. But beginning in 1981, first alone and later with the naïve assistance of dozens of scholars from all over the world, Fujimura extended Japanese prehistory deep into the Asian Stone Age, easily matching the antiquity of its continental neighbors and increasing the depth of Japanese prehistory by a factor of sixteen. A grateful nation proud of its past and an admiring cohort of colleagues lauded Fujimura, making him the most famous archaeologist in Japan—the man they called God's Hand. Fujimura became a metaphorical rock star (yeah, that's sort of a play on words, you know, archaeologists and rocks. Never mind).

God's Hand, indeed. Fujimura, ultimately, was as much a fool as a fabricator, never learning one of the cardinal rules of the archaeological hoaxer:

Don't appear too lucky. Whether fueled by jealousy, resentment, or scientific skepticism over his seemingly uncanny ability to find extraordinarily ancient sites, a few archaeologists quietly felt that Fujimura must have had something more than mere luck going for him. Whatever luck he did have ran out when on October 22, 2000, a team of investigative reporters from one of Japan's national daily newspapers, *Mainichi Shimbun,* took the extraordinary step of positioning a hidden video camera at the Kamitakamori site Fujimura was excavating (Holden 2000; Normile 2001a, 2001b; Yamada 2002). Blissfully unaware that he had been caught on tape, Fujimura sprung the trap on himself the very next day when he announced at a press conference his discovery of yet another astoundingly ancient site, with clusters of stone tools found under, and therefore older than, a volcanic deposit dated to 570,000 years ago. *Mainichi Shimbun* held its fire until November 5, when it printed still images from the video clearly showing Fujimura on the night before the discovery and press conference, carefully placing artifacts that obviously came from somewhere else into the excavation where he was to "find" them on the following day (Figure 3.1).

Figure 3.1 Caught in the act. Japanese archaeologist Shinichi Fujimura, whose incredible luck at finding astonishingly ancient artifacts in Japan earned him the nickname "God's Hand," is here caught by a hidden camera showing that neither luck nor God had anything to do with it. Fujimura is planting genuine artifacts from the Asian mainland at a Japanese site that, in reality, is not nearly as old as the artifacts. (© Mainichi Newspapers/Aflo Co. Ltd.)

In a word: busted. Within hours of the revelation of fraud, a contrite and emotionally decimated Fujimura held a press conference where he confessed, explaining his behavior as the result of the enormous pressure placed on him by his colleagues, his countrymen, and himself to find ever older and more impressive evidence of ancient Japanese culture. He maintained at the time that he had planted artifacts at only two sites and had never before fabricated data. It was only the result of bad luck, it seemed, that in one of the two instances where he committed an archaeological fraud, a hidden camera was watching and recording his actions.

Fujimura's colleagues in Japanese archaeology were aghast, certainly, at their unintentional complicity in the affair: by not more carefully monitoring Fujimura's fieldwork, by not asking enough questions, and, simply, by not being skeptical enough. In a discipline usually characterized by skepticism, it is difficult to find even a single Japanese archaeologist who wondered, at least in print, how one man could be so lucky. Takeoka Toshiki of Kyoritsu Women's University was one of the few who suspected something; in fact, he alerted the *Mainichi Shimbun* to the story in the first place. Fujimura's colleagues understood that whatever damage had been done to their own professional reputations, the damage to Japanese prehistory was far more significant (Lepper 2001). When did Fujimura's lies begin—and had they really stopped? Was he being honest in maintaining that he had falsified only two sites? What about all the other sites he had worked on? Could archaeologists accept any as legitimate? Were there, in fact, any Japanese sites older than 35,000 years that could be trusted? Were all the textbooks— the ones rewritten to accommodate a far deeper Japanese prehistory as a result of Fujimura's discoveries—wrong and in need of serious *re*-revision? Or was Fujimura just a pitiable figure, once an important researcher, whose work should not be dismissed simply because he had made a single, significant, but understandable, mistake?

Additional investigation, very regrettably, proved that Fujimura's insistence that he had faked just two sites was yet another falsification in a fabric of deceit. It was far worse than two sites. By October 2001, the *Mainichi Shimbun* reporters (Dirty-Digger Scandal 2001) had documented not two, but *forty-two* sites where Fujimura had obtained older artifacts, often from China or Korea, where sites of greater age are well known, and planted them in deep and ancient soil layers at Japanese sites. Japanese archaeologists now recognize that Fujimura's fakery had begun, not as a recent attempt to maintain a genuinely dazzling record of discovery, but almost from the beginning, as early as 1981, right at the outset of his archaeological career (Yamada 2002). For many now, none of the more than 180 sites he worked on can be trusted. Indeed, the textbooks would have to be rewritten by a contrite, deeply saddened, and, to be honest, humbled archaeological community.

Consider the list of reasons for archaeological fakery presented in Chapter 1. Was it fame, pride, the respect of his colleagues, a desire to provide his nation with a depth of antiquity the equal of its neighbors, or, more likely, some complex combination of all of these that led to Shinichi Fujimura's descent into first deceit and then disgrace? At least there doesn't seem to be any evidence of another rationale for archaeological hoaxes listed in Chapter 1—the desire for wealth. Fujimura does not appear to have been in it for the money.

The same cannot be said for George Hull or Stub Newell in New York State, in 1869. Unlike Fujimura, the rationale for their hoax cannot be explained as the result of a genuine love for and interest in archaeology, their nation, or even a desire for fame. Their singular archaeological hoax was done for a singular reason: money (Tribble 2009).

The Cardiff Giant: The Goliath of New York

As shown by Scott Tribble (2009) in his marvelous biography of the Cardiff Giant (*A Colossal Hoax*), Hull and Newell's hoax succeeded, if only briefly, for the rather peculiar reason that many people in the nineteenth century believed in the past existence of a race of giant human beings, 8, 9, or even 10 feet tall. They believed this because the Bible clearly stated that giant people inhabited the earth in ancient times.

There is an explicit description of one of these "giants" in the Bible's Book of Samuel. In relating the famous story of David and Goliath, the writers provide this very detailed description of Goliath's truly mammoth proportions:

> And there went out a champion out of the camp of the Philistines
> named Goliath of Gotha whose height was six cubits and a span. And he
> had a helmet of brass upon his head, and he was armed with a coat of
> mail, and the weight of the coat was five thousand shekels of brass . . .
> his spear's head weighed six hundred shekels of iron. (1 Samuel 17:4–7)

We do not measure things in *cubits, spans,* or *shekels,* so you'll need some help here. A cubit, the distance from the tip of the middle finger to the elbow, has had a number of slightly varying definitions in different cultures and times. The range has been between 17 and 21 inches. The nearest guess for biblical times is about 18 inches. A span is defined as the distance between your thumb and pinky with your palm spread, which should be half a cubit or about 9 inches. A shekel, an ancient Hebrew measure of weight, was about one-half of one of our ounces.

If we translate Goliath's measurements into our modern system, we can calculate that, according to the authors of the Old Testament, Goliath stood 9 feet 9 inches in height, his armor weighed more than 150 pounds, and his spearhead alone tipped the scales at close to 19 pounds.

Remember, in the nineteenth century the literal truth of everything in the Bible was believed by more than just a small minority of zealous fundamentalists. For many, Bible stories were not seen as legends, myths, or allegorical tales. They were instead viewed as revelations simply to accept and believe as historical truths. For believers, there was no question about it; Adam and Eve were the first human beings, Jonah was swallowed by a whale, and a nearly 10-foot-tall giant named Goliath had truly existed.

Not surprisingly, during this time rumors circulated concerning the discovery of evidence of ancient giant men. In New York State there was a rumor that the skeletons of five enormous human beings had been found during the building of a railroad grade (Silverberg 1989). In the early 1700s Cotton Mather, who previously had helped inspire the Salem witch trials, claimed that some huge bones sent to him by the governor of Massachusetts were the remains of "sinful giants" drowned in Noah's Flood (Howard 1975).

As folklorist Adrienne Mayor (2000) points out in her terrific book *The First Fossil Hunters,* such tales of the historical discovery of the remains of giants may have a simple explanation. The unearthing of the fossil bones of genuine, large, and extinct *animals* by people in the past may have inspired stories of the existence in antiquity of mythical giant *humans.* Without even a cursory understanding of skeletal anatomy, people in the past likely misinterpreted animal bones as human. Mayor shows that at least some ancient myths concerning giant humans can be traced directly to the Greek discovery of the fossil bones of animals; in some cases, the mythmakers identify the geographic locations where such giants supposedly lived, and these turn out to be places in the Mediterranean where fossil animal bones are readily found. Historical references in America to the discovery of the bones of "sinful giants" and the like may very well reflect a similar process of mythologizing the fossil bones of extinct animals (Mayor 2005).

So, it would seem, with fossil bones being interpreted as proving biblical stories of pre-Flood giants, there could be no question about it: There was physical evidence for the existence of giant humans in antiquity.

The Discovery

On Saturday, October 16, 1869, a farmer by the name of Stub Newell hired some men to dig a well behind the barn on his farm in Cardiff, New York, just south of Syracuse. While digging, the workers came across something very hard and large at a depth of about 3 feet. Though curious, Newell was said to be "annoyed and perplexed" by the discovery—it was reported in the *Syracuse Daily Journal* on Wednesday, October 20, 1869, that he had even suggested filling up the pit and keeping the whole thing quiet. Nevertheless, Newell had the workers expand their excavations. When they were done, the

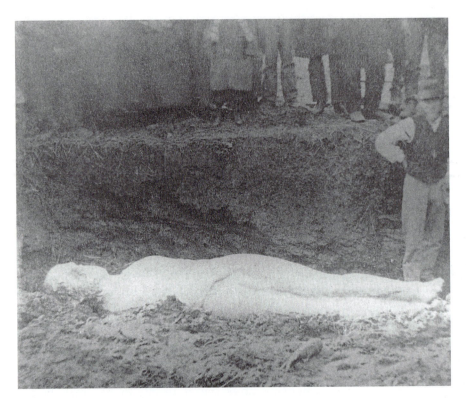

Figure 3.2   An 1869 photograph of the Cardiff Giant in its place of discovery on the Stub Newell farm. An unidentified digger who is, in all likelihood, Stub Newell himself stands to the right of the Giant, and curious onlookers gaze down at the remarkable discovery. (Courtesy the New York State Historical Association, Cooperstown)

group of men looked down with amazement on their thoroughly remarkable discovery. Lying at their feet in the pit was a man of enormous size and proportions whose body, it seemed, had turned to stone (Figure 3.2). He appeared to be "petrified" like the trees in Petrified Forest National Park in eastern Arizona (Figure 3.3).

There, more than 200 million years ago, trees growing in what was then a marshland were buried by sediment rich in silica. The silica leached into the downed trees, filling in the spaces both between and within the individual cells of wood, solidifying and replacing the wood as it decayed away. In some cases the silica faithfully reproduced the appearance of the original tree rings and even the actual cells of the ancient trees. If it could happen to trees, so the argument went, perhaps it could have happened to a person. Thus was the "discovery" of the Cardiff Giant made and the legend of a petrified giant man born.

Word quickly spread in the sleepy little town of a few hundred, and soon, that very afternoon and the next day in fact, local people were gazing

Figure 3.3   Petrified wood, like these remarkably preserved specimens of fossilized trees from Arizona, were seen as models for what might have happened to the Cardiff Giant. If wood could turn to stone, the argument went, so might the body of a giant man from before Noah's Flood. (K. Feder)

with astonishment at the spectacular find in the bottom of the pit behind Stub Newell's barn. As a reporter for the *Syracuse Daily Journal* put it, "Men left their work, women caught up their babies, and children in numbers all hurried to the scene where the interest of that little community centered" (The Lafayette Wonder, 1869).

Newell then exhibited a remarkable degree of business acumen as well as surprising intuition concerning the marketability of the unique discovery on his property. No more than two days passed before Newell obtained a license to exhibit the Giant and purchased and erected a tent over the slumbering, petrified man. He then began to charge twenty-five cents, soon upping the fee to fifty cents for a peek, and the paying public came in droves (Figure 3.4).

From all over New York State, the Northeast, and even beyond, 300 to 500 people daily flocked to the Newell farm. On the first few weekends after its discovery, thousands showed up, all more than ready to wait in line and pay their half-dollar to get a brief glimpse of the petrified "Goliath" of Cardiff (it was actually called that in advertisements). All thoughts of farming on the Newell homestead were abandoned as the crowd of carriages carrying the curious from the train station in Syracuse to the Newell farm increased. The entire farm was transformed virtually overnight into a highly

Figure 3.4   Just days after his "discovery," Stub Newell forgot about farming, erected a tent over the giant petrified man, and began charging people fifty cents to view its remains. (Courtesy of the Onondaga Historical Association, Syracuse)

profitable tourist enterprise, with a food tent, carriage service, cider stand, and, of course, the center of attraction—the awe-inspiring Giant himself (Figure 3.5). One of Newell's relatives, George Hull, estimated in a later report that appeared in the *Ithaca Daily Journal* (The Cardiff Giant, January 4, 1898) that by not quite three weeks after the discovery Newell had collected approximately $7,000 in admission fees, the equivalent of more than $100,000 in modern purchasing power according to the calculations of modern economists (Officer and Williamson 2007).

Stub Newell was not the only one profiting from this lucky discovery on his property. Although the two small hotels in town were benefiting from a great influx of business, Cardiff was simply too small to accommodate the incredible surge of tourists who were making the trek to see the Giant. These people needed to be fed and housed, and that job fell to the businessmen of nearby Syracuse. In a very short time, the Cardiff Giant became a major factor in the economy of that city. Pilgrims streamed into town to pay homage to the Giant and, at the same time, to pay their dollars for the services such a tourist attraction demanded.

The economic impact of the Giant on Syracuse cannot be underestimated and was enough to convince two syndicates of Syracuse businessmen and professional people to initiate a bidding war, each in an effort to make

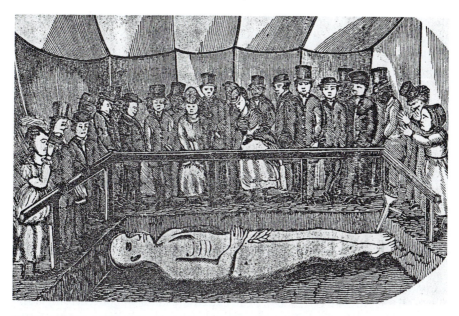

Figure 3.5   From *The Onondaga Giant,* a pamphlet published in 1869, this engraving shows a crowd of people viewing the Giant in the tent on the Newell farm. Note the strategically placed fig leaf.

Stub an offer he couldn't refuse. On October 23, just one week after its discovery, the successful group paid Newell $37,000 for a three-fourths interest in the Giant. Although difficult to calculate, a colleague (John Coyle) estimates that in modern currency this would translate to about half a million dollars. Amazing. By purchasing a controlling share in the Giant, these businessmen were ensuring that it would stay near Syracuse, where it could continue to boost the local economy. At the same time they were assuring themselves a part of the enormous profits the Giant seemed certain to produce.

They were almost right. Between October 23 and November 5, the Syracuse investors had already made back $12,000 of their investment exhibiting the Giant at the Newell farm (Franco 1969:431). I'll save you the math—at fifty cents admission and three-fourths ownership of the Giant and its profits, in that short period about 32,000 people paid for the privilege of seeing the Cardiff Giant.

With no sign of "Giant mania" abating the Syracuse businessmen decided to move the Giant to Syracuse itself, where it would be easier for even greater numbers of people to see it. With great pomp and ceremony, not to mention free publicity through local newspaper coverage, the Giant was disinterred and transported to an exhibition hall in Syracuse. Tribble (2009) determined that in the three weeks of display in Cardiff and the first three weeks in Syracuse, 60,000 people viewed the Giant. Among its admirers was the circus entrepreneur P. T. Barnum, who made an attempt to buy the Giant but was turned down. According to the *Ithaca Daily Journal* article mentioned earlier, Barnum then offered the syndicate of owners $60,000 (about $800,000 in modern dollars) merely for the use of the Giant for three months. Again he was rebuffed. Barnum was not to give up trying to make a circus attraction out of the Giant, however. His unique solution to the problem will be discussed later.

The Beginning of the End

Everything seemed to be going well. Newspapers were printing feature articles about the Giant. The local railroad even made a regular, 10-minute stop across the street from where it was being exhibited in Syracuse to enable people just passing through to run in to see the giant petrified man.

But all was not well. Slowly at first, but then at an accelerating rate, rumors began to surface that the Giant was a fake. A local resident, Daniel Luce, provided a detailed report, recounted in the *Syracuse Standard* (The Stone Giant, November 1, 1869), of an extremely large wagon, carrying a sizable and obviously heavy load, that he remembered traveling toward Cardiff the previous year. Some wondered out loud whether the very large wagon had been carrying a giant statue of a man.

There is also some testimony, as indicated in the *Ithaca Daily Journal* article already cited, that Stub Newell had begun bragging to relatives about the profitable fraud he had perpetrated on the American public. The major stakeholders in the Giant were so concerned by Newell's behavior, they had him sign a statement swearing that he would return the money they paid him if the Giant were proven to be a fraud, even setting a deadline (January 24, 1870) by which the fraud would have to be proven in order for them to recoup their money (Tribble 2009).

Beyond this—and this is very important—professional scientists, including geologists and paleontologists, and even artists who had traveled to Cardiff or Syracuse to examine the Giant in detail, almost without exception immediately declared it to be at best a statue and at worst a fraud. J. F. Boynton, a geologist at the University of Pennsylvania, stated after carefully examining the Giant:

> It is positively absurd to consider this a fossil man. It has none of the indications that would designate it as such, when examined by a practical chemist, geologist, or naturalist. (The Lafayette Wonder, 1869)

Like a few other scientists who examined it, Boynton initially thought it not a fraud, but an actual historical artifact of some antiquity, a statue produced by a community of Jesuits who had lived in the area between 1520 and 1760. Boynton was suspicious, however, after noting the presence of fresh plant material mixed in with the soil from above the Giant, indicating a probable recent burial.

Following a more detailed analysis of the Giant, Boynton declared to a reporter for *Harper's Weekly* magazine (The Cardiff Giant, December 4, 1869) that it was carved of a soft stone called gypsum. He went on to say in that same article that the soft nature of the stone and the amount of weathering on its surface suggested that the Giant had been buried *not more than three years* previous to its disinterment. He even went on to calculate more precisely that the Giant had most likely been in the ground only a little more than one year (approximately 370 days), based on his precise analysis of the rate of weathering of the gypsum from which it was made. As we will see, Boynton's calculation was amazingly accurate.

Othniel C. Marsh, a professor at Yale University and one of the best-known paleontologists of his time, probably was the most important of the scientific skeptics. Marsh examined the Giant and declared it to be "very remarkable." When asked by one of the Giant's owners if they could quote Marsh on that, Marsh is supposed to have said, "No. You may quote me on this though: a very remarkable fake!" (Howard 1975:208). Later, Marsh stated, "I am surprised that any scientific observers should not have at once detected the unmistakable evidence against its antiquity" (as cited in Rose 2005).

Like Boynton, Marsh correctly noted that the Giant was made of gypsum, a soft stone that would not last long in the wet soil of the Newell farm. (Gypsum is a sedimentary rock and exhibits layering, unlike petrified wood.) Previous to Marsh's investigation, a well-known sculptor, Eratus Dow Palmer, had examined the Giant, identifying the marks of a sculptor's tools on its surface. Marsh confirmed the existence of tool marks on the alleged petrified man.

The skepticism of so highly respected a scientist as Marsh had some impact, and a number of the New York City newspapers (in particular, the *New York Herald*) that had previously praised the Giant now changed their opinions. But the statements of Marsh and other, less well-known scientists could not alone dissuade the public from the notion that the Cardiff Giant was a real, petrified man whose existence supported biblical stories of human giants before Noah's Flood.

Hull's Confession

The meteoric rise to fame of the Cardiff Giant was cut short, and his fall from grace was just as quick. A previously shadowy figure involved with promoting the Giant confessed in December 1869 to perpetrating a fraud on the American public. George Hull, a distant relation of Stub Newell, unburdened his soul, and the Giant's value dropped from that of a spectacular archaeological find to that of one slightly worn chunk of gypsum.

George Hull was a cigar manufacturer in Binghamton, New York. Ironically, he also was a devout atheist. He revealed the entire story toward the end of his life in an interview he gave to the *Ithaca Daily Journal* (The Cardiff Giant, 1898).

During a visit to his wife's sister's house in Iowa in 1866, Hull had a long and heated conversation with a Methodist minister traveling through the area. Apparently, the conversation focused on extraordinary biblical stories, like those mentioned at the beginning of this chapter concerning the existence of an ancient race of giant men. Hull suggested to the minister that the Bible was filled with such tall tales, impossibilities that only the gullible would believe. The minister took strong exception to this characterization, maintaining the literal truth of every Bible story. At midnight Hull retired to bed and, in his own words, "I lay wide awake wondering why people would believe those remarkable stories in the Bible about giants, when I suddenly thought of making a stone giant, and passing it off as a petrified man" (The Cardiff Giant, 1898).

In a subsequent visit to the Midwest in June 1868, Hull purchased an acre of land in Fort Dodge, Iowa, from which he quarried a 5-ton block of gypsum. He then had the block shipped to Chicago, where, swearing them to secrecy, he hired sculptors to produce a statue of a giant, slumbering man.

After work had gone on for a couple of months, the Giant was almost complete. On viewing it, however, Hull was unhappy. Initially, the face of the giant statue looked just like George Hull's own! The sculptors had even given the Giant hair and a beard to match Hull's.

But all was not lost. Hull first had the sculptors remove the hair on the head and face. Still not satisfied, he next got some blocks of wood into which he hammered a bunch of knitting needles so that just their tips protruded from the wood. Hull proceeded to pound on the Giant with these blocks. You can imagine the expression on the faces of the sculptors, seeing this madman attack the artistic creation he had just paid them to produce. Hull liked the effect though; it gave the surface of the statue the porelike appearance of skin. As if this weren't enough, Hull next rubbed acid all over the sculpture, which further reinforced its ancient appearance.

Hull had the Giant shipped in a wooden box by railroad to Union, New York. In November 1868 it was finally brought by wagon to his cousin Stub Newell's farm and secretly buried behind the barn (with Newell's knowledge and cooperation). To make certain that no one would connect the shipment with the discovery of the Giant, it was left to lie in the ground for about a year—nearly the exact length of time geologist J. F. Boynton had suggested. Then, according to plan, nearly twelve months later, Hull instructed Newell to hire a crew of men to dig a well where they were both very much aware the Giant would be discovered. The rest is embarrassing history. It should finally be pointed out that it was apparently Newell's bragging to friends and relatives about the fraud that induced Hull to come clean before the whole thing blew up in their faces.

The syndicate of owners initially tried to quash the confession or at least discredit it. But Hull's story was too detailed and reasonable to ignore. When the sculptors in Chicago came forward to verify Hull's confession, the Giant's days as a major tourist attraction were at an end.

The End of the Giant

The Giant's demise was not without its ironies. After P. T. Barnum had been turned down in his initial attempt to purchase the Giant, he simply went out and had a duplicate made. He even billed the statue as the "real" Cardiff Giant, claiming that the owners had sold him the original and that they were exhibiting the copy. In truth, however, Barnum was charging people to see the Cardiff Giant, but his Cardiff Giant was the fake; it was, put bluntly, a fake of a fake! Needless to say, lawsuits were filed. After revenues dropped as a result of the Hull confession, the owners of the "real" fake took the Giant on the road, hoping to drum up some business and maybe even turn the whole fiasco of the confession to their advantage (Figure 3.6). Coincidentally, the real fake and Barnum's fake of the fake were both displayed at the same time in New York City—and Barnum's copy outdrew the real Cardiff Giant.

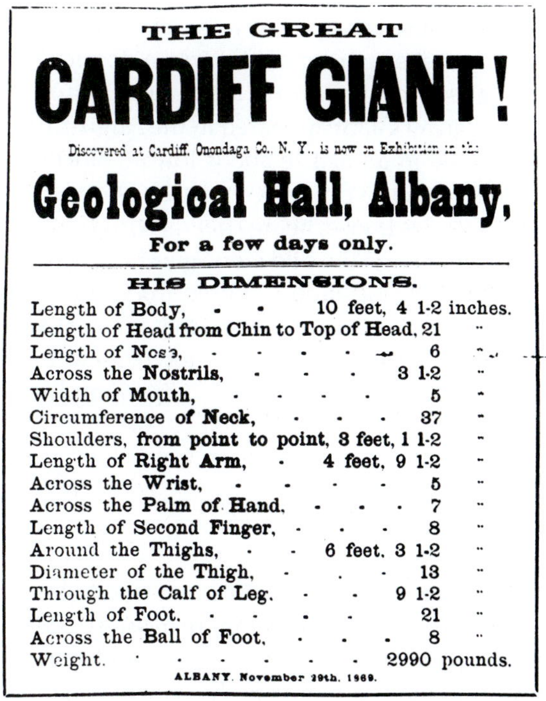

THE GREAT

CARDIFF GIANT!

Discovered at Cardiff, Onondaga Co., N. Y., is now on Exhibition in the

Geological Hall, Albany,

For a few days only.

HIS DIMENSIONS.

Length of Body,	· ·	10 feet, 4 1-2 inches.	
Length of Head from Chin to Top of Head,	21		"
Length of Nose,	· · · ·	6	"
Across the Nostrils,	· · ·	3 1-2	"
Width of Mouth,	· · · ·	5	"
Circumference of Neck,	· · ·	37	"
Shoulders, from point to point,	3 feet, 1 1-2		"
Length of Right Arm,	·	4 feet, 9 1-2	"
Across the Wrist,	· · · ·	5	"
Across the Palm of Hand,	· · ·	7	"
Length of Second Finger,	· · ·	8	"
Around the Thighs,	·	6 feet, 3 1-2	"
Diameter of the Thigh,	· ·	13	"
Through the Calf of Leg,	· ·	9 1-2	"
Length of Foot,	· · · ·	21	"
Across the Ball of Foot,	· · ·	8	"
Weight,	· · · · ·	2990 pounds.	

ALBANY, November 29th, 1869.

Figure 3.6   The Giant on tour. After serious questions were raised regarding the Giant's authenticity, the consortium of owners decided to take their show on the road. This handout advertised the Giant's appearance in Albany, New York, on November 29, 1869. (Courtesy of the New York State Historical Association, Cooperstown)

Mark Twain was so amused by the whole mess that he wrote a short story about it. "A Ghost Story" concerns a man who takes a room at a hotel in New York City and is then terrorized by the ghost of a poor, tormented, giant man. The ghost turns out to be, in fact, the spirit of the Cardiff Giant. The Giant's soul has been condemned to wander the earth until his physical remains are once again laid to rest. He nightly wanders the corridors of the hotel as his fossilized body is cruelly displayed in the exhibit hall across the street. But, as luck would have it, the poor tormented soul of the Giant has made a grievous error. As the hotel resident informed him, "Why you poor blundering old fossil, you have had all your trouble for nothing—you have been haunting a plaster cast of yourself." The ghost of the poor Giant was haunting Barnum's fake. Even he was fooled.

Needless to say, once the hoax had been revealed, the lawsuits settled, and much fun poked, interest in the Giant waned. Though, thankfully, it was not broken up for road fill or some other use, the Giant faded into near oblivion, for decades stored in a barn and sadly awaiting, we can only imagine, his terrible fate. The Giant was not forgotten entirely, however, and on occasion he was trotted out for state fairs in New York, where he had achieved his initial fame, and Iowa, the place of his birth. Gardner Cowles, Jr., a newspaper publisher in Des Moines, Iowa, saw the Giant on one of its midwestern excursions and felt strongly that as a great American archaeological humbug it deserved a better fate. Cowles managed to purchase the Giant and brought it to Des Moines, where for a time it rested in repose in the recreation room of his house as what has to be one of the most peculiar conversation pieces that has ever graced an American domicile. It regained enough of its fame there as a local curiosity that a photograph of the Cowles rec room showing the Cardiff Giant appeared in the August 1939 issue of *National Geographic* magazine in an article about Iowa (coincidentally, a retired dean at my university, James Fox, grew up in the Des Moines area, was a frequent visitor to the Cowles house, being friends with Gardner Cowles's young son, and clearly remembers the odd stone giant in the basement). The New York State Historical Association acquired the Giant from Cowles in 1947, returning it, so to speak, to the scene of the crime. It was installed as an exhibit at the Farmers' Museum in Cooperstown, New York, not far from the location of its greatest, though short-lived, triumph—in fooling people.

Why Did They Do It?

It's easy enough to show that the motive for the Cardiff Giant fraud was, of course, money. George Hull and Stub Newell made far more money displaying the Giant than they ever could have through selling cigars or farming—their usual professions. Money continued to motivate those who benefited from the Giant but who played no part in perpetrating the fraud in the first place. The businessmen of Syracuse grew rich as a result of the Giant, and a small town in rural New York was put on the map.

There also is an explanation for why people with no monetary investment wished to believe that the Cardiff Giant was genuine. Certainly, the religious element behind the public's desire to believe in the validity of the Giant cannot be overestimated. When publications in 1869 referred to the discovery as a "Goliath," they were not making a simple analogy; they were making a serious comparison between the Cardiff discovery and the biblical story of Goliath of Gotha.

Moreover, I would also include the love of a mystery as an explanation for why people chose to accept the Giant even though scientists who studied it declared it to be, at best, a statue and, at worst, a fraud. Whether the Giant lent proof to a biblical claim or not, perhaps it was the simple romance of such an amazing discovery that played at least a secondary role in convincing people to part with their hard-earned money to see what was clearly a gypsum statue.

The lesson of the Cardiff Giant is one that you will see repeated in this book. It is a vitally important lesson; trained observers, professional scientists, had viewed the Giant and pronounced it to be an impossibility, a statue, a clumsy fraud, and just plain silly. Such objective, rational, logical, and scientific conclusions, however, had little impact. A chord had been struck in the hearts and minds of many otherwise levelheaded people, and little could dissuade them from believing in the truth of the Giant. Their acceptance of the validity of the Giant was based on their desire, religious or not, to believe it.

Though one might have hoped for their rehabilitation after the Cardiff Giant debacle, neither Hull nor Barnum was finished with giant hoaxes. Despite being competitors and even enemies in the case of the Cardiff Giant, they apparently called a truce, joined forces, and together produced yet another supposed petrified giant. Hull was the idea man; Barnum supplied the financial backing. Called the "Solid Muldoon," it was planted in Beulah, Colorado, in 1877 and "discovered" by a co-conspirator in the hoax in that same year. It looked a bit more authentic than that other member of its species, but its career was equally short-lived. One of Hull's associates revealed the Solid Muldoon's fraudulent origins when, perhaps not coincidentally, it was being shown in New York, the home state of its predecessor.

Finally, after laughing at all those silly people who in 1869 paid fifty cents to see the Giant, you can now all laugh at me; I recently paid several dollars to see him at the Farmers' Museum in Cooperstown—actually a wonderful place, well worth the price of admission (Figure 3.7). The poor, tortured Giant has at last found a final resting place in a recently refurbished exhibit there. Do I detect a hint of a smile on his face? I guess the Cardiff Giant has the last laugh after all (Figure 3.8).

Figure 3.7   Today, the Farmers' Museum in Cooperstown, New York, displays the Cardiff Giant in a tent blazing the title "America's Greatest Hoax." Who can argue with that? (K. Feder)

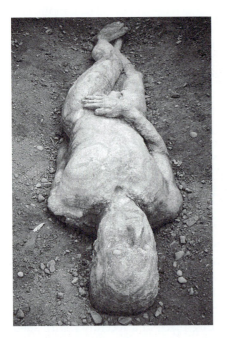

Figure 3.8   In silent repose, the Giant has at last found his eternal rest at the Farmers' Museum in Cooperstown, New York. (K. Feder)

Current Perspectives: Frauds

A clumsy fraud like the Cardiff Giant didn't fool scientists in the nineteenth century and certainly would fool no one today, but the hoaxers keep on trying. Consider this example. The artifacts that Connecticut State Archaeologist Nick Bellantoni and his crew recovered in their excavation of one corner of an otherwise unremarkable 3,000-year-old site in Pachaug State Forest in Voluntown, Connecticut, were unlike anything he had ever encountered in the state (Bellantoni 2002). To be frank, the objects Nick had excavated were equally perplexing to the other archaeologists he called in for counsel (Stowe 2001). Nothing like the twenty oddly carved stone effigies of birds, snakes, sperm whales, and people had ever been found by any of us at any native or colonial site in the state (Figure 3.9).

Nick had been directed to the site by a local hunter in 1997. While most of the 1997 excavation was uneventful, revealing the usual array of stone spearpoints and ancient pottery, a handful of objects including a clay pipe, stone pendant, and copper beads didn't match the age of the site. Intrigued, Nick and his crew returned in 2000 and discovered twenty strange stone carvings in a series of soil-filled pits in a location somewhat removed from the 1997 excavation.

Nick is a careful, methodical, meticulous, and experienced excavator. None of those adjectives could be applied to whoever clearly had buried

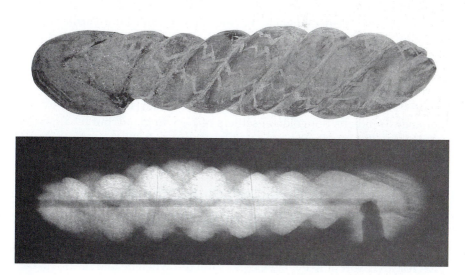

Figure 3.9 One of the Pachaug State Forest fake artifacts. The top photograph is of a supposed smoking pipe; the bottom is an x ray of the artifact. The x-ray image shows a single, continuous drill hole running across the length of the pipe. This hole almost certainly was made with a mechanical, metal drill bit, applying technology unknown to the ancient inhabitants of Connecticut. (Courtesy Connecticut Archaeology Center)

the objects found in the 2000 dig. Nick's careful examination of the soil convinced him that the exotic artifacts they found that year had been planted only very recently. The soil in the general area where the objects were found was compact and hard, but the specific locations where the artifacts were recovered were much looser and softer, clearly having been dug up in the not-too-distant past.

Something else about the places where the objects were excavated betrayed the ineptitude of the hoaxer. The forest soil of Connecticut is universally rooty. Anybody digging through that soil, today or a thousand years ago, will, as a matter of course, cut through roots. For a period of a year or so after infilling, the interior surfaces of soil-filled pits will be dotted by the roots of trees and bushes incidentally cut through by whatever tool was used to dig the pit in the first place. After a time, however, some of the cut roots will die and disintegrate, some will regrow, and, over the years, new root growth will cut through the soil in the filled hole. But the soil-filled holes in which the Pachaug State Forest artifacts were found showed little or no regrowth of roots and no new roots cutting through the surfaces of the now soil-filled pits. In fact, cut roots, still relatively fresh, were visible when Nick excavated the pits, and there even were a couple of fairly fresh oak leaves mixed in the soil matrix. It was Fujimura (with planted artifacts) and the Cardiff Giant (with fresh plant material underlying the statue) all over again. There was no way the pits into which the artifacts had been placed could have been dug more than a year or two before Nick excavated the site. Microscopic evidence of the use of power tools with metal blades to carve some of the stone artifacts clinched it; the Pachaug State Forest artifacts were a modern, very recent archaeological hoax.

The only remaining mysteries underlying the Pachaug State Forest artifacts concern the identity and motive of the hoaxer. It might be nice to solve those mysteries, but the far more important issue is resolved. We need not rewrite the history books; the Pachaug Forest artifacts were made by neither ancient Indians nor colonial settlers of New England, but by a modern prankster with far too much time on his or her hands, in an attempt, apparently, to waste the time of our state archaeologist.

The Rules for a Successful Archaeological Hoax

1. *Give the people what they want.*

   One of the keys to a successful archaeological hoax is marketing research, sort of like what George Hull did when he had his discussion with the Iowa minister. Find out what your market wants and give it to them. A hoax works best when the public has a predisposition to accept it in the first place. The unexpectedly ancient sites Fujimura unearthed, the Cardiff Giant, Piltdown Man (Chapter 4), the

Vinland Map (Chapter 6), and the Newark Holy Stones (Chapter 7) were successful in large measure because people very much wanted them to be genuine; they wanted their implications—of a very ancient human presence in Japan, of proof of the Old Testament of the Bible, of an ancient English component to human evolution, of the Norse discovery of America, and of the presence of ancient Hebrews in the New World—to be true. All of these examples show that hoaxes work best when people are not just willing to, but also longing to, suspend their disbelief, to leave their skepticism at the door because of a desire to embrace a discovery and its implications.

2. *Don't be too successful.*

On a personal level, while it might be nice to be called by your friends and colleagues, as well as by the general public, "God's Hand" (like Fujimura in this chapter) or the "Wizard of Sussex" (like Charles Dawson in Chapter 4), that level of personal recognition is not good for an archaeological hoaxer. "Gods" and "wizards" can generate resentment and suspicion. Resentment and suspicion lead to skepticism and investigations with hidden cameras, police searches, and even subpoenas, all things archaeological hoaxers do well to avoid. Successful hoaxers let others take at least some of the credit and revel in the success of their frauds in private.

Consider the seemingly incredible luck of Curzio Inghirami, a young and wealthy Italian who, in 1634, discovered a miniature time capsule buried on the grounds of his family's estate in Tuscany (Rowland 2004). The capsule, called a "scarith," contained a scroll, ostensibly written in the ancient Etruscan language by "Prospero of Fiesole." At the time of the scroll's writing (in theory, about 2,500 years before its discovery), the Etruscans were about to be defeated and subjugated by ancient Rome. Inghirami's scarith fascinated the inhabitants of Tuscany, who viewed themselves as the descendants of the Etruscans and who still held a powerful grudge against the Romans.

There had been previous discoveries of documents written in Etruscan that might have provided the details of the history of that group but for a significant problem: Etruscan had not been deciphered. The good news for seventeenth-century inhabitants of Tuscany was that Prospero had, very conveniently, provided on the scarith documents a Latin translation of his Etruscan. As a result, the scarith was viewed as an enormously significant historical document and a source of pride by local people.

Perhaps if Inghirami had found just the one scarith, it might have remained a historical curiosity and he might have successfully pulled off a pretty good joke. But he found more than one; in fact, over the next few years he found more than 200 of the scarith, presenting a body of written work which, together, presented a lengthy and detailed history of the Etruscan people. That kind of success, that kind of amazing luck at finding historically important artifacts, of course, drew the interest of scholars and inspired their skepticism. How could one young man be so incredibly, singularly, uniquely lucky at finding just precisely this kind of artifact? Well, luck had nothing to do with it. A detailed analysis showed that Prospero's and Inghirami's handwriting were one and the same! A later analysis clinched the diagnosis that the scarith had all been fakes: the paper on which the scarith documents had been written bore the watermark of a seventeenth-century paper manufacturer (Rowland 2004:135).

Inghirami's initial success stems from the fact that he followed the suggestion in rule 1: he had given his countrymen what they wanted, a noble history, but his failing was in not adhering to rule 2. He was just too lucky at finding scarith and that luck, in part, is what inspired the investigation that revealed the fraud.

3. *Learn from your mistakes.*

There is a learning curve for archaeological fakery, and hoaxers need to listen to criticisms leveled at their early work. It may be ironic, but when professional archaeologists and historians debunk archaeological and historical fakes, they are, in a sense, providing a primer to hoaxers about mistakes to avoid in the future. The fact that the Solid Muldoon was more realistic than the Cardiff Giant, that the second Newark Holy Stone found by David Wyrick exhibited an inscription with a more appropriate version of Hebrew than had the first (see Chapter 7), and that the second batch of the so-called Michigan Relics didn't reflect the rookie mistakes seen in the first batch (see Chapter 7) all seem to indicate that the hoaxers understood that the information supplied by the debunking of their first attempts could be used to their advantage the second time around.

Of course, I am not really trying to help out archaeological hoaxers here. In fact, the previous rules actually represent a cautionary list reflecting what successful hoaxers commonly do and how they hide their tracks. So, when the archaeological discovery you read about in the newspaper, view on a television special, or glance at online just seems too wonderful, a little too good at fulfilling a basic desire about what the past shows; when the discoveries always seem to be made by the same individual or group and never by others—especially not by even open-minded skeptics; and when each criticism or debunking is met by discoveries that astonishingly appear to improve sequentially in their apparent authenticity, be on your guard. You may very well be faced with an archaeological hoax. It's one of the most important things hoaxers have working against them: Nobody likes being fooled.

FREQUENTLY ASKED QUESTIONS

1. The Cardiff Giant was a hoax, but can a human body turn to stone?

No, not really. Wood cells are resilient enough, under the right circumstances, to preserve long enough for minerals to penetrate them, solidify, and take on their appearance. Bones, including human bones, can become mineralized in much the same way. Soft tissue—skin and muscle—simply is too soft for this process to work on it.

2. Can human bodies be preserved for long periods of time?

Yes, under the right, very rare circumstances, they can be preserved for thousands of years. Found in 1991, the so-called Ice Man, a remarkably well preserved body frozen in glacial ice near the border between Austria and Italy, was approximately 5,300 years old. The bodies of the so-called Bog People of Denmark were preserved for more than 3,000 years by moisture and a combination of natural chemicals in the peat in which they were buried. Also, natural mummification under very dry conditions (in either warm or very cold climates) has preserved bodies for millennia. Ancient bodies have been found in Greenland and in the higher elevations of the Andes in South America. Waterlogged human brain tissue was preserved for more than 7,000 years at the Windover site in Florida. The key to the preservation of animal (including human) bodies rests in keeping away those organisms that ordinarily would recycle them. Bacteria that eat dead flesh do not do well under very cold, very wet (waterlogged), or very dry conditions. Keep bacteria away, and human bodies can be preserved for millennia.

3. Whatever happened to Barnum's fake of the Cardiff Giant?

Barnum's copy has turned up and can be seen at Marvin's Marvelous Mechanical Museum in Farmington Hills, Michigan. Further, it turns out that there is a replica of Barnum's copy (making it a fake of a fake of a fake) at Circus World Museum in Baraboo, Wisconsin. I thought you might like to know.

  BEST OF THE WEB

http://www.lhup.edu/~dsimanek/cardiff.htm

Chapter from Andrew White's autobiography detailing the author's experiences in upstate New York when the Cardiff Giant was discovered.

http://www.roadsideamerica.com/attract/NYCOOgiant.html

Very cool site dealing with offbeat tourist sites, here discussing the Cardiff Giant.

http://www.marvin3m.com/cardiff.php

Marvin's Marvelous Mechanical Museum's home page. Visit to see
P. T. Barnum's fake of the Cardiff Giant.

http://www.kickstarter.com/projects/tymarshal/syracuse-cardiff-giant

In a lovely combination of art, history, humbug, and commerce, artist Ty
Marshall recreated the discovery of the Cardiff Giant in October 2011. It
must have been a hoot.

    CRITICAL THINKING EXERCISE

Which groups of people were immediate believers in the Cardiff Giant? On
what did they base their acceptance of the "petrified man"? Which groups
of people were immediately skeptical? On what did they base their skepticism? How can we explain the Giant's acceptance by the former groups and
its rejection by the latter? What lessons in this story are applicable to other
instances of frauds or hoaxes in science?

4

Dawson's Dawn Man:
The Hoax at Piltdown

I first visited the Natural History Museum in London in the summer of 1996, hoping to see the actual remains of Piltdown Man, the most famous—and infamous—fraud in the annals of paleoanthropology. I knew the fossil was in the museum's possession—some of the museum's scientists had played an important, though likely unintentional role, in the hoax—so, naturally, I assumed that this most famous of frauds would be prominently displayed.

When I had trouble finding the fossil in a museum case, I approached a woman at the front desk, asking where I might see the Piltdown remains. "Oh, that is not on display sir," she said, and went on to inform me, rather condescendingly, "It was all rubbish, you know." Well, I guess I knew that. It seems that the Piltdown Man fossil has been a literal skeleton in the closet of prehistoric archaeology and human paleontology.

Things have improved since 1996. Today, when you visit the website of the British Museum of Natural History, you can interactively explore some of the details of the case of Piltdown Man (http://www.nhm.ac.uk/nature-online/life/human-origins/piltdown-man/index.html). The story of Piltdown has been presented in detail by Ronald Millar in his 1972 book *The Piltdown Men*, by J. S. Weiner in his 1955 work *The Piltdown Forgery*, in 1986 by Charles Blinderman in *The Piltdown Inquest*, in 1990 by Frank Spencer in *Piltdown: A Scientific Forgery*, and by John E. Walsh in 1996 in *Unraveling Piltdown: The Science Fraud of the Century and Its Solution*. The story is useful in its telling if only to show that, as seen in the Fujimura case, even scientific observers can be fooled. This is particularly the case when trained scientists are faced with something they are not trained to detect—intellectual criminality. But let us begin before the beginning, before the discovery of the Piltdown fossil.

The Evolutionary Context

We need to turn the clock back to Europe of the late nineteenth and early twentieth centuries. The concept of evolution—the notion that all animal and plant forms seen in the modern world had descended or evolved from earlier, ancestral forms—had been debated by scientists for quite some time (Greene 1959). It was not until Charles Darwin's *On the Origin of Species* was published in 1859, however, that a viable mechanism for evolution was proposed and supported with an enormous body of data. Darwin had meticulously studied his subject, compiling evidence from all over the world for more than thirty years in support of his evolutionary mechanism called *natural selection.* Darwin's arguments were so well reasoned that most scientists soon became convinced of the explanatory power of his theory. Darwin went on to apply his general theory to humanity in *The Descent of Man*, published in 1871. This book was also enormously successful, and more thinkers came to accept the notion of human evolution.

Around the same time that Darwin was theorizing about the biological origin of humanity, discoveries were being made in Europe and Asia that seemed to provide concrete evidence supporting the concept of human evolution from ancestral forms. In 1856 workers building a roadway in the Neander Valley of Germany came upon a piece of a remarkable-looking fossil bone. Though just a "skull cap"—technically a *calvarium*, lacking the face and lower jaw—it clearly was no ape, but it was no modern human either. Though no smaller than a modern human's, the top of the skull was much flatter, the bone was thicker and heavier, and there was a massive ridge of bone across the eyebrows of a size unseen in modern populations. Around the same time, other, similar-looking but more complete fossils were found in Belgium and Spain. As well as being flat and massive and bearing thick brow ridges, these skulls exhibited sloping foreheads and jutting, snoutlike faces, quite distinct from those of modern human beings. However, the postcranial bones (all the bones below the skull) of these fossils were similar to those of modern humans.

There was some initial confusion about how to label these specimens. Some scientists concluded that they simply represented pathological freaks. Rudolf Virchow, the world's preeminent anatomist, explained the curious bony ridges above the eyes as the result of "stupendous blows" to the foreheads of the creatures (Kennedy 1975). Eventually, however, scientists realized that these creatures, then and now called *Neandertals* after the Neander Valley, represented an ancient form of humanity.

The growing acceptance of Darwin's theory of evolution and the discovery of primitive-looking, though humanlike, fossils combined to radically shift people's opinions about human origins. In fact, the initial abhorrence many felt concerning the entire notion of human evolution from lower, more primitive forms was remarkably changed in just a few decades

(Greene 1959). By the turn of the twentieth century, not only were many people comfortable with the general concept of human evolution but there actually also developed a feeling of national pride concerning the discovery of a human ancestor within one's borders.

The Germans could point to their Neandertal skeletons and claim that the first primitive human being was a German. The French could counter that their own Cro-Magnon—ancient, though not as old as the German Neandertals—was a more modern-looking and advanced ancestor; therefore, the first true human was a Frenchman. Fossils had also been found in Belgium and Spain, so Belgians and Spaniards could claim for themselves a place within the saga of human origin and development. Even so small a nation as Holland could lay claim to a place in human evolutionary history; in 1891 a Dutchman, Eugene Dubois, had discovered the fossilized remains of a primitive human ancestor in Java, an island in the Dutch colony of Dutch East India (now Indonesia).

However, one great European nation did not and could not materially contribute to the debate over the ultimate origins of humanity. That nation was England. Very simply, by the beginning of the second decade of the twentieth century, no fossils of human evolutionary significance had been located in England. This lack of fossils led French scientists to label English human paleontology mere "pebble-collecting" (Blinderman 1986). The conclusion reached by most was completely unpalatable to the proud English— no one had evolved in England. The English must have originally arrived from somewhere else.

Remember the Fujimura hoax discussed in Chapter 3. By planting genuinely ancient artifacts at Japanese sites, Fujimura gave Japanese archaeologists as well as the Japanese public precisely what they wanted: archaeological sites apparently as ancient as anything found on the Asian mainland. The sites Fujimura ostensibly found—and, in reality, fabricated—were embraced by the Japanese, fulfilling their desire for evidence of the great antiquity of their people and culture. In a sense, England was in a similar position in the late nineteenth and early twentieth centuries. The nation's sites and fossils simply were not as old as those found on mainland Europe. Public and professional disappointment about this produced a fertile field for an archaeological hoax.

The Brain-Centered Paradigm

At the same time that the English were feeling like a people with no evolutionary roots of their own, many other Europeans were still uncomfortable with the fossil record as it stood in the first decade of the twentieth century. Although most were happy to have human fossils in their countries, they generally were not happy with what those fossils looked like and what their appearance implied about the course of human evolution.

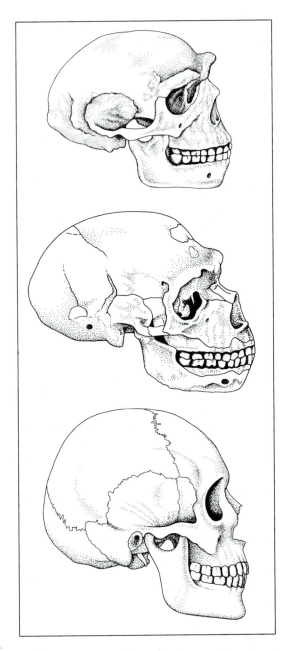

Figure 4.1 Drawings showing the general differences in skull size and form among *top, Homo erectus* ("Peking Man," 500,000 years ago); *center,* "Neandertal Man" (100,000 years ago); and *bottom,* a modern human being. Note the large brow ridges and forward-thrusting faces of *Homo erectus* and Neandertal, the rounded outline of the modern skull, and the absence of a projecting chin in earlier forms. (Carolyn White)

"Java Man" seemed quite apelike, with its large eyebrow ridges and small cranium—a volume of about 940 cubic centimeters (cc) compared with an average of 1,450 cc for modern humans (Figure 4.1). "Neandertal Man," with his sloping forehead and thick, heavy brow ridges, appeared to many to be quite ugly, stupid, and brutish: think those hairy cavemen in the GEICO television commercials. (Check out a compilation of the ads on YouTube: http://www.youtube.com/watch?v=3F3qzfTCDG4&feature=related.)

The skulls of these fossil types were clearly not those of apes, but they were equally clearly not fully human. In contrast, the femur (thigh bone) of "Java Man" seemed identical to the modern form. Although some emphasized what they perceived to be primitive characteristics of the postcranial skeleton of the Neandertals, this species clearly had walked on two feet; apes do not.

All this evidence suggested that ancient human ancestors had primitive apelike heads and, by implication, primitive apelike brains, seated atop rather modern-looking human bodies. This further implied that the human body evolved first, followed only later by the development of the brain and associated human intelligence.

Such a picture was precisely the opposite of what many people had expected and hoped for (Feder 1990b, 2006). After all, it was argued, it is intelligence that most clearly and absolutely differentiates humanity from the rest of the animal kingdom. It is in our ability to think, to communicate, and to invent that we are most distant from our animal cousins. This being the case, it was assumed that such abilities must have been evolving the longest; in other words, the human brain and the ability to think must have evolved first. Thus, the argument went, the fossil evidence for evolution should show that the brain had expanded first, followed by the modernization of the body.

Such a view is exemplified in the writings of anatomist Grafton Elliot Smith. Smith said that what most characterized human evolution must have been the "steady and uniform development of the brain along a well-defined course" (as quoted in Blinderman 1986:36). Arthur Smith Woodward, ichthyologist and paleontologist at the British Museum of Natural History, tellingly characterized the human brain as "the most complex mechanism in existence." He reiterated the contemporary argument: "The growth of the brain preceded the refinement of the features and of the somatic characters in general" (Dawson and Woodward 1913).

Put most simply, many researchers in evolution were looking for fossil evidence of a creature with the body of an ape and a brain near that of a human being. This, in simplest terms, represents the brain-centered paradigm. What was being discovered, however, was the reverse; both Java and Neandertal Man seemed more to represent creatures with skulls that enclosed apelike, or certainly not humanlike, brains perched atop quite humanlike bodies. Many were uncomfortable with such a picture.

A Remarkable Discovery in Sussex

Thus was the stage set for the initially rather innocuous announcement that appeared in the British science journal *Nature* (News, December 5, 1912) concerning a fossil find in the Piltdown section of Sussex in southern England. The notice read, in part:

> Remains of a human skull and mandible, considered to belong to the early Pleistocene period, have been discovered by Mr. Charles Dawson

in a gravel-deposit in the basin of the River Ouse, north of Lewes, Sussex. Much interest has been aroused in the specimen owing to the exactitude with which its geological age is said to have been fixed. (p. 390)

In *Nature* two weeks later (Paleolithic Man, December 19, 1912), further details were provided concerning the important find:

The fossil human skull and mandible to be described by Mr. Charles Dawson and Dr. Arthur Smith Woodward at the Geological Society as we go to press is the most important discovery of its kind hitherto made in England. The specimen was found in circumstances which seem to leave no doubt of its geological age, and the characters it shows are themselves sufficient to denote its extreme antiquity. (p. 438)

According to the story later told by those principally involved, in February 1912 Arthur Smith Woodward at the British Museum received a letter from Charles Dawson, a Sussex lawyer and an amateur scientist. Woodward had previously worked with Dawson and knew him to be an extremely intelligent man with a keen interest in natural history. Dawson informed Woodward in the letter that he had in his possession several fragments of a remarkable and ancient fossil human skull. The first piece had been discovered in 1908 by workers near the Barcombe Manor in the Piltdown region of Sussex, England. In 1911, four more pieces of the skull came to light in the same pit, along with a fossil animal bone and tooth.

In the letter to Woodward, Dawson expressed excitement over the discovery and claimed to Woodward that the find was quite important and might even surpass the significance of Heidelberg Man, an important specimen found in Germany just the previous year.

Because of bad weather, Woodward was not immediately able to visit Piltdown. Dawson, undaunted, continued to work in the pit, finding fossil hippo and elephant teeth. Unable to contain his excitement and eager for Woodward's reaction, he brought the fossil to Woodward at the museum in May 1912. What Woodward saw was a skull that matched his own expectations and those of many others concerning what a human ancestor should look like. The skull, stained a dark brown from apparent age, seemed to be modern in many of its characteristics. The thickness of the bones however, argued for a certain primitiveness. The association of the skull fragments with the bones of extinct animals implied that an ancient human ancestor indeed had inhabited England. By itself this was enormous news; at long last England had a human fossil (Figure 4.2).

Things were to get even more exciting for English paleontologists. On June 2, 1912, Woodward arrived at Piltdown together with Dawson and Pierre Teilhard de Chardin, a priest at the local Jesuit seminary whom Dawson had befriended in 1909 after finding him collecting fossils in the same pit where the skull fragments had been found the previous year. Along

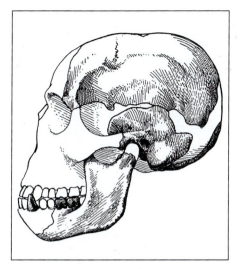

Figure 4.2 Drawn reconstruction of the Piltdown skull. The portion of the skull actually recovered is shaded. As reconstructed, the cranium shows hominid (human) traits and the mandible shows pongid (ape) traits. Compare this drawing to those in Figure 4.1. With its humanlike head and apelike jaw, the overall appearance of the Piltdown fossil is far different from that of *Homo erectus,* Neandertal, or modern humans.

with a workman, the three excavated in the same location unsuccessfully for several hours when, at last, Dawson found another fragment of the skull. Very soon thereafter, Teilhard recovered an elephant tooth.

Woodward was so impressed by their success that he decided to spend the remainder of his summer weekends at Piltdown, excavating alongside Dawson (Figure 4.3). Though work went slowly, in the ensuing weeks the pair found four additional large pieces of the cranium, along with some possible stone tools, animal teeth, and a fossilized deer antler. Altogether, the fragments of fifteen animal teeth were recovered by the excavators. Among the identifiable remains were the teeth of extinct forms of beaver and elephant, both of which were thought to have become extinct sometime between 400,000 and 500,000 years ago. The deduction was made, therefore, that the Piltdown remains likely dated to that same time period and represented the oldest known human ancestor in the world.

Then, to add to the excitement, when Dawson and Woodward returned later in the summer, Dawson discovered what seemed to be half of the lower jaw that belonged to the cranium. Though two key areas—the chin and the condyle, where the jaw connects to the cranium—were missing, the preserved part did not look human. The upright portion, or *ramus,* was too wide, and the bone was too thick. In fact, the jaw looked remarkably like that of an ape (Figure 4.4). Nonetheless, and quite significantly, the two intact molar teeth exhibited humanlike wear. The human jaw, lacking the large canines of apes, is free to move from side to side while chewing. The molars can grind in a sideways motion in a manner impossible in monkeys or apes. As a result, the molar surfaces of monkeys and apes are far rougher than those of humans, which become much smoother as they wear down through time. The relative smoothness or flatness of the

Figure 4.3   Paleontological excavations proceed at Piltdown. From left to right: Robert Kenward, Jr., a tenant of Barcombe Manor; Charles Dawson; workman Venus Hargreaves; the goose "Chipper"; and Arthur Smith Woodward. (© Natural History Museum, London)

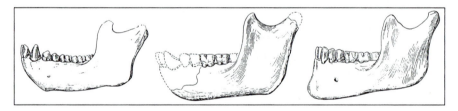

Figure 4.4   Comparison of the mandibles (lower jaws) of a young chimpanzee (left), a modern human (right), and Piltdown (center). Note how much more similar the Piltdown mandible is to that of the chimp, particularly in the form of the reconstructed chin. The presence of a projecting chin is a uniquely human trait.

Piltdown molar surfaces was a clear match with those of modern humans in a jaw that was otherwise quite apelike in form.

That the cranium and the jaw had been found close together in the same geologically ancient deposit seemed to argue for the obvious conclusion that they belonged to the same ancient creature. But what kind of creature could it have been? There were no large brow ridges like those of Java or Neandertal Man. The face was interpreted as having been flat as in modern humans and not snoutlike as in the Neandertals. The profile of the cranium was round as it is in modern humans, not flattened as it appeared to be in the Java and Neandertal specimens (see Figures 4.1 and 4.2). According to Woodward, the size of the skull indicated a cranial capacity, or brain size, of about 1,070 cc (Dawson and Woodward 1913), larger than Java Man's and within the lower range for modern humanity. Anatomist Arthur Keith (1913) suggested that the capacity of the skull was actually much larger, as much as 1,500 cc, placing it almost exactly at the modern mean. But the jaw, as described earlier, was entirely ape-like. Therefore, although only two molar teeth were recovered initially, Woodward reconstructed the Piltdown jaw with large, projecting canine teeth, similar to those of the apes.

The conclusion drawn first by Dawson, the discoverer, and then by Woodward, the professional scientist, was that the Piltdown fossil—named for its discoverer *Eoanthropus dawsoni,* meaning Dawson's Dawn Man—was the single most important fossil find yet made anywhere in the world. *The New York Times* headline of December 19, 1912, proclaimed "Paleolithic Skull Is a Missing Link." Three days later the *Times* headline read even more definitively: "Darwin Theory Is Proved True."

The implications were clear. Piltdown Man, with its modern skull, primitive jaw, and great age, was the evidence many human paleontologists had been searching for: an ancient man with a large brain, a modern-looking head, and primitive characteristics below the important brain. As anatomist G. E. Smith summarized it:

> The brain attained what may be termed the human rank when the jaws and face, and no doubt the body also, still retained much of the uncouthness of Man's simian ancestors. In other words, Man at first, so far as his general appearance and "build" are concerned, was merely an Ape with an overgrown brain. The importance of the Piltdown skull lies in the fact that it affords tangible confirmation of these inferences. (Smith 1927:105–6)

If Piltdown were the evolutionary "missing link" between apes and people, then neither Neandertal nor Java Man could be. Because Piltdown and Java Man lived at approximately the same time, Java might have been a more primitive offshoot of humanity that had become extinct. As Neandertal was much more recent than Piltdown, yet looked more primitive where it really counted (that is, the head), Neandertal must have represented some sort of primitive throwback, a slip down the evolutionary ladder (Figure 4.5).

By paleontological standards the implications were breathtaking. In one sweeping blow Piltdown had presented England with its first ancestral human fossil, it had shown that human fossils found elsewhere in the world were either primitive evolutionary offshoots or later throwbacks to a more primitive type, and it had forced the rewriting of the entire story of human evolution. Many paleontologists, especially those in England, were

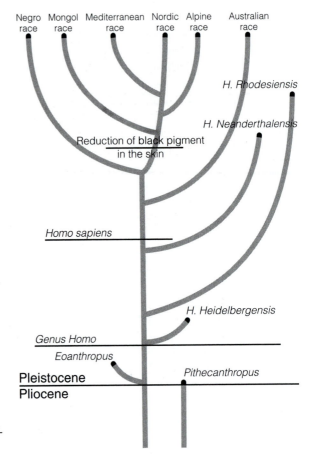

Figure 4.5   Among its supporters, *Eoanthropus* (Piltdown Man) was seen as more directly ancestral to modern humanity than either *Pithecanthropus*—now called *Homo erectus* and depicted as an entirely separate evolutionary pathway—or Neandertal, shown here as a short-lived diversion off the main branch of human evolution. Note also on this diagram the implied racism in its depiction of the "Australian," "Negro," and "Mongol" races as representative of earlier off-shoots of humanity.

enthralled by the discovery in Sussex. An artist's conception of "the first Englishman" was published in a popular weekly magazine, *The Illustrated London News* (Figure 4.6).

In March 1913, Dawson and Woodward published the first detailed account of the characteristics and evolutionary implications of the Piltdown fossil. In their discussion they repeatedly pointed out the modern characteristics of the skull and the simian appearance of the mandible. Their comments regarding the modernity of the skull and the apelike characteristics of the jaw, as you will see, turned out to be accurate in a way that few suspected at the time.

Additional discoveries were made at Piltdown. In 1913 a right canine tooth apparently belonging to the jaw was discovered by Teilhard de Chardin. It matched almost exactly the canine that had previously been proposed by Woodward for the Piltdown skull and that appeared in the reconstruction produced at the British Museum of Natural History. Its apelike form and wear were precisely what had been expected: "If a comparative anatomist

Figure 4.6   Artist's conception of Piltdown Man. Note how the illustrator has depicted the lower part of the face, with jaw thrust forward, just like an ape. (From *The Illustrated London News,* January 11, 1913, New York Edition)

were fitting out *Eoanthropus* with a set of canines, he could not ask for anything more suitable than the tooth in question," stated Yale University professor George Grant MacCurdy (1914:159).

Additional artifacts were found in the Piltdown pit in 1914, the most astonishing of which was almost immediately called the "cricket bat." It was a flat piece of carved bone that, indeed, looked a bit like the bat used to strike the ball in the British game of cricket. It seemed that at Piltdown, not only had the British found the missing link and not only could they assert that he was British, but he had played the British national sport as well!

Certainly, Dawson's discovery at Piltdown inspired a vigorous search for confirming evidence, especially in the form of other fossils that looked like *Eoanthropus* and that dated to a similar time period. For a while, no one could find any such evidence. Then, in what appeared to be a spectacular stroke of luck, in January 1915 none other than Charles Dawson found that evidence in the form of fragments of another fossil human cranium located on Netherhall Farm, about 2 miles from Piltdown. This cranium, dubbed Piltdown II, looked just like the first with a rounded profile and thick bones. Though no jaw was discovered, a molar recovered at the site bore a pattern of wear similar to that seen in the first specimen. You should now understand why, as noted in

Chapter 3, Dawson was called the "Wizard of Sussex" for his amazing luck at finding the only ostensible confirmation of the original discovery.

Dawson died in 1916 and, in part due to a serious illness suffered by his own son, Woodward held back announcement of the second discovery until the following year. When the existence of a second specimen became known, many of those skeptical after the discovery of the first Piltdown fossil became supporters. As Henry Fairfield Osborn, president of the American Museum of Natural History, suggested:

> If there is a Providence hanging over the affairs of prehistoric man, it certainly manifested itself in this case, because the three minute fragments of this second Piltdown man found by Dawson are exactly those which we should have selected to confirm the comparison with the original type. (1921:581)

The Piltdown Enigma

There was no unanimity of opinion, however, concerning the significance of the Piltdown discoveries. The cranium was so humanlike and the jaw so apelike that some scientists maintained that they simply were the fossils of two different creatures; the skeptics suggested that the association of the human cranium and the ape jaw was entirely coincidental. Gerrit S. Miller, Jr. (1915), of the Smithsonian Institution conducted a detailed analysis of casts of Piltdown I and concluded that the jaw was certainly that of an ape (see Figure 4.4). Many other scientists in the United States and Europe agreed. Anatomy professor David Waterston (1913) at the University of London, King's College, thought the mandible was that of a chimpanzee. The very well-known German scientist Franz Weidenreich concluded that Piltdown I was "the artificial combination of fragments of a modern-human braincase with an orangutan-like mandible and teeth" (1943:273).

Though some viewed the combination of a humanlike cranium and an apelike jaw as "an improbable monster" (Spencer 1990:113), the only other possibility being considered seemed even more improbable. As anatomist Grafton Elliot Smith put it:

> This [other possibility] would involve the supposition that a hitherto unknown and extremely primitive ape-man, and an equally unknown manlike ape, died on the same spot, and that one of them left his skull without the jaw and the other his jaw without the skull. (In Spencer 1990:101)

This seemed a strong argument against the hypothesis that Piltdown represented the accidental and coincidental discovery in precisely the same place of the remains of two creatures neither of which had ever been found in England before. As we shall see, accident and coincidence had nothing to do with the Piltdown discovery.

After Dawson's death no further discoveries were made in either the Piltdown I or II localities. Elsewhere in the world, however, human paleontology became an increasingly exciting and fruitful endeavor. Beginning in the late 1920s as many as forty individuals of a species now called *Homo erectus* were unearthed at Zhoukoudian, a cave near Beijing in China (see Figure 4.1). Ironically, Davidson Black, anatomist at the Peking Union Medical College, who was instrumental in obtaining financial support for the excavation, had visited Grafton Elliot Smith's laboratory in 1914 and had become fascinated by the Piltdown find (Shapiro 1974). Further, the Jesuit priest who had dug at Piltdown, Teilhard de Chardin, participated in the excavation at the Chinese cave. The Zhoukoudian fossils were estimated to be one-half million years old, an age quite similar to that assigned to the Piltdown remains. Also, on Java, another large group of fossils (close to twenty) were found at Sangiran; these were similar to those from Zhoukoudian.

Also in the 1920s, in Africa, a fossil given the name *Australopithecus africanus* was discovered. It was initially estimated to be more than one million years old and, therefore, older than Piltdown. In the 1930s and 1940s additional finds of this and other varieties of *Australopithecus* were made. In Europe the number of Neandertal specimens kept increasing; and even in England, in 1935, a fossil human ancestor was discovered at a place called Swanscombe.

Though *Eoanthropus* had inspired much of this research, all of these discoveries seemed to contradict its validity and the validity of the brain-centered paradigm. The Chinese and Sangiran *Homo erectus* evidence pointed to a fossil ancestor with a humanlike body and a primitive head; these specimens were similar to "Java Man" in appearance ("Java Man" is also now considered to belong to the species *Homo erectus*), possessing large brow ridges, a flat skull, and a thrust-forward face while being quite modern from the neck down. Even the much older australopithecines showed clear evidence of walking on two feet; their skeletons were remarkably humanlike from the neck down, though their heads were quite apelike. Together, both of these species seemed to confirm the notion that human beings began their evolutionary history as upright apes, not as apelike people. *Eoanthropus* seemed increasingly to be the evolutionary "odd man out."

How could Piltdown be explained in light of the new fossil evidence from China, Java, Europe, and Africa? Either Piltdown was the one, true human ancestor, rendering all the manifold other discoveries members of extinct offshoots of the main line of human evolution, or else Piltdown was the remarkable coincidental find of the only known ape fossil in England within a few feet of a rather modern human skull that seemed to date back 500,000 years. Neither explanation sat well with many people.

Unmasking the Hoax

This sort of confusion characterized the status of Piltdown for nearly forty years, until 1949, when a chemical dating procedure was finally applied to the fossil. A measurement was made of the amount of the element fluorine in the bones. This was known to be a relative measure of the amount of time bone had been in the ground. Bones pick up fluorine in groundwater; the longer they have been buried, the more fluorine they have.

Kenneth Oakley of the British Museum of Natural History conducted the test. The fossil animal bones from the site showed varying amounts of fluorine, but they exhibited as much as ten times more than did either the cranium or the jaw of the fossil human. Piltdown Man, Oakley concluded, based on comparison to fluorine concentrations in bones at other sites in England, was no more than 50,000 years old (Oakley and Weiner 1955).

Although this cast Piltdown in a new light, the implications were just as mysterious; what was a fossil human doing with an entirely apelike jaw at a date as recent as 50,000 years ago? Then, in 1953, a more precise test was applied to larger samples of the cranium and the jaw. The results were conclusive; the cranium and jaw were of entirely different ages. The cranium possessed 0.10 percent fluorine, the mandible less than 0.03 percent (Oakley 1976). The inevitable conclusion was reached that the cranium and the jaw must have belonged to two different creatures.

As a result of this determination, a detailed reexamination of the fossil was conducted, and the sad truth was finally revealed. The entire thing had been a hoax. The cranium was that of a modern human being. Its appearance of age was due, at least in part, to its having been artificially chemically stained. It has been suggested that the thickness of the bone may have been due to a pathological condition (Spencer 1984) or the result of a chemical treatment that had been applied, perhaps to make it appear older than it was (Montague 1960).

Those scientific supporters of *Eoanthropus* who previously had pointed out the apelike character of the jaw were more right than they could have imagined; it was, indeed, an ape jaw, probably that of an orangutan. When Gerrit Miller of the Smithsonian Institution had commented on the broken condyle of the mandible by saying, "Deliberate malice could hardly have been more successful than the hazards of deposition in so breaking the fossils as to give free scope to individual judgement in fitting the parts together" (1915:1), he was using a literary device and not suggesting that anyone had purposely broken the jaw. But that is likely precisely what

Figure 4.7 A photomicrograph of one of Piltdown Man's teeth shows a series of mostly parallel scratch marks across the enamel of its occlusal surface. These scratch marks are not natural or accidental; they are the result of intentional filing in order to make the tooth appear to be more humanlike within the context of an otherwise very apelike jaw. The jaw was apelike in appearance for a good reason: it was, in fact, the jaw of an ape. (Natural History Museum, London)

happened. An ape's jaw could never articulate with the base of a human cranium, and so the area of connection had to be removed to give "free scope" to researchers to hypothesize how the cranium and the jaw went together. Otherwise the hoax would never have succeeded. Beyond this, the molars had been filed down to artificially create the humanlike wear pattern. Scanning electron microscopy has revealed the metal file marks quite clearly (Figure 4.7). The hoaxer knew that smooth molar surfaces were needed to give the orangutan jaw a more human or "missing link" appearance and, apparently, had used a simple metal file to accomplish the task. The canine tooth had been stained with an artist's pigment and filed down to simulate human wear; the pulp cavity had been filled with a substance not unlike chewing gum.

It was further determined that at least one of the fragments of the Piltdown II skull was simply another piece of the first one. Oakley (1976) further concluded that all the other paleontological specimens had been planted at the site; some were probably found in England, but others had likely originated as far away as Malta and Tunisia. Some of the ostensible bone artifacts—including the cricket bat—had been carved with a metal knife. Altogether forty faked objects (items simply found somewhere else and planted at the site as well as items actually fabricated or altered by the hoaxer), including animal bones and teeth, stone and bone tools, and the Piltdown cranial remains (nine of the forty), were recovered in the dig.

The verdict was clear; as Weidenreich (1943) put it, Piltdown was like the chimera of Greek mythology—a monstrous combination of different creatures. The question of Piltdown's place in human evolution had been answered; it had no place. That left still open two important questions: Who did it, and why?

Whodunnit?

The most succinct and honest answer to the question "Whodunnit?" is, No one knows. Many of those directly involved with the discoveries made at Piltdown or the analysis of the fossils—and even some who were very indirectly connected to the site—have been accused as perpetrators or co-conspirators in the hoax (Figure 4.8). Tobias (1992) lists twenty-one possible suspects. We can assess the cases against some of the more likely of them.

Suspect: Charles Dawson

Charles Dawson was a well-known and highly respected amateur scientist whose great diligence and luck at finding rare or unique specimens was both admired and envied (Russell 2003). Though he had no university degree or specialized training, even before his discovery at Piltdown he had been named a "fellow" of two very prestigious scientific societies: the Geological Society and the Society of Antiquaries of London. Dawson donated much of his geological, paleontological, and archaeological collection to the British Museum (Natural History) and was given the title "honorary collector" by that institution. Further, *Eoanthropus dawsoni* was not the first fossil named

Figure 4.8   Portrait of scientists examining a number of specimens, including *Eoanthropus*, in 1915. From left to right, standing: F. O. Barlowe, G. E. Smith, Charles Dawson, and A. S. Woodward; from left to right, seated: A. S. Underwood, A. Keith, W. P. Pycraft, and E. R. Lankester. Charles Darwin peers over their shoulders in the portrait hanging on the wall behind them. (© Natural History Museum, London)

for him; one fossil plant, one dinosaur, and a fossil mammal species all bore the species name *dawsoni,* each having been brought to light by Dawson (Russell 2003:28). Certainly not "God's Hand" (like Shinichi Fujimura; see Chapter 3) but Dawson's great luck at finding significant specimens earned him, in archaeological circles, the nickname "the Wizard of Sussex" (Russell 2003:10).

Dawson is the prime suspect in the case of Piltdown. He is the only person who was present at every discovery, including Piltdown II. In fact, his apparently spectacular luck in being the only researcher able to find any confirming evidence for the original discovery, also made by him, raises a red flag. As noted in Chapter 3, being too lucky in paleoanthropology or archaeology arouses suspicion. Also, it should be mentioned that Dawson served as steward on both Barcombe Manor, where Piltdown I was discovered, and Netherhall Farm, the site of Piltdown II, so he had access to and familiarity with both locations of "discovery." This circumstantial evidence alone strongly implicates Dawson in the hoax. It would have required incredible luck for someone else to have planted the bones and, both times, to have Dawson find them. Dawson's motive may have been rooted in his desire for acceptance within the scientific community. He certainly gained notoriety; even the species name is *dawsoni.*

With all of this in mind, it is difficult to dispute Russell's (2003:208) conclusion: "In short, Dawson *cannot* have been innocent of the Piltdown hoax. From the start to the finish, he is implicated at every single stage."

Suspect: Arthur Smith Woodward

Arthur Smith Woodward was the professional scientist most intimately involved with Piltdown, co-announcing its discovery, co-authoring the first scientific publication describing the find, and participating in the discovery of additional materials in later excavations at the site. His association with Dawson can be traced for thirty years before Piltdown.

Woodward's behavior toward the end of his life, however, seems not to reflect that of a co-conspirator in the hoax, or even of someone who was aware that Piltdown might have been a fake. Upon retirement from the museum, Woodward actually moved close to Piltdown and continued to excavate at the site in the summer. That would seem to indicate that Woodward maintained a belief that Piltdown was genuine and that additional research at the site might reveal additional proof of the significance of the original find.

Suspect: Pierre Teilhard de Chardin

Pierre Teilhard de Chardin has come under scrutiny as well, most recently by Harvard paleontologist and chronicler of science Stephen Jay Gould (1980). Teilhard is a reasonable suspect because he was present during many of the key discoveries at Piltdown. It is also the case, as Gould points out, that Teilhard's later reconstruction of the chronology of his involvement with Piltdown was suspicious; at one point he asserted that he had seen the remains of Piltdown II and had been taken to the site in 1913, which was two years before Dawson supposedly found them. It is also somewhat perplexing that, after the hoax was unmasked toward the end of his life, Teilhard became increasingly reluctant to comment on the entire affair or to clarify his role in it.

But the mere facts that an embarrassed Teilhard mentioned Piltdown but little in his later writings on evolution and was confused about the precise chronology of discoveries in the pit do not add up to a convincing case.

Suspect: Sir Grafton Elliot Smith

The evidence for involvement by G. E. Smith in the hoax is slim, and all of it is circumstantial. Smith was born in Australia, and his arrival in England was followed relatively quickly by the appearance of the Piltdown skull; thus, a connection has been suggested. But Smith did not visit the Piltdown location until 1915–16 and would have had no opportunity to have planted the fossils. Similarly, he would have had no motive for doing so, save to support his fundamental perspective of human evolution. His view of the temporal priority of brain expansion in human evolution was similar to that of many of his colleagues, so this in no way distinguishes Smith from a multitude of scientists who welcomed the implications of Piltdown, but who had nothing to do with the hoax itself.

Suspect: Sir Arthur Keith

Anatomist Arthur Keith has been accused of participation in the hoax (Spencer 1990; Tobias 1992). According to Keith's own diary, on December 16, 1912, he had written an anonymous article describing events at Piltdown for the *British Medical Journal*. Curiously, this was two days *before* some of the events discussed took place (Spencer 1990:189). Also, the article contained information that, ostensibly, no one but Woodward, Dawson, and the hoaxer could have known. Further, Keith knew or at least had met Dawson before he told people he had, and later he destroyed his correspondence with Dawson.

This may show that Keith was guilty of obtaining additional information about the discovery from someone else (perhaps one of the workers at the excavation) and then of publishing it, but it is not convincing evidence of participation in the hoax. The rest seems attributable to a faulty memory and an innocent mistake in recording a date in a personal log. Again, there is no direct evidence of involvement.

Suspect: Martin A. C. Hinton

Martin A. C. Hinton was a curator of zoology at the Natural History Museum in London. Hinton had worked under Arthur Smith Woodward at the time of the hoax, and some have claimed that before the Piltdown affair they had a falling out about payment for some work Hinton had done at the museum. So, conceivably, Hinton may have had a motive for embarrassing Woodward.

More important, some have pointed to what they consider to be a smoking gun with Hinton's fingerprints—a trunk found at the museum in the mid-1970s bearing Hinton's initials (Gee 1996). The trunk contained an assemblage of fossil hippopotamus and elephant teeth stained and carved in a fashion similar to the fake animal fossils found with Piltdown Man. In fact, the proportions of chemicals that had been used in staining the bones found in Hinton's trunk were the same as those used to make the Piltdown specimens look old.

However, there is no evidence that Hinton had been to Piltdown before Dawson's discovery, so there is no direct evidence of his having any opportunity to plant the bones.

Suspect: Lewis Abbott

Blinderman (1986) argues that Lewis Abbott, another amateur scientist and artifact collector, is the most likely perpetrator. He had an enormous ego and felt slighted by professional scientists. He claimed to have been the one who directed Dawson to the pit at Piltdown and may even have been with Dawson when Piltdown II was discovered (Dawson said only that he had been with a friend when the bones were found). Abbott knew how to make stone tools and so was capable of forging those found at Piltdown. Again, however, the evidence, though tantalizing, includes no smoking gun.

Suspect: Sir Arthur Conan Doyle

Even Sir Arthur Conan Doyle has come under the scrutiny of would-be Piltdown detectives. Doyle lived just seven miles from Piltdown, golfed nearby, and is known to have visited the site at least once. This provides him with the opportunity, but what would have been his motive to perpetrate the hoax?

Ironically, though Doyle was the creator of Sherlock Holmes, possessor of the most logical, rational mind in literature, Doyle himself was quite credulous when it came to spiritualism. He became an ardent supporter of two young English girls who claimed that fairies regularly visited their garden. They even concocted some outrageously bad photographs to prove their point, and Doyle accepted these obvious fakes without reservation.

One of Doyle's chief critics in this arena was British anatomist and zoologist Ray Lankester. Lankester had been for some time publicly contemptuous of Doyle's belief in spirits and fairies. If Doyle were truly involved in the Piltdown hoax, Lankester would have been one obvious target. In this scenario, Doyle crafted the hoax hoping that Lankester would fall for it and then be humiliated when Doyle revealed that it was all a fraud.

But this is quite a stretch; after all, how would Doyle know that Lankester would become deeply involved in Piltdown? He is depicted in the painting showing scientists examining the Piltdown specimen (see Figure 4.8; Lancester is sitting at the far right), but he wasn't all that involved in the research. Finally, there is no direct evidence to implicate Doyle. In the final analysis, he is an unlikely suspect.

The Lesson of Piltdown

Certainly, in the case of the Piltdown hoax, there is no shortage of suspects, and there is plenty of circumstantial evidence implicating many of them. Unfortunately, nothing has yet surfaced that definitively eliminates any of them or that would lead us confidently to a guilty verdict for any one of them either. But does that matter now, nearly a century after the first of the bones came into Charles Dawson's possession? If the Piltdown tale were a detective mystery, the question of "whodunnit" would be at the core of the story. However, in his review of Frank Spencer's book accusing Sir Arthur Keith, British prehistorian Christopher Chippindale (1990) has expressed the opinion of many anthropologists in his title: "Piltdown: Who Dunit? Who Cares?" Chippindale doubts that definitive evidence of anyone's guilt exists and suggests that this is beside the point anyway. His skepticism, however, isn't stopping people from trying to solve this part of the mystery. As I write this in March 2012, British scientists are having yet another go at it. The Piltdown remains are being analyzed once again, this time in an effort to find a smoking gun—in particular, any trace of chemical alteration that might connect the bones to the laboratories of any of those in any way associated with the discovery. I am not confident that a clear answer is forthcoming, but I don't think that will ever stop people from trying to solve this part of the mystery.

Of far greater significance than "whodunnit" is the reason for Piltdown's acceptance by such a broad group of scientists. Piltdown provided validation for a preferred view of human evolution, one in which the development of the brain preceded other aspects of human evolution. The hoaxer may never be known, but we do know that he or they almost certainly crafted the fraud to conform to this "brain-centered" perspective of human evolution. He or they gave people a fossil they would want to accept, and many fell into their trap.

The lesson of Piltdown is clear. Unlike the case of the Cardiff Giant, where scientists were not fooled, but just as was the case in the Fujimura hoaxes, here many were convinced by what appears to be, in hindsight, an inelegant fake. It shows quite clearly that scientists, though striving to be objective observers and explainers of the world around them, are, in the end, human. Many accepted the Piltdown evidence because they wished to—it supported a more comfortable view of human evolution. The perpetrator provided the British with an ancient ancestor and also a prehistory with a time depth at least the equal to and perhaps even greater than that of other nations. In his archaeological hoaxes, Fujimura provided much the same to the people of Japan. In fact, the widespread acceptance of Piltdown and, more recently, of Fujimura's planted sites may be attributable, in part, to the desire on the part of the British and the Japanese for a national connection to a more ancient period of time. Furthermore, perhaps out of naïveté, scientists could not even conceive that a fellow thinker about human origins would wish to trick them; the possibility that Piltdown was a fraud probably occurred to few, if any, of them.

Nevertheless, the Piltdown story, rather than being a black mark against science, instead shows how well it ultimately works. Even before its unmasking, Piltdown had been consigned by most to a netherworld of doubt. There was simply too much evidence supporting a different human pedigree than that implied by Piltdown. Proving it a hoax was just the final nail in the coffin lid for this fallacious fossil. As a result, though we may never know the hoaxer's name, at least we know this: If the goal was to forever confuse our understanding of the human evolutionary story, the hoax ultimately was a failure.

Current Perspectives: Human Evolution

With little more than a handful of cranial fragments, scientists defined an entire species, *Eoanthropus*, and recast the story of human evolution. Today, the situation in human paleontology is quite different. The tapestry of our human evolutionary history is no longer woven with the filaments of a small handful of gauzy threads. We can now base our evolutionary scenarios (Figure 4.9) on enormous quantities of data supplied by several fields of science (see Feder 2011 for a detailed summary of current thinking on human evolution).

It is rare, indeed, to find even the fragmentary remains of human ancestors dating back millions of years. It is astonishing in the extreme to find a nearly complete ancestral human fossil. And it is almost unheard of that such a skeleton is found along with the fragmentary remains of three dozen or so of its cohorts. Yet this is precisely the case for the finds made in Aramis, Ethiopia (White et al. 2009). The fossils date to 4.4 million years ago and are labeled *Ardipithecus ramidus*.

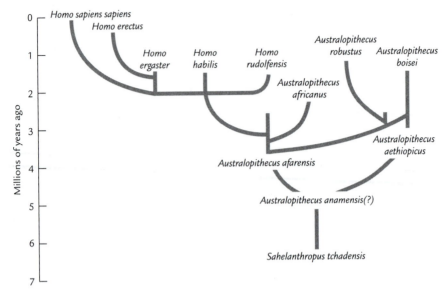

Figure 4.9   The chronology and connections of fossil hominids over the past 6.5 million years are depicted here. Each of the named species is represented by a number of fossil specimens. As can be seen, though many hominids existed in the past—and some lived at the same time—there currently is only a single species, *Homo sapiens*. All living people are members of this group.

The nearly complete skeleton is of a female. Her brain size is quite small; at about 350 cc it's only about one-quarter the size of a modern human's. It's smaller, in fact, even than that of a modern chimpanzee. But her face has a more human appearance. It's more vertical, showing less protrusion than a chimp's.

From analysis of the remains of her pelvis and leg bones, unlike chimps but like modern humans, "Ardi" clearly was an efficient upright walker. Also, she shows no evidence in her hand and finger bones for the specialized knuckle-walking of the modern apes; in all likelihood, at least on the ground, *Ardipithecus* was a fully committed biped. However, her skeleton shows that she was, at the same time, a proficient climber; her arms were proportionally long, like an ape's, and she also had a "divergent," highly separated big toe, another apelike feature. Long arms are useful for reaching for and pulling up on branches and a separated big toe (configured more like our thumbs than our big toes) is useful for grabbing onto branches while climbing. Her long fingers would also have been valuable in grasping onto tree limbs when climbing. Analysis of her teeth suggests a plant-based diet and the *Ardipithecus* adaptation to moving around in trees suggests that that's where much of its food was gathered. "Ardi" is so cool, precisely because she doesn't meet our expectations. She's not a neat form intermediate between ape and human from an early chapter in our evolution. She exhibits a mosaic of human and apelike traits that reflect a far more complex picture of the evolution of our earliest human ancestors. Very cool. And admittedly challenging.

Following *Ardipithecus* and dating to about 4 million years ago, *Australopithecus afarensis* is represented by more than a dozen fossil individuals from East Africa. The most famous specimen, known as "Lucy," is more than 40 percent complete. Its discovery by a team led by paleoanthropologist Donald Johanson was far more exciting than any hoax possibly could have been (Johanson and Edey 1982). Lucy's pelvis is remarkably modern and provides clear evidence of its upright, and therefore humanlike, posture. One of the defining characteristics of the human foot is the presence of an arch. The arch provides what is effectively a shock absorber because our full body weight is focused on each foot as it separately and sequentially contacts the ground during walking. The arch further allows for flexibility in negotiating uneven ground, and it provides an effective bounce-back, which aids in taking the next stride. Watch the bottom of a human foot closely as a person walks barefoot, and you'll see what I mean. A recently discovered *afarensis* metatarsal (one of the long bones in the foot) is wholly unlike the same bone in an ape and looks, instead, just like a modern human metatarsal (Ward, Kimbel, and Johanson 2011). This shows that *afarensis* possessed an arched foot and confirms that it was, in fact, an efficient upright walker.

If that's not enough for you, how about this: At a place called Laetoli, researchers discovered a pathway of fossilized *Australopithecus* footprints preserved in hardened volcanic ash (White and Suwa 1987). At least two individuals, walking in an entirely human pattern, crossed the soft ash, leaving an unmistakably human trail (Figure 4.10). The chemical makeup of the ash caused it to harden and preserve the footprints. The ash itself has been directly dated to more than 3.5 million years ago. By the way, though *Australopithecus* walked in a humanlike fashion, its skull was quite apelike and contained a brain the size of a chimpanzee's. The fossil evidence, contrary to Piltdown and the brain-centered view of evolution, shows quite clearly that human evolution proceeded from the feet up, not the head down.

Alan Walker and Richard Leakey (1993) excavated the 80-percent-complete skeleton of a 9- or 10-year-old boy who died on the shore of a lake more than 1.5 million years ago. He clearly walked upright and possessed a brain far larger than that of *Australopithecus* and about two-thirds the modern human size. That the so-called Nariokotome boy exhibits evidence of physical immaturity at the age of 9 or 10 reflects how human he was. Compared to most other animals, human beings have an extended period of maturation during which we master the skills we need as creatures who rely on learned behavior to a far greater degree than physical characteristics or instinct. The Nariokotome boy is placed in the taxonomic category *Homo ergaster. Homo ergaster*'s Asian descendant, *Homo erectus,* is known from

Figure 4.10   The dioramas at the American Museum of Natural History in New York City are glowing windows to other worlds, other places, and other times. Here, you can gaze through one of those magical windows and see two australopithecines, walking just like us, leaving their footprint trails in volcanic ash at Laetoli more than 3.5 million years ago.

dozens of individuals—forty from Zhoukoudian alone, nearly twenty from Java, and more than a dozen from Africa.

Recovered Neandertal skeletons number in the hundreds, allowing detailed comparisons between this extinct form of human being and us (Wynn and Coolidge 2012). Advances in technology have now allowed scientists to recover and isolate enough Neandertal nuclear DNA—the DNA found in the nucleus of the cell—from preserved bones to reconstruct the genome (the full DNA sequence) of this variety of human being (Green et al. 2010). Though we can't yet (and maybe never will be able to) clone one, the Neandertals can now talk to us directly through their own genetic code (Figure 4.11).

The scientists in this project began by identifying and then extracting nuclear DNA from the bones of three separate Neandertal individuals from Vindija Cave in Croatia, dating to around 40,000 years ago. They then were able to do the same for three more individual Neandertals, one from Spain (dating to 49,000 years ago), one from Germany (dating to 42,000 years ago),

Figure 4.11   Though past reconstructions of the Neandertals emphasized their "primitive" appearance, recent work, based on their actual skeletal morphology rather than preconceptions of their primitiveness, have resulted in a more accurate look. In the recent reconstruction shown here, Neandertals looked quite a bit like modern humans, albeit modern humans with sloping foreheads and big brow ridges; surprisingly similar in appearance, for what it's worth, to the actor John Travolta. (© Volker Steger/Nordstar "4 Million Years of Man"/ Photo Researchers)

and one from Russia (dating somewhere between 60,000 and 70,000 years ago), expanding the geographical database to cover much of the European homeland of the Neandertals.

The researchers then analyzed the genomes of five modern human beings, spread broadly across the globe, including an individual from southern Africa, one from western Africa, another from New Guinea (the large island just north of Australia), one from China, and, finally, an individual from France. When researchers compared all of the Neandertal and modern human DNA sequences, it was seen that the genetic makeup of all six of the Neandertals was internally consistent; in other words, Neandertals across Europe were genetically quite similar. Interestingly, however, they were also pretty similar to the modern humans, but there were significant exceptions. In fact, in 212 specific regions of our genetic instructions, modern humans possessed forms not seen in any of the Neandertal sequences (Green et al. 2010:717). Interestingly, one of those differences causes features of the cranium, including a large and protruding forehead, that are characteristic of modern humans but not of Neandertals, who had flat, sloping foreheads. Different genetic instructions like that one must have evolved since the evolutionary split between Neandertals and the ancestors of modern human beings.

Researchers estimate that the 212 differences seen between modern humans and Neandertals took between 270,000 and 440,000 years to accumulate (Green et al. 2010:718). In other words, Neandertals and our anatomically modern-looking ancestors appear to have diverged as evolutionary lines about that long ago. Derived from DNA, this date is a very good match for the date of divergence based on our skeletal anatomy: individuals with Neandertal-like features appear in the fossil record about 400,000 years ago and the oldest examples of anatomically modern human beings date to about 200,000 years ago. Science is at its best when entirely different lines of evidence converge to tell a similar story; that is precisely what we see in this research project.

There's one more fascinating implication of the recent Neandertal DNA research: Somewhere between 1 percent to 4 percent of the modern human genome can can be identified as "Neandertal." This Neandertal DNA may be present in modern human populations as a result of inter-breeding when anatomically modern humans left Africa after 100,000 years ago and encountered Neandertal populations already in place in the Middle East. So I guess you could say that the next time someone calls you a "Neandertal," it may very well be, at least in part, an accurate accusation, at least if you can trace your ancestry to Asia or Europe; there does not appear to be any Neandertal genetic admixture with people of African descent.

The Neandertal DNA research is cutting edge, and there is much more work that needs to be done. The conclusions reached by these researchers will need to be tested, reevaluated, refined, revised, and maybe even over-turned. That's exciting, far more exciting, in fact, than a fake concocted from stained skull bones and an ape jaw.

◈ ◈ ◈ FREQUENTLY ASKED QUESTIONS ◈ ◈ ◈

1. *Why didn't they just radiocarbon-date the Piltdown cranium and jaw to show how old they were?*

Radiocarbon dating was not developed until the 1950s, nearly forty years after Piltdown's discovery. If the Piltdown skull had been a genuine million-year-old fossil, carbon dating would have been useless anyway. Carbon dating works only on organic material (all the organic material in fossilized bone has been replaced with minerals) and can be applied to specimens no more than about 50,000 years old. After scientists realized that Piltdown had been a hoax, they did radiocarbon-date the cranium; it was about six hundred years old. The jaw was only ninety years old (Spencer and Stringer 1989).

2. *Isn't the theory of human evolution based on the discovery of just a handful of tiny bone fragments that could mean just about anything?*

Not at all. Paleoanthropologists have recovered thousands upon thousands of bones of our human ancestors. There are more than a dozen partial skeletons of *Australopithecus* and more than three hundred partial skeletons of Neandertals. Beyond this, some ancient skeletons—the Nariokotome boy from Africa and Jinniushan Man from China are two examples—are nearly complete, giving us a very detailed picture of what some of our extinct ancestors looked like. Modern scenarios of human evolution are based on a solid, large, and expanding database that includes DNA, ancient tools, and geology as well as bones—another reason why today a Piltdown hoax would be unlikely to fool anyone.

BEST OF THE WEB

http://www.nhm.ac.uk/nature-online/life/human-origins/piltdown-man/index.html

As mentioned at the beginning of the chapter, the Natural History Museum in London has an interactive guide to the Piltdown hoax.

http://home.tiac.net/~cri_a/piltdown/piltdown.html

Detailed discussion of the hoax; enormous bibliography is linked.

http://home.tiac.net/~cri_a/piltdown/readinglist.html

Piltdown bibliography with an extensive section on possible perpetrators.

http://home.tiac.net/~cri_a/piltdown/winslow.html

Presents the argument that Conan Doyle was the Piltdown "perp."

http://home.tiac.net/~cri_a/piltdown/drawhorn.html

Gerrell Drawhorn's paper presenting the argument that Arthur Smith Woodward was the perpetrator of the Piltdown hoax.

http://www.lhup.edu/~dsimanek/piltdown.htm

Website arguing that Martin Hinton was the perpetrator of the Piltdown hoax.

CRITICAL THINKING EXERCISE

The Cardiff Giant and Piltdown Man hoaxes were similar in that both related to archaeology and the study of human prehistory. However, they were quite different in terms of motives, the reasons for their success, and their impacts. Compare the motives for these two hoaxes. What were the goals of the hoaxers? Compare the reasons each was successful. Why did people want to believe them? Compare the impacts of the Cardiff Giant and Piltdown hoaxes on the *scientific* understanding of the human past. Do you think archaeologists would be fooled by these hoaxes today? Can modern archaeologists be fooled by any hoaxes considering the modern technology we now have available to assess the legitimacy of artifacts and skeletons?

Which of these two implications drawn from the Piltdown hoax do you agree with and why?

- Piltdown shows that even "objective" scientists cannot be trusted to apply a skeptical eye to data when those data fulfill their expectations and desires.

- Piltdown exemplifies the self-corrective nature of science.

5

Who Discovered America?

America's First People

Each October, on Columbus Day, pundits ponder the significance of the voyages of Christopher Columbus to the New World and debate whether, in fact, Columbus "discovered" America. Heated arguments ensue, and ink, if not blood, is spilled. But the issue of who discovered America is and should be a simple question of scientific fact. Did Columbus "discover" America in the true sense of that term? No, certainly not.

The scientific facts are clear. When Columbus arrived in the Caribbean in 1492, he found people already there. In fact, it is estimated that at the time of Columbus's voyages the New World was home to tens of millions of people exhibiting a broad spectrum of cultural diversity. There were hunters and gatherers in the Arctic, farmers in the midwestern United States who constructed enormous pyramids of earth (Chapter 7), mobile hunter-gatherers in the desert West, and corn-farming town dwellers in the Southwest. The New World also was home to a number of full-blown civilizations including the Aztec, Inca, and Maya (Chapter 13). These cultures were, in the view of the invading Spaniards themselves, the equal to any in the Old World. What the Aztec, Inca, Maya, and others were lacking, however, was gunpowder (a Chinese, not European, invention) and, even more significantly, immunity to European diseases, which killed more of them than did any conquistadors with swords or guns (Ramenofsky 1987).

The unanswered question, then, is not, Who discovered America? but, Where did the true discoverers, the Indians, come from? This very question was, in fact, asked by European scholars soon after they became aware of the inhabitants of the New World.

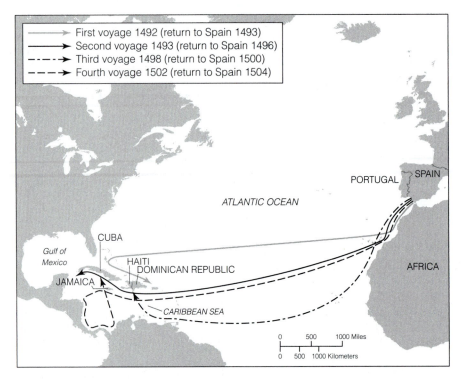

- → First voyage 1492 (return to Spain 1493)
- → Second voyage 1493 (return to Spain 1496)
- —·—·→ Third voyage 1498 (return to Spain 1500)
- ———→ Fourth voyage 1502 (return to Spain 1504)

SPAIN

PORTUGAL

ATLANTIC OCEAN

CUBA

Gulf of Mexico

HAITI
DOMINICAN REPUBLIC

AFRICA

JAMAICA

CARIBBEAN SEA

0   500   1000 Miles

0   500   1000 Kilometers

Figure 5.1 Routes taken by Columbus in his four voyages of exploration of the New World in 1492, 1493, 1498, and 1502. Columbus never gave up hope that he had discovered the coast of either Japan or China or lands immediately adjacent to the Orient.

A New World—To Europeans

Between 1492 and 1502, Christopher Columbus made four separate voyages to the New World searching for a shortcut to the riches of China and Japan (Figure 5.1). On the first and second of these he made landfalls on "San Salvador" (today identified as Watling Island or, possibly, Samana Cay), Cuba, and Haiti (Marden 1986). On the third and fourth voyages, a landfall was made on the coast of South America, and a large section of the coast of Middle America (Panama, Costa Rica, and Honduras) was explored (Fernandez-Armesto 1974).

Columbus never fully understood that he had accidentally discovered the Western Hemisphere, but he did come to realize that he had not successfully reached his hoped-for destination of Cathay (China) or Cipangu (Japan). For a short time during the first voyage, he thought Cuba was part of mainland Asia (Fuson 1987), but he soon concluded that it was, in fact, an island. Nevertheless, Columbus remained convinced that Cuba and the other islands he explored lay in proximity to the Asian mainland. As a result, he thought that the people he encountered during his voyages were Asians (Figure 5.2).

Figure 5.2   Woodcut image showing an artist's conception of the landing of Christopher Columbus on San Salvador, in the Caribbean, on October 12, 1492. (Library of Congress)

Others in Europe, however, believed that Columbus had discovered something far more intriguing than a handful of inhabited islands off the Chinese coast. It seemed clear to many that Columbus had discovered, as Amerigo Vespucci called it for the first time in print in 1503, "*a new world, because none of these countries were known to our ancestors*" (Vespucci 1904). Mapmaker Martin Waldseemüller may have clinched it in 1507 when he produced the first map that both labeled at least part of this new world "America" and depicted the Pacific Ocean as a substantial and distinct body of water separating it from Asia (Holden 2006b). When Magellan circumnavigated the globe in 1519–22, any lingering doubts that Columbus had indeed discovered a "new world" were erased.

Biblical Exegesis and American Indians

If the lands explored by Columbus were not part of Asia, then the people he encountered were not actual Asians, but some heretofore unknown group. This idea was problematical to sixteenth-century scholars and clerics. In their worldview, all people could be traced to Adam and Eve. Beyond this, all people could be more recently traced to Noah and his family (his wife, sons, and daughters-in-law), for all other descendants of the first couple had been wiped out in a great flood (see Chapter 12).

According to the Book of Genesis in the Old Testament, Noah had three sons, Shem, Ham, and Japheth. Biblical scholars had long since decided that each of the three sons represented the source for the three "races" of humanity recognized by Europeans: European, Oriental, and African. Japheth, apparently the best of the lot, was, naturally enough, considered to be the patriarch of the European people. Shem gave rise to the Asians, and Ham was the source for Africans. This was a neat enough arrangement for biblical literalists, but the recognition that the people Columbus had encountered were not Chinese or Japanese—and the initial assumption that they were neither European nor African—created a problem. There simply was no *fourth son* of Noah to provide a source for a *fourth race* of people. Though some, like Isaac de la Peyrère in 1655, suggested that Indians were part of a separate "pre-adamite" creation that had been unaffected by the biblical Flood (Greene 1959), notions of polygenesis were never particularly popular. For most, Indians were ordinary human beings descended first from Adam and later from Noah.

That led to the only conclusion possible: the natives of the New World must have reached its shores sometime after the Flood and could, therefore, be traced to one of Noah's three sons through a historically known group of people. For some three hundred years, European thinkers speculated about who that group might be.

American Indians: From Israelites to Atlanteans

Some early New World explorers noticed a clear physical similarity between the native people of the New World and Asians. Giovanni da Verrazano, an Italian navigator sailing for France in 1524, spent almost three weeks exploring the interior of Rhode Island and had an opportunity to examine local natives closely. He concluded:

> They tend to be rather broad in the face. . . . They have big black
> eyes. . . . From what we could tell in the last two respects they resemble
> the Orientals. (Quinn 1979:182)

Though Verrazano and others were quite perceptive in noticing these physical similarities, many others suggested different sources for the Native American population. In his *General and Natural History of the Indies* published in 1535, Spanish writer Oviedo (Huddleston 1967) suggested two sources for indigenous American populations: lost merchants from Carthage, a Mediterranean city-state of 2,000 years before, or the followers of King Héspero, a Spanish monarch who fled Europe in 1658 b.c. The latter hypothesis was appealing to the Spanish, who could therefore assert that Columbus had only rediscovered and reclaimed what the Spanish had already discovered and claimed.

Speculation concerning the source of American Indians accelerated after 1550. As shown in Chapter 8, Lopez de Gomara believed they were a remnant population from the Lost Continent of Atlantis. In 1580 Diego Duran suggested that the New World natives were descendants of the so-called Lost Tribes of Israel—ten of the twelve Hebrew tribes mentioned in the Bible were historically "lost." Duran enumerated traits that he believed Indians and Jews had in common: circumcision, stories about plagues, long journeys, and the like.

José de Acosta   Perhaps the most important work examining the origin of the Indians was *The Natural and Moral History of the Indies,* by Friar José de Acosta, published in 1590. The book is a remarkably perceptive, scientific examination of the question of Indian origins.

Acosta spent seventeen years as a Jesuit missionary in Peru beginning in 1570. He recognized that however people came to the New World and wherever they came from, wild animals came with them. Acosta suggested that people might have brought with them economically useful animals, but others—predators like wolves or foxes, for example—would not have been purposely imported and must have traveled to the New World by themselves.

Acosta then made a simple yet significant deduction: If animals could migrate on their own to the New World from the Old—as they must have after the Flood, since Noah's Ark came to rest on "the mountains of Ararat," somewhere in western Asia—then "the new world we call the Indies is not completely divided and separated from the other world" (Acosta, as cited in Huddleston 1967:50).

Acosta deduced that the Old and New Worlds must be connected; animals could simply walk from the Old World to the New, and people could have come to the Americas the same way. Based on geographical knowledge of his day, Acosta even proposed where such a connection might be found—northeast Asia/northwest North America. European explorers would not verify that northeastern Asia and northwestern North America were separated by only a narrow strait (in fact, only about 51 miles [82 kilometers] of open sea) until the second half of the eighteenth century (Figure 5.3).

Acosta's argument was remarkable for its objectivity and solid reasoning. Furthermore, it did not contradict a literal interpretation of the Bible—it was, after all, based on the assumption that all animals in the New World were descended from those saved on board the Ark.

Tracing the Source of Native Americans

As firmly grounded in fact and good deductive reasoning as Acosta's argument was, most European scholars rejected his conclusions and looked for

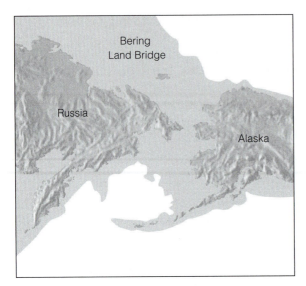

Figure 5.3 During parts of the Pleistocene epoch, sea level dropped substantially as water evaporated from the world's oceans, fell as snow in northern latitudes and higher elevations, and did not melt but produced glaciers. This drop in sea level produced land connections like the Bering Land Bridge—an almost 1,000-mile-(1,500 kilometer-) wide platform of land connecting northeast Asia and northwest North America. The Bering Land Bridge provided access to the New World for animals and people in the Old World.

sources other than Asia for the native population of the New World. Most such thinkers based their tracing of American Indian cultures on *trait list comparisons.* They hunted through descriptions of Indian cultures, seeking practices, beliefs, and even linguistic elements that were reminiscent of those in some Old World group. Where similarities were found, it was thought that a source for the American population had been identified.

Certainly, there is some logic to cultural comparison. Within the context of American society, we recognize that immigrants and their descendants often maintain traditions from their homelands. Religious practices, holiday celebrations, craftwork, clothing, and even language may persist for generations. Chinese immigrants celebrating the Chinese New Year, African Americans giving their children African names, and Puerto Ricans living in the United States celebrating Three Kings Day are all examples of such cultural persistence.

In these examples and in the myriad others that could be presented, the connections between the practices of immigrants and those of their homelands are clear, specific, and detailed. Each occurs within an overall cultural context of many other persistent practices.

The evidence marshalled by European scholars in previous centuries regarding the source of American Indian populations is very different. Often, the similarities they saw were vague, generic, and biased. For example, sixteenth-century Spanish cleric Gregoria Garcia contended that both Jews and Indians were cowardly, that neither believed in the miracles of Christ, that both were uncharitable, that they were ungrateful, that they loved silver, and so on (as cited in Steward 1973). These aspersions, which reflect more on Garcia's attitudes than on either Native American or Jewish behavior, were taken as strong evidence of a connection between the two peoples.

It isn't at all uncommon—surprising—that people with no close historical connection practice some similar behaviors. For example, a simple trait like circumcision, practiced by Jews as well as the Inca, does not, by itself, necessarily prove a connection between the two peoples. The cultural/religious context and meaning of the practice in the two groups turn out to be entirely different. It is such a general trait and so many people all over the world practice it that we would quickly run out of Lost Tribes if we tried to trace them to all world cultures that circumcised their male infants.

Out of Asia

Though Acosta was ahead of his time in tracing the human population of the New World to Asia, his reasoning in *The Natural and Moral History of the Indies* was so sound that it could not be ignored. Rather than relying on scattershot cultural comparisons or unverifiable transoceanic crossings, his theory was constructed on a solid geographical foundation. Slowly, as knowledge of the northern Pacific grew, it gained acceptance. By the middle of the eighteenth century, most scholars agreed that the indigenous people of the New World were, in fact, descendants of Asians.

By 1794 Father Ignaz Pfefferkorn could say in reference to the narrow slip of water separating Asia from America, "It is almost certain that the first inhabitants of America really came by way of the strait" (as cited in Ives 1956:421). The people whom Columbus encountered had been Asians after all—but separated by thousands of miles and thousands of years from the people of Cathay and Cipangu.

An "American Genesis"?

Though archaeologists still argue about the timing of migration of people to the New World, they virtually all agree that American Indians are Asians who arrived via the area today known as the Bering Strait. This narrow and shallow part of the Bering Sea is today a minor impediment to human movement between the Asian and North American mainlands. In the past, during the geological epoch known as the *Pleistocene* (Ice Age), travel between the two continents was even easier. During this epoch, marked by episodes of worldwide climate much colder than those that occur at present, large bodies of ice called glaciers covered much of the surface of North America and Europe (Figure 5.4). This ice came from water that had evaporated from the world's oceans. As a result, worldwide sea level dropped as much as 400 feet (almost 125 meters), exposing large amounts of land previously and presently under water (Josenhans et al. 1997). A 1,500-kilometer-wide (almost 1,000-mile) land platform called *Beringia* or the Bering Land Bridge was exposed, connecting Asia and North America (see Figure 5.3). Analysis of submarine sediments suggests a late glacial maximum sometime between

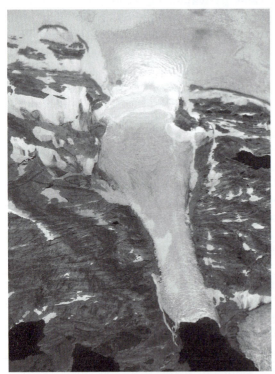

Figure 5.4   Much of North America, as well as Europe and the higher elevations of South America and Asia, were once dominated by a glaciated landscape characterized by large sheets (top) and tongues of ice (bottom) like these that currently cover much of Greenland. (K. Feder)

22,000 and 19,000 years ago (Yokoyama et al. 2000). Sea level was at a low point for a period of a few hundred years sometime during this time span, and Beringia would have been at its most extensive. This same evidence indicates a general warming accompanied by sea level rise in the period immediately following 19,000 years ago. So, sometime between 22,000 and 19,000 years ago, as well as during subsequent glacial readvances between 19,000 and 10,000 years ago, the Old and the New Worlds were connected by a broad swath of land, and it would have been possible for people and animals to walk from one to the other. It should also be pointed out that when Beringia was exposed, there would have been one continuous coast arcing across from Asia to America. A maritime people living on the northeast Asian coast could have expanded east following the Beringian coast into Alaska and then south into the rest of the New World. Whether by land, through the interior of Beringia, or by sea, along its coast, the movement of people into the New World via the Land Bridge is well supported by geological, meteorological, biological, anthropological, and archaeological evidence (Derenko et al. 2001; Dillehay 2000; Meltzer 2009; Yokoyama et al. 2000).

Some Native Americans object strenuously to the Land Bridge scenario because, as one told me directly, "It makes us immigrants, no different from you and your ancestors." Maybe that is the case, but the most conservative scientific view places Native Americans in the New World more than 13,000 years ago—"immigrants" they may be, but certainly not latecomers!

Current Perspectives

Tracing People by Their Morphology

Modern anthropologists can trace the origins of a people through their morphology. The human species is polymorphic; we come in different colors, shapes, and sizes. There are variations in blood type, skeletal form, tooth shape, head shape, genetic conditions, and so on. These variations are not distributed randomly across the earth, but are geographically patterned.

Sixteenth-century explorers like Verrazano recognized this geographic patterning, noted the physical similarities between Asians and Native Americans, and hypothesized an Asian source for the indigenous human population of the New World. Today, biological anthropologists can test and verify this hypothesis through application of sophisticated analytical procedures.

For example, physical anthropologist Christy Turner examined some 200,000 teeth from the New World (Turner 1987) and found that American Indian teeth are most similar to the teeth of Asian people. Among American Indians, a particular form of incisor—so-called shovel-shaped—is found in between 65 and 100 percent of Indian populations in different parts of North and South America (Figure 5.5). The frequency of shovel-shaping in

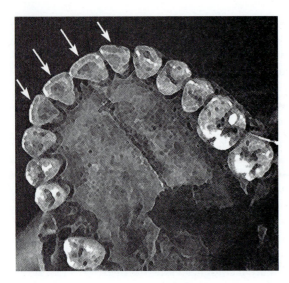

Figure 5.5   Upper jaw (maxilla) showing shoveling in the incisor teeth. This morphology is seen in a high percentage of the native peoples of East Asia and the Americas, evidencing the common biological heritage of people living on either side of the Bering Strait. (Courtesy John Seidel)

Africans and Europeans has been measured at less than 20 percent. In eastern Asia, 65 to 90 percent of the people exhibit the trait.

Other features of the skeleton exhibit the same pattern; thus, archaeologists can be fairly certain that the skeletons excavated from prehistoric sites in the Americas are those of Indians and that Indians are derived from Asia (Turner 1987:6).

Kennewick Chronicles   We do not know his name, and yet different groups assert that they know who he was. He has no known genealogy, yet various people claim to be his descendants. He left no last will and testament, but some assert that they are his heirs. To the best of our knowledge, he provided no instructions as to how his body was to be treated upon death, but various factions today wish to speak for him on this very point. To the Umatilla, Yakama, Confederated Tribes of Colville, Nez Perce, and the Wanapum Tribe of the Columbia River valley of Washington State, where his remains were discovered, he is simply the "Ancient One." To members of the Asatru Folk Assembly, a group of latter-day Vikings, his remains belong to their ancient ancestor, a brave Norse explorer of the New World, dating to long before the voyages of Christopher Columbus. To Paramount Chieftain Faumuina, he is the ancestor of modern Polynesians, his descendants having migrated from the American Northwest to South America, and from there by boat to Samoa. To scientists, both archaeologists and biological anthropologists, the bones of the individual they call "Kennewick Man" present a nearly unprecedented opportunity to peer closely at the remains of an early human inhabitant of the New World, one whose bones have been radiocarbon-dated to more than 9,000 years ago (Chatters 2002).

Though we can never know his name, his scientific study has allowed for a detailed postmortem (the description of the skeletal remains that follows comes from Powell and Rose 1999). He—and careful analysis of his bones provides a high degree of certainty that he was a male—lived a long and not uneventful life. He could never have conceived, however, the debate that his bones would generate more than 9,000 years after he breathed his last breath.

One of the surprising and controversial results of the analysis of Kennewick Man has been how different his bones look from those of modern Native Americans. In fact, he was initially identified as a white settler, largely because of the shape of his skull; his is long and narrow, while modern Native Americans tend to have short, broad skulls with tall, wide faces and broad cheekbones.

Does this mean that Kennewick Man is not related to modern Native Americans and may represent a migration of a different people to the New World? That is a fascinating possibility, but, in fact, the skeletal morphology of modern people often doesn't match that of ancient bones found in their regions, even when the bones are those of their ancestors. Skeletal morphology can change from one generation to the next as a result of changed diet and behavior. Certainly, over the course of 9,000 years or more, evolutionary processes can alter skeletal morphology as well, producing descendants whose bones are markedly different from those of their ancestors.

Though Kennewick Man did not look like a modern Native American (Figure 5.6), his skeletal remains do resemble those of Asian people, particularly

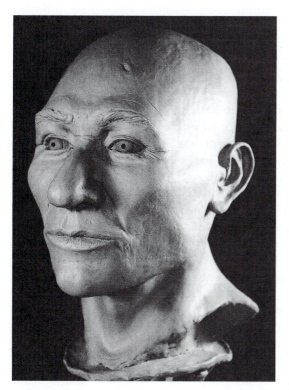

Figure 5.6 An artist's conception of the face of Kennewick Man based on a detailed analysis of his cranial anatomy. Perhaps because of its lack of hair, this version of the Ancient One bears a striking resemblance to Patrick Stewart, the actor who portrayed Jean-Luc Picard, the captain of the *Enterprise* in the television series *Star Trek: Next Generation* and Professor Charles Xavier in the X-Men movies. (© AP/Perfect Image, James Chatters, HO)

the Ainu of Japan and native people of Polynesia; and there are similarities to Chukchi Eskimo of Siberia as well.

Beyond his ethnicity, we know a bit about his life. He appears to have been between 45 and 50 years old when he died. At about 5 feet 9 inches, he was physically powerful; his bones bear unmistakable marks of extensive use, looking like those of a modern weight lifter or construction worker. Also, he was a quite healthy individual; his bones show scant evidence of illness (other than a little bit of arthritis), and there is no hint of nutritional deficiency. However, his bones also tell the story of a devastating physical trauma sometime between his fifteenth and twentieth year. In what may have been a single, terrible incident, his right forearm was broken; he cracked at least a couple of the ribs on the right side of his body; and, certainly most traumatic of all, he was stabbed by a stone-tipped spear that entered from the front; someone standing somewhat above impaled the young man, thrashing down on him at a 77-degree angle, and the stone tip lodged in his innominate (the flat blade of bone) of the right side of his pelvis. The spearpoint sliced into his pelvic bone before it was fully developed and actually affected its growth. By reference to standard human developmental patterns, his pelvis was likely that of a teenager when it sustained the wound. Because other indicators of the skeleton show that he lived to be at least 45, we know this severe wound did not kill him. In fact, he lived for about thirty years after the injuries and, based on the location of the wounds and the degree of healing, he likely suffered no permanent disabilities. His right arm healed completely, his ribs fused as best they could, and the pierced bone of his pelvis mended itself. The spearpoint remained in his body, healing bone growing around it, from the time the wound was inflicted until his death—and even beyond. In fact, it remains there still, more than 9,000 years after his life ended.

The aforementioned Native American groups in Washington State would like to reconsecrate the bones of the Ancient One to the earth, where he had been intentionally buried by those who likely knew and loved him more than nine millennia ago. They view him as an ancestor whose grave has been plundered and want no part of additional scientific analysis. Scientists, on the other hand, have asked to be allowed to study his remains, to learn what they can of his life and times from the story that has been coded into the bones he left behind. Scientists view him as an exceptionally important source of information whose reburial would be a tragic loss to our scientific understanding of the early settlement of America.

Unfortunately, these divergent desires have led to litigation and hard feelings on both sides. The two most recent court decisions, in February and April 2004, upheld the right of scientists to study the bones and rejected the Indians' claim of ownership of the remains. Essentially, the court ruled that modern tribal members cannot show that the 9,000-year-old individual we now call Kennewick Man was a member of their tribe, so they have no legal standing to claim his remains. Nevertheless, members of the previously men-tioned tribes continue to assert kinship with the person they call the Ancient One and periodically request and are granted access to pray over his remains.

It is a bit of a conundrum after all. Native people have objected to anal-ysis of the bones, but the results of this analysis may show that these mod-ern Indians are Kennewick's descendants and, therefore, of legal standing to demand his reinterment without analysis. In other words, the Indians might be able to prove their legal standing as direct descendants definitively only through the application of the very kinds of forensic examination to which they object. Object though they might, the court has granted scientists the continued right to examine the bones. The bones are housed at the Burke Museum in Seattle where they are well cared for. Unfortunately, though a morphological analysis of the skeleton has revealed much about his eventful life, the attempt to peer directly into the genes of Kennewick Man has so far been unsuccessful. No intact DNA was recovered from small samples taken from one of his ribs and a metacarpal (one of the long bones in the palm of the hand) (Merriwether, Cabana, and Reed 2000). Scientists continue to hope that further analysis—perhaps the same extraction method used on additional skeletal elements or new, yet-to-be-developed methods of extraction—might result in the successful extraction of DNA.

Anthropologist and Choctaw Indian Dorothy Lippert has walked in both worlds as a Native American who also is a scientist. She has seen the often-callous disregard with which some scientists have treated the physical remains of beloved ancestors, and she has been appalled and angered. But she also is troubled by the ironic loss of information that would be valuable especially to the modern descendants who might wish to return the bones of their ancestors to the earth. Lippert (1997:126) phrases it beautifully when she argues that "for many of our ancestors, skeletal analysis is one of the only ways that they are able to tell us their stories." As she maintains, these ancestors can teach us all if only we listen to their "voice made of bone." Let us all hope that, someday, we can all listen to this voice and that the Ancient One will continue to tell us about the life he lived more than 9,000 years ago. For additional information about the many issues concerning Kennewick Man, read James Chatters's (2002) *Ancient Encounters*, David Hurst Thomas's (2000) *Skull Wars*, and Roger Downey's (2000) *Riddle of the Bones*.

Tracing People by Their DNA

It has been called "molecular archaeology," and it involves the metaphorical excavation for information hidden deep within the genes of living people. To connect a modern group of human beings to its initial population source, these archaeologists of our chromosomes sift through the genetic instructions of living people to determine which groups share unique codes, often repre-senting minor genetic mistakes or small idiosyncrasies that don't mean much and that don't have an impact on a person's appearance or health status. There are so many different possible clusters and variants, it is a virtual certainty that those living groups who share the same cluster of minor differences must share a biological ancestor from whom they inherited it. It's the equivalent of what happens in the movies when long-lost siblings verify their biological connection by comparing a tiny mole, a gap in their front teeth, or a bent little toe each one possesses like a tiny badge that identifies them as members of the same family; only here that badge is a set of genetic instructions.

For example, when researchers investigate the mitochondrial DNA (mtDNA; a variety of DNA that appears not in the nucleus of cells, but in their mitochondria, the energy factories that provide them with power) of living people across the globe, they find a number of variants called haplogroups. Native Americans exhibit a total of five such distinct haplogroups: A, B, C, D, and X. Those five variants have so far turned up in only one other human group in only one geographic location: specifically, the Atlatians, a group of Asian natives who live along the shores of Lake Baikal in central Siberia (Derenko et al. 2001). The appearance of the five distinct haplogroups among New World natives and Asian natives provides strong evidence of close familial ties.

In an analysis of the mtDNA haplogroups extracted from a sample of ancient skeletons found at archaeological sites in eastern North America and from a group of living Native Americans, Bolnick and Smith (2007; and see Bolnick et al. 2012) found an astonishing degree of similarity (Figure 5.7). As you can see, haplogroups A, B, C, and D were found in similar frequencies

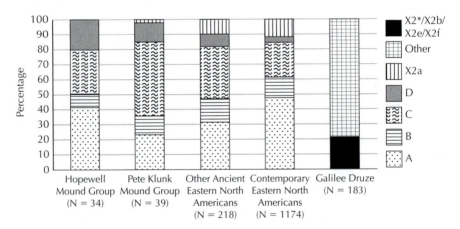

Figure 5.7 This bar chart shows the prevalence of various mitochondrial DNA haplogroups in a number of Native American populations, both modern and ancient. The haplogroups A, B, C, D, and X2a are common in Native American populations as well as among the native people of northeast Asia, clearly indicating their historical and biological connection. The bar on the far right represents a population in the Middle East and reflects an entirely different haplogroup pattern.

in all Native American groups they sampled, and a specific version of haplogroup X (specifically, X2a) was found in two of the archaeological samples as well as in living Native Americans. Also in Figure 5.7, note how utterly different the Native American mtDNA haplogroups are from those seen in a Middle Eastern population. This mtDNA research provides no support for claims that Native Americans are descendants of the Lost Tribes of Israel, or any other Middle Eastern population (see Chapter 6).

Mitochondrial DNA is passed down only in the female line, so the mtDNA evidence relates only to females. Analysis of specific variants in the Y-chromosome, obviously present only in males, has shown results similar to those of mtDNA. Maria-Catira Bortolini and her colleagues (2003) have identified two specific mutations on the Y-chromosome that allow us, again, to connect native Asians and Native Americans. These researchers found the two Y-chromosome mutations in native populations in the New World and in central Siberia. This, like the mtDNA data, provides strong evidence for an ancient biological connection between the aboriginal people of the New World and those living in central Siberia.

In another study, anthropologist Deborah Bolnick and her colleagues (2006) examined the Y-chromosomes of 261 Native American men representing 16 different population groups indigenous to eastern North America. Their research shows that if European or African explorers or settlers were traipsing around eastern North America before Columbus, they tread lightly, leaving behind no genetic footprint. Bolnick et al. conclude that there is no evidence of the admixture of African or European Y-chromosomes in Native American populations in eastern North America before A.D. 1492.

It is truly remarkable that researchers can investigate our genes much in the way archaeologists can excavate ancient sites. Our genes, it seems, much like ancient artifacts, preserve the stories of our ancestors and define who we are and where we have come from. Those stories are being read by the molecular archaeologists and are telling us the story of the migration of people into the New World.

It is further interesting to point out that archaeological sites dating close to 20,000 years ago have been excavated in central Siberia, specifically near Lake Baikal where the five mtDNA haplogroups present in America have been identified, producing artifacts that bear a similarity to some of the earliest tools found in the New World. Artifacts, as well as genes, point to the people of central Siberia as the most likely source for the native people of the New World.

Though the most direct way of studying an ancient population's history is through the genetic analysis of its peoples' ancient skeletons, it's a lot easier to find and collect DNA from living descendants. Through analysis of the DNA of the living, researchers attempt to extrapolate back in time to determine the source and history of their ancestors. In just such a study, geneticist David Reich and his colleagues (Reich et al. 2012) examined the DNA of a large sample of living Native Americans of thirty-four different groups or tribes in North and South America. They found three genetic, geographically patterned clusters sufficiently distinct to suggest that each group had a different population history and had entered the New World from Asia in a separate wave of migration in antiquity. They labeled the groups First American (this was the most abundant and geographically widespread group in their sample), Eskimo/Aleut (spread across Alaska, Canada, and Greenland), and Chipewyan (in Canada). The challenge now is to find ancient skeletons to assess this hypothesized scenario.

Tracing People by Their Archaeology

Archaeologists define ancient cultures on the basis of the unique combination of artifacts the people who practiced that culture made and left behind. On that basis, archaeologists named and defined the Clovis culture, characterized especially (and uniquely) by large stone spear tips (called Clovis points) with broad channels or "flutes" (as in "fluted columns") on both faces (Figure 5.8). Clovis points look like none other found anywhere in the world and are found at sites that date to the very narrow time period between 13,200 and 11,900 years ago (as determined by the application of radiocarbon dating, not to the spearpoints themselves—stone can't be dated in this way—but to organic remains, especially burned wood, found in association with the spearpoints).

Figure 5.8 Channeled or "fluted" points are found only in the New World and are associated with a rather narrow range of radiocarbon dates: 13,200 to 11,900 years ago. Varieties of so-called Clovis points are found all over the United States and Canada. (K. Feder)

Clovis appears to have been the first broadly successful human adaptation to the New World with archaeological evidence of their presence spread across much of North America. At last count (Toner 2006:41), some 16,000 Clovis points have been found in the United States alone. But Clovis points are not the oldest artifacts found in the New World, leaving us with the question, Who preceded Clovis? Ted Goebel, Michael Waters, and Dennis O'Rourke (2008) present the current archaeological consensus about the initial, pre-Clovis settlement of the Americas:

1. Comparing the mtDNA of modern northeast Asians and the native people of the New World, those two groups appear to have separated sometime between 25,000 and 20,000 years ago.

2. The Y-chromosomes of northeast Asians and Native Americans confirm that period as the time during which the two populations went their separate ways.

3. A land connection between northeast Asia and northwest North America was available continuously between 22,000 and 19,000 years ago and then intermittently between 19,000 and 10,000 years ago.

4. A migration route along the Pacific coast of North America was navigable by about 15,000 years ago.

5. An interior route from northeast Asia into the interior of Alaska and Canada and then south through an ice-free corridor between the Laurentide and Cordilleran glaciers into the American Great Plains opened up by about 14,000 years ago.

The archaeological record lends support to the hypothesis that movement into the New World from northeast Asia occurred soon after the coastal and interior routes noted in points 4 and 5 became available. Evidence for the movement of a coastal people with a subsistence focus on the resources of the sea—first east along the southern Bering Land Bridge coast and then south along the western shore of North America—is seen at Paisley 5 Mile Point Caves in coastal Oregon (Gilbert et al. 2008). Along with stemmed stone spearpoints, researchers there found the rather unromantic, though very important, remnants of human fecal deposits or "coprolites." The field of coprolite studies isn't what gets most kids excited about becoming an archaeologist (and I am certain that the next *Indiana Jones* movie will not be about the search for the precious petrified poop), but they are a fascinating source of information about human diet and disease. They also provide sufficient organic residue for carbon dating: the Paisley 5 Mile Point Caves coprolites are certainly human and date to 14,300 years ago, about 700 years after the Beringian coastal route became available for travel.

Archaeological sites are often characterized by the discovery of tools and bones. It is extremely rare, however, to find a tool actually embedded in the bone of an animal hunted and killed by ancient people. The Manis site, located in Washington State has produced precisely that kind of snapshot of antiquity (Waters et al. 2011b). There, the remains of what appears to be a butchered mastodon were found; there are cutting and scraping marks on its bones, almost certainly made by stone tools. Deeply embedded in one of its ribs, archaeologists found a sharpened bone spear tip, a weapon that at least contributed to the animal's death. Radiocarbon dating indicates that the mastodon was alive 13,800 years ago when it was killed by ancient hunters.

Moving south, three sites dating to between 12,200 and 11,200 years ago have been excavated on the Channel Islands off the coast of southern California (Erlandson et al. 2011). Archaeologists working there found finely made stone tools, including stemmed points somewhat similar to those at Paisley 5 Mile Point Caves (Figure 5.9). There's clear evidence at the Channel Island sites of a maritime adaptation. Food remains that excavators recovered from hearths at the sites include the bones of sea birds like cormorants as well as the remains of finfish, the shells of various kinds of shellfish, and the bones of sea mammals. This is exactly what we should expect for a people migrating along a coastal route.

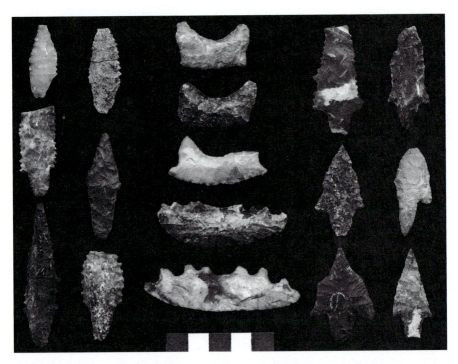

Figure 5.9   Stone tools, including projectile points and possible scraping tools found at two sites on the Channel Islands, located off the coast of southern California. These sites represent a 12,200-year-old occupation along the likely coastal route from northeast Asia into the New World. (Courtesy of Jon Erlandson)

Additional evidence of early migration into the New World along a coastal route has been found by archaeologists working in South America. At a place called Monte Verde, near Chile's Pacific coast, researchers have discovered artifacts dating back to 14,600 years ago (Dillehay 1989, 1997; Dillehay and Collins 1988; Dillehay et al. 2008). The major cultural level at that site has produced spearpoints and a number of other stone tools. Organic preservation at the site is remarkable, with pieces of mastodon meat, wooden hut foundations, and plant remains recovered in the excavation.

Sites that represent the settlements of those who took an interior route into the New World from the Old include the Debra L. Friedkin site in Texas (Waters et al. 2011). The site produced more than 15,000 artifacts, including finely made spear points in a soil layer underneath (and, therefore, older than) a layer in which researchers found Clovis artifacts (Figure 5.10). A date of about 15,500 years ago was derived for the pre-Clovis layer. Twelve of the pre-Clovis tools are, in many ways, similar to Clovis points in how they were produced, but they lack the diagnostic flute. This may mean that tools found at the Debra L. Friedkin site could be, directly or indirectly, ancestral to Clovis.

Figure 5.10 Stone tools from the 15,500-year-old Debra L. Friedkin site in Texas. Pictured here are sharpedged blades, a stone core from which blades have been removed, a chopping tool, and a number of other cutting and scraping tools. (Courtesy of Michael Waters)

In the eastern United States, at Meadowcroft Rockshelter in Pennsylvania, excavators recovered material that has produced the oldest radiocarbon dates associated with human-made material in northeastern North America (Adovasio, Donahue, and Stuckenrath 1990). Sealed beneath a rockfall from the roof of the shelter dated to 15,000 years ago were some four hundred lithic artifacts, including blades, knives with retouched edges, and a pentagonal, bifacial projectile point, looking nothing at all like a Clovis point (Figure 5.11). Six dates in excess of 13,500 years ago were derived from material at or below this level.

At Cactus Hill in Virginia, stone projectile points were found in an undisturbed soil layer 15 centimeters (nearly 6 inches) below a stratum in which Clovis-type artifacts were found. This implies strongly that the points in question are older than Clovis.

There is a growing consensus that Clovis points do not date to the earliest settlement of the New World. Though certainly the people responsible for Clovis can be traced to northeast Asia, no fluted points have been found there. Further, fluted points are both rare in Alaska and northwestern Canada and relatively late in time. Fluting or channeling points appears to have been an innovation of the native people of North America, perhaps a

Figure 5.11   The projectile point at the far left was recovered at Meadowcroft Rockshelter in western Pennsylvania. The other artifacts here are quite similar in appearance and were also found in western Pennsylvania, at other sites. (Courtesy James Adovasio)

couple of millennia *after* they first arrived in the New World. It seems increasingly likely, therefore, that Clovis was developed by people who were the descendants of those who migrated to the New World sometime after about 16,000 years ago. The explosion of Clovis appears not to have been the result of a new migration, but the result of an indigenous development—the invention of fluting—which allowed for a great leap forward in the ability to hunt large-game animals.

Though it must be admitted that debate regarding the age of the earliest occupation of the New World has sometimes been acrimonious, at least those on either side, and those in between, adhere to the scientific method. There are no appeals to divine inspiration and no references to nonexistent lost continents. All the players in the game agree that the search for the first Americans is a worthwhile endeavor. And all abide by the rules of science.

◈ ◈ ◈ FREQUENTLY ASKED QUESTION ◈ ◈ ◈

Where did the Clovis culture come from?

Whether they were the first people to enter the New World or not, archaeologists have long agreed that the bearers of the Clovis culture were certainly among the ancestors of modern American Indians, could be traced to northeast Asia, and had migrated here via the Bering Land Bridge. Archaeologists Dennis Stanford and Bruce Bradley (2000; 2012), however, have questioned this assumption and hypothesized that, in fact, the bearers of Clovis culture were Europeans who journeyed by watercraft to the New World during the period known there as the Upper Paleolithic (think big-game hunters and cave painters). Stanford and Bradley (2012) make their case in their book *Across the Atlantic: The Origin of America's Clovis Culture.*

Their argument is based primarily on similarities they see in the stone tool technologies of Clovis and, in particular, the European Solutrean culture. Bradley is an extremely well respected expert on stone tool making—he is spectacularly good at replicating stone tools, so he knows the technology well—and his opinion is taken quite seriously. However, as Upper Paleolithic specialist Lawrence Straus (2000) points out, beyond the fact that there's no evidence that they had boats, the Solutrean culture was short-lived, disappearing about 17,000 years ago, 5,000 years before Clovis appears. That fact alone implies that we must look elsewhere for a source for Clovis. It is still believed by the vast majority of archaeologists that Clovis was "home grown," a technology developed by ancient Americans in America.

BEST OF THE WEB

http://www.beringia.com

The very informative web presence of the Yukon Beringia Interpretive Center, focusing on the story of Beringia.

http://instaar.colorado.edu/QGISL/bering_land_bridge/

A very cool animation of the change in the configuration of Beringia from 21,000 years ago when sea level was at its low point and the Land Bridge was at its maximum to the establishment of the modern coastline about 8,000 years ago.

http://csfa.tamu.edu/

Perhaps the best place online to find information about the earliest human settlement of the New World is the website of the Center for the Study of the First Americans. Click the link, Who Were the First Americans (http://csfa.tamu.edu/who.php), for a terrific summary of the current archaeological thinking on the subject.

 CRITICAL THINKING EXERCISE

Using the deductive approach outlined in Chapter 2, how would you test these hypotheses? In each case, what archaeological and biological data must you find to conclude that the hypothetical statement is an accurate assertion, that it describes what actually happened in the ancient human past?

- The first discoverers of America were Asians who crossed over from the Old World via a land connection.

- The first Americans were big-game hunters who entered the New World by following migratory herds of animals.

- The original settlers of America were a diverse group not limited to northeast Asians, but also including Africans, Australians, and Europeans.

6

Who's Next? After the Indians, Before Columbus

We saw in Chapter 5 that the ancestors of modern American Indians were the first humans to walk on the soil of the New World, perhaps more than 20,000 and probably by no later than 15,000 years ago. Further, we know that Christopher Columbus arrived in the New World in 1492, though he did not know it was a "new" world. The question that remains to be addressed is, Were there any other visitors or migrants to the New World from the Old World after the Indians arrived from Asia and before Columbus arrived from Europe? We can answer this question by examining the archaeological record.

Artifact Trails: Evidence of Visitors to the New World

The late comedian George Carlin performed a hilarious routine about human beings and their possessions. An archaeologist might characterize the bit as being focused on human "material culture," but for Carlin, it's all about your "stuff" (Carlin 1997). People everywhere have stuff—the things you own, use, carry with you, and so on. In Carlin's comedy bit, a house is just a place for your stuff.

Carlin talked about what happens when you leave on vacation. Of course, you take some of your stuff—a second, smaller version—along with you. We do it today, and people in the past did it as well. And, as archaeologists can show, people invariably leave some of that stuff behind: It gets lost, stolen, used up, and discarded. This "left-behind stuff" constitutes archaeological evidence for the presence of these people in those places.

There is an important rule that resides at the core of archaeology: Everybody's stuff is different, unique, distinguishing, and diagnostic. In other words, the material remains produced by each culture are recognizable and, at the same time, recognizably different from the material remains produced by every other culture. Different cultures have different ways of doing things. They use different raw materials and use the same raw materials differently. They make different styles of tools and different kinds of pottery; they use different construction materials and use the same construction materials differently to produce very different kinds of structures. They have different rules concerning burial of the dead or even disposal of their trash. As a result, archaeological sites, because they constitute the physical remains of these unique, culture-specific practices, uniquely reflect the cultures of the particular people who produced them.

In a sense, then, archaeological sites are like fossils. The sites produced by different cultures are distinguishable much in the way that the fossils of different animal species are. When members of a foreign group enter into a new territory, they bring elements of their material culture with them. The sudden, intrusive appearance of their own unique brand of "stuff" is precisely the way archaeologists detect the presence of such intruders in the territories of other people.

The New England Model

Consider the archaeological record of New England as a model. Dig virtually anywhere in habitats attractive to human settlement here and you will find, in the deepest, oldest layers in the stratigraphic sequence, clear evidence of a people whose primary raw material for making tools was stone and whose primary food sources were local wild animals and plants. As you move up that stratigraphic sequence and, therefore, forward in time, you will recognize slow, incremental changes in, for example, the style of the stone tools and the species on which subsistence was focused You will see the development of new technologies; for example, ceramics show up and slowly develop through time. In virtually any such hypothetical excavation in New England, at a certain point in the soil layers, you will find the abrupt appearance of artifacts that look nothing like those seen previously in lower layers (Figure 6.1a & b). Without any neat sequence of development, suddenly you find ceramics exhibiting evidence of having been made on a wheel; some of the new ceramics exhibit elaborate painted or printed designs and images, with a hard glaze applied to the surface. But no wheel-made or glazed ceramic objects are seen in previous soil layers. Also, you will find a sudden abundance of artifacts made of iron, brass, and glass where, again, no such material was found in lower (older) stratigraphic layers. What you are seeing in the New England archaeological record, of course, is the arrival of seventeenth-century European colonists, along with all their stuff. This example of the abrupt appearance of different looking "stuff" in the soils of New England, without any evidence of the development of these "new" technologies, provides a model for what the abrupt appearance of a group of invaders should look like in any archaeological, stratigraphic sequence.

Figure 6.1a   Typical sherds of native earthenware ceramics. There are no painted designs, no glaze, and the pots were coil made. The design was incised into the surface when the clay was dry and before firing. Ceramics like this are commonly found in native archaeological sites in New England dating to the last 1,000 years. (K. Feder)

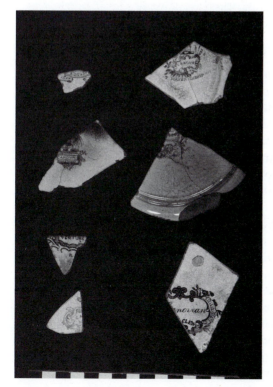

Figure 6.1b   Reflecting a very different technology, these are wheel-made, glazed ceramic shards made by potters in England in the nineteenth century. The sudden appearance of ceramics like these in archaeological contexts in America provides us with a model for an artifact footprint reflecting the entry of a group of people into an area, bringing their own unique "stuff" along with them. (K. Feder)

The Archaeology of Columbus

This model applies even to the exploration of the New World by Christopher Columbus. Columbus and his men left behind a trove of artifacts that were, in fact, representative of their own, unique brand of stuff. Archaeologist Charles Hoffman has recovered an enormous assemblage of European artifacts at Long Bay on Watling Island that date to Columbus's first expedition (Hoffman 1987). Also, archaeologist Kathleen Deagan has found some possible traces of the settlement of La Navidad, established by Columbus on Christmas Day in 1492 after one of his ships, the *Santa Maria*, was wrecked off the coast of what we today call Haiti.

La Navidad was, in effect, an accidental colony, peopled by only a handful of Spaniards with a small sample of their own material culture. Deagan has recovered burned wood at what is the most likely location of their fort. That wood has been radiocarbon-dated to the second half of the fifteenth century, making it a good match with the known date of La Navidad's settlement.

The 1493 expedition was an attempt to establish a large-scale, permanent Spanish colony in the New World. The resulting settlement, located in what is now the Dominican Republic, was called La Isabela. Kathleen Deagan and José María Cruxent have excavated this site, finding a vast array of evidence of this Spanish colony, including glazed ceramics, nails, glassware, horse gear, knives, dated coins, a key, and even a crucifix (Deagan and Cruxent 2002).

The Spanish *Entrada* into the American Southeast

This same pattern is seen in other, historically known European visits to the New World. For example, consider the sixteenth-century investigation of North America by Hernando de Soto in A.D. 1538. His contingent of more than six hundred men made landfall on May 30 of that year on the west coast of Florida south of Tampa Bay. During the course of the next four years, members of this expedition passed through most of the southeastern United States, crossing more than 3,500 miles of territory (de la Vega 1605; Swanton 1939).

The archaeological evidence found to date in the American Southeast presents us with a virtual trail of the de Soto expedition (Figure 6.2; Feder 1994b). The discovery of Nueva Cadiz beads, brass bells, silver and gold disks, assorted iron objects (scissors, swords), and even dated coins shows the clear imprint of a Spanish presence in the Southeast in the early sixteenth century (Feder 1994b). For example, Nueva Cadiz beads have been found at the Little Egypt site in northwestern Georgia, a village probably visited by de Soto, as well as at the Martin site in Florida, identified as the Anhaica village of the Apalachee people, also visited by de Soto (Ewen 1989). Wrought-iron nails, chain-mail links, a crossbow dart, and five Spanish coins that date to an earlier Spanish expedition were also found at the Martin site (Ewen 1989).

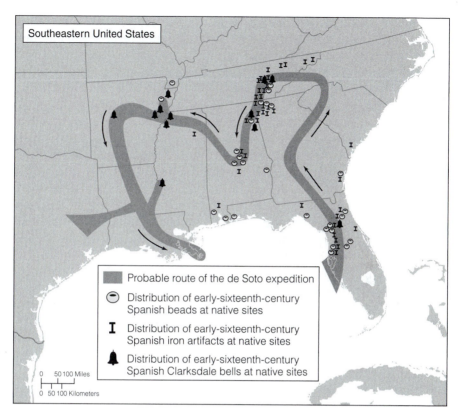

Figure 6.2   Map showing the historically documented route of the de Soto expedition (1538–42) through the American Southeast and locations where archaeological evidence of his expedition, as well as previous and subsequent Spanish expeditions, has been found.

Compare the maps of the archaeological find spots of these artifacts and the actual route de Soto and his men followed (Figure 6.2). The message can be no clearer and the lesson for us no more obvious: Foreign visitors bring with them a recognizable, foreign material culture. Their unique and alien material culture represents, in fact, a signature of their presence, and similar evidence should be found in any other case where such a presence is to be verified.

A Chinese Discovery of the New World?

Now, how about other possible visits to the New World from the Old, visits that predate Columbus? A large number of claims about such visits have been made, but is there evidence to support them—can we find any of their stuff in archaeological context? For example, there is a long-standing debate concerning the possibility of Chinese sailors, accidentally or intentionally, making it to the shores of the New World before Columbus. The story begins with the legend of the land of Fusang, a distant place, the story tells, visited by a Buddhist monk about 1,500 years ago. Depending on how you interpret the story, Fusang was real, mythical, or some combination of the two.

As Frost (1982) points out, Fusang was placed on the Asian coast by ancient Chinese mapmakers. Nevertheless, some have tried to identify Fusang as America, carefully selecting elements of the legend that seem to reflect the biogeography of the California coast. But is there any physical evidence for the presence of Chinese explorers or lost fishermen in the New World that dates to 1,500 years ago? For a time, it was thought that there was. In 1973 a vessel dredging off the coast of California brought up a sizable rock, carved into the shape of a doughnut. In 1975, twenty or so similar stones were found by divers off the Palos Verdes peninsula in southern California. These discoveries generated a great deal of publicity at the time. Some suggested that the stones were identical to anchor stones used on Chinese sailing vessels as far back as A.D. 500.

The Palos Verdes stones were examined by the geology department at the University of California, Santa Barbara, in 1980. If the anchor stones could be shown to have been made from rock present only in China, the case for a Chinese presence in the New World before Columbus would be much stronger. Unfortunately for the supporters of this hypothesis, it was determined that the alleged Chinese anchors were made of California rock (Frost 1982:26), most likely Monterey shale, a common local rock type.

The stones looked like Chinese anchors, however, because that is precisely what they were. Chinese American fishermen commonly trawled the waters off California in the nineteenth century. They sailed in their traditional craft, the junk. Indeed, the Palos Verdes stones are almost certainly the anchors, moorings, and net weights of these fishermen. They provide no help to those who wish to prove that Fusang is, in reality, ancient California.

The hypothesis proposed by Gavin Menzies (2002) in his book *1421: The Year China Discovered America* (the original, hardcover version was more accurately titled *1421: The Year China Discovered the World*) is breathtaking: Menzies proposes that between A.D. 1421 and 1423, an armada of more than one hundred Chinese ships with a contingent of 10,000 men circumnavigated the globe, encountering and, in some instances, colonizing Africa, North America, South America, and assorted Pacific Islands, as well as Australia.

Menzies begins with the fascinating historical account—largely ignored in the West (did you ever hear about this in social studies?)—of the voyages of Chinese Admiral Zheng He, who commanded a huge fleet of ships in his seven epic voyages dating from 1405 to 1433. During these voyages, Zheng He ventured westward from China along the south Asian coast, traveling as far as the east coast of Africa and then north into the Persian Gulf, a truly remarkable feat of navigation decades before Columbus or Magellan. So far, so good; but from there, Menzies, to put it mildly, extrapolates. He suggests that when Zheng He returned home after exploring the east coast of Africa in 1421, a part of the fleet, commanded by four of Zheng He's rear admirals, didn't return, as most historians contend, but continued the journey, following the African coast to the south, turning to the north after circling the southern tip of Africa, exploring the west coast of that continent, and then making a beeline to the east coast of the New World.

To be sure, Menzies tells a ripping good sea tale, but the evidence for Zheng He's fleet circumnavigating the globe is quite thin. Much of his evidence consists of a number of fifteenth- and sixteenth-century maps known to have been in the possession of European explorers. Menzies interprets these maps as exhibiting a preexisting knowledge of the New World. That knowledge, he proposes, came to Europe from the Chinese.

Is there any physical evidence to back up the Menzies hypothesis; is there any of that archaeologically crucial—and expected—fifteenth-century Chinese stuff in archaeological contexts in North America? In a word, no. Make no mistake, the fifteenth-century Chinese were certainly up to the task of circumnavigating the globe and "discovering" those places we in the West give credit to European explorers for discovering. Until definitive physical evidence like the material left behind by Columbus is found, however, the claim that China discovered the world in 1421 remains unproven.

Africans in Ancient America?

Others have suggested that Africans journeyed to the Americas long before Columbus, made contact with the native people, and may have had an enormous impact on the development of New World civilization. Although not the first to suggest it, a professor of anthropology, Ivan Van Sertima (1976), has been the most eloquent proponent of these claims.

In his book *They Came Before Columbus* Van Sertima presents the following evidence in support of his claim of an African presence in the pre-Columbian New World:

1. References in Columbus's writings to the presence of "black Indians" in the New World

2. The presence of a metal (*gua-nin*) purported to be African in origin, reported by Columbus

3. Pre-Columbian skeletons with "Negroid" characteristics

4. Artistic representations of black Africans at sites in the New World that predate the voyages of Columbus

While some of the kinds of evidence cited by Van Sertima are in line with the discussion earlier in this chapter concerning what is necessary to trace the prehistoric movement of people, the actual data presented fall far short of that needed for a convincing case.

For instance, Columbus does not claim to have seen black-skinned Indians; he merely passes along a story told to him by a group of Indians he did contact. Columbus also passed on the report of Indians with tails, so such evidence is highly suspect.

The report of the metal called *gua-nin* is similarly unconvincing. We do not have the metal to examine, none has ever been found in archaeological excavations in the New World, and we certainly cannot rely on five-hundred-year-old assays of the metal that Van Sertima maintains indicate its African identity.

As stated earlier, one way to trace the movement of prehistoric people focuses on skeletal analysis. Van Sertima cites analysis of a small number of skeletons found in the New World, particularly in Mesoamerica, that ostensibly have indicated the African origin of some individuals. Here again the evidence is quite weak, with either the African character of the skeletons being questionable or the dating of the bones uncertain. Europeans brought black slaves to the New World as early as the sixteenth century, and some of the skeletons found in the New World cited by Van Sertima, if actually of African origin, would most likely be those of early, but post-Columbian, slaves.

Van Sertima's assertion that there is ample evidence of the presence of black Africans in the New World in the form of artistic representations of individuals who look African is, perhaps, the weakest link in an already weak chain of reasoning. The weakness lies in the subjective nature of the assertion. For example, Van Sertima points to the physiognomies of the so-called Olmec heads of lowland Mesoamerica—huge pieces of basalt carved into human heads between 3,200 and 2,900 years ago by the bearers of what is almost certainly the first complex culture in Mesoamerica (Stuart 1993) (Figure 6.3). To date, just seventeen of these carved heads have been found; they range from about 5 to 11 feet in height.

Van Sertima asserts that they are clearly African in appearance, and indeed they do possess full lips and broad noses. Van Sertima, however, ignores the fact that many of the Olmec heads also have flat faces like American Indians, not prognathic profiles (jutting-out lower faces) like Africans. He also chooses not to see what appear to be epicanthic folds on the eyelids of the statues—these are typical of Old World Asians and American Indians. It is also the case that American Indians exhibit a broad range of features and some, in fact, have full lips and broad noses—at the same time, they possess other, more typically Indian physical features (Sabloff 1989). Most archaeologists interpret the Olmec heads as stylized sculptures, perhaps representing the faces of their rulers or chiefs.

Many other specific responses could be provided to refute particular claims made by Van Sertima. It is more important, however, to point out the deductive implications of his hypothesis and the lack of confirming evidence. If Africans truly were present in the New World in large numbers before Columbus and if they had a substantial impact on indigenous

Figure 6.3   An example of a giant carved stone head of the Olmec culture of Mesoamerica. These carvings in hard volcanic rock—weighing up to 20 tons—are evidence of an advanced society in Mesoamerica three thousand years ago. For some, the facial features of the Olmec heads are evidence of an African origin for that advanced culture. However, there is no evidence for an African presence in ancient Mesoamerica. (Alberto Rios Szalay/Sexto Sol/Getty Images)

cultures, there should be ample evidence in the archaeological record of artifacts, raw materials, and skeletons—the kinds of cultural and biological evidence that archaeologists regularly find and analyze—to support this claim. We would find more than enigmatic statues and vague historical references. Archaeologists should find clear evidence of material remains reflecting an African rather than an Indian pattern in housing, tool making, burial of the dead, ceremonies, and so on.

Furthermore, to assess the origin of things like the huge Olmec sculptures, we must focus not on subjective assertions about what or whom they may look like but on the cultural context of these artifacts within Olmec society. Artifacts like the basalt heads that Van Sertima cites as evidence of an African influence cannot be viewed in a vacuum. Surely such things demanded a level of technical competence, but they also required a complex social/political/economic infrastructure. Labor had to be conscripted to quarry the stone, to transport it across many miles, and to carve it. Workers needed to be fed and housed, and their labor had to be organized and overseen. It is highly unlikely that a small group of interlopers, even if they had been present, could possibly have so altered a society over a short period of time to produce all of the manifold cultural systems needed to create the stone heads—and the pyramids, jade carvings, earthen platforms, and so on that characterize the Olmec culture. Of necessity, the sculpted heads could have been produced only as one part of a complex pattern of behaviors and abilities that must have evolved together over a lengthy period of time.

This is precisely what the archaeological record shows. In fact, there is no physical evidence to validate the claimed presence of African visitors to Mesoamerica before Columbus. Having conducted research in Mesoamerica for more than thirty years and specializing in the Olmec for nearly that long, archaeologist Richard A. Diehl (2004:14) dismisses claims about an African presence in ancient Mesoamerica in this way: "Not a single bona fide artifact of Old World origin has ever appeared in an Olmec archaeological site, or for that matter anywhere else in Mesoamerica." For a detailed and comprehensive critique of Van Sertima's assertion that the Olmec were inspired by West African voyagers to the New World, see the articles by Mesoamericanist Bernard Ortiz de Montellano in the journals *The Skeptical Inquirer* (Ortiz de Montellano 1991, 1992), *Current Anthropology* (Ortiz de Montellano et al. 1997a), and *Ethnohistory* (Ortiz de Montellano et al. 1997b).

Other Europeans in the New World Before Columbus?

Evidence for the presence of other European visitors to the New World before Columbus is not nearly as strong as for the Norse. For example, according to legend, the Irish priest St. Brendan was supposed to have embarked on a seven-year trip westward into the Atlantic Ocean sometime in the late fifth and early sixth centuries A.D. Three centuries later, his adventures were recorded in a work called the *Navigatio* (Ashe 1971).

Based on documentary and archaeological evidence, it is clear that wandering Irish monks called *anchorites* had indeed accomplished some rather remarkable feats of navigation in the sixth through eighth centuries A.D. (Figure 6.4). Searching for places of quiet solitude where they could worship God, they settled the Orkney Islands in A.D. 579, the Shetlands in 620, and the Faroes in 670 (Ashe 1971:24). They even beat the Vikings to Iceland, settling it in A.D. 795.

Some assert that a place mentioned in the *Navigatio*—the so-called Land Promised to the Saints—is actually North America. Could Brendan have visited the New World? Adventurer Tim Severin (1977) attempted to replicate such a hypothesized voyage by sailing across the Atlantic in a replica of a *curragh*, the name given to the hide boats of the Irish. But replicative experiments of historical events merely show what may have been possible; they cannot prove that such events actually did take place. The only way to prove that Brendan made it to the shores of North America would be to find physical, archaeological evidence of a sixth-century Irish presence here—to find some of their stuff, like crosses, iron rings, or buttons—and no such confirmation

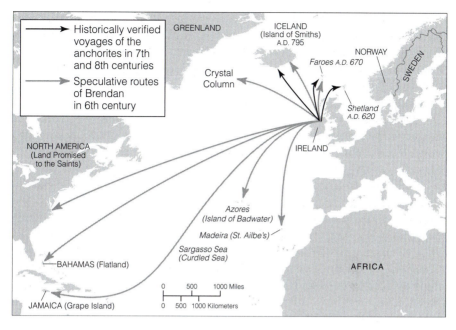

Figure 6.4 Map depicting the actual routes of exploration of Irish priests and proposed routes of Brendan in the sixth century A.D.

has ever been found. Without such evidence, the story of Brendan remains simply an interesting legend.

Another purported European visitor to the New World is Prince Madoc. Madoc himself appears to have been an actual historical personality who lived in the twelfth century A.D. He was a renowned or, more accurately, legendary sailor. In one of the stories about his exploits, he allegedly sailed westward from Wales in about A.D. 1170 and discovered a new land. Depending on which version of the story suits you, either he never returned, or he did come back, making several trips to this new land and bringing hundreds of Welsh settlers to the territory he had discovered.

Unfortunately, many of the stories the Madoc supporters provide are secondhand and contradict each other. We can read accounts published in the eighteenth century of the Navajo, Cherokee, Aztec, or Mandan Indians being indistinguishable in culture, language, and skin tone from Welshmen. In many of these stories we see an underlying racist theme similar to what we will see in reference to the Moundbuilder myth in Chapter 7; where Indian villages are clean, where their houses are well made and streets neatly laid out, even where agriculture is the primary mode of subsistence, it is presumed that the Indians must really be Europeans. With a ready-made legend like that of the Welsh voyage(s), it was natural to associate those groups with Madoc and his band of travelers.

There is, however, one variety of physical, archaeological evidence presented by the Madoc supporters. These supposed confirming data consist of the ridgetop stone forts of Kentucky and Tennessee. In fact, Deacon (1966:202) attempts to trace Madoc's route in America from Mobile Bay, up the Alabama River into Kentucky and Tennessee, by the distribution of these sites.

Clearly the discovery of a single iron sword, a datable Welsh inscription, artifacts made from a raw material present in Wales, or the skeleton of a western European would have gone further in support of the Welsh hypothesis than would all the stories of Welsh-speaking, light-skinned Indians. But archaeologist Charles Faulkner (1971) found no physical evidence supporting the Welsh hypothesis when he excavated one of the better-known forts in central Tennessee. Instead, the fort, which is really little more than a hilltop enclosed with a stone wall, contained artifacts made by American Indians, not Europeans. Included among the very few artifacts actually recovered were stone spearpoints and cutting and scraping tools. Carbon dates derived from charcoal found at the site and associated with its construction and use indicate that the stone fort was built and used sometime between A.D. 30 and 430.

In the mid-1960s the Daughters of the American Revolution erected a historical marker on the shore of Mobile Bay in Alabama. It reads, in part: "In memory of Prince Madoc, a world explorer who landed on the shores of Mobile Bay in 1170 and left behind, with the Indians, the Welsh language." If Madoc, indeed, did sail across the Atlantic into the Gulf of Mexico, into Mobile Bay, up the Alabama River, and eventually into Tennessee, he might have seen the stone forts credited to him and today presented as material evidence for his visits in the twelfth century. The Indians had already beaten him to it, having built them as much as one thousand years before. Here again, there is no physical evidence—no support in the archaeological record—for a Welsh presence in America before Columbus.

America B.C.?

Harvard marine biologist Barry Fell (*America B.C.*, *Saga America*, and *Bronze Age America*) provides ostensible evidence, not just for the discovery but also for the exploration and colonization of the Americas by Iberians (people from Spain and Portugal) 3,000 years ago, Celts 2,800 years ago, Greeks 2,500 years ago, ancient Hebrews about 2,000 years ago, and Egyptians 1,500 years ago.

Most archaeologists and historians in the New and Old Worlds who have had something to say concerning Fell's claims have been skeptical, and some have been downright hostile (Cole 1979; Daniel 1977; Dincauze 1982; Hole 1981; McKusick 1976; Ross and Reynolds 1978).

Mystery Hill: A Convergence of Evidence?

Remember in Chapter 2 the discussion of how historical sciences like archaeology rely on Michael Shermer and Alex Grobman's (2000) concept of a "convergence of evidence." It would be preferable—not to mention, beyond cool—if we could travel back in time to witness the ancient past, but we can't. So we rely on multiple, diverse, and independent streams of evidence available in the here and now to metaphorically time travel. When those streams converge on the same interpretation, when they point us in the same direction, we can be confident that our reconstruction reflects how the past really was.

Consider this "convergence of evidence" concept in reference to a large stone artifact exhibited at the Mystery Hill site, a key place in Fell's argument. The North Salem, New Hampshire, site consists of numerous stone structures and features (Figure 6.5). William Goodwin (1946), a retired insurance executive from Hartford, Connecticut, purchased the site in 1935 and spent the rest of his life rebuilding parts of it and trying to prove that it was the settlement of ancient Europeans—specifically, Irish Culdee monks in the tenth century A.D. His attempt at remaking the place in the image he expected is more than a little problematic; a comparison of the "before" photographs in his 1946 book and photos taken more recently reveals a clear problem. For years it was called Mystery Hill, though now the owners refer to it as America's Stonehenge, believing it was built by even more ancient seafarers from Great Britain.

Figure 6.5   The admittedly strange stone structures of Mystery Hill, North Salem, New Hampshire, are part of an idiosyncratic site most likely built by colonists in the eighteenth or nineteenth century. Some insist that the site is far older, built by European settlers of the New World more than three thousand years ago. (K. Feder)

Certainly, the owners of the site have little doubt concerning the function and purpose of the artifact in question; they direct you to the slab of stone with a sign saying: TO THE SACRIFICIAL TABLE. Awesome (Figure 6.6). We can only imagine the horror as the desperate victim, perhaps a virgin whose blood was needed to propitiate some vengeful Celtic god, was led to the table. Held down, her carotid artery was severed. Screams gurgled from her slit throat as her lifeblood surged across the surface of the stone. Running freely, it accumulated in red pools in the finely chiseled channels etched into the margins of its surface where it coursed through another carved channel serving as an outlet. Finally, the blood was collected in a pot placed beneath for some terrible ceremony it sickens us even to consider. It's a grotesque and fascinating scenario—and I appear to have gotten way too carried away writing about it.

But on what do they base their supposition that the object in question was used for human sacrifice? Is there a "convergence of evidence"—multiple independent sources of information—that leads to this inevitable conclusion? For example, are there very similar sacrificial tables dated to antiquity in Ireland, Scotland, Wales, or England? Has human blood residue been found in the interstices of crystals in the stone? Have sacrificial daggers of bronze been found at the site or nearby in New Hampshire? Is the Mystery Hill stone table a unique object found in a clearly ceremonial context?

Figure 6.6   The so-called sacrificial altar stone at Mystery Hill is presented by some as a unique and romantic artifact, evidence of a population of pre-Columbian interlopers practicing ceremonial sacrifices. However, the grooved stone platform at Mystery Hill is anything but unique; it is a common artifact found in historical New England farming communities, used in the rather unromantic production of apple cider or soap. (K. Feder)

Unfortunately, the answer to all of these questions is no. In fact, the only argument presented for the artifact being a sacrificial table is that some people think it looks like what they expect a sacrificial table to look like. Nothing more. And that's not nearly enough.

Viewed more closely, the "sacrificial table" presents us with a convergence of evidence leading to a far different interpretation. In fact, stone slabs with channels etched or carved on their surfaces, including apparent exit channels for collection of whatever liquid had accumulated on the stone's surface, are widely known in colonial New England and recognized for what they were. Their context, when they have been found in place, shows their use in farm industries; not sacrifice, but in the rather more mundane production of lye soap and apple cider!

Let's begin with one stream of evidence; historical descriptions of cider making. Before the modern era, a hand-cranked cider press commonly was placed on top of a flat table of wood or stone with channels carved around the perimeter (Figure 6.7). When stone was used, the base was called a "cider-press bedstone." Crushed apples were placed on the bedstone in flat sheets between layers of filtering fabric. Workers applied pressure to the apple mash using a screw press, squeezing out the liquid, whereupon it accumulated in the channels along the bedstone's margins. The cider was collected in a pot or bucket when it poured out of the outlet channel. I'll

Figure 6.7 An authentic, historical cider press located at Old Sturbridge Village restoration in Massachusetts. Note the screw press on top which would have been turned to move a top plate down against the crushed apples resting in layers on the base. The wooden base is a close match for cider-press bedstones like those seen in Figure 6.8. (K. Feder)

admit, it's a lot less "romantic" than the image of blood collection attendant to a human sacrifice, but the end result tastes much better.

After historical descriptions of cider production, including the use of a wooden base or bedstone looking a lot like the sacrificial altar stone at Mystery Hill, another stream of evidence is the material record with surviving examples of similar artifacts, all originally found in farming contexts (Figure 6.8). The Mystery Hill artifact is not unique, mysterious, or surprising; similar artifacts have been found, all dating to the eighteenth and nineteenth centuries, and their historical context suggests their use as cider-press bedstones. Oh, and there's no indication of an ongoing, widespread practice of human sacrifice and blood collection on the part of New England's colonial farmers.

Then, in yet another stream of converging evidence, re-enactors using original artifacts or replicas have actually produced cider the old-fashioned way, using the wooden bases and bedstones as the tables on which cider was squeezed from apples and then collected in carved channels (Quinion 2008).

In a final convergence of evidence, it should be pointed out that using durable stones as platforms for collecting liquids was common in colonial times. Flat stones, usually smaller than the cider-press bedstones just discussed, but with similar channeling, were used in the production of lye soap. In this application, a wooden bucket was centered on a stone, just inside the circumference of a carved, circular channel. A layer of filtering material was placed at the bottom of the bucket, which had a series of holes drilled into its base. The bucket was then filled with wood ash. Water poured over the ash would leach out the lye, which would then accumulate in the channel and pour into a container placed beneath an exit channel (Figure 6.9). The collected lye was used in the production of soap.

It is ironic to point out that another artifact in the production of apple cider has been called a ceremonial object made by ancient Celtic migrants to New England. A double ring of carved stones found at the Gungywamp site located in Groton, Connecticut, has been proposed as an ancient Celtic worship site (Figure 6.10 top). However, relying on the same convergence of evidence just presented for the cider-press bedstone at Mystery Hill (we don't have to keep calling it a "sacrificial altar stone," unless you are referring to sacrificing defenseless apples), we can conclude that its use can be more simply explained. Remember the crushed apples placed on the bedstones in cider production? One common way in which that "mash" was produced was in an animal-powered mill. A heavy, vertically set mill wheel would have been positioned between the double ring of stones at the Gungywamp site. With apples poured into the circular channel between stones on the ground, the mill wheel would have been turned by a horse (or other draft animal) walking in a circle. As the wheel moved around the circle, it crushed the apples, preparing the mash for the bedstone (Figure 6.10 bottom). The

a

b

Figure 6.8 Cider-press bedstones: (**a**) is located on the grounds of the Hadley Farm Museum in Massachusetts; (**b**) is located at Old Sturbridge Village, Massachusetts. Both were located at local farms and were used in cidering operations. Note their similarity to the artifact called "the sacrificial table" at Mystery Hill (K. Feder)

Figure 6.9 An authentic lyestone with a replica barrel for containing the wood ashes used in soap production. Note that the barrel is centered within the circular groove on the surface of the stone. Also note the exit channel. The lyestone is one of several in the collection at Old Sturbridge Village. (K. Feder)

convergence of evidence clearly shows that these artifacts, far from being mysterious indicators of ancient Celtic human sacrifice, are, instead, fascinating remnants of farm industry in the eighteenth and nineteenth centuries.

The Archaeological Verdict

While on a visit to Mystery Hill, I asked the guide why their small museum had one large glass case of stone artifacts found at the site and clearly of local Indian manufacture and one glass case filled with the pottery, brick, and iron nails of nineteenth-century inhabitants, but no case filled with the European bronze tools of the supposed "Bronze Age" European settlers of the site. The guide responded, "You don't think those ancient people would have left all those valuable bronze tools just lying around, do you?" I responded that they most certainly had left "all those valuable bronze tools" lying around in Europe; that's how we know it was the Bronze Age—archaeologists find such objects. In other words, I was simply asking that the archaeological context be considered. I was told, in essence, that there was no archaeological context.

An archaeological excavation was conducted at Mystery Hill. In the 1950s the organization that controlled the site, the Early Sites Foundation,

Figure 6.10 Some claim that the seemingly mysterious circle of stones at Gungywamp, Connecticut (**top**) has mystical significance within an early European religious context—proof, therefore, that pre-Columbian Europeans had settled Connecticut. However, other, similar historically documented—and photographed— features are known to have been used by more recent settlers of New England as bark mills for the extraction of chemicals for hide tanning (**bottom**). (K. Feder)

hired Gary Vescelius, a Yale University graduate student in archaeology, to excavate. Their hope was that artifacts would be found that would support the hypothesis that the site had been built and occupied by ancient European immigrants to the New World. In hiring an archaeologist to excavate at the site, they were recognizing that an archaeological context was necessary. They were admitting, in a sense, that architectural similarity was not enough, that it merely suggested the possibility of a connection between the Old and New Worlds. Archaeological evidence of the kind of people who lived at the site was necessary to support the hypothesis—the kind of evidence discussed earlier in the chapter, including entire complexes of artifacts found only in ancient Europe, the skeletal remains of identifiable Europeans, and artifacts made of raw materials from European sources, all in a context that could be dated to before Columbus.

Vescelius (1956) found nothing of the kind. He recovered some seven thousand artifacts in his excavation. They all were clearly of either prehistoric Indian manufacture (dating to an occupation of the site before the stone structures were built) or nineteenth-century European manufacture—ceramics, nails, chunks of plaster, and brick fragments. No ancient Celtic stuff was found in the excavations. The archaeological evidence clearly pointed to a nineteenth-century construction date for the site.

Finally, regional surveys have been performed on sites in Massachusetts (Cole 1982) and Vermont (Neudorfer 1980), where stone structures suggested by some to be of ancient Celtic origin are found. Both projects show quite clearly and definitively that the stone structures were part of historic, colonial patterns of land use and construction.

Neudorfer (1980) conducted a three-year project, examining forty-four stone chambers in Vermont, taking measurements and searching for historic contexts for the structures (Figure 6.11).

Neudorfer found that the stone chambers, far from being enigmatic, were a common part of farm culture in historic New England. She found in some cases that the style of masonry of the chambers was identical to that of the foundations of nearby historic farmhouses. Further, she found eighteenth- and nineteenth-century publications describing the best methods for building such structures for cold storage of fruits and vegetables. Whereas Fell claims that the southerly or easterly orientation of the chamber entrances reflects ancient Celtic ceremonies, the farm publications Neudorfer located advised eighteenth- and nineteenth-century farmers to orient the openings of their root cellars to take advantage of the position of the winter sun in the southern sky, thereby preventing freezing in the cellars.

Inscriptions

As we'll talk about in Chapter 7, the nineteenth century in North America was a period rich in archaeological speculation and fakery, especially regarding the discovery of inscriptions in ostensible Old World languages found in

Figure 6.11   A stone chamber at the Gungywamp site, similar to those studied by Neudorfer in Vermont. (K. Feder)

contexts that suggested the presence of visitors from Europe, Asia, and Africa long before the voyages of Columbus (Table 6.1). Linguists and epigraphers have argued long and hard about the authenticity of such inscriptions, but all of these artifacts are lacking that which is most important from an archaeological perspective: archaeological context. People traveling through an alien territory with enough time on their hands to leave behind a note etched onto a rock were certainly around long enough to drop, lose, discard, or hide for safekeeping some of what we began this chapter talking about: bits of their stuff. If visitors were present in North America, they must have camped along their way and, as a result, left behind archaeological remains of their presence. Individual, inscribed objects are certainly easier to fabricate than are entire archaeological sites, so "one-offs" (or even "two-offs") like the Kensington Stone, the Grave Creek Tablet, the Bat Creek Stone, the Newark Holy Stones, the Los Lunas Stone, and Dighton Rock (I have shown and summarized four of these in Table 6.1) are not, by themselves, terribly convincing to most archaeologists. In none of the instances in which such inscribed artifacts have been found has any archaeological context been forthcoming to support their authenticity. In each case, it is as if ancient Old World explorers had hovered over a place in North America, dropped their etched note, and then skirted off, leaving behind no archaeological footprint. Needless to say, archaeologists are skeptical of the possibility that any group could be that pathologically neat and so are skeptical of the authenticity of the claims of visits based on inscribed artifacts alone.

Table 6.1 *Inscribed Stones*

Bat Creek Stone: An inscribed stone excavated in 1889 in eastern Tennessee. A definitive debunking of the artifact was written by Mainfort and Kwas (2004).

Dighton Rock: An inscribed 40-ton boulder located in eastern Massachusetts. Its first historical reference is dated to 1680. Some of the markings appear to be genuine petroglyphs. Some writers "read" the inscriptions, but can't agree on what it says or even on what language it's written in (Norse? Chinese?).

Los Lunas Stone: A Hebrew inscription on an 80-ton slab of rock, found 35 miles south of Albuquerque, New Mexico, in 1933. The inscription is of the Ten Commandments. The inscription is crisp with little evidence of weathering. There is no supporting evidence for the presence of ancient Hebrews in New Mexico.

Grave Creek Stone: A strangely inscribed stone reflecting no particular language found in West Virginia in 1838 (Barnhart 1985–86). David Oestreicher (2008) has shown that this is clearly a fake.

Archaeological Context: Digging Pits and Recovering Evidence

Every year in the United States, archaeologists excavate tens of thousands of test pits in compliance with the requirements of federal, state, and local regulations regarding historic preservation, environmental protection (including the historical or cultural environment), and zoning. A state may decide to build, re-align, or widen a highway; a municipality may want to construct a sewage treatment plant; or a town may deem it necessary to build a new school. In all of these cases, when federal funding is requested or federal permits are needed, federal regulations come into play. These regulations often require research to determine whether important historical sites—especially sites on or eligible for a national "honor roll" called the National Register of Historic Places (http://www.nps.gov/nr/)—will be adversely affected by the project. States and municipalities often have similar requirements. Of course, in order to determine if an important archaeological site will be damaged or even destroyed by a construction project, archaeologists first need to determine if there are sites in a project's footprint or right-of-way. We accomplish this by digging test excavations sampling the subsurface within a project area. We dig holes, screen the dirt, and look for evidence of ancient activity in an area.

The number of test pits excavated as part of this process is stagger-ing. I recently surveyed some of my colleagues in southern New England concerning this. Table 6.2 was the result. One column presents an estimate for the number of test pits excavated in each state in 2011. The next column extrapolates that number out over the past decade. Though I cannot pretend that the numbers are absolutely precise, this gives you a good estimate for test pit frequency. As you can see from Table 6.2, even in the relatively small area of southern New England, we dig, not hundreds, but thousands of test pits each year to comply with historic preservation regulations. And here's the point: Thousands of archaeological sites have been found in these test pit surveys, including very rare, very ancient sites (some more than 10,000 years old) of extremely low archaeological visibility: 9,000-year-old sites rep-resenting the villages of native people who were adjusting to the post–Ice Age environment of southern New England; far more abundant so-called Late Archaic sites representing a florescence of human population in the region between 6,000 and 4,000 years ago; larger, more permanent and, there-fore, more archaeologically visible sites of the so-called Woodland period, late in whose sequence we find native people planting the traditional Native American triad of corn, beans, and squash; native sites of the seventeenth century showing clear evidence of contact with European settlers; and the

Table 6.2 *Estimated Number of Test Pits Excavated in Southern New England State Mandated Archaeological Surveys in 2011 and Over the Past 10 Years*

	2011 Estimated Count	Over 10 Years
Connecticut	4,000	40,000
Massachusetts	2,500	25,000
Rhode Island	1,200	12,000

villages, camps, burial grounds, quarries, mines, and the like of these new European inhabitants of southern New England.

Remember our discussion earlier in this chapter of our human proclivity to bring along some of what George Carlin called our "stuff" wherever we travel and our habit of losing and discarding some of that stuff along the way? There is no reason to believe ancient visitors to the New World would have been any different. With that in mind, it must be reported that in none of the thousands of test pits excavated in New England over the past decade did any archaeologist report the discovery of even a single artifact attributable to the ancient Welsh, Chinese, Celts, Africans, or other non–Native American group and dating to the dim mists of antiquity. We have found none of the stuff that they would have brought along on their voyage. This alone is strong evidence that these groups were not here before Columbus.

Current Perspectives: The Norse Discovery of America

An assessment of the purported Norse discovery of the New World before Columbus begins not with artifact trails or people's stuff, but with a series of stories—the so-called Viking Sagas—passed down through oral tradition and eventually put to paper decades and even centuries later.

The *sagas* are compelling tales of adventure and discovery, life and death. The stories were handed down orally for generations and recorded hundreds of years after the events they celebrated actually transpired. Among the tales told in the sagas are a number concerning the Viking discovery, exploration, and settlement of Iceland and Greenland. Also described in the sagas is a story of the discovery of another new country. That country, it has been claimed, was North America.

Two sagas in particular tell the story of this new land: the *Greenlander's Saga* and *Eirik the Red's Saga*. The *Greenlander's Saga* relates the following tale (*Eirik the Red's Saga* differs in some particulars but describes essentially the same events); the summary is based on the English translation of the sagas by Magnusson and Paulsson (1965).

Soon after A.D. 980, Eirik Thorvaldsson, known as Eirik (Erik) the Red, was banished from his home on Iceland for having killed two men (his father before him had been banished from Norway for the same offense). The dispute had likely resulted from the growing struggle for land and power on the island nation (McGovern 1980–81). Discovered in A.D. 860 and settled initially by the Vikings in A.D. 870, Iceland's population had grown to nearly fifty thousand, and land was at a premium (Jones 1982).

Outlawed because of his crime, Eirik left his home on Iceland and sailed westward, searching for and verifying the existence of a land that had previously been sighted. Eirik, in an attempt to reestablish a land and power base, returned to Iceland, encouraging people to follow him to this newly discovered land. He called it *Greenland*. Though it was largely covered by glacial ice, Eirik gave the land its name in an early case of deceptive advertising; as the saga writers stated, "People would be more tempted to go there if it had an attractive name" (Magnusson and Paulsson 1965:50).

Established in A.D. 985–86, the Greenland colony attracted many disenchanted with the political turmoil of Iceland and grew to a population of about 5,000 (McGovern 1982). The Norse succeeded in carving out a life for themselves in Greenland for 500 years; their archaeological sites are plentiful, represented by the remains of some four hundred farmsteads and seventeen churches clustered in two major settlements (the Western and Eastern) with a combined population of between 4,000 and 5,000 people (Ingstad 1982:24). The archaeological remains of the Greenland Norse provide a model for what such a colony in the New World might look like.

The mystery of the Greenland colony is not why it failed but, as archaeologist Tom McGovern points out, how it survived for five hundred years (Pringle 1997). In Greenland, at least initially, it seems that the Norse attempted to adhere to their traditional dairy farming economy in a place only marginally suited to that way of life. When the climate of Greenland grew dramatically cooler in the fourteenth century, that way of life became not just uncertain, but also untenable. The skeletal remains of the Norse show a major shift in their diet from the agricultural produce they previously relied on but could no longer grow to food from the sea. Chemical analysis of their bones shows that in the 1300s, fish and marine mammals made up an increasingly large portion of their diet (Richardson 2000).

A Newfound Land

The same year the Greenland colony was established, a Viking ship captained by Bjarni Herjolfsson got lost in a storm on the journey from Iceland to Greenland. After about four days of sailing he sighted land. Bjarni could not identify the country and continued to sail, sighting at least two other lands before finally reaching Greenland by sailing *east*. Bjarni and his men did not set foot on these new unidentified lands. Later, he was to be criticized for not exploring these possibly valuable territories. Bjarni was more a farmer than an explorer, yet this relatively unknown Viking is likely the first European to have sighted America.

Despite the fact that the Greenland settlement was prospering and growing at the end of the tenth century, or maybe because of its success and growth, the possibility that new lands might be found to the west intrigued many. Eirik's son, Leif, spoke to Bjarni about his accidental discovery and even purchased his boat—apparently, Leif hoped that the boat would remember the route back to the new lands. He set sail with thirty-five men around A.D. 1000 to search for these new lands. According to the *Greenlander's Saga*, following

Bjarni's directions backward, Leif made landfalls on the three new lands. He called them Helluland (flat-stone or slab land), Markland (forest land), and Vinland (wine land) (McGovern 1980–81). On Vinland, Leif built some sod houses (called *booths*) and used these as a base from which Vinland could be explored (Figure 6.12).

After this initial exploration, Leif returned to Greenland and told of the richness of Vinland; there were salmon in the rivers, wild grains (probably wild rice) in the meadows, abundant grapes, and so on. Soon thereafter, Leif's brother, Thorvald, traveled to these newfound lands and investigated them for about a year. He encountered natives of the new land, called them *Skraelings*, and was killed in a battle with them. He was buried on Vinland, and the rest of his men returned to Greenland.

In A.D. 1022, Thorfinn Karlsefni led at least 65 and perhaps as many as 160 colonists from Greenland to attempt a permanent settlement of Vinland. Families came, and farm animals were brought along. They built homes and began farming the land. After about a year, however, following a bitter battle with the Skraelings, the colony was abandoned. This first attempt to establish a permanent European settlement in the New World failed, according to *Eirik the Red's Saga*, because "although the land was excellent they could never live there in safety or freedom from fear, because of the native inhabitants" (Magnusson and Paulsson 1965:100). History might have been substantially

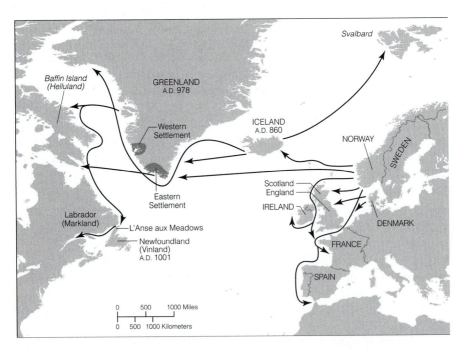

Figure 6.12   Map of Viking explorations of the North Atlantic, including their probable route to the New World in the late tenth and early eleventh centuries A.D.

different had this not been the case. One final attempt was made to settle Vinland, but this too ended in failure.

Where Was Vinland and Who Were the Skraelings?

McGhee (1984) points out that the sailing directions in the sagas, as well as the geographical and environmental descriptions of the islands Leif explored, suggest quite strongly that Helluland is Baffin Island, Markland is Labrador, and Vinland is Newfoundland, all in Canada. The Skraelings, then, were American natives, most likely Indians rather than Eskimos (Fitzhugh 1972:191–95; Jones 1986:130–34).

Norse Discovery of America: The Physical Evidence

Historical or legendary claims of the discovery and settlement of new lands, like those made in the sagas, can be notoriously difficult to prove. Making ancient tales fit our modern knowledge of geography, superimposing modern maps over ancient ones and trying to finesse similarities, and attempting to mine nuggets of historical truth from legendary tales are all interesting exercises, but they often fall far short of proof. We need to find physical evidence in the New World of the presence of travelers and settlers like the Norse, their unique material culture, their "stuff." And, in fact, Norse stuff, dating to as much as five centuries before Columbus, has been found throughout northeastern North America.

A growing number of native sites in Arctic Canada show evidence of widespread, occasional, but sometimes intimate contact for centuries between local people and Norse visitors (McGhee 1984, 2000; Sutherland 2000a). For example, a substantial collection of Norse material culture has been recovered from a native site on Ellesmere Island and includes pieces of European chain-mail armor, iron ship rivets, iron wedges, and a wooden carpenter's plane (Schledermann 1981, 2000). The local inhabitants of the site may have obtained these objects through trade or as plunder, or they may merely have found items left behind by a party of Norse explorers.

Archaeologist Patricia Sutherland (2000a) notes a copper pendant of native design but made from smelted (and, therefore, nonnative) copper, excavated at a site located on the east shore of Hudson Bay, dating to the twelfth century A.D. Also in the Canadian Arctic, archaeologists have found scattered and small quantities of smelted iron, copper, and even a cast bronze pot at native sites (Sutherland 2000a). Sutherland attributes the presence of this Viking stuff to direct trade between the Norse and natives, trade of Norse objects among native groups, and even native scavenging of places where the Norse had visited and left some of their stuff behind.

Sutherland (2000b) also has discovered physical evidence at the Nunguvik site on northern Baffin Island indicating more significant contact between the Norse and native people of northeastern Canada dated to the thirteenth century

A.D. She excavated artifacts there that can be traced to the Norse, including a span of about 3 meters of spun yarn made from a mixture of Arctic hare fur and goat hair. The local people did not spin yarn; there are no goats on Baffin Island; and the yarn itself is a very close match to specimens found in Norse Greenland. In addition, fragments of wooden objects were found at two sites on Baffin Island that show wood joinery techniques—for example, mortising—unknown to the native people aboriginally, but well known to the Norse. Also, red-stained holes in the wood are the remnants of corroded, square-cut iron nails, again reflecting the technology of Europe and not aboriginal America.

L'Anse aux Meadows   Finally, one of the villages where these Norse visitors stayed has been found. In 1960 writer and explorer Helge Ingstad (1964, 1971, 1982), convinced that Newfoundland was the Vinland of the sagas, initiated a systematic search of its bays and harbors for evidence of the Viking settlement. At least the sizable colony of Karlsefni would still be archaeologically visible less than one thousand years after its abandonment. If the sagas were based on an actual attempt at colonization, the site could be found. It was only a matter of figuring out where it was.

On a promontory of land, at the northern tip of the northwestern peninsula of Newfoundland, Ingstad made his remarkable discovery. There he located the

Figure 6.13   House remains at L'Anse aux Meadows, Newfoundland, Canada. Archaeological evidence at this site, including the house patterns, artifacts like soapstone spindle whorls and iron nails, as well as radiocarbon dates, supports the hypothesis that this was a genuine Viking settlement of the New World some five centuries before Columbus. (Photo by B. Schonback, courtesy Birgitta Wallace, Canadian Parks Service)

remains of what appeared to be eight typically Norse turf houses (Figure 6.13). Between 1961 and 1968 the site was excavated under the direction of Ingstad's wife, archaeologist Anne Stine Ingstad (1977, 1982). The archaeological evidence was more than sufficient to identify the site at L'Anse aux Meadows as Viking. This interpretation was based not on vague similarities between the excavated structures and those known from Viking colonial settlements on Greenland but on detailed identities of the artifacts and structural remains.

Along with the turf houses—the so-called booths of the sagas—they found four Norse boatsheds, iron nails and rivets, an iron smithy where local bog iron was worked into tools, a ring-headed bronze pin (Figure 6.14), and a soapstone spindle whorl used in spinning wool. As the local prehistoric Eskimos and Indians did not build boatsheds, smelt iron, produce bronze, or spin wool with spindle whorls, the evidence of an alien culture was definitive (Ingstad and Ingstad 2000).

Chunks of jasper, a flintlike stone that, when struck, produces sparks and was used by the Norse to start fires, were recovered at L'Anse aux Meadows. The jasper has been examined through trace element chemistry; its source is not Newfoundland but Greenland and Iceland, which, of course, are where the Norse inhabitants of L'Anse aux Meadows originated. We also know that the Norse who lived here traveled farther south in the New World because butternut fragments were found in the L'Anse aux Meadows hearths. Butternuts are a kind of walnut that does not grow on Newfoundland and did not grow there

Figure 6.14   A ring-headed bronze pin found at L'Anse aux Meadows. The raw material of the artifact and its form are purely Norse. Its recovery within an overall archaeological pattern that matches Viking sites in Greenland and Iceland and its clear association with a turn-of-the-eleventh-century date further support the hypothesis that the site is Viking. (Photo by G. Vandervloogt, courtesy Birgitta Wallace, Canadian Parks Service)

during the Norse occupation. Their source is Nova Scotia. The Newfoundland Norse must have visited there or traded with others to obtain them.

In the floor of one of the house structures the excavators discovered a small, stone-lined box. Called an "ember box," it was for storing embers of the night fire. Remains of a very similar ember box have been found at Eirik's farmstead on Greenland (Ingstad 1982:33). Twenty-one carbon dates provide a mean age of A.D. 920 ± 30 for the settlement—a bit old by saga accounts, but some of the burned wood used for dating purposes likely was driftwood that already was old when used by the Viking settlers (Ingstad 1977:233). Nevertheless, a number of the carbon dates fit the chronology of the sagas quite well.

More recent excavations at L'Anse aux Meadows have recovered additional material of Norse manufacture dating to about a thousand years ago. In water-logged areas of the site where preservation was good, a team led by Parks Canada archaeologist Birgitta Wallace (2000) recovered a fragment of a notched bow, a piece of what appears to be a ship patch, a pedal-shaped object, and the top of a barrel, all made of wood. All of these objects exhibited evidence that they had been carved or cut with metal tools. Also, a glass bead, a piece of gilded brass, and a needle hone—all of typical Norse design—were found.

Was L'Anse aux Meadows the settlement initiated by Leif, occupied by his brother Thorvald, and expanded in the hope of permanency by Karlsefni? The archaeological data do not conform perfectly to the sagas. No human burials were found, though the sagas indicate that a number of Vikings died in Vinland. No evidence of European domesticated animals was recovered in the excavations, though the sagas relate that such animals were brought by the settlers. Wallace (2000) concludes that L'Anse aux Meadows is not Vinland, but that Vinland was a region with L'Anse aux Meadows located at its northern margin. The site, she suggests, was used as a base of operations (called Straumfjord in the sagas) from which Norse exploration of points farther south was initiated.

It will likely never be known for certain whether L'Anse aux Meadows is the archaeological site of Eiriksson's and later Karlsefni's settlement, but perhaps this is not so important. What is important and what is indisputable is the archaeological evidence at L'Anse aux Meadows of a Viking settlement, the westernmost outpost of their far-flung world. The settlement was planted in the fertile soil of America. It withered and died for reasons largely beyond the control of those hardy folk who attempted it: a worsening climate that would render Greenland uninhabitable for Viking farmers and render the voyage from the west coast of Greenland to Vinland virtually impossible, and a native population willing to fight to protect themselves and their lands. In the final analysis, the saga of the Vinland settlement may be a tragic story of failure. But, most important in terms of the focus of this chapter and perhaps in terms of human history as well, the physical evidence indicates quite clearly that it was a drama played out on the world stage five hundred years before Columbus set sail.

Other Evidence of the Viking Presence?

The Newport Tower   Is there evidence for a pre-Columbian Norse presence south of the modern border between Canada and the United States? The Newport Tower in Newport, Rhode Island, has been proposed as an ancient Viking construction (Figure 6.15). It is singular in appearance, at least in the New World, and has been the focus of both inquiry and speculation.

There is a significant problem, however, with the hypothesis that the tower is Viking and predates the accepted period of European settlement of the region. The English settled the area around Newport in A.D. 1639, and there is no mention made by these settlers of a mysterious and already existing stone tower. They almost certainly would have noted it had there been one.

However, there was enough controversy about the possibility of a pre-Columbus Viking connection to the tower that an archaeological investigation was conducted around and *under* the tower (Godfrey 1951). Most of the artifacts were pieces of pottery, iron nails, clay tobacco pipes, buttons, and buckles. All of these items can be traced to Scotland, England, or the English colonies in America and were manufactured between the seventeenth and nineteenth centuries (Hattendorf 1997). The investigators even found the preserved impression of a colonial bootprint in the soil beneath the stone

Figure 6.15   The Newport Tower in Newport, Rhode Island, claimed by some to be an ancient Viking church. Historical and archaeological evidence indicates quite clearly that the tower was built during colonial times. (K. Feder)

foundation of the tower. For a seventeenth-century bootprint to have been left under the tower, the tower must have been built either sometime during or sometime after the seventeenth century.

The most recent excavations in the vicinity of the tower were conducted between 2006 and 2008, partially as the result of the replacement of a paved path around the structure. Once again, and confirming the earlier archaeology, the oldest artifacts found in the recent study date to the seventeenth century, a time we know that Europeans were settling the region. "Not a coin, nail, or piece of pottery" was found to support an earlier date or a connection to ancient Norse visitors to or settlers of Rhode Island (Flynn 2006).

Finally, the lime mortar bonding the stones used to build the tower has been radiocarbon-dated. The carbon date matches quite precisely the historical record and the artifacts recovered, A.D. 1665 (Hertz 1997). The mysterious tower turns out to be a windmill likely built by the then governor of Rhode Island, Benedict Arnold, the grandfather and namesake of the famous traitor (it is even mentioned in his will, dated to 1677). The architecture of the tower turns out not to be unique after all; it is a close match for a windmill built in A.D. 1632 in Chesterton, England (Hertz 1997). The senior Benedict Arnold was brought up within just a few kilometers of Chesterton; perhaps he liked the unique design and decided to have a copy built on his property in Rhode Island.

The Kensington Stone   A large stone slab with ostensible Viking writing, or *runes,* was found near Kensington, Minnesota, by Olof Ohman in 1898 (Kehoe 2005). If legitimate, the stone would represent physical evidence of the westernmost exploration by the Norse in the New World. The stone bore a short message concerning a voyage of thirty men—"eight Goths and twenty-two Norwegians"—who had sailed west from Vinland in A.D. 1362. Ten of the men were found by their comrades "red with blood and dead," and the survivors carved the runes to mark the spot and tell their brief story.

In her book *The Kensington Runestone* archaeologist Alice Kehoe (2005) makes the case for the artifact's authenticity and, therefore, a Norse presence in Minnesota in the mid-fourteenth century, based on the degree of weathering reported within the runes, the form of the runes themselves, and the lack, in her opinion, of a credible hoaxer. However, Kehoe also reveals the lack of any confirming archaeological evidence for the Norse being anywhere in the area during the time mentioned on the stone. Excavations were carried out at the runestone's place of discovery in 1899 and 1964; there was an archaeological survey in the general area in 1981, as well as additional subsurface testing in 2001. Kehoe reports that no confirming archaeological evidence was found—no discarded or lost Norse tools or weapons, no fireplace where they cooked their food, and not the skeletons of any of the ten men killed at the spot where the stone was erected. Simply stated, no additional archaeological evidence has been found that might lend support to the claim that a band of Norse was present in Minnesota more than 100 years before Columbus's first voyage to the Caribbean.

Along with the lack of any confirming archaeological evidence of a Norse presence in Minnesota in the fourteenth century, the skepticism of rune experts like Anatoly Liberman, who characterizes the writing on the Kensington Stone as "bizarre" (Powell 2010:69), and the fact that some of the "bizarre" forms of the writing may be traceable, not to the fourteenth century but to much later, perhaps the late nineteenth century, you can understand the skepticism of many scientists and historians concerning the Kensington Stone.

The Vinland Map   When the so-called Vinland map first surfaced in 1957, a few historians and cartographers thought it might be genuine, dating to about A.D. 1440, more than fifty years before the first voyage of Columbus to the New World. It was initially suggested by those who accepted the authenticity of the map that it was a copy of an even older work based on Viking knowledge of the geography of northern Canada (Skelton, Marston, and Painter 1995). Greenland is shown and named on the map. To the west of Greenland is an island called Winilanda Insula; this is thought by some to be the earliest—and a pre-Columbian—depiction of Vinland (Figure 6.16).

Many, however, were immediately skeptical of the map's authenticity. As map scholar Douglas McNaughton (2000) has summarized, the map displayed a general style and appearance that was unlike any known fifteenth-century map: Its orientation was wrong, and it lacked the border delineating Heaven and Earth seen in other maps of this time period. Beyond this, although some thought the map's authenticity was supported by the fact that it was discovered bound into a fifteenth-century book, there is no mention of the map in the book itself, supporting the hypothesis that the map may have been added long after the book was published.

In 2002 researchers radiocarbon-dated a small piece of the parchment on which the map was drawn. The result: The parchment dates to approximately A.D. 1434 (Donahue, Olin, and Harbottle 2002). If the map showing Newfoundland truly dates to fifty-eight years or so before Columbus set sail, it would seem to support its authenticity, but skeptics have a response; suppose the forger cleverly used an old piece of parchment which, they claim, would have been readily available?

In a book that reads like a detective novel, historian Kirsten A. Seaver (2004) deconstructs the story of the Vinland map, concludes that it was a twentieth-century fake, and even presents a strong argument as to who did it and why. Seaver points out a clarifying fact ignored by those who support the map's authenticity: If the Vinland map is genuine, it's unique, but not only because it depicts the New World. The map would be unique as the sole example of Norse cartography! Simply stated, the Norse didn't produce or use maps in navigation; none other have been found.

Though the authenticity of the map is of great concern to cartographers and to Yale University (the current owner of the map), its significance relative to the question of a Viking presence in the New World actually has diminished over the years. After all, as shown in this chapter, we know from

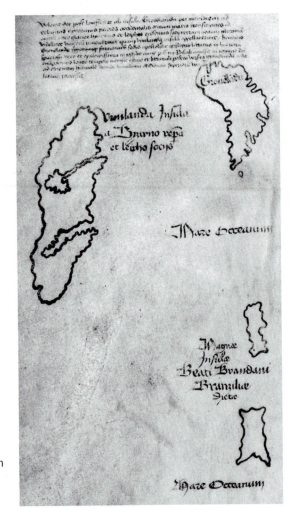

Figure 6.16 Section of the Vinland map that depicts the New World. The parchment on which the map was drawn appears to date to before Columbus, but the ink used to draw the map has been shown to be modern. (Beinecke Rare Book and Manuscript Library, Yale University)

the archaeological record that the Norse explored and attempted to settle the northeast coast of the New World 500 years before Columbus. Whether or not they drew a map of their exploits is, at least in this regard, largely beside the point.

      FREQUENTLY ASKED QUESTION

How could the Vikings navigate to the New World without devices like a compass or a sextant?

The Vikings navigated by ocean currents, winds, and positions of stars in the sky. It was a knowledge informed by centuries of exploration.

An attempt to replicate the Norse voyage to Vinland was carried out in 2000, close enough in time to call it the millennial celebration of the original voyage. The replica ship, the *Islendingur* (Icelander), sailed from Reykjavík, Iceland, on June 17, 2000, that island nation's Independence Day. It arrived safely at L'Anse aux Meadows on July 28 to an enthusiastic welcome. The ship's design was based on that of a well-preserved Norse boat built in the ninth century A.D. and discovered by archaeologists in 1882.

  BEST OF THE WEB

http://www.geraceresearchcentre.com/

Home page of the Gerace Research Center, College of the Bahamas. The site has links to a listing of archaeological research and publications related to Bahamian archaeology, including the work of Charles Hoffman at the Long Bay site, where late Spanish artifacts have been found dating to the early voyages of Christopher Columbus.

http://www.columbusnavigation.com

An interesting site produced by Keith A. Pickering, presenting a discussion of the many possible locations of Columbus's Caribbean landfalls.

http://www.pc.gc.ca/lhn-nhs/nl/meadows/index.aspx

The Canadian government's official L'Anse aux Meadows website, with links to brief discussions of the village's founding by the Norse in the late tenth century, the Viking sagas, and the archaeological research conducted at the site that confirms definitively the site's identification as a Norse outpost in the New World five centuries before Columbus.

http://www.mnh.si.edu/vikings/voyage/

This is the companion website for the museum exhibit Vikings, The North Atlantic Saga, produced by the Smithsonian Institution. Extremely informative and well produced, the site provides an enormous amount of information about the archaeology, history, genetics, and environment of the Norse.

  CRITICAL THINKING EXERCISE

Research the expeditions of Martin Frobisher or Francisco Vasquez de Coronado. How can their visits to the New World provide us with insights about the archaeological trail left by a small group of visitors to the New World?

❖❖❖❖❖❖❖❖ *7* ❖❖❖❖❖❖❖❖

The Myth of
the Moundbuilders

Today, the intriguing culture archaeologists know as the Moundbuilders is one of the best-kept secrets in American history. That a complex American Indian society with great population centers, powerful rulers, pyramids, and fine works of art evolved in the midwestern and southeastern United States comes as a surprising revelation, even to those in whose backyards the ruins lie.

Yet the archaeological evidence of the villages and monuments left by these Native Americans is nearly ubiquitous. The most obvious manifestation of their culture is their earthworks (Figures 7.1 and 7.2): conical mounds of earth, up to nearly 100 feet in height, containing the burials of perhaps great rulers or priests with fine grave goods in stone, clay, copper, and shell; great flat-topped pyramids up to 100 feet in height, covering many acres, and containing millions of cubic feet of earth and on which ancient temples once stood; and effigy earthworks in the shapes of great snakes, birds, and bears.

Few of us seem to be aware of the remarkable cultural legacy of this indigenous American culture. This became sadly clear to me when attending an archaeology conference in St. Louis more than thirty years ago. Much of my excitement about the conference resulted from its location. The largest and most impressive Moundbuilder site, Cahokia, an ancient settlement with thousands of inhabitants, sits on the Illinois side of the Mississippi River, in the town of Collinsville, just east of St. Louis. Wishing to take advantage of my proximity to the site, I asked the gentleman at the hotel front desk how I might get to Cahokia. The response: a blank stare. He had never heard of it. "You know," I explained, "the big Indian site." "No, no," he responded, "There haven't been any Indians around here for many years."

No one in the hotel had heard of Cahokia, and even at the bus station people thought I was just another confused out-of-towner. Luckily, I ran into a colleague who knew the way, and I finally got to the site.

Figure 7.1   Examples of mounds: Serpent Mound, an effigy earthwork in southern Ohio in the form of a coiled 1,500-foot-long snake (**top**). A huge, conical burial mound close to 100 feet high in Miamisburg, Ohio (**bottom**). (*Top:* photo by Major Dache M. Reeves. Courtesy National Museum of the American Indian, Smithsonian Institution; *bottom:* K. Feder)

Figure 7.2   Monks Mound is an enormous, tiered pyramid of earth, the centerpiece of mound construction at Cahokia in Illinois. By any measure, Monks Mound is one of the largest pyramids in the world. Monks Mound served as a platform on top of which a wooden temple once stood. (K. Feder)

It was worth the trouble. About 70 of the 200 or so original mounds remain (Fowler 1989). Several of these demarcate a large plaza where ceremonies were likely held during Cahokia's peak between A.D. 1050 and 1250. Monks Mound (see Figure 7.2), containing more than 20 million cubic feet of earth, is one of the largest pyramids in the world (including those of Egypt and Mesoamerica). It dominates the plaza. The highest of its four platforms is raised to a height of 100 feet, where it once held a great temple. Surrounding the central part of this ancient settlement was a massive log wall, or palisade, with evenly spaced bastions and watchtowers. The palisade enclosed an area of about 200 acres in which eighteen of the largest and most impressive of Cahokia's earthworks were built. The log wall itself may have been the most monumental of the many large-scale construction projects undertaken by Cahokia's inhabitants; it consisted of some 20,000 logs, each one about 1 foot in diameter and 20 feet tall, and was rebuilt virtually in its entirety at least three times during the site's occupation.

Cahokia must have been a splendid place (Iseminger 2010; Pauketat 2009). Based on the density of house remains in the excavated areas, archaeologist Tim Pauketat (2009) estimates Cahokia's peak population at something between 10,000 and 16,000 inhabitants, with an additional 20,000 to 30,000 people living in a 50-mile radius of the site owing allegiance to

Figure 7.3   An artist's rendition of Cahokia at its cultural peak. With a population estimated in the thousands, Cahokia was a virtual prehistoric American Indian city on the Mississippi River more than seven hundred and fifty years ago. (Painting by William Iseminger, courtesy Cahokia Mounds State Historic Site)

what he justifiably calls "ancient America's one true city north of Mexico" (2009:1–2). Cahokia was an economic, social, and religious center, a teeming metropolis that was a city in every sense of the word, and the predominant political force of its time (Iseminger 1996, 2010; Lawler 2011; Milner 2004; Pauketat 1994, 2009). It was, by the reckoning of many, an emerging civilization created by American Indians whose lives were far different from the stereotype of primitive, nomadic hunters too many of us envision (Figure 7.3).

From atop Monks Mound one can peer into two worlds and two different times. To the west rises the modern city of St. Louis, framed by its Gateway Arch of steel. Below rests the ancient city of Cahokia with its monuments of earth, shadows of a long-ignored Indian culture.

How could people not know of this wonderful place? Suffice it to say that if people today living twenty minutes from Cahokia haven't heard of it, most New Englanders, Californians, Southerners—in fact, most Americans— are completely unaware of it and the archaeological legacy of the indigenous American society that produced it and hundreds of other sites.

Cahokia and Moundbuilder culture, however, were not always an invisible part of the history of this continent. In fact, the remains of their culture once commanded the attention of the American public and scientists alike. It was not only that the mounds themselves, the fine ceramics, sumptuous burials, carved statues, and copper ornaments were so impressive, though this was part of the fascination. Unfortunately, much of the intense interest generated by the remains of this culture resulted from a supposed enigma perceived by most; the Moundbuilders clearly lived before Columbus, the Indians were the only known inhabitants of North America before the coming of the Europeans, and it was commonly assumed that the Indians were simply incapable of having produced the splendid works of art and monumental construction projects that characterized Moundbuilder culture. With the rejection of the possibility that American Indians had produced the culture, the myth evolved of an ancient, vanished American race (see especially Silverberg 1989 for a very useful and succinct account of the evolution of the Moundbuilder myth).

The myths of a petrified giant (Chapter 3) and of a human ancestor with a modern brain and simian jaw (Chapter 4) were based on hoaxes, clever or otherwise. People suspended their critical faculties and were fooled by these frauds. The Moundbuilder myth, in contrast, was not predicated on a hoax (though, as you will see, hoaxes did play a role) but rather on a nearly complete and sometimes willful misunderstanding of genuine data.

The Myth of a Vanished Race

The myth of a vanished race of Moundbuilders was accepted by many Americans in the eighteenth and nineteenth centuries. Five basic arguments were presented to support the notion that American Indians could not have been the bearers of Moundbuilder culture. Let's deal with each in turn.

1. *Indians were too primitive to have built the mounds and produced the works in stone, metal, and clay attributed to the Moundbuilder culture.*

   The attitude of J. W. Foster, president of the Chicago Academy of Sciences, was prevalent. Describing the Indian, he states:

   > He was never known voluntarily to engage in an enterprise requiring methodical labor; he dwells in temporary and movable habitations, he follows the game in their migrations. To suppose that such a race threw up the symmetrical mounds which crown so many of our river terraces is as preposterous, almost, as to suppose that they built the pyramids of Egypt. (1873, as cited in Silverberg 1989:117)

   In his 1872 work, *Ancient America*, J. D. Baldwin is even more direct: "It is absurd to suppose a relationship or connection between the original barbarism of these Indians and the civilization of the moundbuilders" (as cited in Thomas 1894:615).

   These arguments can be fairly characterized as racist and unfortunately held sway among many people.

2. *The mounds and associated artifacts were very much more ancient than even the earliest remnants of Indian culture.*

Though the analysis of soil layering known as stratigraphy was not to become an established part of archaeology until later in the nineteenth century (for example, Dall 1877), in 1820 Caleb Atwater used a simple form of stratigraphic analysis to support the notion that the Moundbuilders were from a period far before the Indians arrived in the New World. He maintained in his book *Antiquities Discovered in the Western States:*

> Indian Antiquities are always either on, or a very small distance below the surface, unless buried in some grave; whilst articles, evidently belonging to that people who raised our mounds, are frequently found many feet below the surface, especially in river bottoms. (1820:125)

3. *Stone tablets were found in the mounds that bore inscriptions in European, Asian, or African alphabets.*

The best known of such artifacts were the Grave Creek Mound Stone from West Virginia (Schoolcraft 1854), the Newark Holy Stones from Ohio, the Bat Creek Stone from Tennessee (Manifort and Kwas 2004), and the Cook Farm Mound Tablets in Davenport, Iowa: see Table 6.1 for the Grave Creek and Bat Creek Stones and Figure 7.6 for the Holy Stones (Putnam 1886). Because American Indians north of Mexico were not known to have possessed a writing system before European colonization, the presence of writing in the mounds seemed to provide validation of the hypothesis that a non-Indian culture had been responsible for their construction. Where characters from specific alphabets could be discerned, sources for Moundbuilder culture could be, and were, hypothesized.

4. *American Indians were not building mounds when first contacted by European explorers and settlers. When queries were made of the local Indians concerning mound construction or use, they invariably professed complete ignorance.*

Very simply, the argument was presented that if Indians were responsible for the mounds, they should have been building such earthworks when Europeans first came into contact with them. If no longer building mounds, living Indians should remember a time when their ancestors had built them. It was claimed by many, however, that the Indians themselves did not claim a historical connection to the mounds. For example, French writer François René Vicomte de Chateaubriand (1801) maintained that "all the tribes uniformly say that when their ancestors arrived in the West, in order to settle in seclusion, they found the ruins there such as we see them today." The belief that Indians were not building mounds when first contacted by Europeans combined with the fact that most Indians did not claim that their ancestors had built the mounds was seen by many as definitive, empirical evidence against any claim of Indian responsibility for Moundbuilder culture.

5. *Metal artifacts made of iron, silver, ore-derived copper, and various alloys had been found in the mounds.*

Historic Indian cultures north of Mexico were not known to use metal other than copper, which could be found in pure veins and nuggets in parts of Michigan; silver, also found in pure, natural deposits that required no further metallurgical refinement; and iron from meteorites. Smelting ore to produce copper, silver, or iron and techniques of alloying metal (mixing copper and tin, for example, to produce bronze) were unknown. Therefore, the discovery of artifacts of these materials in the mounds was a further indication that a people other than and more technologically sophisticated than American Indians had been the Moundbuilders.

With these five presumably well-supported "truths" in hand, it was clear to the satisfaction of many that Indians had nothing to do with mound building or Moundbuilder culture. This left open the question of who, in fact, the Moundbuilders were.

Who Were the Moundbuilders? Identifying the Vanished Race

From our vantage point in the early years of the twenty-first century, it is extremely difficult to imagine how intensely interested many were in the origins of the mounds and Moundbuilder culture. The fledgling Smithsonian Institution devoted several of its early publications to the ostensible Moundbuilder enigma. Another government agency, the Bureau of American Ethnology, whose job it was to preserve information concerning rapidly changing Native American cultures, devoted a considerable part of its resources to the Moundbuilder issue. Influential private organizations like the American Philosophical Society also supported research into the question and published works reporting on such research.

The mystery of the mounds was a subject that virtually all thinking people were drawn to. Books, pamphlets, magazine pieces, and newspaper articles abounded, written by those who had something to say, sensible or not, on the question that seemed so important to answer: Who had built the mounds? Though few could agree on who was responsible for construction of the mounds, there was no lack of opinions.

In one of the earliest published conjectures, Benjamin Smith Barton wrote in 1787 that the Moundbuilders were Vikings who had long ago journeyed to the New World, settled, and then died out. Josiah Priest in his 1833 work variously posited that the mounds had been built by wandering Egyptians, Israelites, Greeks, Chinese, Polynesians, or Norwegians (Silverberg 1989:66). Others suggested that the mounds had been fashioned by the Welsh, Belgians, Phoenicians, Tartars, Saxons, or Africans. In his previously mentioned article, Chateaubriand (1801) enumerated all of those he considered as possible builders of the mounds—Mexicans, members of the Hernando de Soto expeditionary force, Prince Madoc (see Chapter 6), the Vikings, the Phoenicians, Carthaginians, ancient Israelites, and Egyptians. He concludes that none of those groups were responsible and doesn't suggest an alternative. In *The Commercial*, a Cincinnati newspaper, Lafcadio Hearn made a number of interesting suggestions concerning the source of the mysterious midwestern Moundbuilders. In an article published in 1876, he proposed that, though their source was uncertain,

> it is at least generally recognized that they were not Indians. Their monumental record little resembles that of the Aztec people; and indeed no other American Nation has left traces satisfactorily analogous to those left by the Mound-builders. But it is worthy of note that very similar remains have been left by the European Mound-builders.

So, maybe they were Europeans. Then again, in the very same article, Hearn proposed another, even more speculative origin for the Moundbuilders; he suggested that the Moundbuilders came from the Lost Continent of Atlantis (see Chapter 8)!

An Atlantean source might sound impressive, but one thinker went further still, attributing one of the mounds to a divine architect. The Reverend Landon West maintained that Serpent Mound (Figure 7.1, top) represented the snake that tempted Eve in the Genesis story in the Old Testament of the Bible (Lepper 1998b). Not content merely to make this literary connection, Reverend West went on to claim that God himself had constructed Serpent Mound to memorialize the event and placed the monument in Eden itself. Yes, that is correct; Reverend West suggested that Eden was located in Bush Creek valley, Ohio.

The Archaeology of the Myth

Caleb Atwater, an Ohio lawyer, performed a detailed analysis of the earthworks in his state in an attempt to establish the identity of the vanished race. Though Atwater's conclusions were typical for the time, his methods were far more scientific than the speculations of some of his contemporaries. In his work *Antiquities Discovered in the Western States* (yes, Ohio was then considered a "western" state), Atwater divided the archaeological remains found there into three categories: Indian, European Colonial, and Moundbuilder. The last of these he ascribed to "a people far more civilized than our Indians, but far less so than Europeans" (1820:120).

To his credit, Atwater was not an armchair speculator concerning the Moundbuilders. He personally inspected many sites in Ohio and produced detailed drawings and descriptions of artifacts and earthworks. But his myopia about American Indian cultural achievement clearly fashioned his view:

> Have our present race of Indians ever buried their dead in mounds?
> Have they constructed such works as described in the preceding pages?
> Were they acquainted with the use of silver, iron, or copper? Did the
> North American Indians erect anything like the "walled town" on Paint
> Creek? (Atwater 1820:208)

For Atwater the answer to these questions was a clear "no." American Indians simply were too primitive. He concluded his discourse on the question by suggesting that the Moundbuilders had actually been "Hindoos" from India.

To be sure, there were a few prescient thinkers on the question of the origin of Moundbuilder culture. Perhaps the first to approach the question objectively was Thomas Jefferson, framer of the Declaration of Independence and third president of the United States. Jefferson was curious about the ancient earthworks on and adjacent to his property in Virginia. Not content to merely speculate about them, in 1784 Jefferson conducted what is almost certainly the first archaeological excavation in North America, carefully digging a trench through a mound that contained many human skeletons (Willey and Sabloff 1993). Jefferson drew no conclusion concerning who the Moundbuilders were, calling for more work on the mystery. As the president of the American Philosophical Society, he later would encourage others to explore this question.

Interest in the mounds and debate over the source of the culture that had produced the tens of thousands of these earthworks continued to increase during the nineteenth century as white settlement expanded into the American Midwest, the heartland of Moundbuilder culture. American archaeology developed as a discipline largely in response to questions about the mounds (as well as to questions concerning the origins of the Indians; see Chapter 5).

In their chronicle of the history of American archaeology, Willey and Sabloff (1993) select 1840 as the benchmark for a shift in American archaeology from a period of speculation to one characterized by research—with a goal of description and classification. The work of Ephraim G. Squier and Edwin H. Davis on the Moundbuilder mystery is a good example of this shift in emphasis. Squier was a civil engineer and writer from Connecticut. Davis was an Ohio doctor. Both were interested in the Moundbuilder culture and between 1845 and 1847 carried out intensive investigation of some two hundred sites. They conducted excavations and produced detailed maps of the sites and drawings of the artifacts. Their research culminated in a book, *Ancient Monuments of the Mississippi Valley,* which was selected as the first publication of the recently established Smithsonian Institution.

Squier and Davis approached their task without many of the preconceptions and pet theories of their predecessors on the Moundbuilder question: "With no hypothesis to combat or sustain, and with a desire only to arrive at truth, whatever its bearings upon received theories and current prejudices, everything like mere speculation has been avoided" (1848: xxxviii).

Ancient Monuments of the Mississippi Valley is a descriptive work, with more than two hundred drawings in its three hundred or so pages (Figure 7.4). Squier and Davis were quite systematic in their investigations. Generally, they classified the various kinds of earthworks according to the empirical data of form and content as deduced from their detailed surveys and excavations. However, they also made unwarranted assumptions concerning the function of the different earthwork types.

Squier and Davis describe in great detail and depict in beautifully rendered drawings the artifacts that are found in association with the mounds: ceramics, metal implements and ornaments, stone and bone objects, sculptures, and inscribed stones (Figure 7.5). In a number of places in their book,

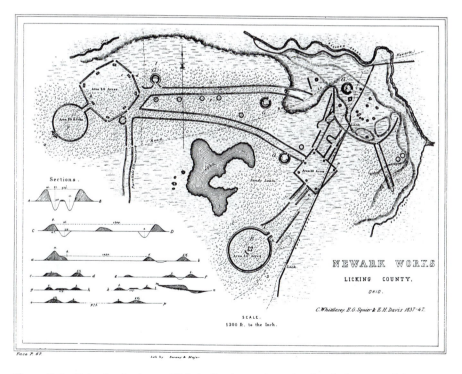

Figure 7.4 Ephraim Squier and Edwin Davis conducted a detailed survey of the mounds of the Ohio Valley and "western" United States in the 1840s, producing beautiful drawings of earthworks like these enclosures in Newark, Ohio. (From *Ancient Monuments of the Mississippi Valley*, AMS Press and Peabody Museum of Archaeology and Ethnology, Harvard University)

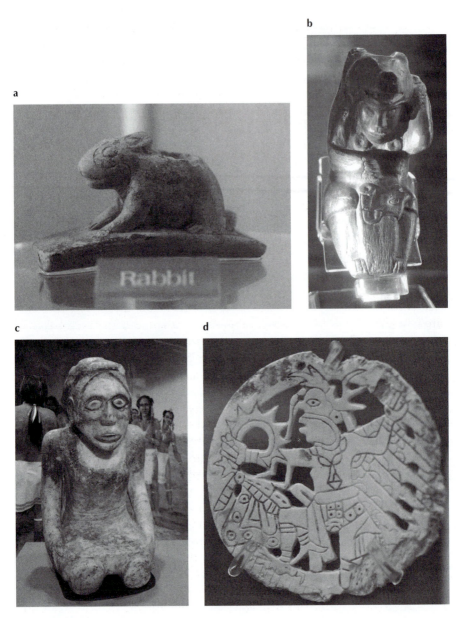

Figure 7.5   The artistic skills of native artisans of the New World are exemplified in the artifacts shown here: (**a**) an effigy pipe carved into the shape of a rabbit, found in a burial mound in central Ohio; (**b**) the Wray Figurine, found in a mound in Newark, Ohio, depicting what appears to be a shaman or priest dressed in a bear skin; (**c**) a sculpture of a kneeling woman, complete with makeup and a headdress, found at the Etowah site, in Georgia; and (**d**) a piece of shell intricately and beautifully carved into the form of a weapon-wielding man wearing what appears to be a bird cloak and mask (also from Etowah). (K. Feder)

they compare these objects with those found in other parts of the world, but never attempt to make a direct connection. Nevertheless, Squier and Davis are explicit in maintaining that the quality of artwork found in the mounds is "immeasurably beyond anything which the North American Indians are known to produce, even to this day" (1848:272).

Squier and Davis conclude their report by suggesting a "connection, more or less intimate" (p. 301) between the Moundbuilders and the civilizations of Mexico, Central America, and Peru. So they do subscribe to the idea that the Moundbuilders were a group separate from and culturally superior to the North American Indians, but at least they ascribe an indigenous, New World source for the Moundbuilders.

The Moundbuilder Mystery Solved

The late nineteenth century saw a continuation of interest in the Moundbuilders. Then, in 1882, an entomologist from Illinois, Cyrus Thomas, was hired to direct a Division of Mound Exploration within the Bureau of American Ethnology. An amendment to a federal appropriations bill in the U.S. House of Representatives directed that $5,000 of the $25,000 BAE budget be devoted solely to the solution of the Moundbuilder mystery. With this funding, Thomas initiated the most extensive and intensive study yet conducted on the Moundbuilder question. The result was more than seven hundred pages submitted as an annual report of the Bureau in 1894 (Thomas 1894).

Above all else, Thomas's approach was empirical; he thought it necessary to collect as much information as possible before suggesting hypotheses about mound function, age, origins, and cultural affiliation. Whereas Squier and Davis focused on about 200 mounds mostly in Ohio, Thomas and his assistants investigated 2,000 mound sites in twenty-one states. He gathered more than 40,000 artifacts, which became part of the Smithsonian Institution's collection. After amassing so much information, Thomas was not afraid to come to a conclusion on the Moundbuilder mystery. Whereas Squier and Davis devote six pages to their conclusions regarding the mounds, Thomas provides a 136-page discussion on the identity of the Moundbuilder culture. Thomas's work was a watershed, both in terms of answering the specific question of who had built the mounds and in terms of the development of American archaeology.

For Thomas the important question was simple and succinct: "Were the mounds built by the Indians?" (1894:21). He went about answering this question by responding to the arguments—presented earlier in this chapter— against identifying Indians as the Moundbuilders.

1. *Indian culture was too primitive.*

To the claim that Indians were too primitive to have attained the level of civilization reached by the Moundbuilders, Thomas responded that it was difficult to conceive

> why writers should so speak of them who had access to older records giving accounts of the habits and customs of the Indian tribes when first observed by European navigators and explorers . . . when the records, almost without exception notice the fact that . . . they were generally found from the Mississippi to the Atlantic dwelling in settled villages and cultivating the soil. (p. 615)

For example, Hernando de Soto's chronicler, known to us only as the "Gentleman of Elvas," described encountering great walled towns of as many as five or six thousand people (1611:122). It is clear from his descriptions of Indian settlements that there was a large, sedentary, "civilized" population in the American Southeast in the sixteenth century.

In another example, William Bartram, a botanist from Philadelphia, began his travels through the Southeast in 1773. In his book enumerating his experiences, he also describes scores of heavily populated Indian towns; in one case he mentions traveling through nearly two continuous miles of cultivated fields of corn and beans (1791:285). He estimates the population of a large town called *Uche* to be as many as fifteen hundred people (p. 313), and he was very much impressed with how substantially built their structures were.

So, in Thomas's view and in fact, evidence indicated that at least some Indian cultures were agricultural and sedentary, with people living in large population centers. They clearly would have been culturally capable of constructing monumental earthworks.

2. *Mound culture was older than Indian culture.*

In reference to the presumed great age of the earthworks, Thomas was wrong; the age of at least some of the mounds may have been more accurately estimated by some of the ancient race enthusiasts. Thomas incorrectly thought many had been built after European arrival in the New World. Ultimately, however, the age of the mounds was only a problem if one accepted the then-current notion that the Indians were relatively recent arrivals. We now know that Native Americans first arrived in the New World more than 13,000 years ago (see Chapter 5), and the mounds are all substantially younger.

3. *There were alphabetically inscribed tablets in the mounds.*

Thomas had quite a bit to say concerning the supposed inscribed stone tablets. Though the myth of a vanished race of Moundbuilders was based largely on misinterpretation of actual archaeological and ethnographic data, hoaxes involving inscribed tablets also were woven into its fabric.

For example, in 1838, during an excavation of a large mound in Grave Creek, West Virginia, two burial chambers were found containing three human skeletons, thousands of shell beads, copper ornaments, and other artifacts. Among these other artifacts was a sandstone disk with more than twenty alphabetic characters variously identified as Celtic, Greek, Anglo-Saxon, Phoenician, Runic, and Etruscan (Schoolcraft 1854). Translations varied tremendously and had in common only the fact that they were meaningless. The disk was certainly a fraud (Oestreicher 2008; and see Table 6.1).

Given the popularity of the notion that the Indians may have descended from one of the Lost Tribes of Israel (Chapter 6), it is not surprising that suggestions were made that at least some of the Moundbuilders themselves represented a group of ancient Jewish migrants from the Holy Land. The so-called Newark Holy Stones (Figure 7.6) seemed to support this notion (Applebaum 1996).

In the summer of 1860, David Wyrick, a professional land surveyor and ardent amateur archaeologist, continued his ongoing explorations of the impressive group of ancient mounds and enclosures located in Newark, Ohio (Lepper and Gill 2000). Immediately to the east of the large octagonal enclosure (seen on the left of Figure 7.4), Wyrick discovered a roughly triangular, polished stone object, 6 inches long by 2½ inches at its widest. It looked somewhat like a plumb bob and was labeled the "Keystone." What made the object so intensely interesting was the fact that there was a series of clearly recognizable Hebrew letters etched onto its surface (Figure 7.6a). Wyrick must have been ecstatic at this discovery because it seemed to supply proof for his own deeply held belief that the New World Moundbuilders were members of the Lost Tribes of Israel. Hebrew writing on an object found in association with an ancient earthwork in Ohio would lend dramatic support to this hypothesis.

Unschooled in the Hebrew language, Wyrick brought the object to a local reverend, John W. McCarty, who could translate it. Reverend McCarty determined that on each of its four faces, the messages read in Hebrew, respectively: "the laws of Jehovah"; "the Word of the Lord"; "the Holy of Holies"; and "the King of the Earth."

Some were immediately skeptical of the object's antiquity, pointing out that the Hebrew writing on this supposedly antique object was quite modern. Beyond this, Wyrick had made the discovery of

a

b

c

Figure 7.6   The so-called Keystone, the first of the Newark Holy Stones found in Ohio, was presumed by some to have been produced by ancient Israelites who visited the American Midwest some 2,000 years ago (**a**); The Decalogue, the second of the Newark Holy Stones, was written in a more ancient version of Hebrew than the Keystone, bearing an enumeration of the Ten Commandments (**b**); Just one example of the literally hundreds of the so-called Michigan Relics, a tablet with a childish drawing and a nonsensical inscription (**c**). (**a** and **b**: Courtesy Johnson-Humrickhouse Museum, Coshocton, Ohio; **c**: © Thom Bell, From the documentary "The Michigan Relics").

the Keystone without witnesses who could verify its context in the ground. As a result, the Keystone was judged by many to be a fake.

In the September issue of the *Masonic Review,* the editor Cornelius Moore (1860:379) mentions the discovery of the Keystone and goes on to report that near its find spot a skeleton had subsequently been found, which, it was suggested, might be that of Moses himself! Perhaps that was merely a joke, but Moore then notes quite seriously that Wyrick and his crew were now looking for "two tablets of stone on which the law was engraved"!—that law being the Ten Commandments.

By a remarkable coincidence—well, likely it wasn't a coincidence at all—several months after the discovery of the Keystone, amid growing skepticism concerning its age, and about two months after the *Masonic Review* article mentioned that Wyrick was now on the hunt specifically for tablets bearing an inscription of the Ten Commandments, Wyrick found exactly that just a few miles away, this time under the watchful gaze of a retinue of witnesses (Wallbridge 1861).

This new discovery was a far more elaborately carved object: a limestone tablet, covered on all of its faces with Hebrew letters of an entirely different, apparently older vintage than the characters on the Keystone. This stone became known as the "Decalogue" when its translation revealed it to be a version of the Ten Commandments; the person around whom the commandments were carved was identified as Moses (Figure 7.6b).

Some hailed these artifacts as proof of an ancient Jewish presence in Ohio. Others were still skeptical. If both stones were legitimate, how is it that ancient Jews in North America were, at the same time, writing in two different versions of Hebrew traceable to different time periods in their homeland? Perhaps only the first stone with its modern writing was a fake and the Decalogue was the real thing? How likely was it that a genuine stone with ancient Hebrew writing would coincidentally be found by the same searcher just a few miles from the spot where hoaxers had recently planted a fake stone with modern Hebrew on it? The Decalogue stone seemed to reflect a Hebrew script dating to the presumed antiquity of the mounds, but, nevertheless, it contained apparent anachronisms that suggested that it had been carved in the nineteenth century. These questions do not even begin to approach broader, cultural issues: There is no ancient (or modern) Jewish practice of constructing conical burial mounds or earth enclosures, yet it was being proposed that the ancient Jews who had left behind the Holy Stones had also built the earthworks found in Ohio.

In a wonderful piece of detective work, Brad Lepper and Jeff Gill (2000) have traced the cast of characters in this story. They point out that in 1839, Reverend McCarty's bishop, Charles Petit McIlvaine, had already predicted that artifacts linking the Moundbuilders to the Bible would one day be found. In Lepper and Gill's solution to the mystery, McCarty simply supplied the "proof" that realized his bishop's prediction. The ambitious Reverend McCarty was demonstrably deeply involved *after* the discovery of the Holy Stones, both translating them and championing their authenticity. Lepper and Gill suggest that he was also deeply involved *before* they were "found." In other words, McCarty faked the stones, planted them, and made sure Wyrick found them. McCarty's motive may have been to lend support to his and McIlvaine's belief in the unity of the native inhabitants of the Old and New Worlds as descendants of the people of the Bible. As Lepper and Gill suggest, in a general sense, the purpose of planting artifacts bearing Hebrew writing may have been "to encompass the prehistory of the New World with the biblical history of the Old" and to show that all people could be traced to the first people whom God had created and placed in the Garden of Eden (Lepper and Gill 2000:25).

The fact that the second Newark Holy Stone (the Decalogue) seemed specifically and precisely to challenge the reaction of skeptics to the first discovery is not terribly surprising. The Decalogue stone was written in a form of the Hebrew script more appropriate for the time period of mound building in the American Midwest, and this time the artifact was found while witnesses looked on; in both of these circumstances, the Decalogue seemed to respond a little too conveniently to the complaints of those skeptical of the Keystone's authenticity.

As noted in Chapter 3, it is pretty typical for archaeological hoaxers to use the criticisms of skeptics to improve the quality of their fakes. Consider the example of the Michigan Relics, a series of some 800 faked artifacts of clay, copper, and slate discovered throughout Michigan between 1890 and 1920 (Halsey 2009). In their initial attempt to produce objects that seemed to show that the mounds were tied to ancient Egyptians, Israelites, Christians, and others, the fakers, led, apparently, by James Scotford, a local man in west-central Michigan, made some fundamental errors. For example, some of the first objects discovered were unfired clay cups. Anyone who has worked with clay can testify that if they remain unfired, clay objects will begin disintegrating soon after they are made. They will dry out, crack, and fracture in the sun and under moist conditions—for example, when embedded in soil—will simply become wet and mushy, lose their shape, and, eventually, fall apart. Unfired clay artifacts certainly would not have remained intact for hundreds or even thousands of years in the Michigan soil, so, skeptics argued, the unfired clay artifacts among the Michigan Relics were recently made and demonstrably fake. To make matters even a bit worse, in at least one instance, one of the fabricators of an unfired clay bowl apparently had set the object down on what was clearly a machine-sawed wooden board. The board left the telltale imprint of mechanized sawing on the bottom of the bowl. Because ancient "whoevers" did not have machine-sawed boards, but nineteenth-century Michiganers did, the recent origin of the bowl was clinched.

Almost as soon as this inconsistency was pointed out by skeptics, however, people began finding, certainly not coincidentally, fired clay artifacts to add to the Michigan Relics assemblage. In fact, it may be a general rule of archaeological fakery: When skeptics point out the obvious errors in the first artifacts made by hoaxers, the hoaxers learn from their mistakes and produce specimens that are more convincing.

As archaeologist John Halsey (2009), who has extensively investigated the Michigan Relics, points out, there was a plan to show some of them as part of an archaeological exhibit being prepared for the World's Columbian Exposition, the world's fair held in Chicago in 1893. The man charged with putting together the exhibit for the fair, Walter Wyman, became suspicious of the proponents of the Relics and actually paid one of them a surreptitious visit, using a false name to gain entry to his workshop. According to Wyman, when he entered the workshop of James Scotford, he found it filled with relics in the making! Scotford was pumping out fakes and even at that point shamelessly offered to sell some to Wyman. Not surprisingly, Wyman turned him down. Later, in 1911, Scotford's stepdaughter signed a statement in which she admitted that she had seen her stepfather manufacturing relics in copper, clay, and slate and she further knew that he had buried the objects in order to later pretend to discover them.

If contemporary, eyewitness testimony concerning the fraudulent nature of the Michigan Relics were not enough, recently, one of the objects was subjected to luminescence dating, a technique applicable to baked clay objects (Lepper 2009; Lipo and Sakai 2009). The artifact in question is a clay tablet covered with all manner of incomprehensible glyphs and odd etchings clearly intended by its fabricator to appear to be Old World, possibly Mesopotamian or Babylonian (though it is nothing of the sort; Figure 7.6c). The result of the applied dating method merely confirms the fraudulent nature of the object. In fact, the tablet is not an ancient artifact at all. The clay was baked either in the middle of the nineteenth century (about A.D. 1840, if the artifact was never buried in the soil) or the beginning of the twentieth century (A.D. 1901, if it had been buried in the soil, which it almost certainly was). It is no small coincidence that the second luminescence date matches quite nicely with the date of the object's purported discovery. Like the whole assemblage of the Michigan Relics, it's not an ancient artifact, it's a late nineteenth-century or early twentieth-century fake.

4. *Indians were never witnessed building mounds and had no knowledge of who had built them.*

We next come to the claim that Indians were not Moundbuilders at the time of European contact, nor did they know who had built the mounds in their own territories. Thomas shows that this is, quite simply, false. De Soto's chronicler, the Gentleman of Elvas, mentions the construction and use of mounds almost immediately in his sixteenth-century narrative. Describing the Indian town of Ucita, he writes, "The lordes house stoode neere the shore upon a very hie mount, made by hand for strength" (1611:25). From the same journal, we know that de Soto visited what today is called the Etowah site, in Georgia. Now a state park, Etowah is characterized by monumental and beautifully crafted pyramidal mounds in the heart of a vast, ancient native settlement (Figure 7.7a). De Soto did not doubt that Indians built and used the mounds.

Garcilaso de la Vega compiled the notes of some of the 311 survivors of the de Soto expedition. He describes how the Indians constructed the mounds on which temples and the houses of chiefs were placed: "They built up such sites with the strength of their arms, piling up large quantities of earth and stamping on it with great force until they have formed a mound from twenty-eight to forty-two feet in height" (cited in Silverberg 1989:19).

Nearly two hundred years later, at the turn of the eighteenth century, French travelers lived among the Natchez Indians at the mouth of the Mississippi River. They described the principal town of these agricultural Indians as possessing a mound 100 feet around at its base, with the houses of leaders located on smaller mounds (Figure 7.7b; Du Pratz 1774). William Bartram, at the end of the eighteenth century, mentions the fact that the houses of chiefs are placed on eminences. Even as late as the beginning of the nineteenth century, William Clark, co-leader of the Lewis and Clark expedition to the American West, noted:

> I observed artificial mounds (or as I may more justly term graves) which to me is strong evidence of this country being once thickly settled. The Indians of the Missouris still keep up the custom of burying their dead on high ground. (Bakeless 1964:34)

There clearly was ample historical evidence of Indians building and using mounds. The reason for the demise of at least some of the mound-building cultures of the Southeast was that de Soto accidentally introduced smallpox into these populations (Ramenofsky 1987). Exposed to this deadly disease for the first time, the indigenous people had no immunity to it and died in great numbers. Large mound

Figure 7.7   These two enormous platform mounds are the largest at the Etowah site in Georgia. (**top**) The larger of the mounds shown here is more than 18 meters (60 feet) tall; (**bottom**) The platform mound shown here is located at the Emerald Mounds site in Louisiana. It, in turn, was built on top of a monumentally scaled, artificial earth platform, itself 10.7 meters (35 feet) high and covering more than 7.5 acres. Emerald Mounds was in use well into the seventeenth century. (K. Feder)

Figure 7.8   So-called native copper—metal found in an almost pure state in nature and which, therefore, did not need to be extracted from an ore—was widely used by the native people of eastern North America, and especially by various mound-building people. Here, an artist in ancient Ohio produced a splendid image of a bird—possibly a Peregrine falcon—by hammering the copper into a flat sheet, and cutting it into its final shape with stone tools and by hammering in details like the eyes and feathers. This artifact was found at Mound City, located in Chillicothe, Ohio, but the copper was most likely obtained from a source in Michigan, nearly 1,000 kilometers (600 miles) away (see Figure 7.10). (K. Feder)

sites were abandoned as a result of the tragic consequences of this deadly epidemic.

5. *Metal objects found in the mounds were beyond the metallurgical skills of the Indians.*

Thomas carefully assessed the claim that some mound artifacts exhibited a sophistication in metallurgy attained only by Old World cultures. Not relying on rumors, Thomas actually examined many of the artifacts in question. His conclusion: All such artifacts were made of so-called native copper (Figure 7.8). Certainly this implied extensive trade networks. Michigan was the source for much of the raw material used in copper artifacts found as far away as Florida. There was no evidence, however, for metallurgical skills the Indians were not known to have possessed.

Thomas clearly had marshalled more evidence on the Moundbuilder question than had anyone before him. In a rather restrained fashion, he comes to this conclusion: "It is proper to state at this point, however, that the author believes the theory which attributes these works to the Indians . . . to be the correct one" (1894:610).

With the publication of Thomas's *Report on the Mound Explorations of the Bureau of American Ethnology,* Moundbuilder archaeology had come of age. Its content was so detailed, its conclusions so reasonable that, though not accepted by all, the myth of a vanished race had been dealt a fatal blow.

Rationale for the Myth of a Vanished Race

The myth of a non-Indian, vanished race of Moundbuilders was predicated not on a hoax or series of hoaxes but on ignorance and selective acceptance of the data. Silverberg's thesis that the vanished race myth was politically motivated is well founded; it was, as he says, "comforting to the conquerors" (1989:48).

If the Indians were not the builders of the mounds and the bearers of a culture that impressed even the rather ethnocentric European colonizers of America, it made eliminating the presumably savage and primitive natives less troublesome. And, if Europeans could further convince themselves that the Indians were very recent interlopers—in fact, the very invaders who had savagely destroyed the gentle and civilized Moundbuilders—so much the better. Finally, if it could be shown that the Moundbuilders were, in actuality, ancient European travelers to the Western Hemisphere, the circle was complete. In displacing the Indian people, Europeans in the eighteenth and nineteenth centuries could rationalize that they were merely reclaiming territory once held by ancient Europe. The Moundbuilder myth was not just the result of a harmless prank or a confusing hoax. It was part of an attempt to justify the destruction of American Indian societies. We owe it to them to set the record straight.

Current Perspectives: The Moundbuilders

An enormous amount of research has been conducted on the Moundbuilder culture in the last hundred years. See George R. Milner's (2004) book *The Moundbuilders: Ancient Peoples of Eastern North America* for a terrific summary of what we now know about Moundbuilder society, and see Brad Lepper's (2005) *Ohio Archaeology: An Illustrated Chronicle of Ohio's Ancient American Indian* for a detailed and beautifully illustrated discussion of the Ohio contingent of Moundbuilders. We now realize that there was not one Moundbuilder culture but several (Figure 7.9). The oldest evidence for mound building in North America has been found at the Watson Brake site in Louisiana and dates to 5,500 years ago (Saunders et al. 1997). There, a people reliant on

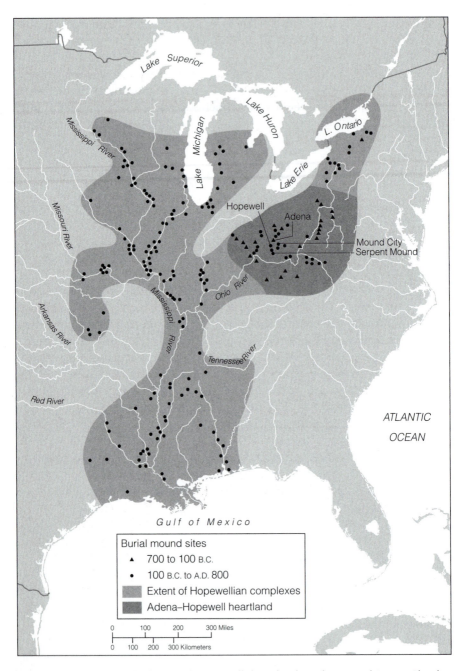

Figure 7.9 Location of Adena and Hopewell, heartlands in the United States. Clearly, the geographical focus of Moundbuilder culture was the river valleys of the American Midwest and Southeast.

hunting and gathering for their subsistence constructed a complex of eleven earthworks, including mounds and enclosures. The largest among the mounds is 25 feet (6.5 meters) in height. The great antiquity of Watson Brake is a clear indication that mound building has a very long history in North America. It also is geographically widespread, with ancient earthworks found throughout the American Southeast, Midwest, and northern plains.

Also in Louisiana, dating to a little before 3,250 years ago, are the Poverty Point earthworks (Gibson 2000). Monumental in scale, they consist of a series of six segmented, concentric earth ridges enclosing a rough half-circle with a radius of 2,100 feet (0.65 kilometer) (Figure 7.10). Each of the ridges is about 80 feet (24 meters) wide at its base, 3.5 meters (10 feet) tall, and separated from adjacent ridges by about 150 feet (45 meters). Altogether there are 6 miles (9.65 kilometers) of these ridges at Poverty Point enclosing a central plaza of about 37 acres. If the soil to produce Poverty Point had been mounded up in 50-pound basket loads, it would have taken 30 million such loads to complete the monument (Kopper 1986).

The tops of the earth ridges were living surfaces where archaeologists have found the remains of hearths and trash pits. Though there is evidence of domesticated squash at Poverty Point, wild foods, especially fish and

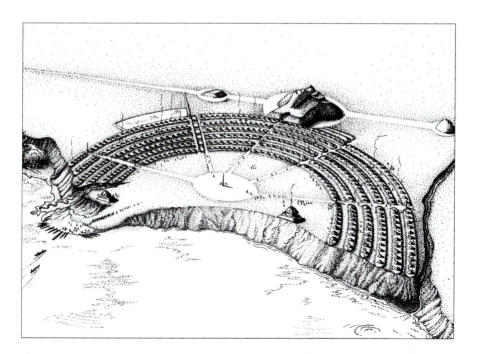

Figure 7.10   The concentric mounds of the Poverty Point site in Louisiana are more than 3,200 years old and reflect the work of a large, organized labor force among the native people whom we today call the Moundbuilders. (Drawing courtesy Jon Gibson, State of Louisiana Division of Archaeology)

other aquatic resources, seem to have been the mainstays of the diet. The construction of the Poverty Point earthworks necessitated the existence of a large labor force coordinated through a complex social and political structure more than 3,000 years ago.

The conical burial mounds that developed in the Ohio River valley have been divided into two cultures: the *Adena* and the *Hopewell* (Lepper 1995a). These both involved burial cults, long-distance trade, and the production of fine crafts and artwork and are differentiated on the basis of certain artifact types. Adena is earlier, dating to as much as 2,800 years ago. Hopewell emerged from Adena about 2,200 years ago and likely represents what is essentially a flowering of Adena culture, though there is extensive chronological overlap between the two patterns. (In other words, not all of those we call Adena developed into Hopewell at the same time.)

Adena and Hopewell people lived in small towns located across much of southern and central Ohio and surrounding states to the south and west. Though we usually think of Native American subsistence as based on corn, very little evidence for that crop has been found at either Adena or Hopewell sites. The Hopewell people especially are known to have relied on the cultivation of local seed plants like sunflower, knotweed, maygrass, goosefoot, and marsh elder, as well as squash, crops that were part of an indigenous agricultural revolution that took place before the movement of corn into the region from Mexico (Smith 1995). Hunting and gathering wild plant foods continued to contribute to the subsistence quest.

The burial mounds themselves mark the remains of either individuals or groups of people, almost certainly the "important" religious, social, and political leaders of Adena or Hopewell society. These "important people" include both men and women and people of a broad range of ages from young children to older adults. Some of these mounds are quite impressive, covering several acres and reaching 70 or 80 feet (20 to 25 meters) in height. Mound 25 at the Hopewell Mound Group in Ohio is particularly striking; it is 500 feet (150 meters) long, 180 feet (55 meters) wide, and 30 feet (9 meters) high (Lepper 1995a). Mound City in Chillicothe, Ohio, is another significant site, a virtual necropolis, or "city of the dead," consisting of twenty-three burial mounds surrounded by an earth embankment.

A widespread trade network brought natural resources to the Adena/Hopewell from all over the United States: Copper and silver from the Great Lakes region were made into finely crafted goods and placed in the graves of those buried in the mounds; turtle shells, pearls, and conch shells from the Gulf of Mexico traveled up the major river systems of eastern North America and were also included in the burials of the Adena and Hopewell; obsidian from the Rocky Mountains, quartz crystals and mica from the Appalachian Mountains, alligator teeth from the lower Mississippi Valley, and chalcedony from North Dakota all made long journeys into the hands of the elite of Adena/Hopewell society.

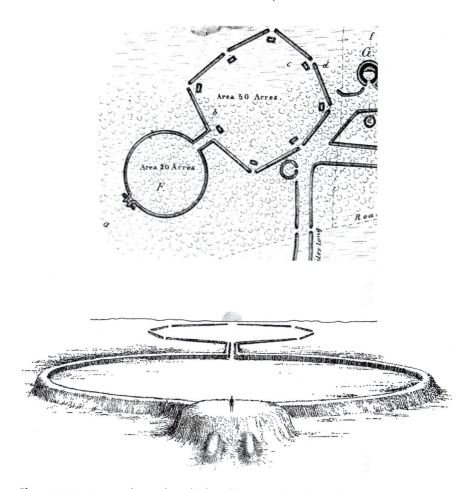

Figure 7.11   Among the earthworks found in Newark, Ohio, is this double enclosure consisting of a 20-acre circle connected to a 50-acre octagon (**top**). If an observer stands on the earthwork located along the bottom left of the circle, looks out through the earth-walled connection between the circular and octagonal enclosures, and straight across the octagon, the line of sight encounters the horizon at a compass direction of 51.5°, the precise location of the rising of the moon at its furthest northern location during its 18.6-year cycle (**bottom**). (*Top:* From Squier and Davis, *Ancient Monuments of the Mississippi Valley* [1848]; *bottom:* From the article "Ancient Astronomers of the Ohio Valley," by Brad Lepper [1998]. Courtesy Brad Lepper and *Timeline,* a publication of the Ohio Historical Society.)

Some of these sites of extensive earthworks include earthen-wall-enclosed spaces of unknown purpose. For example, in Newark, Ohio, near where David Wyrick found the first of the Newark Holy Stones, a series of long, narrow, earthen walls about 5 feet high encloses an octagonal plot of approximately 50 acres, which is in turn connected by two parallel earthen walls to an enormous circular area of more than 20 acres, also enclosed with an earth wall several feet high (Lepper 2002; Figure 7.11, top). This large earthwork is located at the endpoint of what appears to have been a 60-mile-long ceremonial road demarcated by two earthen walls approximately 200 feet apart and perhaps as much as 8 to 10 feet in height (Lepper 1995b, 1995c). Altogether, archaeologist Brad Lepper (2002) estimates, the builders of the Newark earthworks piled up more than seven million cubic feet of dirt to produce the mounds, enclosures, and walls that characterize the site. Connecting sacred or ceremonial mound sites and enclosures, these "roads" may have been used by pilgrims visiting the sites for religious observances—perhaps burial ceremonies or worship services.

The earthworks located along these ceremonial roads appear to have been aligned in reference to important locations along the horizon, places where the sun and moon rise and set at certain dates during the year. For example, go outside and watch the moon rise each night during the course of the twenty-seven and a third days of a lunar "sidereal" month. The moon will appear to rise on the eastern horizon each night at a slightly different location, from a maximum northerly point to a maximum southerly point midway through the month. Moonrise then returns to the north along the horizon until it reaches a northern maximum by the first day of the next month, but that maximum is slightly different from the last one. In fact, the northerly and southerly maxima are a little different in each subsequent month during the course of a much longer cycle, one that lasts 18.6 years. From a vantage point in central Ohio during those 18.6 years, the furthest north moonrise for that entire period occurs at a compass direction of 51.5° (38.5° north of due east). That location represents an important part of a lengthy lunar pattern and astronomical cycle. I don't know about you, but I had no knowledge of it until I read about the alignments of Hopewell earthworks (Lepper 1998a). It seems that the Hopewell recognized that the location of moonrise was patterned and memorialized it in the positioning of some of their monuments. I've already mentioned the Newark earthworks where the Hopewell constructed two enclosures, one circular and one octagonal, joined by an earth-walled corridor (Figure 7.11, top). An observer standing on the raised mound located along the circular mound directly opposite the connecting corridor can look down that corridor and into the center of the octagon; that observer's line of sight neatly bisects both mounds and represents a compass direction of 51.5°. That same line of sight continues past the octagon enclosure and crosses the horizon at precisely the location, therefore, of the maximum northerly rising of the moon in its 18.6-year cycle (Figure 7.11, bottom).

Lepper (1998a, 2002) suggests that such astronomical alignments are not coincidental but indicate a detailed knowledge of the movements of the sun and moon, perhaps incorporated into calendar ceremonies practiced by the Moundbuilder people. These sites and the ceremonial roadways are examples of the ability of the Adena/Hopewell to organize a large labor force and produce works of monumental proportions.

Later developments in the Mississippi River valley and the American Southeast represent a different pattern. During this period, called the Mississippian, the major temple mound sites were not just places of burial but were also the central places or capital towns of increasingly complex societies, called "chiefdoms." The labor of a sizable population was conscripted by the leaders of temple mound societies to construct large, truncated (cut off at the top) pyramids of earth. Cahokia was the largest and most impressive of these, a true metropolis and the only one with a resident population of a size and density that approach an urban character. There were, however, many others like Etowah in Georgia, Moundville in Alabama, Town Creek Mound in North Carolina, and Crystal River in Florida that, though smaller in size and complexity, with fewer and smaller monumental earthworks, nevertheless represent development of complex, indigenous societies in the period after A.D. 1000 (Figure 7.12).

Figure 7.12   Examples of the great diversity and geographic spread of mound building: (**a**) The two primary mounds at Toltec Mounds in Arkansas. Mound A is 15 meters (50 feet) high, and mound B is about 12 meters (40 feet) high; (**b**) a wide expanse with more than a dozen temple mounds at Moundville in Alabama; (**c**) Town Creek Mound in North Carolina (with a reconstructed temple at the apex of the primary mound); and (**d**) the primary mound at Pinson Mounds in Tennessee is more than 21 meters (70 feet) high. (K. Feder)

The temple Moundbuilders grew maize and squash and later added domesticated beans to their diet. The chemical analysis of their bones shows a dramatic shift to a diet reliant on maize at around A.D. 1000 (Smith 1995). They fished in the rivers and hunted in the forests and continued to gather wild plant foods, including acorn and hickory. The enormous food surplus made possible by agriculture likely allowed for the support of a class of priests and the attendant nobility and artisans.

Old World civilizations such as those of ancient Egypt and Sumer and New World civilizations including the Aztec and Maya are marked by stratified social systems. Kings, emperors, or pharaohs ruled with the help of noble and priestly classes. The nature of social stratification is exhibited quite clearly in the archaeology of their deaths; the tombs of pharaohs and kings are large and sumptuous with concentrations of finely crafted artwork, rare or exotic (and presumably expensive) materials, and even the presence of sacrificed human beings—people killed and buried with the ruler to accompany him or her to the afterlife.

Cahokia, too, has evidence of just such a burial (Fowler 1974:20–22, 1975:7–8). Mound 72 represents the interment of members of a royal family of Cahokia (Figure 7.13). The primary burial was of a man in his mid-forties

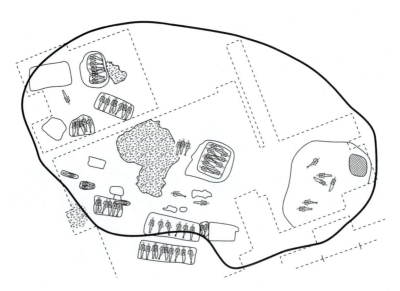

Figure 7.13 Map showing the location of the burials at Mound 72 at Cahokia. The primary burial is that of a man in his mid-forties, laid out on a bed of more than 20,000 mother-of-pearl shell beads. The great wealth reflected in the materials with which he was buried and the likelihood that some of the secondary burials represent human sacrifices suggest that the primary burial in Mound 72 was that of an important person, perhaps a ruler of ancient Cahokia. (Courtesy William Fowler)

when he died, laid out on a platform of 20,000 perforated mother-of-pearl shell beads that had, perhaps, been woven into a burial cloak. A cache of more than 700 arrowpoints made from stone from as far away as Wisconsin had been placed in his tomb (Figure 7.14). Nearby, three women and three men were buried, accompanied by stone weapons made from materials imported from Oklahoma and Arkansas as well as by sheets of mica from North Carolina. A 2-foot by 3-foot sheet of copper from Michigan had also been included in their burial.

Another part of the mound contained the burials of four men, decapitated and with their hands cut off. Close by were the remains of fifty-three women, all but one of whom had been in their late teens and early twenties when they were killed. These almost certainly were individuals whose lives were sacrificed for the presumed needs of the rulers in their lives after death. Altogether, archaeologists have found 272 burials in Mound 72. There likely are more human remains in the unexcavated area around the mound itself (Iseminger 2010:80).

Just as in the tombs of ancient Egypt's pharaohs, the abundance of finely made objects crafted from rare, precious, and difficult to obtain raw materials and, maybe especially, the presence of human sacrifice victims are

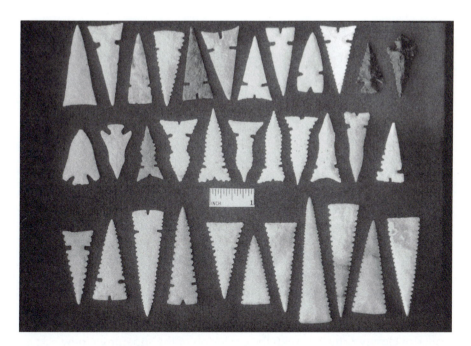

Figure 7.14   A small sample of the more than 700 finely crafted stone projectile points buried with one of Cahokia's leaders in Mound 72. (Courtesy Cahokia Mounds State Historic Site)

clear indications of the enormous importance and great power wielded by of some of the people buried in Mound 72 at Cahokia. It is ironically the case that such evidence of vast social, political, and economic inequality are all hallmarks of what we commonly call "civilization."

The evidence at Cahokia and other temple mound sites, as well as at sites of the Adena and Hopewell cultures, is clear. American Indians produced cultures of great sophistication and complexity. The only mystery that remains is why more Americans are not aware of the legacy of these indigenous civilizations.

    FREQUENTLY ASKED QUESTIONS

1. *Some of the mounds are huge. Where did all the dirt come from to build the mounds?*

The dirt came from the immediate vicinity of the mounds. Huge quantities were excavated using wooden shovels and stone- and shell-bladed hoes. The dirt was carried by basket. In the vicinity of some of the larger mounds, enormous borrow pits (extensive, but not terribly deep) represent the source areas for the dirt used to build the mounds.

2. *Was Cahokia the result of a supernova?*

The ascendancy of Cahokia presents a fascinating challenge. Why, in what appears to be a very sudden break with previous practice, did a city develop in western Illinois that came to dominate the lives of people living in the American heartland? Why is it that, beginning in about A.D. 1050, Cahokia arose in what archaeologist Tim Pauketat (2009) describes as a "big bang" that essentially reconfigured the native culture of a vast swath of North America in a very short time?

Pauketat proposes an interesting speculation. A.D. 1054 marks a momentous astronomical event: the explosion of a supernova visible from Earth and recorded in art and text in antiquity (Chinese sky-watchers actually referred to the new light in the sky as a "guest star"). In an otherwise predictable and consistent heaven, the supernova suddenly appeared as an unexpected, frightening, and brilliant stranger in the night sky. The supernova was four times brighter than the planet Venus and shone so incandescently, it was visible even during the day for close to a month.

The explosion of Cahokia as a dominant cultural force in North America closely coincides with the explosion of the supernova (now visible through telescopes as the Crab Nebula). It might be just a coincidence, but Pauketat suggests that, perhaps, as a result of a feeling of awe—or maybe fear, or a mixture of both emotions—ancient farmers in the American Midwest responded to this portent in the sky by heavily investing their faith in rulers who, they may have believed, could protect them from the threat posed by the astonishing blast of light. In this scenario, those rulers became the nobility of Cahokia and great material wealth, political power, and social status accrued to them. They lived in luxury and when they died, people were sacrificed to accompany them to the afterlife.

Pauketat's hypothesis is difficult to test, and we should be skeptical as we are of all untested hypotheses. But clearly something momentous happened at Cahokia after A.D. 1050 and proposed explanations like Pauketat's provide us with pathways to follow as we attempt to solve this mystery.

   BEST OF THE WEB

Most of the big mound sites have their own web page. Several of the official web pages for some of the most important sites are listed here.

http://cahokiamounds.org/
Cahokia

http://moundville.ua.edu/
Moundville

http://ngeorgia.com/ang/Etowah_Indian_Mounds_State_Historic_Site
Etowah

http://www.nchistoricsites.org/town/town.htm
Town Creek Mound

http://www.nps.gov/ocmu/index.htm
Ocmulgee Mounds

http://www.nps.gov/hocu/historyculture/index.htm
Hopewell Culture National Park (Mound City)

http://www.nps.gov/history/archeology/feature/builder.htm
This site provides a detailed discussion of Moundbuilder culture.

CRITICAL THINKING EXERCISE

Using the deductive approach outlined in Chapter 2, how would you test these hypotheses? In each case, what archaeological and biological data must you find to conclude that the hypothetical statement is an accurate assertion, that it describes what actually happened in the ancient human past?

- The mounds found throughout the American Midwest and Southeast were the product of an indigenous people.
- The mounds found throughout the American Midwest and Southeast were the product of invaders from Europe who later were displaced by the ancestors of American Indians.

8

Lost: One Continent—Reward

It was a beautiful land. Its people, gentle and fair, artistic and intelligent, created the most wonderful society the world has ever known. Their cities were splendid places, interwoven with blue canals and framed by crystal towers gently arching skyward. From its seaports, ships were sent out to the corners of the globe, gathering in abundant raw materials needed by its artisans and giving in return something far more valuable—civilization. The wondrous achievements of the archaic world can be traced to the genius of this singular ancient land. The cultures of the ancient Egyptians and the Maya, the civilizations of China and India, the Inca, the Moundbuilders, and the Sumerians were all derived from this source of civilization (Figure 8.1).

But tragedy was to strike down this great nation. In a cataclysmic upheaval of incomprehensible proportions, this beautiful land and its people were destroyed in a day and a night. Earthquakes, volcanic eruptions, and tidal waves, with forces never before or since unleashed by nature, shattered the crystal towers, sank the great navy, and created a holocaust of incalculable sorrow.

All that remains are the traces of those derivative cultures that benefited from contact with this most spectacular source of all culture. But ancient Egypt, the Aztecs, the Maya, the Chinese Shang, the Moundbuilders, and the rest, as impressive as they were, could have been only the palest of shadows, the most tepid of imitations of the source of all human civilization.

This is the great irony of prehistoric archaeology; the most important of ancient cultures is beyond the grasp of even those archaeologists who investigate the corpses of great civilizations. The original civilization of which I speak, the source of all human achievement, is *Atlantis*, the island continent whose people were obliterated beneath the seething waters of the Atlantic more than 11,000 years ago: Atlantis the fair; Atlantis the beautiful; Atlantis the source. But Atlantis the myth. Such a place never actually existed.

Figure 8.1 Artists have long imagined what Atlantis may have looked like. In this rendering, the artist has remained true to the Greek philosopher Plato's description, depicting a series of concentric rings of habitation, separated by canals but linked by gracefully arching bridges. (© AKG Images/Peter Connolly)

Atlantis: Where Are You?

I live in a charming, bucolic, and rather woodsy part of Connecticut, tucked into the green and lush Farmington River valley. Along with terrific schools, wonderful people, and The Tulmeadow farm store which sells the best ice cream anywhere, my little town has another thing going for it. West Simsbury, Connecticut, zip code 06092, appears to be almost the only place left on the planet that someone has *not* claimed is the actual location of the Lost Continent of Atlantis. Or so it seems.

I am exaggerating here a bit, but check it out (Figure 8.2). According to Plato, the lost civilization of Atlantis was located on a continent-size landmass positioned outside of the Straits of Gibraltar, in the Atlantic Ocean, and was destroyed in a natural cataclysm more than 11,000 years ago (Plato in Hutchins 1952). But no, that can't be right. Atlantis must have been located on the island of Crete in the Mediterranean, and it was destroyed by a volcanic eruption 3,600 years ago (Galanopoulos and Bacon 1969). No, that's not right either; instead, it was located on the much smaller island of Santorini, also in the Mediterranean, and destroyed by the aforementioned volcanic eruption (Pellegrino 1991). If that doesn't work for you, how about moving it a bit north and to the east, and make it not an island continent, but a city in western Turkey (James 1998)? No? Maybe it was actually situated in the Antarctic, of course during a time when the climate of the South Pole was far more

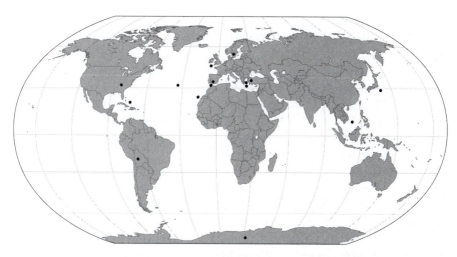

Figure 8.2   Where has Atlantis been found? Better to ask, Where hasn't Atlantis been found? This map shows just some of the better-known locations where assorted researchers have claimed Atlantis has definitely been located. All of these places share one important characteristic: There is no archaeological evidence indicating that any one of them represents the actual location of Plato's Atlantis, which was, after all, an invention of his imaginative mind.

hospitable and a lot less "arctic" than it is now (Flem-Ath and Flem-Ath 1995). No, that's not right either; I've it: Atlantis was located on Spartel Island, a tiny, not-so-continent-size landmass, located immediately west of the Straits of Gibraltar, between Morocco and Spain (Collina-Girard 2001). No, forget the island; Atlantis was in Spain proper, right there on the mainland of Europe (Kühne 2004). A recent National Geographic special (Ball 2011) features an archaeologist who believes that Atlantis has been found in a Spanish marsh. Maybe it's there. How about further north, in Scandinavia as some have claimed (Spanuth 1979). I suppose that would make the Atlanteans Vikings. You don't like that? Okay, let's push it to the west and locate Atlantis in the North Atlantic, about 160 kilometers (100 miles) from the coast of Great Britain, on an island just off Cornwall (a claim made by unspecified Russian scientists and reported by the BBC in 1997). No, wrong ocean; the continent of Atlantis was actually situated in the South China Sea (dos Santos 1997). No, it's not there either. I've got it: Atlantis was in North America (Lopez de Gomara back in 1555 as cited in Huddleston 1967). No, not there? How about this: Atlantis was located in South America, specifically, Bolivia (Allen 1999). No, not Bolivia or anywhere in South America, but perhaps farther north, just off the coast of Cuba (Collins 2002). Or was it (or something very much like Atlantis) located off the coast of Japan (Hancock 2003)? Wait. I just found it. Of course, Atlantis is on an island in the Bahamas, just offshore of the island of Bimini (Cayce 1968). No, wait; we can trace it, not to Bimini, but to another island in the Bahamas. I have documentary evidence right here in this brochure. Whoops; that "Atlantis" is just a modern and rather pricey resort that calls itself Atlantis, but it isn't really Atlantis. Maybe it's back in the Mediterranean after all. The spectacular architectural remains of walls, a canal, and even an acropolis have been found beneath the sea, just 97 miles off the coast of Cyprus (as announced in late 2004 by the explorer Robert Sarmast; Hamilton 2004). No; it's not there either. Hold on! Atlantis has been found by an aeronautical engineer fiddling around on Google Earth (which, okay, might be the coolest thing ever). Check it out for yourself. Type in the following location in the Google Earth search box: 31 15'15.53N 24 15'30.53W (McCarthy 2009). When you get there, set the "eye alt" or "eye altitude" seen on the bottom right of the Google Earth screen to about 200 miles and you will indeed see a pattern of lines all crossing at right angles. Are these the criss-crossing broad avenues of fair Atlantis? The party poopers at Google Earth say no, that the lines aren't real but an artifact of how the sea floor is mapped (by boats crossing back and forth in a right angle grid).

Assessing assertions about the discovery of Atlantis is like a game of Whac-A-Mole. Claims keep popping up from assorted holes, and historians, geologists, and archaeologists keep whacking them back down, only to have another claim pop up from another hole.

Atlantis isn't in any of the claimed locations because it wasn't anywhere. Like Oz, Middle Earth, or Tatooine, it was a mythical place, concocted to tell a story. In fact, Atlantis was simply a literary tool to convey a lesson about the political, social, and economic organization of a well-run society. When looking for Atlantis, it turns out that satellite photographs, sonar, ground-penetrating radar, deep-sea submersibles, and other modern tools of the archaeologist are of no help. Atlantis can't be traced underwater or under mud or rock or volcanic ash. In fact, Atlantis is traceable to no geographical place at all, but to the mind and imagination of one of the world's best-known and most highly respected thinkers (Jordan 2001). That mind belonged to the Greek philosopher Plato.

Atlantis: The Source of the Legend

Plato was born in 429 or 428 B.C. He became a disciple of another great philosopher, Socrates, in about 410 B.C. and established his own academy in 387 B.C. He was well known in his own time and is, of course, still studied and considered a great thinker more than 2,000 years after his death.

Plato apparently believed that the best way to teach was to engage his students in dialogues. Plato wrote many of his philosophical treatises in a dialogue format as well. Readers who insist that the entire Atlantean dialogues are genuine history may be unaware, however, that even the context of Plato's dialogues is fictitious. The dialogues were largely imaginary conversations between Socrates and *his* students. The actual discussions Plato reported on never really took place; the published dialogues were not simply stenographic records. They usually included real people, but some of them lived at different times. In fact, the Critias who tells the Atlantis story has been identified as Plato's maternal great-grandfather (Lee 1965).

The late entertainer and writer Steve Allen once produced a fascinating television show using a similar device. In his *Meeting of Minds,* actors and actresses portraying famous historical figures discussed and debated important philosophical issues. In one episode nineteenth-century evolutionist Charles Darwin, nineteenth-century poet Emily Dickinson, renowned sixteenth- and seventeenth-century scientist Galileo, and fifth-century general and king Attila the Hun sat down together for a chat. And wouldn't you have liked to have been a fly on the wall when Plato himself showed up to thrash out a few ideas with eighteenth-century French author and philosopher Voltaire, sixteenth-century church reformer Martin Luther, and late-nineteenth-/ early-twentieth-century medical pioneer Florence Nightingale? Each of these historical figures was portrayed by an actor or actress well versed in the perspective of the individual he or she was playing. Of course, the real people being depicted never actually had these discussions. The point was to imagine how such conversations might have gone (you can read the transcripts of some of the shows in Allen 1989). Plato used a similar technique to challenge, teach, and entertain his readers.

The story of Atlantis was presented in two of Plato's dialogues: *Timaeus* and *Critias,* named, respectively, after the major participant in each conversation. We know that Timaeus and Critias were real people; Timaeus was an astronomer from Italy, and Critias was an Athenian poet and teacher. The dialogues that bear their names were written sometime after 355 B.C. and before Plato's death in 347 B.C. and describe conversations that supposedly occurred in 421 B.C. (Jordan 2001:11). If you have already done the math, you realize that Plato would have been only seven or eight years old at the time; the dialogues certainly could not have been stenographic transcriptions written by an eight-year-old who listened in on a real conversation.

The Timaeus Dialogue

The Timaeus dialogue begins, oddly enough, with Socrates taking attendance. Socrates then refers to the previous day's discussion of the "perfect" society. It is clear in this context that the discourse Plato is referring to is his most famous dialogue, the *Republic,* actually written several years before *Timaeus.* Here, we are being asked by Plato to go along with the fiction that the *Republic* dialogue, where the nature of a perfect society had been discussed in great detail, was the product of yesterday's conversation.

Socrates next summarizes the characteristics of the conjectural perfect culture presented in the *Republic.* Artisans and husbandmen would be separated from the military; and those in the military would be merciful, would be trained in "gymnastic" and music, would live communally, and would own no gold or silver or any private property.

Socrates, however, then despairs of hypothetical discussions, like the one presented in the *Republic,* of such a perfect society:

> I might compare myself to a person who, on beholding beautiful animals either created by the painter's art or, better still, alive but at rest, is seized with a desire of seeing them in motion or engaged in some struggle or conflict to which their forms appear suited. (Hutchins 1952:443; all quotations from Plato's dialogues are from this translation)

Socrates next gives what amounts to an assignment:

> I should like to hear some one tell of our own city [his hypothetical perfect society] carrying on a struggle against her neighbors, and how she went out to war in a becoming manner, and when at war showed by the greatness of her actions and the magnanimity of her words, in dealing with other cities a result worthy of her training and education. (p. 443)

Socrates even explicitly instructs his students to engage "our city in a suitable war" to show how the perfect society would perform. One of those present, Hermocrates, tells Socrates that a fellow student, Critias, knows the perfect story. Critias then begins to give the account: "Then listen, Socrates, to a tale which though strange, is certainly true . . ." (p. 444).

Critias says that he heard this "true" story from his grandfather, who related the tale at a public gathering on a holiday called Apatouria that Plato scholar Paul Friedlander refers to as a kind of April Fool's Day (1969:383) when prizes are awarded for the best narrative. If this is true, doing the math, Critias's grandfather was 90 when he told the story and our Critias was just 10 years old. Critias's grandfather (also named Critias) said that he heard it from his father, Dropides, who heard it from the Greek sage Solon, who heard it from some unnamed priests in Egypt when he was there about 590 B.C. (Figure 8.3). So at best, when we read Plato, we are reading a very indirect account of a story that had originated about 240 years earlier.

According to the tale told by Critias, the Egyptian priests tell Solon that the Greeks are little more than "children" and know nothing of the many cataclysms that befell humanity in ancient times. They then go on to tell him of ancient Athens, which "was first in war and in every way the best governed of all cities" (p. 445). In fact, it is this ancient Athens which in Critias's story will serve as the model of the perfect state.

The priests tell Solon of the most heroic deed of the ancient city of Athens; it defeated in battle "a mighty power which unprovoked made an expedition against the whole of Europe and Asia" (pp. 445–46). They continue by describing and identifying the evil power that so threatened the rest

Plato (355 B.C.)

↑

Critias, the Younger (421 B.C.)

↑

Critias, the Elder

↑

Dropides

↑

Greek Sage Solon (590 B.C.)

↑

Egyptian Priests

Figure 8.3 A version of "telephone tag" that Plato presents as the pedigree of the Atlantis story. By making it so indirect—the story Critias tells Socrates has already passed through several filters over the course of more than 150 years—with obvious opportunities for embellishment and error, Plato is likely letting the reader know that the story is not meant to be taken as a veritable history.

of the world: "This power came forth out of the Atlantic Ocean . . . an island situated in front of the straits, which are by you called the Pillars of Heracles" (p. 446). (Today they are called the Straits of Gibraltar.) The Egyptian priests told Solon the name of this great power in the Atlantic Ocean: the island nation of Atlantis.

Ancient Athens was able to subdue mighty Atlantis, which had held sway across northern Africa all the way to Egypt. After her defeat in battle, all of Atlantis was destroyed in a tremendous cataclysm of earthquakes and floods. Unfortunately, ancient Athens also was destroyed in the same catastrophe.

After outlining the Atlantis story, Critias remarks to Socrates:

> When you were speaking yesterday about your city and citizens, the tale which I have just been repeating to you came into my mind, and I remarked with astonishment how, *by some mysterious coincidence,* you agreed in almost every particular with the narrative of Solon. (p. 446, emphasis mine)

Of course, it was no coincidence; it was how Plato worked Atlantis and ancient Athens into the dialogue.

Following this brief introduction to the story, Critias cedes the floor to Timaeus, who provides a very detailed discussion of his theory of the origins of the universe. In the next dialogue, *Critias,* details of the Atlantis story are provided.

The Critias Dialogue

Critias appears to have listened well to his teacher's description of the perfect society; for in his tale ancient Athens, even in detail, matches precisely the hypothetical society of Socrates. According to the story Critias told, in ancient Athens, artisans and husbandmen were set apart from the military, military men owned no private property and possessed no gold or silver, and so on.

Only after first describing ancient Athens does Critias describe Atlantis, a 15-mile-wide city of concentric rings of alternating land and water, with palaces, huge canals, towers, and bridges. The Atlanteans produced artworks in silver and gold and traded far and wide. They possessed a great navy of twelve hundred ships and an army with ten thousand chariots. Their empire and their influence expanded exponentially.

After a time, however, the "divine portion" of their ancestry became diluted and the human portion became dominant. As a result, their civilization became decadent, the people depraved and greedy. The dialogue relates that after Athens defeated the Atlanteans in war, Zeus, the chief god in the Greek pantheon, decided to teach the inhabitants of Atlantis a lesson for their avarice and prideful desire to rule the world. Zeus gathered the other gods together to relate his plan. The dialogue ends unfinished at just this point, and Plato never returned to it, dying just a few years later.

The Source and Meaning
of Timaeus and Critias

Though briefly summarized here, this is the entire story of Atlantis as related in Plato's dialogues. All else written about Atlantis is derivative, contrived, extrapolated, imagined, or invented.

It is ironic, however, that this source of the popular myth of Atlantis, while having spawned some two thousand books and articles (de Camp 1970) along with a number of periodicals (*Atlantis*, the *Atlantis Quarterly*, and *Atlantis Rising*), isn't really about Atlantis at all. The lost continent is little more than a plot device. The story is about an ostensible ancient *Athens*. Athens is the protagonist, the hero, and the focus of Plato's tale. Atlantis is the antagonist, the empire gone bad in whose military defeat by Athens the functioning of a perfect society as defined by Socrates can be exemplified.

Now consider the story that Plato tells: A technologically sophisticated but morally bankrupt, evil empire—Atlantis—attempts world domination by force. The only thing standing in its way is a relatively small group of spiritually pure, morally principled, and incorruptible people—the ancient Athenians. Overcoming overwhelming numerical and technological odds, the Athenians are able to defeat their far more powerful adversary simply through the force of their spirit.

Sound familiar? Plato's Atlantean dialogues are essentially an ancient Greek version of *Star Wars!* Think about it: Plato placed Atlantis nine thousand years before his time, off in the little-known (to the ancient Greeks) Atlantic Ocean. *Star Wars* takes place "a long time ago, in a galaxy far, far away." Atlantis, with its sophisticated military and enormous navy, parallels the Empire with its Stormtroopers and Death Star. The Athenians are the counterparts of the ragtag group of rebels led (eventually) by Luke Skywalker. The rebels and the Athenians both are victorious, certainly not because they are militarily superior, but—why?—because "the Force" is with them both. One more connection can be made; if 9,000 years from now people ask whether the *Star Wars* saga is actual history, not fiction, it would not be too different from our suggesting today that Plato's story of Atlantis really happened. Both stories are myths, used to entertain and to convey moral lessons. They are both equally fantastical.

Who Invented Atlantis?

In the Timaeus dialogue, Plato has Critias state that Atlantis was destroyed more than 9,000 years before Solon's time (590 b.c.). But there are no records of the Atlantis story in Egypt, where Solon is supposed to have been told the tale. It is equally instructive to point out that chroniclers of the history of Athens, including those who discussed that city's military triumphs in great detail, do not mention a war with a nation called or even vaguely sounding like Atlantis. The best-known Greek historian, Herodotus, who lived 100 years before Plato, never mentions Atlantis. Also in the fifth century b.c., Thucydides provides a detailed discourse on the military and political struggles of ancient Athens in his book *Archaeology,* yet he is absolutely silent about Atlantis.

Imagine that the War of Independence in the United States had become a dimly remembered event, discussed only occasionally by people, many of whom were skeptical that it had actually occurred. Now, imagine that, many years after that war took place, a respected scholar found an ancient manuscript that focused entirely on that war, providing a wealth of information about the roots of our nation, the heroism of its founders, as well as the nature of the empire that held us in subjugation. In revealing a crucial part of our history and detailing events that formed us as a nation, that manuscript certainly would generate intense discussion after its discovery. Even those who were aware of the "legend" of such a war, but still skeptical it had actually taken place, would be expected to talk or write about the newly discovered document, presenting their arguments for why they were still skeptical about the historicity of the war.

Now consider Plato's story of a conflict between Athens and Atlantis, which surely would have been viewed as being as singularly formative for Athens as the War of Independence was for the United States. It is inconceivable that there would be no mention of a great military victory by ancient Athens over Atlantis—or anyplace even vaguely like it—in the works of Greek historians who followed Plato (Fears 1978). Yet this is precisely the case. Greek historians didn't mention Plato's story of Atlantis because they didn't view the story as anything more than the fiction Plato intended it to be. They felt no more need to discuss it in their histories—even to refute it—than a modern historian feels compelled to mention the Evil Empire of the *Star Wars* saga, even to remind readers that it didn't actually exist. Everyone already knows that; and, it appears, Greek writers of history and their readers already knew that about Atlantis too.

But wait; Plato has Critias assert that the story of Atlantis was true. Isn't this evidence that Plato believed he was relating genuine history? Absolutely not. As historian William Stiebing, Jr., states, "Virtually every myth Plato relates in his dialogues is introduced by statements claiming it is true" (1984:51). It is not only the Atlantis account but also tales about heaven and hell (Isles of the Blessed and Tartarus) in *Georgias,* immortality and reincarnation in *Meno,* antiquity in *Laws,* and the afterlife in the *Republic* that are prefaced with statements attesting to their truth (Stiebing 1984:52).

Remember also that the story Critias relates here is the direct result of Socrates having asked his students the previous day to come up with a tale in which his hypothetical perfect state is put to the test by warfare. In other words, it's a homework assignment! Critias relates the story of a civilization conveniently enormously distant from his Athens in both time and space, whose remnants are below the Atlantic, certainly beyond recovery or testing by the Greeks of Plato's time. He also has ancient Athens, which would not have been beyond the purview of contemporary Athenians to study, conveniently destroyed. Finally, though maintaining it is a true tale, he admits that "by some mysterious coincidence" it matches Socrates' hypothetical society almost exactly. As A. E. Taylor has said, "We could not be told much more plainly that the whole narrative of Solon's conversation with the priests and his intention of writing the poem about Atlantis are an invention of Plato's fancy" (1962:50).

Where Did Plato Get the Details of the Story? A Minoan Source

The final question to be asked is, If the Atlantis story was Plato's invention, did he at least base it on a real event or a series of events? In other words, did Plato construct elements of his story—of a great civilization destroyed by a cataclysm—from historical events, perhaps only dimly remembered by the Greeks at the time he was writing? The answer is almost certainly yes; in a sense, all fiction must be based on fact. All writers begin with knowledge of the real world and construct their literary fantasies with the raw material of that knowledge. Plato was no different, and there were plenty of historical events of which Plato was well aware that he could have used in constructing his Atlantis tale.

For example, as early as 1909, a scholar at Queen's University in Belfast suggested a connection between historical Minoan Crete and the Atlantis legend (cited in Luce 1969:47).

Figure 8.4   Those who support the hypothesis that the eruption on Thera is the source of the story of the destruction of Atlantis have suggested that the Minoan civilization on Crete was the historical model for Atlantis culture. Pictured here is the ancient temple at Knossos on Crete, dating to Minoan times. (M. H. Feder)

The spectacular temple at the Minoan capital of Knossos was built beginning about 3,800 years ago (Figure 8.4). At its peak the temple covered an area of some 20,000 square meters (more than 210,000 square feet or about 5 acres), contained about one thousand separate rooms, and had a central courtyard with a pillar-lined hallway, a ceremonial bath, and grand staircases. Some parts of the temple were three and even four stories tall. The walls of some of the living quarters and large halls were covered with artfully produced fresco paintings of dolphins and bulls. Where the Minoans depicted themselves in these paintings, we see a graceful and athletic people. The Greeks of Plato's time were aware of this even more ancient and impressive culture.

There are, however, many problems in attempting to assign a Minoan source to Atlantis. Crete is far too small and in the wrong place to conform with Plato's description of Atlantis. Further, it is not nearly as old as Atlantis is purported to be. In addition, there are no elephants on Crete, though Plato maintains that the Atlanteans had a large stock of elephants.

A key element in the argument linking Plato's fictional Atlantis with the historical Minoan civilization relies on a catastrophe that affected the Mediterranean and its environs specifically and, it is no exaggeration to say, the broader world, generally. I refer here to the massive volcanic eruption on

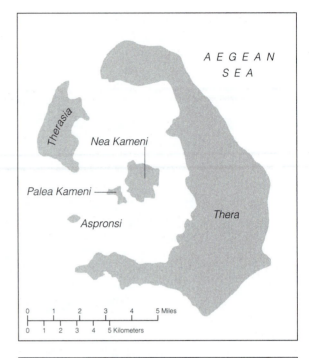

Figure 8.5   The island of Thera in the Mediterranean today is the remnant of a volcano that erupted more than 3,600 years ago. It has been suggested that the historical eruption of the volcano served as a model for Plato's story of the destruction of Atlantis.

the island of Santorini (the Greeks called it Thera), 120 kilometers (72 miles) north of Crete (Figure 8.5). The eruption produced enough ash to affect global climate by blocking out the sun's rays; evidence indicates that as a result of this eruption, there was frost damage to trees in places as far removed geographically as Ireland and California (Friedrich et al. 2006). The explosive force of the eruption was four times as powerful as that of Krakatoa in the Dutch East Indies in 1883 (Marinatos 1972:718), which killed some 36,000 people.

Radiocarbon dating conducted by two separate research projects has provided an accurate indicator of the timing of the eruption. In the research led by William Friedrich (Friedrich et al. 2006), the branch of an olive tree that was killed by the eruption and recovered in an excavation on Santorini produced a calendar date of between 1627 and 1600 B.C. In a project directed by Stuart Manning, twenty-eight samples including seeds and a twig produced a calendar date of between 1639 and 1616 B.C.

It should come as no surprise that the obliteration of Thera did have a significant impact on the Minoan civilization (Marinatos 1972). The eruption itself, accompanied by severe earthquakes, badly damaged many settlements on Crete. Devastating waves, or tsunamis, produced by the eruption of Thera wiped out Minoan port settlements on the north coast of Crete.

The Minoan civilization developed, at least in part, as a result of trade. The loss of ports through which trade items passed and the probable destruction of the Minoan fleet of trading vessels must have had a tremendous impact on the Minoan economy. Also of great significance for the Minoans over the long term was the thick deposit of white volcanic ash that blanketed the rich farmland of Crete, interrupting for a time the agricultural economy of the Minoan people.

Despite being adversely affected by the eruption on Thera, however, Minoan Crete was not destroyed by it. In fact, the Minoan civilization continued to thrive for 100 years after the eruption on Thera—actually, for a time, rising to new heights. It did not collapse until 1320 B.C., about 300 years after the eruption on Thera. As the instantaneous obliteration of Atlantis is a key component of Plato's story, this alone would seem to rule out Crete as the model for Atlantis in anything but the most general sense.

There is another major problem with identifying Minoan Crete as the single source for Plato's Atlantis. Significantly, the major theme of Plato's story, the defeat by Athens of a great military power, remains unexplained here. Minoan Crete did not suffer a major military defeat at the hands of Athens. If Minoan Crete was Plato's inspiration for the Atlantis story, this key aspect of the tale was entirely fictional.

As long ago as 1872, the French writer Louis Figuier made the correlation between Atlantis and the very impressive Minoan settlement on Santorini/Thera (Castleden 1998). Others have followed (Pellegrino 1991). Though this site better conforms to Plato's description of Atlantis's fate, having been utterly destroyed by the volcanic eruption there in 1628 B.C., it is plagued by all of the other objections to any direct correlation between the Minoan civilization and Atlantis. Clearly, Thera is far too small, it is far too recent, and it is still in the wrong location to be Plato's Atlantis.

Most of the attempts to directly correlate a historical place with Atlantis are afflicted by the same problem; large chunks of Plato's story must be entirely changed or thoroughly ignored to make a reasonable fit.

This raises a key question: How many alterations does it take to make Critias's description of Atlantis match Minoan Crete? I attempted to find out by writing down every specific, materially (in other words, archaeologically) testable piece of information that Critias provides for Atlantis's appearance: its size and location, what the walls of the city looked like, Atlantean metallurgy, what animals were present there, and so on. I found six specific, testable descriptions in Timmaeus and forty-seven in Critias, for a total of fifty-three details about Atlantis that Minoan Crete should show archaeologically if it were the inspiration for the Atlantis tale (Table 8.1). The results after a comparison to Minoan archaeology: Only one description in Plato clearly matches Minoan Crete, and that one is so general as to be meaningless (Critias describes the palace as being "a marvel to behold for size and beauty"). That's it. Big deal. Three other of Critias's descriptions can be made to sort of resemble the real Minoan civilization, but only by special pleading and hand-waving. Even granting those, and counting six specific descriptions that, in fairness, cannot be assessed, this leaves forty-three of fifty-three (more than 80 percent) of Critias's descriptions of Atlantis that are flatly contradicted by the archaeological record of Minoan Crete. That doesn't sound like a very good match to me.

Table 8.1

			Yes	Special Pleading	Unknown	No
Timmaeus	1	Located in the Atlantic.				X
	2	Larger than Libya and Asia combined.				X
	3	A boundless continent.				X
	4	Controlled parts of Europe, Africa (Egypt), and Asia.				X
	5	Disappeared in a single day and night.				X
	6	The sea is "impassable and impenetrable" in the area as a result of shoals left behind by the sinking of the great landmass.				X
Critias	1	Happened 9,000 years before Critias's telling of the story.				X
	2	Atlantis was the size of Libya and Asia combined.				X
	3	As a result of its destruction, the sea was an "impassable barrier of mud."				X
	4	The center of Atlantis was marked by a plain.				X
	5	30 stadia (3.28 miles) from the island's center was a mountain.				X

		Yes	Special Pleading	Unknown	No
6	Concentric rings of sea and dry land; specifically, two rings of land, three of water (Critias says Poseidon made it that way).		X		
7	Great number of elephants on the island.				X
8	Valuable metal mined on Atlantis: *orichalcum* "now only a name."				X
9	All sorts of other animals lived on the island.			X	
10	Lots of crops, various plants.			X	
11	Bridges built to connect the rings of land separated by rings of sea.				X
12	Palace was a "marvel to behold for size and for beauty."	X			
13	A canal was dug from the sea to the central island: 300 feet wide, 100 feet deep, and 50 stadia in length (close to 30,000 feet: nearly 5.5 miles).				X
14	The central island on which the palace was located was 5 stadia in diameter (about a half a mile).				X
15	The central island was surrounded by a stone wall on every side, with towers and gates.				X
16	The masons of Atlantis quarried native stone to build the walls and buildings; the stone was red, black, and white.				X
17	The exterior wall of the outermost island ring was coated with brass.				X
18	The exterior wall of the central island ring was coated with tin.				X
19	The exterior wall of the inner island on which the palace was located was covered with *orichalcum*.				X
20	Holy temple dedicated to Poseidon and Cleito.				X
21	Posiedon's temple was 1 stadium × .5 stadium (577 feet × 288 feet).				X
22	The walls of Poseidon's temple were covered in silver.				X

Continued

Table 8.1   *(continued)*

		Yes	Special Pleading	Unknown	No
23	The pinnacles of the temple were covered in gold.				X
24	The roof of the temple was made of ivory.				X
25	Gold, silver, and *orichalcum* elaborations covered the place.				X
26	Huge statue of Poseidon in the center.				X
27	Dolphins statues surrounded Poseidon.		X		
28	Gold statues of the descendants of the first kings of Atlantis.				X
29	Nearby was a palace of fountains.				X
30	Cisterns surrounded this temple.				X
31	Separate baths for men, women, and for horses and cattle.				X
32	Beautiful grove surrounded the fountain temple.				X
33	Many smaller temples nearby.				X
34	A stadium for racing horses, a stadium 175 meters (577 feet) in width and length.				X
35	Guard towers at intervals along the walls.				X
36	Docks filled with triremes.			X	
37	Whole country "lofty and precipitous."				X
38	The flat part of the country was oblong in shape and 3,000 stadia by 2,000 stadia (328 × 218 miles).				X
39	This part of the island "looked towards the south, and was sheltered from the north."				X
40	The plain was artificial and incredible in scope: excavated to a depth of 100 feet, a stadium in breadth, and 10,000 stadia in length (577 feet by nearly 1,100 miles long).				X
41	Canals of 100 feet in width everywhere cut through the plain for water transportation. These canals are placed at intervals of 100 stadia (11 miles).				X

		Yes	Special Pleading	Unknown	No
42	Divided up into lots that were 10 square stadia, and there were 60,000 such lots in the plain (nearly 72,000 square miles).				X
43	10,000 chariots.			X	
44	1,200 ships. ("Such was the order of the royal city—the order of the other nine governments varied and it would be wearisome to recount their several differences.")			X	
45	Pillar of *orichalcum* in the center of the city inscribed with laws.				X
46	Bulls had free range in the temple of Poseidon and were hunted ritually there. (Note: No reference to paintings or other bovine artwork.)		X		
47	Bull sacrifice by the ten Atlantean kings detailed description of the process.			X	

Searching *Critias* for characteristics of Atlantis that closely parallel specific ancient societies almost certainly misses Plato's primary point. The specifics that Plato has Critias speak are not intended as history but as part of the parable. To make his point, Plato makes Atlantis sound like a nearly insurmountable adversary. Plato's detailed description of Atlantis was intended to impress the reader with its material wealth, technological sophistication, and military power. That the smaller, materially poorer, technologically less well endowed, and militarily weaker Athenians could defeat the Atlanteans imparts the fundamental message of *Critias:* It is not just wealth or power that is important in history; even more important is the way a people govern themselves. For Plato, the intellectual achievement of a perfect government and society is far more important—and triumphs over—material wealth or power.

After Plato

As noted, Plato's contemporaries knew he was telling a tall tale. It was not until the Age of Exploration and the discovery of the New World that consideration of the veracity of the Atlantis story became popular. For example, as we saw in Chapter 5, Huddleston (1967) points out that in 1552 the Spaniard Lopez de Gomara suggested that American Indians were a remnant population of emigrés from the Lost Continent of Atlantis. Gomara based his

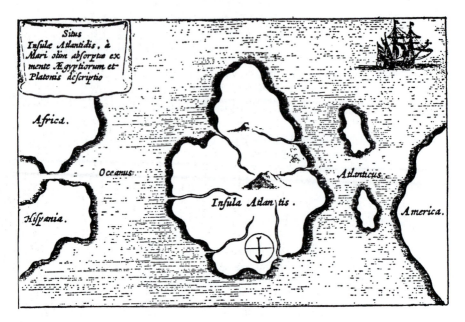

Figure 8.6   This 1644 map shows the location of Atlantis in the Atlantic Ocean. Note that south is to the top of the map. (From *Mundus Subterraneous* by Athanasius Kircher)

interpretation on a linguistic argument concerning a single word; in the Aztec language of Nahuatl, the word *atl* means water (Huddleston 1967:25).

Later, in 1572, Pedro Sarmiento de Gamboa maintained that the great civilizations of the New World were partially derived from Atlantis. In the seventeenth century, maps were drawn placing Atlantis in the Atlantic Ocean (Figure 8.6). Some, like Englishman John Josselyn (1674), even identified the New World *as* Atlantis.

French scholar Abbé Charles-Étienne Brasseur (called de Bourbourg) "translated" a Maya Indian book, the Troano Codex, in 1864. It was a complete fantasy and contained elements of the Atlantis story, particularly destruction by flood. Using the same delusional alphabet, Augustus Le Plongeon also translated the Codex, coming up with an entirely different story, connecting the Maya to the ancient Egyptians. It was all complete fabrication, but it kept alive the notion that perhaps the civilizations of the Old and New Worlds could somehow be connected and explained by reference to Atlantis.

Ignatius Donnelly:
The Minnesota Congressman

Speculation concerning the possible reality of Plato's Atlantis story might have ended in the eighteenth or nineteenth century, as other myths were abandoned when scientific knowledge expanded (see Chapters 5 and 6). We have one man to thank, or blame, for this not happening: Ignatius Donnelly.

Donnelly was born in 1831. He studied law, and at only twenty-eight years of age became the lieutenant governor of Minnesota. He later went on to serve several terms in the federal House of Representatives and twice ran for vice president of the United States.

By all accounts, Donnelly was an exceptional individual. Politically progressive, he was a voracious reader who collected an enormous body of information concerning world history, mythology, and geography. Clearly, however, he was less than selective in his studies and seemingly was incapable in his research of discriminating between the meaningful and the meaningless. Donnelly is the father of modern Atlantis studies; and, as writer Daniel Cohen (1969) has aptly put it, Donnelly's book *Atlantis: The Antediluvian World,* published first in 1882, is the "bible" of belief in the legend.

Donnelly begins by asserting he will prove that the Atlantis story as told by Plato is not legend but "veritable history" (1882:1); that Atlantis "was the region where man first rose from a state of barbarism to civilization" (p. 1); and that it was the source of civilization in Egypt, South America, Mexico, Europe, and North America, where he specifies the Moundbuilder culture (Figure 8.7).

Reasoning based on *cultural* comparisons is central to Donnelly's methodology. He maintains: "If then we prove that, on both sides of the Atlantic, civilizations were found substantially identical, we have demonstrated that they must have descended one from the other, or have radiated from some common source" (1882:135).

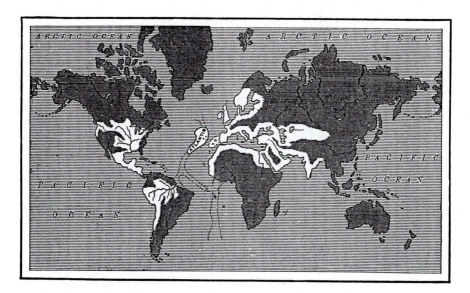

Figure 8.7 Ignatius Donnelly saw all of the world's ancient civilizations as having been derived from that of Atlantis. Here, Donnelly maps (in white) the extent of Atlantis's influence, including the cultures of ancient Egypt, Mesopotamia, Mesoamerica, and the Moundbuilders of the United States.

This argument for the significant role of *diffusion* in cultural development was common in anthropology in the late nineteenth and early twentieth centuries (Harris 1968). The presumption seems to have been that cultures are basically uninventive and that new ideas are developed in very few or even single places. They then move out or "diffuse" from these source areas. It was fairly common to suggest that Egypt was the source of all civilization, that agriculture, writing, monumental architecture, and the like were all invented only there. These characteristics, it was maintained, diffused from Egypt and were adopted by other groups.

Donnelly was a diffusionist. For him the common source of all civilization was Atlantis, rather than Egypt, Sumer, or some other known culture. In his attempt to prove this, he presents a series of artifacts or practices that he finds to be identical among the civilizations of the Old and New Worlds. In these comparisons, Donnelly presents what he believes is the clearest evidence for the existence of Atlantis. His evidence essentially consists of trait list comparisons of the sort discussed in Chapter 6. Let us look at a few of these and do what Donnelly did not—test the implications of his claims.

1. *Egyptian obelisks and Mesoamerican stelae are derived from the same source* (Donnelly 1882:136).

   Donnelly finds that the inscribed obelisks of Egypt are virtually identical to the inscribed stelae of the Maya civilization. He does little more than make this assertion before he is off on his next topic. But it is necessary to examine the claim more closely and to consider the implications. If it were, in fact, the case that Egyptian obelisks and Maya stelae were derived from a common source, we would expect that they possessed similarities both specific and general. Yet, their method of construction is different; they are different in shape, size, and raw materials; and the languages inscribed on them are entirely different (Figure 8.8). They are similar only in that they are upright slabs of inscribed rock. It is not reasonable to claim that they must have been derived from a common source. They are simply too different.

2. *The pyramids of Egypt and the pyramids of Mesoamerica can be traced to the same source* (Donnelly 1882:317–41).

   Here again, if this hypothesis were true, we would expect that these pyramids would share many specific features. The pyramids of the Old and New Worlds, however, do not look the same (Figure 8.9). New World pyramids are all truncated with flat tops, whereas the Egyptian monuments are true geometric pyramids with four triangular faces meeting at a common apex. New World pyramids have stairs ascending their faces; Egyptian pyramids do not. New World pyramids served as platforms for temples, and many also were burial

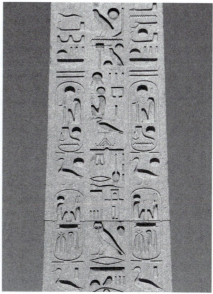

Figure 8.8   Donnelly asserted that Egyptian obelisks and Maya stelae were so similar in form and function, they must have originated in the same place: Atlantis. Yet here it can be seen that obelisks, like this one currently residing in the Piazza del Popolo in Rome and dedicated to the pharaoh Ramses II (**top left**); were quite tall, inscribed, four-sided columns, whereas Maya stelae (**bottom**); were far different, being flat blocks of inscribed limestone. Beyond this, though both bear written inscriptions, Egyptian hieroglyphs (see top right for a closer image of the inscription on Ramses II's obelisk) and Maya hieroglyphs are entirely different. (*Top:* K. Feder; *bottom:* Library of Congress Prints and Photographs Division [LC-USZ62-97814])

Figure 8.9   Egyptian pyramids, like this one from Giza (**top**); and Mesoamerican pyramids, like this one from Chichén Itzá (**bottom**) are quite different in construction, form, function, and chronology. Donnelly was thoroughly unjustified in claiming a connection—via Atlantis—between pyramid building in the Old and New Worlds. (*Top:* M. H. Feder; *bottom:* K. Feder)

chambers for great leaders. Egyptian pyramids had no temples on their summits, and all were burial chambers for dead pharaohs or their wives. Construction methods were different; most Egyptian pyramids represent a single construction episode, whereas Mesoamerican pyramids usually represent several building episodes, one on top of another. Finally, if Mesoamerican and Egyptian pyramids are hypothesized to have been derived from the same source (Atlantis or elsewhere), they should date from the same period. But Egyptian pyramids were built between about 5,000 and 4,000 years ago. Those in Mesoamerica are all less than 3,000 years old—most are considerably younger, dating to less than 1,500 years ago. All pyramids date to well after the supposed destruction of Atlantis some 11,000 years ago.

3. *Ancient cultures in the Old and New Worlds possessed the arch* (Donnelly 1882:140).

This statement reflects an imprecise use of language. Cultures in the Old World possessed the true arch with a keystone—the supporting wedge of stone at the top of the arch that holds the rest of the stones in place. New World cultures did not have knowledge of the load-bearing keystone, constructing, instead, the entirely different corbelled arch where stones are set in layers (Figure 8.10).

4. *Cultures in the Old and New Worlds both produced bronze* (Donnelly 1882:140).

This is true, but Donnelly does not assess the implications of the claim that Old and New World metallurgies are derived from a common source. For this to be the case, we would expect the technologies to share many features in common. Bronze is an alloy of copper and some other element. Old World bronze is usually an alloy of copper and tin. In the New World, bronze was generally produced by alloying copper and arsenic (though there is some tin bronze). With such a basic difference in the alloys, it is unlikely that there is a common source for Old and New World metallurgy.

5. *Civilizations in both the Old and New Worlds were dependent on agricultural economies for their subsistence. This indicates that these cultures were derived from a common source* (Donnelly 1882:141).

It is almost certainly the case that cultures we would label "civilized" are reliant on agriculture to produce the food surplus necessary to free the number of people required to build pyramids, produce fine artworks, be full-time soldiers, and so on. But again, for this to support the hypothesis of a single, Atlantean source for Old and New World agriculture, we would expect there to be many commonalities, not the least of which would be the same or similar crops. That this was not

Figure 8.10   Though Donnelly claims that the arch was present in ancient buildings in both the Old and New Worlds—and that this architectural feature had a single source on Atlantis and spread out from there—even the first assertion is not true. The true arch with a "keystone" was present in the ancient Old World (left, looking out from the interior of the Colosseum in Rome), but it was unknown in the pre-Columbian New World. Native American architects used a corbelled arch, like this one found at the Maya site, Chichén Itzá, in Mexico (right). (K. Feder)

the case certainly was known to Donnelly. Even during his time, it was established that cultures in the Old World domesticated one set of plants and animals, whereas people in the New World domesticated an entirely different set.

We now know that even within the Old World, different ancient societies relied on different mixtures of agricultural crops for their subsistence. In the Middle East, wheat, barley, chick peas, lentils, and vetch were most significant (Henry 1989; Hole, Flannery, and Neely 1969). In the Far East, foxtail millet and rice were major crops (Crawford 1992; Solheim 1972). In Africa, sorghum, pearl and finger millet, and a host of tropical cultigens like the cereals fonio and tef, as well as the banana-like enset, provided subsistence to agricultural people (Harlan 1992; Phillipson 1993). In the Old World, animals like sheep, goats, cattle, and pigs added meat to these various diets.

The list of crops used aboriginally in the New World is just as varied and is entirely different from the lists of Old World domesticates. In Mesoamerica, maize (corn), beans, and squash were predominant with crops like tomato, avocado, chili pepper, amaranth (a grain), and even chocolate rounding out the diet (de Tapia 1992; MacNeish 1967). In South America, maize and beans were important, as were a number of other crops including (most significantly to our modern diets) potato, but so were less well-known crops like oca, jícama, and ulluco (Bruhns 1994; Pearsall 1992). In North America, native people produced their own agricultural revolution, domesticating such crops as sunflower, sumpweed, pigweed, goosefoot, and a local variety of squash (Smith 1995). Turkeys were bred by the ancient inhabitants of the American Southwest. In Mesoamerica, turkeys, Muscovy ducks, and dogs were raised for food, and in South America, llamas, alpacas, and guinea pigs were domesticated and provided meat. The llama was also a serviceable pack animal and the alpaca was a source of wool.

It is readily apparent that the agricultural bases of Old and New World cultures were entirely different. This is far more suggestive of separate evolution of their economies than of their having been derived from a common source.

Archaeological investigations have further supported this fact by showing that, in both the Old and New Worlds, agriculture evolved in place over thousands of years. In several world areas after 12,000 years ago—notably in southwestern Asia, southern Europe, eastern Asia, Africa south of the Sahara, Mesoamerica, the North American Midwest and mid-South, and South America—lengthy evolutionary sequences reflect the slow development of agricultural societies. The archaeology in these areas has revealed long periods during which people hunted wild animals and gathered wild plants that later became domesticated staples of the diet.

The physical evidence in these areas in the form of animal bones and carbonized seeds similarly reflects the slow development of domesticated species. Over centuries and millennia, human beings "artificially selected" those members of wild plant communities that produced the biggest, or densest, or quickest-maturing seeds, allowing only those that possessed these advantageous (from a human perspective) characteristics to survive and propagate. Similarly, the ancient people in these regions selected those individuals in an animal species that were the most docile or that produced the thickest wool or the most meat or milk, again allowing only those that possessed these features to survive, breed, and pass these traits down. The continuum through time visible in the archaeological record of increasing seed size, decreasing size of dangerous animal teeth or horns, and so on is clear evidence of the evolutionary process that resulted in fully agricultural people. Agriculture does not simply appear in the archaeological record of the Old and New Worlds. It has deep roots and a lengthy and distinct history in each. Clearly agriculture was not introduced wholesale from Atlantis; rather, it was developed separately in many world regions (Smith 1995).

By failing to consider the implications of his claims of connections between the cultural practices of Old and New World civilizations, Donnelly was easily led astray by their superficial similarities. Ever hopeful and convinced of the legitimacy of his argument, Donnelly ended *Atlantis: The Antediluvian World* by stating:

> We are on the threshold. Scientific investigation is advancing in great strides. Who shall say that one hundred years from now the great museums of the world may not be adorned with gems, statues, arms, and implements from Atlantis, while the libraries of the world shall contain translations of its inscriptions, throwing new light upon all the past history of the human race, and all the great problems which now perplex the thinkers of our day? (p. 480)

It has been more than 130 years since Donnelly wrote these words, and Atlantis the fair and the beautiful is as distant as it was when Plato constructed it out of the stuff of his imagination more than 2,000 years ago.

Atlantis After Donnelly

The web of Atlantis speculation and fantasy has continued to be spun in the twentieth century. For example, between 1923 and 1945, the so-called sleeping prophet, Edgar Cayce, gave some 2,500 "life readings" to 1,600 people, of whom, according to him, about 700 had lived past lives on Atlantis (Cayce 1968:27). Reading the published transcripts of Cayce's Atlantis ramblings is a real chore (there are portions of a bunch of them in the 1968 book written by his son, Edgar Evans Cayce). Much of it consists of spiritual pronouncements, the validity of which it is impossible to assess. His son admits that some of the language is "awkward" and the meaning must be "deciphered" (Cayce 1968:61), but I think that is a great understatement. Be that as it may, the elder Cayce did provide some material details of life on his Atlantis and they are, it must be admitted, extraordinary. He mentions specifically weapons invented by the Atlanteans that were based on "radioactive forces" (nuclear weapons?), others that used "rays from the sun that turned on crystals" (lasers?), and others still that harnessed "the fires of the inner portions of the earth" (Cayce 1968:74). Also, the Atlanteans seem to have traveled around in lighter-than-air vehicles (Cayce 1968:62) and in tubes powered by compressed air and steam (Cayce 1968:68), something like those containers you use to make bank deposits in the drive-through. It should go without saying that there is nothing like any of this in Plato.

Cayce maintained that at least some Atlanteans who survived the destruction of their homeland migrated to Egypt before 10,000 B.C. and there constructed an underground pyramid in which they housed the historical records of their nation. Cayce said that this "Hall of Records" was located near the Great Sphinx. To date, archaeological research has located no such feature.

Indeed, the legend of Atlantis did not die with Plato, nor did it die with Donnelly. It seems constantly to shift, filling the particular needs of each era for a Golden Age when great warriors, ingenious scientists, astral jellyfish, or egg-laying hermaphrodites walked the earth. Ultimately, in trying to convey a rather simple message, one of the great rational minds of the ancient world produced fodder for the fantasies of some of the less-than-great, nonrational minds of the modern world. If only we could trance-channel Plato, I wonder what he would say. I doubt that he would be pleased.

Current Perspectives: Atlantis

According to Plato's story, Atlantis was defeated in battle by a humble but quite advanced Athenian state some 11,000 years ago. What does modern archaeology tell us about ancient Greece from this period? Is there any physical evidence in the Atlantic Ocean for the civilization of Atlantis? What does modern geology tell us about the possibility of a lost continent in the Atlantic?

Ancient Greece

Simply stated, there was no Athenian state 11,000 years ago. Such a statement is based not on legends and stories but on the material remains of cultures that inhabited Greece. South of Athens, for example, a site has been investigated that dates to around the same time as the claimed Athenian defeat of Atlantis. The site, Franchthi Cave, has been excavated by archaeologist Thomas Jacobsen (1976).

More than 10,000 years ago the inhabitants of the cave were not members of an "advanced" culture. They were simple hunters and gatherers, subsisting on red deer, wild cattle, and pigs. They also collected mollusks, snails, small sea fish, and wild plant foods, including barley and oats. They were a Stone Age people and obtained obsidian—a volcanic glass that can produce extremely sharp tools—from the nearby island of Melos. It is not until 6000 B.C. that there is evidence of the use of domesticated plants and animals by the inhabitants of the cave. Evidence at other sites in Greece conforms to the pattern seen at Franchthi. Cultures that we would label as "civilized" do not appear in Greece for thousands of years. The Greek world of 11,000 years ago is nothing like Plato imagined.

Archaeological Evidence in the Atlantic:
The Bimini Wall

Claims have been made that there is archaeological evidence of submerged walls and roads off the coast of Bimini in the Bahamas. Just as Edgar Cayce maintained that the island of Bimini was a remnant of Atlantis, modern Atlantis popularizers have claimed that the features constitute direct empirical evidence for the existence of the lost continent (Berlitz 1984).

In the 1960s divers found tabular limestone blocks that they interpreted as being parts of a road and wall as well as supposed columns from a submerged building (Figure 8.11). They based this interpretation largely on the assumption that these patterned features of the landscape were not natural. In fact, however, the appearance of patterning may mean very little; natural geological forces and processes are capable of producing extraordinarily symmetrical geometric shapes laid out in precise patterns. The surface of the top of the Devils Postpile National Monument in California exhibits a perfect example (Figure 8.12, top). What might appear to be a floor of hexagonal pavers neatly laid out by a flooring contractor turns out to be, instead, the tops of a series of long and entirely natural columns of volcanic rock. Though the geological process is different, the so-called Bimini Wall also is likely the

Figure 8.11 This underwater rock feature, found off the coast of the island of Bimini, has been identified by some believers in the Atlantis tale as material evidence for its existence. But the so-called Bimini Road or Bimini Wall is an entirely natural formation and nowhere near Plato's Atlantis location. (Courtesy of John Gifford)

Figure 8.12   Devils Postpile National Monument in California (**top**); The patterned jointing seen at the top of the individual columns of the volcanic rock that formed this feature is entirely natural. Not an artificial construction, these rectangular blocks of stone from the southeastern coast of Tasmania (south of Australia) are the result of natural processes of erosion (**bottom**). A similar geological feature located off the Bimini coast in the Caribbean has been misidentified by nongeologists as a wall built by inhabitants of Atlantis. (*Top:* K. Feder; *bottom:* Courtesy Sonja Gray)

product of natural erosional processes. So-called beachrock erodes as a result of tidal forces, and breaks or joints tend to occur at regular intervals and at right angles to each other. Similarly jointed natural beachrock has been observed off the coast of Australia (Figure 8.12, bottom; Randi 1981).

The Geology of the Atlantic

There is no evidence in the Atlantic Ocean for a great submerged continent. In fact, our modern understanding of the geological processes of *plate tectonics* rules out this possibility.

The earth's crust is not a solid shell but consists of a number of geologically separate "plates." The plates move, causing the continents to drift. In fact, we know that the present configuration of the continents was different in the past. More than 200 million years ago, the continents were all part of a single landmass we call *Pangaea*. By 180 million years ago, the continents of the Northern Hemisphere (*Laurasia*) parted company with the southern continents (*Gondwanaland*). The separation of the continents of the Eastern and Western Hemispheres and the formation of the basin of the Atlantic Ocean occurred sometime before 65 million years ago. The Atlantic has been growing ever since, as the European and North American plates have continued to move apart, the result of expansion of the seabed along the intersection of the plates. Movement along the Pacific and North American plates resulted in the destructive earthquake that hit the San Francisco–Oakland area in October 1989.

A ridge of mountains has been building for millions of years at the intersection of the two crustal plates that meet in the Atlantic. Material is coming up out of the plate intersection; landmasses are not being sucked down below the ocean. The geology is clear; there could have been no large land surface that then sank in the area where Plato places Atlantis. Together, modern archaeology and geology provide an unambiguous verdict: There was no Atlantic continent; there was no great civilization called Atlantis.

◈ ◈ ◈ FREQUENTLY ASKED QUESTIONS ◈ ◈ ◈

1. *Could the legend of Atlantis somehow be connected to the mystery of the Bermuda Triangle?*

   The belief that there are mysterious and inexplicable disappearances of boats and planes—and all the people aboard—in a triangular area with Bermuda at its apex and Puerto Rico and the southern tip of Florida as the other two vertices is a myth, just like Atlantis. Writer Lawrence Kusche (1995) has investigated most of the major disappearances in the Triangle and found that all of these supposedly mysterious incidents had rational explanations. Bad weather, equipment failure, dangerous cargo, and pilot error account for virtually all of the occurrences. There is no evidence that the area enclosed by the Bermuda Triangle has experienced worse nautical or aviation luck than any other similar-size part of the globe. Atlantis was supposed to be nowhere near the Bermuda Triangle anyway. The only connection between Atlantis and the Bermuda Triangle mystery is the fact that both are myths.

2. Is there a "lost continent" in the Pacific?

There is a *legend* of a lost continent in the Pacific Ocean: Mu, or Lemuria. Mu is entirely mythological; the geology of the Pacific basin shows that there was no—and could not have been any—large landmass that sank below the waters in a cataclysmic upheaval.

   BEST OF THE WEB

http://www.sacred-texts.com/cla/plato/timaeus.htm
Complete Timaeus dialogue online.

http://www.sacred-texts.com/atl/critias.txt
Complete Critias dialogue online.

   CRITICAL THINKING EXERCISE

Using the deductive approach outlined in Chapter 2, how would you test this hypothesis? In other words, what archaeological and biological data must you find to conclude that this hypothetical statement is an accurate assertion, that it describes what actually happened in the ancient human past?

- The civilizations of ancient Egypt and Mexico share many general cultural similarities. This is most likely the result of both of these societies having been influenced by the civilization of the Lost Continent of Atlantis.

9

Prehistoric E.T.:
The Fantasy of
Ancient Astronauts

I thought I had just flipped onto the History Channel in my unending search for anything decent on cable. After all, the screen did read "History Channel." The narration sounded real enough, too, at least initially: "A lot has been written about the first Thanksgiving between Pilgrims and Native Americans. But what really happened at that first historic dinner?" The accompanying video looked authentic, if a little cheesy, but the next thing that appeared made it clear I was watching, not the History Channel, but a Comedy Central parody of one of the shows on the History Channel. In fact, I was watching an episode of South Park in which the kids were watching the History Channel for a Thanksgiving report. Cartman put it pretty clearly and, as he always does, bluntly: "Who needs to read a bunch of stupid books when we've got History Channel?" Returning to the faux History Channel narration: "We know the first Thanksgiving was in the fall of 1621, but new evidence suggests that the first exchanging of food between the pilgrims and Native Americans may have been visited by Aliens . . ."

Aliens! The extraterrestrial kind! It was hilarious. Matt and Trey had produced a spectacular send up of the complete lunacy of the actual *Ancient Aliens* series on the actual History Channel (http://www.south parkstudios.com/full-episodes/s15e13-a-history-channel-thanksgiving). I bet you didn't know that the presence of stuffing at the first Thanksgiving was evidence of an alien technology. Having seen a couple of episodes of the actual *Ancient Aliens* show, it was clear that Matt and Trey had done their homework. *A History Channel Thanksgiving* was spot on and, to be honest, only slightly sillier than the real show. The claims made in the parody were only a step or two beyond the actual claims made by the supporters of the hypothesis that extraterrestrial aliens were responsible for the technological achievements of ancient human beings. Finally, the evidence presented by Stan, Kyle, Cartman, and even Kenny in the show was every bit as convincing as that offered by the real ancient aliens crowd. In other words, they presented no convincing evidence whatsoever. So, what is the deal about the "ancient-aliens-visited-earth" claim? Can we dismiss it even without considering the possibility? Certainly not. The only important issue here concerns evidence. What does the archaeological record tell us about ancient aliens?

Ancient Astronauts: The Source of the Idea

It was a remarkable, even audacious, suggestion when first made in an article published in 1963. It began with the proposition that even under the most conservative of scenarios, the universe likely is teeming with life. The author based this optimistic assumption on the work of Frank Drake (2003), an astronomer who, in 1961, proposed a simple equation that allowed for a sort of back-of-the-envelope calculation of the number of intelligent life forms that might have evolved throughout our galaxy. It was all guesswork, to be sure, a series of probabilities (the fraction of stars that are circled by planets, the fraction of those planets where life evolved, the fraction where that evolved life developed great intelligence, the fraction that developed technologies sophisticated enough to allow for their exploration of the galaxy, etc.) all multiplied together and then by the number of stars in our galaxy. Though these fractions all might be quite small, the number of stars in our galaxy is enormous, something in the neighborhood of 100 billion. As a result, depending on the numbers you insert, you can still derive a very large number reflecting the possibility that the universe is filled with intelligent life forms who may one day contact us, or we them.

Though the author of the 1963 article admitted there is no evidence that these extraterrestrial civilizations are currently visiting Earth, he went on to maintain that there was a strong likelihood that, at some time during the evolution of the human species, they had explored our planet and that "It is not out of the question that artifacts of these visits still exist" (p. 496). The author was making the incredible suggestion that, perhaps, ensconced in the archaeological record there might be archaeological artifacts that were direct evidence of these extraterrestrial visitations: pieces of Mr. Spock's communicator, Luke Skywalker's light sabre, or even E.T.'s bones.

It was amazing, indeed—an extraterrestrial archaeology on Earth. Who would make such a bold suggestion? Was it a UFO afficionado? A believer in flying saucers, extraterrestrial abductions, and alien invasions? In fact, no. This scenario was drawn up by none other than the late Carl Sagan (1963)— brilliant scientist, prolific writer, noted rationalist, and supreme skeptic (Poundstone 1999; Sagan, 1996).

Gods in Fiery Chariots

Sagan's article, published in a technical journal, *Planetary and Space Science,* read only by astronomers and astrophysicists, made no impression on the nonscientist public and is long forgotten. But five years after its publication, the notion that extraterrestrials had visited Earth at some time in the distant past, leaving evidence of their prehistoric visits in the form of archaeological artifacts, became wildly popular.

The ancient astronaut bubble began inflating in 1968, first in Europe with the publication in German of a book titled *Erinnerungen an die Zukunft (Recollections of the Future)* and then in the United States with the publication in English of the same book, now with the question-mark-bearing title *Chariots of the Gods?* The Swiss author of the book, Erich von Däniken, proposed that there was indisputable and copious archaeological support for his claim that extraterrestrial aliens had visited Earth in prehistory and had played a significant role in the development of humanity.

In *Chariots of the Gods?* it seemed that Sagan's remarkable suggestion had been blown up into a full-scale anthropological fairy tale (though von Däniken does not cite Sagan's article in his book).

There seemed to be three implicit hypotheses behind von Däniken's ideas as he has presented them, relentlessly, for more than forty years in his twenty-nine books which, translated into thirty-two languages, have sold more than 63 million copies (figures take from von Däniken's website: http://www.daniken.com/e/index.html) (1970, 1971, 1973, 1975, 1982, 1989, 1996, 1997a, 1997b, 1998, 2000, 2003, 2009, 2010):

1. All over the world there are prehistoric pictorial and three-dimensional representations—drawings on cave walls, pottery, and sculptures—as well as early written accounts that most reasonably can be interpreted as the drawings, sculptures, or literary descriptions by primitive people of actual extraterrestrial visitors to Earth.

2. The biological evolution of the human species cannot be understood unless we assume the involvement of a scientifically advanced extraterrestrial civilization.

3. Some ancient artifacts and inventions are far too advanced and complex to have resulted from simple, prehistoric human intelligence and ingenuity. These advanced artifacts and great inventions must instead be the direct result of purposeful introduction by extraterrestrial aliens.

It's more than forty years since von Däniken published his first book, but, as the cliché goes, the song remains the same. For example, in *Prometheus,* the latest Ridley Scott blockbuster sci-fi movie, released in the spring of 2012, archaeologists encounter cave paintings in Scotland that show giant aliens visiting the Earth in antiquity. Later in the movie, a host of well-known actual archaeological artifacts are explained as somehow directing humans to the home of these aliens. It's no coincidence; Scott has freely acknowledged that von Däniken's work inspired the underlying theme of the movie, which, by the way, is an incomprehensible suck-fest. And there's more. The three hypotheses I just described underpin the *Ancient Aliens* series currently on cable, this time as espoused by Giorgio Tsoukalos, the current representative of von Däniken's nonsense. Tsoukalos is so over the top and relentless and his claims so absurd, he and they have even become the focus of an entire industry of Internet parodies.

Let's assess the three hypotheses I just enumerated and that so inspired Ridley Scott and Giorgio Tsoukalos one at a time.

The Inkblot Hypothesis

The first implicit claim concerns the existence of prehistoric drawings or sculptures of aliens from outer space and early writings about their visits. It is an intriguing thought. Hundreds, thousands, even tens of thousands of years ago, spaceships landed on our planet in a burst of fire and smoke. Out came space-suited aliens, perhaps to take soil samples or study plant life (just like E.T. in the Spielberg movie). On completion of their mission, they got back into their spaceships and took off for home.

Secreted in the bushes, behind the rocks, an ancient human sat transfixed, having watched the entire scene unbeknownst to our alien friends. This prehistoric witness to extraterrestrial visitation rushed home to tell others of the marvelous sight of the fiery "chariots" of the "gods" (thus, the English title for von Däniken's book) that had come down from heaven. He or she would tell of how the gods had silver skins (space suits) and bubble-heads (space helmets) and wielded marvelous devices (communicators, lasers, and so forth). Artistic renderings would be made on cave walls and pots. Descriptions would be passed down from generation to generation, especially if the space gods came back again and again, reinforcing the entire idea of gods from the heavens. Descriptions would be written of the wondrous spectacle of the gods coming to Earth. Our ancestors would wait for their return, as perhaps we wait to this very day.

Fascinating? Undoubtedly! Wonderful, if true? Absolutely! Would this forever alter our understanding of our place in the universe? Definitely. Backed up by evidence and proof? Absolutely not.

This first von Däniken scenario can be called the *Inkblot Hypothesis.* I am sure you are familiar with "inkblots" used in psychological testing (called Rorschach tests after their originator). A person looks at a series of inkblots (images made by dripping ink on paper, which is then folded and pressed while the ink is still wet) and then describes what he or she sees. The rationale for such an exercise is quite simple. Because there really are no specific, identifiable images in the random inkblot pictures, the image you recognize comes entirely from your imagination. Therefore, your description of what you see in the inkblots should give a psychologist an idea of what is going on in your mind. It might tell him or her something about your personality, feelings, and so on.

The point is that the picture seen in an inkblot is entirely dependent on the mind of the viewer. The images themselves are not necessarily anything in particular. They are whatever you make them out to be, whatever you want them to be.

Von Däniken's approach is analogous to an inkblot test. Although he is describing actual images, these images belong to a different culture. Without an understanding of the religious, artistic, or historical context of the drawings or images within the culture that produced them, von Däniken's descriptions of the images tell us more about what is going on in his mind than about what was in the minds of the ancient artists.

For example, an image identified by von Däniken as an astronaut with a radio antenna might be more easily explained as a shaman or priest with an antler headdress or simply a mythical creature (Figure 9.1). Von Däniken sees spacemen because he wants to, not because they really are there.

Here is another example. On the desert southern coast of Peru, prehistoric people called the *Nazca* constructed a spectacular complex of shapes (Kosok and Reiche 1949; McIntyre 1975; Reiche 1978). Most are long lines, etched into the desert surface, criss-crossing each other at all angles. The most interesting, however, are about three hundred actual drawings, rendered on an enormous scale (some are hundreds of feet across), of animals such as fish, monkeys, birds, snakes and a spider (Figure 9.2).

The figures and lines were made by clearing away the darker surface rocks, exposing the lighter desert soil beneath. They are remarkable achievements because of their great size, but certainly not beyond the capabilities of prehistoric people. Remember, these drawings were not carved into solid rock with extraterrestrial lasers; they were not paved over with some mysterious substance from another world. They were, in essence, "swept" into existence. Science writer Joe Nickell, an investigator of extreme claims whom we will encounter again when we examine the Shroud of Turin in Chapter 12, has duplicated the technique of making Nazca-like designs. With a crew of six people and several bags of lime (the white powder farmers and backyard landscapers use to cut soil acidity; it's also used to lay out lines on athletic fields), Nickell was able to outline a nearly perfect replica of a 120-meter-long (400-foot) Nazca bird in a single day. The other raw materials were some rope and a few pieces of wood (Nickell 1983).

Recent excavations have revealed the presence of raised platforms and tall posts at the endpoints of some of the Nazca lines, providing, in all likelihood, high points from which construction of the patterns could have been directed and also from which the images could have been viewed

Figure 9.1 Applying von Däniken's perspective to artifacts like this ancient rock art (petroglyphs) from Utah (**a**) and California (**b**), one might conclude that they depict space-helmeted aliens, complete with antennae. Could they be? Maybe. But application of Occam's razor demands that we first consider more mundane explanations. Perhaps the "antennae" in the Utah example are merely headdresses used to mimic the look of a bison or other horned animal. The images from California may be representations of spirit beings or gods. The jump from "spirit being" to "ancient alien" is enormous. (K. Feder)

Figure 9.2   This Nazca geoglyph, or earth drawing, depicts a giant spider. Large-scale drawings like those at Nazca are known from a number of places in the world. They likely were intended to please the gods and may have been constructed with the use of scale models. They certainly did not require the intervention of extraterrestrials—and why would aliens from outer space instruct humans to draw giant spiders (and monkeys, condors, snakes, birds, and the like) in the first place? (© Keren Su/Corbis)

(Curry 2007). Beyond this, excavation has also revealed the presence of what appear to be ceremonial activities such as animal sacrifice and offerings including seashells, guinea pigs, crayfish, and maize kernels (Curry 2007:447). Further, the archaeological record shows clear evidence of the kind of social hierarchy that would have made possible organizing the labor of the builders of the Nazca geoglyphs. The elaborate graves of the Nazca elite class have been found at a site called La Muna.

The Nazca markings and drawings are spectacular and exotic-looking, especially to our Western sensibilities, but they were clearly part of a local cultural tradition of ceremony and worship, and well within the capabilities of the ancient people of South America.

What does von Däniken have to say about the Nazca markings? Almost yielding to rationality, he admits that "they could have been laid out on their gigantic scale by working from a model and using a system of coordinates" (1970:17), which is precisely how Nickell accomplished it. Not to disappoint us, however, von Däniken prefers the notion that "they could also have been built according to instructions from an aircraft" (p. 17). Relying on the "ink-blot approach," he says, "Seen from the air, the clear-cut impression that the 37-mile-long plain of Nazca made on me was that of an airfield" (p. 17).

Please remember Occam's razor here. On one hand, for the hypothesis that the ancient people of South America built the lines themselves, we need only assume that they were clever. For von Däniken's preferred hypothesis, on the other hand, we have to assume the existence of extraterrestrial, intelligent life (unproven); assume that they visited Earth in the distant past (unproven and not very likely); assume that they needed to build rather strange airfields (pretty hard to swallow) and then, for added amusement, instructed local Indians to construct enormous representations of birds, spiders, monkeys, fish, and snakes. Those assumptions are bizarre, and the choice under Occam's razor is abundantly clear.

We can go on and deduce some implications for our preferred hypothesis: We should find evidence of small-scale models, we should find the art style of the desert drawings repeated in other artifacts found in the area, and we might expect the Nazca markings to be part of a general tradition in western South America of large-scale ground-drawings called "geoglyphs." When we test these predictions, we do find such supporting evidence: For example, Wilson (1988) has reported on a more recently discovered set of large-scale Earth drawings in Peru. Archaeological and historical information indicates that the lines were ceremonial roads leading to sacred origin places for families or entire communities. Far from being entirely enigmatic or without any cultural or historical context, they were made and used by some local native groups until fairly recently as a regular part of their religious festivities (Bruhns 1994).

Consider another example of the inkblot approach from a more recent von Däniken book, *The Eyes of the Sphinx* (1996). Deep in one of the subterranean chambers of the Egyptian temple dedicated to Hathor, goddess of music, love, and dance, located in Dendera, is a relief sculpture depicting two strange objects (Figure 9.3). In each, a slightly sinuous snake emanates

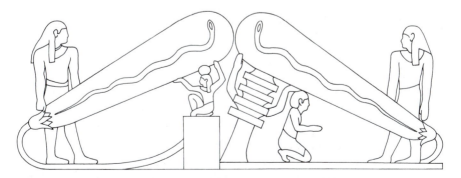

Figure 9.3 Image from a wall deep in the temple of Hathor at Dendera, Egypt. These objects can be interpreted as representations of ancient lightbulbs only by applying von Däniken's inkblot approach. Absolutely no physical evidence supports the claim that ancient Egyptians produced electrically powered lightbulbs.

from a flower and is enclosed in an elongate object attached to the flower. Altogether, the relief looks like two giant eggplants with enclosed snakes facing off against each other. A strange image, to be sure, but what does it mean?

To answer this riddle, von Däniken considers the challenge of providing enough light for Egyptian artisans to have produced the wall reliefs deep in the temple and postulates an extraordinary light source. Egyptologists assume, rather unimaginatively, that these workers used oil lamps and torches to light their way. From Egyptian sources we know that pieces of linen were soaked in oil or animal fat and then twisted into wicks, which, when lit, provided a bright light. Salt was applied to these wicks to reduce smoke and soot. Lamps that burned oil or animal fat also were used; again, salt was added to the mix to cut down on smoke. Beyond this, the ancient Egyptians made candles to light their way in the darkness of subterranean rooms and pyramid tombs. These candles were manufactured to burn a predetermined amount of time. Pyramid and tomb workers knew their shift was complete when the candle began to burn down to its base. Finally, there also is clear physical evidence that the Egyptians constructed clever arrays of polished metal mirrors to bring reflected light down inside deep corridors.

Not one to accept such simple explanations, von Däniken complains that absolutely no lamp soot was found on the walls or ceilings and that the light reflected by mirrors would have been too weak. Occam's razor forces a scientist to suggest the rather mundane possibility that salt was effective in reducing the amount of soot produced and that workers cleaned the soot that was produced from the chamber's surfaces when they were done. Also, experimental testing of mirror replicas shows that they work quite well, and these produced no soot at all.

Von Däniken, however, is not bound by Occam's razor, experimental testing, or any other rule of logic or method of science. His suggestion? The snake encased in an eggplant motif is a depiction of an electric lightbulb! The flower is its socket, the snake the filament, and the eggplant its glass enclosure.

Electrical lights more than 4,000 years ago in ancient Egypt? That is an extraordinary hypothesis. However, like any hypothesis, extraordinary or otherwise, it can be—in fact, must be—tested through the scientific method. Electrically powered lightbulbs in ancient Egypt or anywhere else must have been invented, manufactured, and used within a broader context. What are the deductive implications of the hypothesized existence of such lighting devices in ancient Egypt? What should we find in archaeological excavations to support this interpretation? Even modern lightbulbs burn out or break, so we would expect to find in archaeological excavations in Egypt dead but, perhaps, intact bulbs, fragments of broken glass bulbs, metal sockets, pieces of the necessarily durable filaments, and stretches of the electric cable needed to bring electricity to the bulbs from its source.

This last requirement leads us to the most important and most problematic deduction—we also must find evidence for the production of electric power by ancient Egyptians for these lightbulbs.

Little of this seems to occur to von Däniken, although using a thoroughly discredited interpretation of a 2,000-year-old artifact from Iraq he does claim that electricity was produced in the ancient world (Eggert 1996). (See the Frequently Asked Questions section in this chapter.)

Is there any hard, archaeological evidence of the kind just listed that ancient Egyptians produced electricity and manufactured lightbulbs? The answer is no. In his analysis of the images on the wall in Hathor's Temple in Dendera, von Däniken does not even ask whether such evidence exists. He certainly doesn't prove that Egyptians had electric lighting but merely that his inkblot speculations have become even more wildly imaginative in recent years.

The most infamous example of inkblot hypothesis is von Däniken's interpretation of the sarcophagus lid from the Maya site of Palenque (Figure 9.4). It's one of the ancient artifacts highlighted in a scene in the movie *Prometheus,* as alluded to earlier. Does it evoke in your mind any extraterrestrial images? Probably not. Yet, for von Däniken, the coffin lid is a clear representation of a space-suited alien piloting a spacecraft (1970:100–101).

The inkblot principle is at work again. When you are unfamiliar with the culture, you can make just about anything you want to out of these images, but you are most decidedly not practicing science. Von Däniken does not understand the cultural context of the Palenque artifact. He does not recognize the Maya symbols in the carving of the Ceiba Tree and the Earth Monster. What are mysterious devices for von Däniken are simply common artistic representations of Maya jewelry, including ear and nose plugs. Again, not understanding the context of the artifact, von Däniken apparently does not think it important or even relevant that the person depicted on the sarcophagus lid was a dead Maya king represented in a position between life, the Ceiba Tree above him, and death, the Earth Monster below (Robertson 1974; Sabloff 1989).

As for the individual depicted on the lid and buried in the tomb, he is anything but some mysterious, out-of-place enigma whose origins can be traced to outer space. In fact, we know a great deal about him; the information was provided by the Maya themselves (Schele and Freidel 1990). He was Pacal, ruler of the ancient city of Palenque from A.D. 615 until his death and placement in the tomb at the base of an impressive pyramid in A.D. 683 (Figure 9.5).

Fortunately for students of Maya history, Pacal had a detailed king list inscribed in the temple atop his pyramid tomb, and an additional listing placed on his sarcophagus. We know the names of his ancestors and the names of his descendants. We know what he accomplished during his

Figure 9.4   Using what we here call the inkblot approach, von Däniken interprets the image on the sarcophagus lid from the Temple of Inscriptions at the Maya site of Palenque as depicting an astronaut with antennae and oxygen mask, peering through a telescope and manipulating the controls of a rocket. Maya archaeologists prefer to interpret this scene within the context of Maya cosmogony—a king poised between life and death in his journey to the afterlife. (© 1976 Merle Greene Robertson/Pre-Columbian Art Research Institute)

Figure 9.5 The magnificent Temple of the Inscriptions, the final resting place of Pacal, ruler of Palenque. Pacal's tomb with its famous sarcophagus lid was found at the bottom of a staircase leading from the top to a point beneath the pyramid. (D. Normak/ PhotoLink/Getty RF)

reign as ruler of Palenque. And we have his physical remains in the coffin. Although he was once the all-powerful ruler of a splendid society, nothing is left of Pacal save his very human bones.

Pacal's story needs no tired speculation about extraterrestrial visitors to Earth. Pacal was a dynamic and vibrant historical personage, a real human being who lived, ruled a great city, and died more than 1,300 years ago, and whose story has been revealed by archaeology and history.

One needs to be familiar with Maya cosmogony, writing, and history to recognize the context of the Palenque stone within Maya culture. Von Däniken and his followers, however, seems wholly ignorant of Maya beliefs and therefore can come up with such an unsupported speculation concerning the image on the coffin lid.

The Amorous Astronaut Hypothesis

Von Däniken's second hypothesis suggests that extraterrestrial aliens played an active and important role in the actual biological development of our species. There has been some controversy on this particular point. An episode of the public television series *Nova* ("The Case of the Ancient Astronauts" 1978) focused on von Däniken's ideas. During an interview that was part of the episode, he maintained that he never really made such a claim. Let's see.

In *Chariots of the Gods?* von Däniken proposed the following scenario. A group of extremely advanced, interstellar space travelers land on Earth, for the first time perhaps millions of years ago. They find a primitive race of creatures, very apelike, with small brains, but with a lot of potential. Then, von Däniken claims, "A few specially selected women would be fertilized by the astronauts. Thus a new race would arise that skipped a stage in natural evolution" (1970:11).

If the previous claim can be called the *Inkblot Hypothesis,* I can call this one the *Amorous Astronaut Hypothesis.*

According to this hypothesis, extraterrestrial aliens have streaked at near light speed to get to Earth. The speed of light is fast (186,000 miles per second), but the universe is large, and our space*men* (for von Däniken, the extraterrestrial visitors always seem to be males) have been cooped up in their spaceship, perhaps in suspended animation, for more than four years. The star (Alpha Centauri) nearest to our sun is about 4.3 light-years away, and so—even traveling at the speed of light—four years is the absolute minimum. Our extraterrestrial friends land, are wakened from their deep sleep, and exit their spaceship to explore the new frontiers of an unexplored planet in an alien solar system. And what do you think they do? They look for females to "fertilize." The human species is not the product of evolution, but of interstellar miscegenation.

Even von Däniken's most ardent supporters must admit that he has some very strange ideas concerning the ability of different species to mate and produce offspring. For example, the mummy of ancient Egyptian priestess Makare, daughter of Pharaoh Pingdjem (c. 1075 B.C.), was placed in her tomb with a small mummified bundle. It had been assumed that the bundle was her child until it was x-rayed in 1972. The small mummy turned out to be that of a baboon. This was not so surprising. Egyptians commonly mummified animals, and most Egyptologists assumed that the baboon baby was Makare's pet or, perhaps, a symbolic child entombed with Makare as a surrogate for a human baby. Von Däniken (1996:63) suggests, instead, that Makare may have actually given birth to what he implies was a human–baboon hybrid. Von Däniken recognizes that humans and baboons cannot mate and produce offspring, so he proposes that extraterrestrial aliens conducted genetic experiments, hybridizing a wide variety of earth species. Makare's baby baboon is just one example. The many mythological creatures seen all over the ancient world—Pegasus, the Sphinx, griffins—are not mythological at all for von Däniken but are accurate depictions of these hybrids! Why did ancient astronauts conduct these seemingly bizarre genetic experiments? According to von Däniken (1996), it was solely for entertainment: "The extraterrestrials had found a way to keep themselves busy. They merrily invented one monster after another . . . and they observed with much amusement the reactions of the flabbergasted humans" (p. 58). The extraterrestrials appear to have had a rather twisted sense of humor, if you ask me.

The possibility of two species that evolved on different planets in two different solar systems even having the appropriately matching physical equipment for mating, much less having matching DNA necessary to produce offspring, is so incredibly unlikely that it is beyond calculation. Yet these are precisely the implications that must be deduced from von Däniken's hypothesis. As Carl Sagan pointed out in "The Case of the Ancient Astronauts," a human ancestor would likely have been more successful mating with a petunia than with a creature from outer space; at least the human ancestor and the petunia both evolved here on Earth. Extraterrestrial astronauts, amorous or not, simply could not have mated with our ancestors to produce us.

The "Our Ancestors, the Dummies" Hypothesis

This leads us to the final von Däniken hypothesis, the notion that the archaeological record is replete with evidence of highly advanced artifacts beyond the capability of ancient humans. This can be called the *Our Ancestors, the Dummies Hypothesis* (after Omohundro 1976). Von Däniken is claiming that our human ancestors were too dumb to have, all by themselves, using their own creative abilities, intelligence, and labor, produced the admittedly spectacular works of engineering, architecture, mathematics, astronomy, botany, and zoology evidenced in the archaeological record.

Mind you, von Däniken is not saying that archaeologists are hiding the physical evidence of ancient flying saucer parts or photon torpedoes found at prehistoric Indian villages or ancient Chinese temples. That would be an easy claim to check scientifically; such artifacts either exist or they do not. No, instead, von Däniken simply points to artifacts such as pyramids or temples, statues, or carvings. He makes reference to prehistoric accomplishments such as the domestication of plants and animals, the development of metallurgy, and especially astronomical abilities—all things for which archaeological evidence is abundant. Von Däniken simply cannot understand how, and therefore doesn't believe that, prehistoric people could have managed all this without some sort of outside help. This help, for von Däniken, comes in the form of aliens from outer space.

Extraterrestrial Calendars?

For example, in his third book, *Gold of the Gods* (1973), von Däniken makes reference to the hypothesis of science writer Alexander Marshack (1972). Marshack maintains that some inscribed bone, antler, and ivory tools from

Paleolithic Europe, dating from 30,000 to 10,000 years ago, represent the oldest calendars in the world. He hypothesizes that these first calendars were based on the cycle of changes in the phases of the moon. Amazed as always, von Däniken asks:

> Why did Stone Age men bother about astronomical representations? It is usually claimed that they had their hands full just to procure sufficient nourishment on endless hunts. Who instructed them in this work? Did someone advise them how to make these observations which were far above their "level"? Were they making notes for an expected visit from the cosmos? (1973:203–4)

Von Däniken has lots of questions, but precious few answers. Let's look at one of these artifacts and see if it indeed looks like something only an extraterrestrial alien might have devised. Probably the most famous of the artifacts in question is the Abri Blanchard antler plaque found in southern France and dated to about 30,000 years ago (Figure 9.6). This ancient piece of ivory has close to seventy impressions carved into it along a sinuous arc. If you begin in the center of the antler and work your way along the arc, a rough pattern emerges. Each design element appears to be a fraction of a circle. As you follow the arc of impressions, the marks seem to grow in terms of the proportion of a circle represented and then, once a whole circle is produced, to diminish. The similarity between the sequence of impressions and the phases of the moon is apparent. It is Marshack's

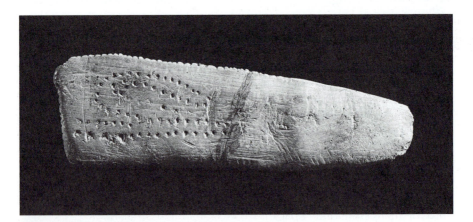

Figure 9.6 Von Däniken sees evidence for knowledge far beyond the capabilities of ancient people in 30,000-year-old bone implements of the Upper Paleolithic. But perhaps the best known of these, the antler plaque at Abri Blanchard in France, though a compelling argument for the great intelligence of our prehistoric ancestors, is really just the simple depiction of lunar phases. The pattern of lunar waxing and waning was likely well known to these people. (© President and Fellows of Harvard College, Peabody Museum of Archaeology and Ethnology, 2005.16.318.38)

well-reasoned, though still-debated, hypothesis that this is precisely what these ancient people were trying to convey.

No one can deny that it is fascinating to think that 30,000 years ago prehistoric people may have looked at the mysterious light in the night sky and wondered about it. Based on this and similar artifacts from the period 30,000 to 10,000 years ago, it appears quite possible that these ancient people recognized the cyclical nature of the lunar phases. But as interesting as it might be, does the antler plaque look like the calendar of an extraterrestrial alien? Wouldn't their calendars and to-do lists be kept on their iPads, and wouldn't archaeologists find those devices? (They're Apple products, so they'd probably still be working!)

Certainly it took intelligence to watch the nightly change in the moon's phases and conclude that it was not random, that it was patterned and predictable. But remember, these were people who, of necessity, were attuned to the natural world around them. Their very survival depended on their observations of nature, and nature is filled with predictable cycles. Day followed by night followed by day is an unending, constant pattern that is easily recognized. The fact that summer follows spring, is replaced by fall and then winter, which leads inevitably back to spring, was a cycle that had to be known, followed, and relied on by our prehistoric ancestors. Long before 30,000 years ago their brains had become as big as ours, and they were just as intelligent as we are. The fact that they may have recognized the phases of the moon as another cycle in nature and that they recorded these changes to be used, perhaps, as a kind of calendar is a wonderful achievement, but not really so unexpected.

Extraterrestrial Aliens in the Pacific?

Easter Island is one of the most remote places on Earth, 3,200 kilometers (2,000 miles) west of the coast of South America and 2,000 kilometers (1,250 miles) southeast of the nearest inhabited Pacific island (Bloch 2012). Called Rapa Nui by its inhabitants, Easter Island was first settled in about A.D. 1200 by Polynesians as part of their own remarkable "age of exploration," the equivalent of the European spread across the Atlantic in the fifteenth and sixteenth centuries.

On the island, more than 950 large stone statues called Moai have been located (Hunt and Lipo 2011). Carved from a relatively soft volcanic rock called *tuff*, they are impressive indeed. The largest is more than 10 meters (33 feet) high and weighs about 72,000 kilograms (80 tons). The "average" statue is more than 14½ feet high and weighs 14 tons. Even the smaller statues would have taken considerable labor to quarry, sculpt, transport, and erect (Figure 9.7).

Not surprisingly, von Däniken does not believe that the Easter Islanders could have accomplished these tasks by themselves. In *Gods from Outer Space* (1971), he suggests that the statues (or at least some of them) were erected

Figure 9.7   Left The remarkable Moai of Easter Island number in the hundreds and reflect the great intelligence, technical skill, and organizational abilities of so-called primitive people. The photograph on the right shows a Moai that was not finished, still lying in place in its quarry. No laser burns have been found in the quarries, only the stone tools the Easter Islanders used to carve out the statues from the surrounding rock. (Courtesy Sonja Gray)

by extraterrestrial aliens marooned on Easter Island. What was their motive for erecting the statues? According to von Däniken, it was simple boredom (p. 118). Between conducting genetics experiments for giggles and carving statues out of a sense of boredom, these extraterrestrials appear to have had way too much time on their hands, and they certainly mucked things up for us archaeologists trying to figure out the human past.

Intensive archaeological investigations have been carried out on Easter Island since 1955 (see Van Tilburg 1994 for a detailed discussion of this work). Quarries with partially completed statues have been discovered—along with hundreds of stone picks, hammers, and chisels used to quarry the rock and carve the images.

Okay, but how were the multi-tonned statues moved as much as 17 kilometers (11 miles)? Archaeologist often use replicative experiments to test hypotheses about how ancient people may have accomplished a task, from something as simple a making a spear point to something quite a bit more challenging and complex like moving a Moai. Among the rules underlying such experiments are the requirements that the replication actually works—you can accomplish the task—and that the archaeological and historical data conform to the results of the experiment.

One of the most interesting attempts at transporting a Moai has been conducted by archaeologists Terry Hunt and Carl Lipo (2011). Unlike some other researchers who believe that the statues were moved on wooden sleds, on their backs, Hunt and Lipo hypothesize that the statues were transported from the quarry in an upright position in a technique they call a "refrigerator walk." If you've ever moved a large, bulky refrigerator, you'll know what that means. Using the fact that the refrigerator has a low center of gravity, you can tilt it from side to side, and twist it at the same time, slowly and safely moving it a little forward with each tilt and twist. Hunt and Lipo showed that with a relatively small crew and ropes, you can build up a pretty good pace of moving a Moai in its upright position using the refrigerator walk approach.

Like all replicative experiments in archaeology, merely being able to accomplish a task using a particular technique does not guarantee that ancient people did it the same way. However, Hunt and Lipo also note actual evidence that conforms to their hypothesis. For example, the statues show grinding wear on their bases, which is what you'd expect if they were moved in an upright position. Also, like a refrigerator with its motor on the bottom, the Moai have a low center of gravity, the result of the potbellies most of them exhibit. Their interesting body shape may have been intentional; a more top-heavy statue would be more likely to fall during transport. Also, a number of statues did break during their trip from the quarry to the shoreline, but the way they broke is interesting. They don't all lie on their backs, as you might expect they would had they been transported that way. While some are found broken on their backs along the many roadways that cross the island from the quarry to the shore, some are found face down. Hunt and Lipo point out that this broken positioning isn't random; statues tend to be found on their backs when they broke while being transported uphill—in other words, they look like they fell backward because of the slope. Broken statues tend to be found face down if they broke during a downhill section of their trip, appearing to have broken in a big, sad face-plant (2011:83). That's exactly what you'd expect to find if the statues were being moved in a vertical or upright position, but not if they were supine during transport.

Along with conforming to the proportions of the statues, the basal grinding, and the correlation between slope and the positioning of broken Moai, the upright transportation hypothesis also conforms to another significant source of evidence—the stories told by the Rapanuians themselves. Islanders have long claimed that the statues "walked" from the quarry to the coast. Though they go on to assert that their ancestors accomplished this through magic, we can suggest that it wasn't magic, but ingenuity on their part. Either way, there's no need or room for anti-gravitation devices wielded by extraterrestrial statue makers.

A Real Mystery

But the absurdity doesn't end there. Not content merely to write preposterous books, von Däniken devised another way to spread the gospel of the ancient astronauts. *It's a theme park!* Disney proclaims Mickey's Magic Kingdom "The Happiest Place on Earth," and I see no reason to dispute that. I would like to here proclaim von Däniken's Mystery Park the *silliest* place on earth, and I dare anyone to dispute that (Powell 2004)! Von Däniken was able to convince a number of major corporations, including Coca-Cola, Sony, Fujitsu, and Swatch, among others, to bankroll (to the tune of $62 million) his Mystery Park, a sort of world's fair of silliness, dedicated to the ancient astronaut hypothesis. Unfortunately, for von Däniken anyway, he apparently wasn't able to convince enough tourists to actually visit the park. Opened in 2003, Mystery Park closed its doors in November 2006 as a result of poor attendance. Mind you, lots of people bought tickets and visited the park—in fact, more than 440,000 in 2004 (its best year)—but the yearly numbers dramatically declined in 2005 to less than half that (Künzle 2006). The park reopened briefly in 2009, closed again, and has now opened under new management. No longer "Mystery Park," "Jungfrau Park" (the park has been renamed after a nearby mountain; "jungfrau" literally means "young girl" and is usually used to signify a virgin in German), the owners are now appealing to a younger audience, adding a small petting zoo, go-karts, and "bouncy castles." The animals in the small zoo include llamas and goats, but nothing extraterrestrial. It remains to be seen whether this rebranding will improve the park's attendance numbers or if it will lead to the fulfillment of von Däniken's expressed wish to open a series of "von Däniken Lands" (okay, that's my snarky name for them) in North America, Thailand, Singapore, and the United Emirates.

The park was built with seven major attractions, each one constructed to represent what is, to von Däniken, a great mystery of the ancient world. For example, one pavilion was built in the shape of an Egyptian pyramid (see Chapter 10), another mimicked the Maya Pyramid of the Feathered Serpent in Chichén Itzá (see Chapter 13). Each pavilion's name represented its theme in von Däniken's universe of absurdity: Maya, Orient (focusing on Egypt), MegaStones (Stonehenge and the like), Contact, Challenge, Nazca (South America), and Vimana (ancient India). Each pavilion's exhibit consisted of a movie, dioramas, and artifacts. The seven main pavilions formed a ring around a central Earth base for the ancient astronauts; von Däniken himself maintained an office and library there. Oh, and don't forget the Mystery Park mascot, "Mysty" (get it?), a bluish, sort-of-extraterrestrial critter who showed up on the website and some of the Mystery Park merchandise.

The park was filled with bizarre juxtapositions and incredible anachronisms. For example, among the exhibits of ancient Mesoamerican cities and Maya stelae within the Maya pavilion, there also was a diorama of a mariachi band (Powell 2004). What, exactly, was von Däniken trying to tell us (or sell us) here? Mariachis of the gods?

As deliciously bizarre as this all was, writer Eric Powell, who attended the grand opening of the park for *Archaeology* magazine, points to a far more serious, depressingly familiar von Däniken theme that permeates Mystery Park. It's "our ancestors, the dummies" all over again. Powell notes that the foundation of amazement that underlies Mystery Park doesn't honor the great capabilities of our ancient human ancestors, but, instead, reflects an assumption of their intellectual incompetence. The great engineering and intellectual achievements of the ancient world were made possible not by human ingenuity and brain power, but by extraterrestrial tutoring. Powell's (2004:66) description of the Mayaland movie reveals the core of the von Däniken mind-set: Ancient astronauts land on Earth, abduct a band of children from the primitive native people, take them to their home planet, instruct them in the ways of pyramid building and calendar making, and then return them to the Mesoamerican jungle where they share their newfound knowledge, pulling their people from a life of savagery up to the pinnacle of intellectual, civilized life. It would be funny, if it were not fundamentally an egregious libel against the human species. I'd like to believe that this is why the park couldn't attract enough visitors to survive; people are too smart to fall for such nonsense.

The Archaeology of Mars

As the result of a single photographic exposure taken by the camera on board the U.S. Viking spacecraft orbiting Mars in 1976, some proclaimed that there is mind-boggling archaeological evidence of monumental proportions for life there in the past (DiPietro and Molenaar 1982). On exposure 35A72, in a grainy pastiche of shadow and light, is the image at the heart of this extraterrestrial archaeological controversy (Figure 9.8). It is called, simply, "the Mars Face," and it is enormous, roughly a mile long from the top of its head to its chin.

Undeniably, it does look like a human face, or at least a part of one. But it also seems to be explainable as an interesting and coincidental play of light and shadows, the kind of image trickery that causes us to see faces, animals, or even household appliances in rock exposures, cave formations, and clouds. These images do not really exist except for our mind's tendency to coax familiar pictures out of natural features. I have been in countless underground caverns where the tour guides have pointed out features like "the Capitol Dome," "Two Eggs, Sunnyside Up," and the "New York City Skyline." A rock face in Wisconsin presents a lifelike, entirely natural profile

Figure 9.8   The so-called Mars Face (upper right) is almost certainly a natural product of Martian geology—a natural feature of the landscape that happens to look like a human face under the right lighting conditions—and not a monument built by an ancient Martian civilization. (Courtesy NASA)

of the Indian leader Black Hawk. None of these often astonishingly real-looking images were conjured up by some ancient geological intelligence. There's a term for seeing patterned images in random wisps of clouds, in geological formations, in dental x rays, or even on a piece of toast: pareidolia (Poole 2007). You might remember a few years ago a woman sold half a grilled-cheese sandwich on eBay for $28,000 because it had what some interpreted to be a miraculous image of the Virgin Mary on the toasted surface of the sandwich. That's pareidolia.

Most geologists who viewed the original Mars Face photograph ascribed it to something like the inkblot effect. Sure, it sort of looked like a face, but so what? The resolution of the image—each tiny pixel on the photograph corresponds to a whopping 43 meters (141 feet) on the ground—is far too low to accurately determine what the feature actually looks like (Malin 1995).

At least partially as a result of public interest about what the photograph depicted, additional images of the Cydonia region were taken in April 1998 by another interplanetary voyager, the Mars Global Surveyor (MGS) satellite. The 1998 photographs taken by the much more sophisticated camera on board were of a resolution ten times higher than that of the original Viking images; each pixel represents only 4.3 meters (14.1 feet) of the Martian surface. This much sharper photograph showed that the feature looked nothing at all like a face, but more like an eroded mesa, entirely natural in

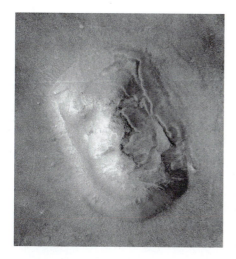

Figure 9.9 The Mars Global Surveyor photographed the Mars Face again in April 2001, producing the highest possible resolution with the camera on board. An object the size of a small building would be discernible in the photograph; genuine cultural features, like a giant, mile-long sculpted face, would be easily recognized. But no such feature is present in the new photograph; the Mars Face has disappeared completely. (Courtesy NASA)

appearance. Then, on April 8, 2001, the MGS photographed the region yet again. The resulting photograph has an even higher resolution than the April 1998 image, with each pixel now representing only about 1.56 meters on the ground (about 5 feet, the maximum resolution possible with this camera; Figure 9.9). According to NASA (2001), an object the size of a small building would be discernible in the photograph; genuine cultural features, like a giant, mile-long sculpted face, would be easily recognized. But no such feature is present in the new photograph; the Mars Face has disappeared completely. All that is left is an eroded mesa with an irregular depression where the "eye" was located and a valley where people saw a mouth. NASA scientist James Garvin (2001) has even determined the easiest trail to the top of the mesa, should astronauts ever make it to Mars and have a desire to stroll around the geological feature once called the Mars Face.

There are other interesting features on the Martian landscape. One looks like the "happy face" symbol (Gardner 1985), but it is simply a meteorite impact crater about 215 kilometers (134 miles) across with fortuitously positioned smaller features located inside it: a smaller crater and a cluster of eminences for eyes and a curved cliff for the smiling mouth (Figure 9.10a).

In June 1999, the Mars orbiter camera photographed a geological feature on Mars that specialists identified as a natural pit formed by collapse within a straight-walled trough. Though it was a bit late for the holiday, the 2.3-kilometer- (1.4-mile-) wide feature looked remarkably like a Valentine's Day heart (Figure 9.10b).

Finally—my personal favorite—another photo of the Martian surface shows a lava flow that bears a remarkable resemblance to Kermit the Frog (Figure 9.10c)! No one has claimed, at least not yet, that this is evidence of an extraterrestrial origin for the Muppets.

a

b

c

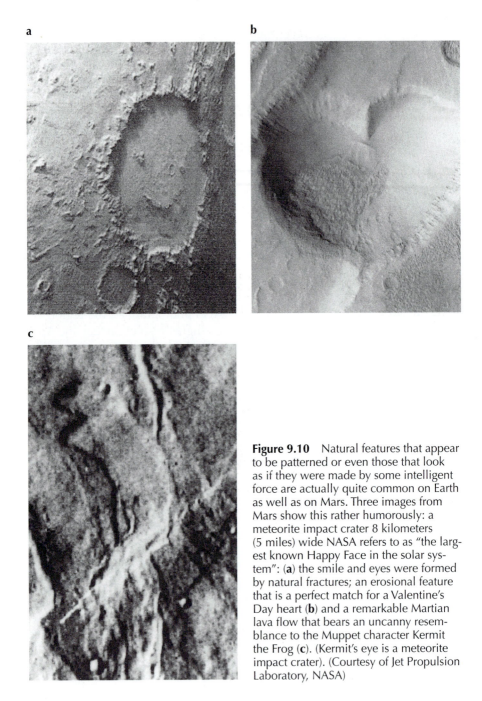

Figure 9.10   Natural features that appear to be patterned or even those that look as if they were made by some intelligent force are actually quite common on Earth as well as on Mars. Three images from Mars show this rather humorously: a meteorite impact crater 8 kilometers (5 miles) wide NASA refers to as "the largest known Happy Face in the solar system": (**a**) the smile and eyes were formed by natural fractures; an erosional feature that is a perfect match for a Valentine's Day heart (**b**) and a remarkable Martian lava flow that bears an uncanny resemblance to the Muppet character Kermit the Frog (**c**). (Kermit's eye is a meteorite impact crater). (Courtesy of Jet Propulsion Laboratory, NASA)

To scientists, the Face, the "happy face," the Valentine heart, and Kermit the Frog are rare, but by no means unique, images of landscape features on a planetary body; the images look artificial, but they are entirely natural.

Current Perspectives:
The von Däniken Phenomenon

Adherents of the Ancient Aliens hypothesis repeatedly underestimate the intelligence and abilities of our ancestors and then proposes an extraordinary hypothesis to explain the past. That is clear. However, what is not so clear is the second reason I have suggested for von Däniken's inability to accept prehistoric peoples' ability to produce the great achievements seen in the archaeological record (the first was simple ignorance). I have already mentioned it briefly—European ethnocentrism.

What I mean by this becomes clear when you read *Chariots of the Gods?* It is curious that von Däniken is ever ready to provide examples as proof of his third hypothesis (Our Ancestors, the Dummies) from archaeological sites in Africa, Asia, North America, and South America; but he is curiously and atypically silent when it comes to Europe. My feeling about this was so strong on reading *Chariots of the Gods?* that I actually went through the book and tallied the specific references to amazing accomplishments of prehistoric people that von Däniken believes were too advanced, too sophisticated, or too remarkable for mere humans to have produced. I paid careful attention to where in the world (which continent) these specific examples were from. The following chart resulted (Feder 1980a):

The great majority of von Däniken's examples here are from places other than Europe. It appears that he is utterly astounded by the archaeological records of ancient Africa, Asia, and North and South America. He is so astounded, in fact, that he thinks that only through the assistance of men from outer space could native Africans, Asians, and Americans have produced the prehistoric works that archaeologists find on these continents.

It is curious that von Däniken never wonders who helped the ancient Minoans build the great temple at Knossos or the Greeks the Parthenon, or which spacemen instructed the Romans in constructing the Colosseum. Why not? These monuments are every bit as impressive as those that von

Table 9.1

Continent of the Example	Number of Examples	Percentage
Africa	16	31
Asia	12	23
Europe	2	4
North America	11	22
South America	10	20
Total	51	100

Däniken does mention. The temple at Knossos is more than 3,500 years old, the Parthenon is almost 2,500 years old, and the Colosseum is close to 2,000. Even in the case of Stonehenge in England, von Däniken is strangely quiet and only briefly mentions it in *Chariots of the Gods?*—though he finally does get around to Stonehenge in a more recent book, *Pathways to the Gods*.

Many people are aware of phenomena like the pyramids of Egypt, the ruins of Mexico, and the ancient Chinese civilization. Some, however, may wonder how the prehistoric ancestors of contemporary people whom they consider to be backward and even intellectually inferior accomplished such spectacular things in the past. After all, today Egypt is a developing nation, many Indians of Mexico are poor and illiterate, and the Chinese are just beginning to catch up with the technology of the modern world. How could the ancestors of such people have been advanced enough to have developed pyramids, writing, agriculture, mathematics, and astronomy all by themselves?

Along comes von Däniken with an easy answer. Those people did not produce those achievements on their own. Some sort of outside help, an extraterrestrial "peace corps," was responsible. If I am correct in this suggestion, it really is a pity; human prehistory is a spectacular story in its own right. All peoples have ancient pasts to be proud of, and there is no place for, nor any need to fall back on, the fantasy of ancient astronauts.

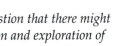 **FREQUENTLY ASKED QUESTIONS**

1. *Carl Sagan predates von Däniken in publishing the suggestion that there might be archaeological artifacts that bear witness to the visitation and exploration of our planet by extraterrestrial astronauts sometime in the distant past. Does that make Sagan a pseudoscientist?*

Of course not. Merely suggesting a potentially fruitful line of investigation—even if other scientists are skeptical—doesn't make somebody a pseudoscientist. Sagan recognized, of course, the kind of evidence needed to uphold his hypothesis and clearly concluded, in the years following his suggestion, that the requisite evidence was not found. Read any of Sagan's more recent works, especially *The Demon-Haunted World* (1996). One of Sagan's great wishes was that, during his lifetime, there would be proof that we are not alone, that our Earth is not the only repository of intelligent life forms in the universe. Disappointed he may have been that this did not happen, but deluded he was not. There is no archaeological evidence for ancient extraterrestrial visits to Earth; Sagan knew and accepted this fact.

2. *Is there any evidence for the use of electricity by ancient people?*

No, but the claim has been made that a primitive 2,000-year-old electrical battery was found in Iraq (Eggert 1996). No one knows precisely what this object was used for, but it certainly was not producing any electrical power when it was found in 1936. The so-called Baghdad Battery is a ceramic vase with a closed bottom, a cylindrical tube of copper inserted through the neck, and a rod of iron inside the copper tube. The metals were held in place with a plug of asphalt. A number of modern experiments, often with inaccurate models of this object, have produced mild and short-lived electrical currents when an appropriate electrolyte (liquid that conducts electricity) is poured into the vessel. However, this will happen whenever two different metals are immersed in an electrolyte, and there is no evidence that any such liquid was ever placed into the original jar. In what has to be considered the definitive experiment with a Baghdad Battery replica, Adam Savage and Jamie Hyneman, the guys from the Discovery Channel's *MythBusters* show—the best show on television at casting a skeptical eye at all sorts of extraordinary claims—along with their "co-busters," made a replica Baghdad Battery from scratch. Their working model actually did produce electricity—all of about 0.269 volt (Packard 2006:122). A single AA battery produces about five-and-a-half times more voltage than that (and most flashlights require more than one of those). The set-up may have been used in electroplating, but there just is no way that the Baghdad Battery could have produced enough juice to power a system of illumination sufficient to light the interior of a pyramid. That part of the myth, indeed, is busted.

 BEST OF THE WEB

ANCIENT ALIENS

http://www.dumbassguide.info/

Okay, it has a really unfortunate name, but the Dumbasses Guide to Knowledge is a terrific place to find a point-by-point refutation of the claims made in the *Ancient Aliens* series. It's a lot of fun, well written, and spot on.

EASTER ISLAND

http://www.netaxs.com/~trance/rapanui.html

Especially useful for an extensive series of links to Easter Island websites as well as breaking news about archaeological work on the island and potential threats to the Moai as a result of recent plans to develop parts of the island.

http://www.pbs.org/wgbh/nova/easter/

PBS companion web page to the *Nova* "Secrets of Easter Island" documentary.

MARS FACE

http://www.msss.com/education/facepage/face.html

Web page dating to 1995 presenting a discussion of the Mars Face based on the 1976 Viking *Orbiter 1* photograph.

http://mars.jpl.nasa.gov/mgs/msss/camera/images/4_6_face_release/

NASA web page revisiting the Mars Face phenomenon on the basis of new, high-resolution photographs taken by the Mars Orbiter camera.

http://www.msss.com/mars_images/moc/extended_may2001/face/index.html

Web page presenting the May 2001 NASA press release announcing the most recent (April 2001) image of the Mars Face. The download is quite amazing, but there's not even a hint of a face.

http://science.nasa.gov/headlines/y2001/ast24may_1.htm?list540155

NASA web page presenting a brief history of the Mars Face phenomenon, including the April 2001 photographs taken by the Mars Global Surveyor, the highest-resolution photos yet taken of the feature. Scroll down to the end of the site for James Garvin's trail map to the top of the mesa.

   CRITICAL THINKING EXERCISE

Using the deductive approach outlined in Chapter 2, how would you test this hypothesis? In other words, what archaeological and biological data must you find to conclude that this hypothetical statement is an accurate assertion, that it describes what actually happened in the ancient human past?

- The prehistoric record contains evidence of enormous and unexpected leaps forward in science and technology—agriculture, pyramid building, writing, and so on. These leaps are evidence of the introduction of such innovations by extraterrestrial aliens.

Mysterious Egypt

Hours before I wrote these words, I stood in the literal shadow of one of the iconic monuments of the ancient world: the Colosseum in Rome. The Colosseum is a building of spectacular beauty, breathtaking majesty, and remarkable functionality, all of which are even the more mind-boggling when one considers that it was built nearly 2,000 years ago (Figure 10.1).

The emperor Vespasian oversaw much of the Colosseum's construction, carried out between A.D. 72 and 80. The walls of the ancient amphitheater rise a dizzying 48.5 meters (almost 160 feet), the equivalent of a modern nearly fifteen-story building. The amphitheater's three tiers of seating could accommodate an audience of upward of 50,000 people, about the capacity of many modern major league baseball stadiums. Like many of its modern counterparts, the Colosseum had a protective partial roof (of cloth) shielding at least some of those in attendance from the sun, something anyone who has endured August in Rome will appreciate. The Colosseum served as the primary Roman venue for gladiatorial matches, staged animal hunts, and even mock naval battles for which the several-acre playing surface and basement were flooded.

When Did People Get That Smart?

It is perfectly reasonable for modern people to marvel at the end products of ancient technologies, structures like the Colosseum, monuments like Stonehenge (see Chapter 13), splendid bits of architectural magic like the Great Houses of the American Southwest (Figure 10.2), and memorials like the Egyptian pyramids (this chapter). When did ancient people get that smart? How could they possibly have developed the engineering, architectural, mathematical, and even the practical skills necessary to build

Figure 10.1 Completed in A.D. 80, the three tiers of seating in the justifiably famous tourist destination, the Colosseum in Rome, could hold nearly 50,000 spectators. Monumental structures like the Colosseum beg the question: "How did ancient people get so smart?" (K. Feder)

things that continue to astound us hundreds and even thousands of years after they were built? Who were the geniuses who first solved the many complex challenges involved in building these remarkable structures, and how did they do it? Scientists and nonscientists alike have long pondered these apparent mysteries.

Grafton Elliot Smith, whom we met in Chapter 4, was one of those thinkers. Smith's intellectual legacy will, perhaps, forever be tainted by his association with the Piltdown Man hoax. You will remember that, though almost certainly not materially involved in perpetrating the fraud, he became one of the false fossil's strongest proponents.

At least as important as his association with Piltdown, however, was Smith's role as one of the chief architects of the diffusionist perspective that characterized the British school of anthropology in the early years of the twentieth century. An underlying theme of this school of thought, put most simply, was that human beings were, in general, dull, unimaginative, and uninventive. From this, Smith deduced that most ancient human groups were, in large measure, culturally static and, if left on their own, would have changed very little through time.

Of course, Smith understood that humanity had, nevertheless, undergone vast cultural changes since human beings first burst onto the scene.

Figure 10.2 Pueblo Bonito, at Chaco Canyon, is a four-story structure containing more than 800 rooms, built nearly a thousand years ago by the ancestral Puebloan people of what is today New Mexico. Great Houses, like Pueblo Bonito and the cliff dwellings also found in the American Southwest, reflect the great intelligence of ancient people as well as their remarkable architectural and engineering abilities. (K. Feder)

He explained these changes as the result of exceptions—or perhaps a single exception—to this characterization of human groups as culturally inert. Smith and the other diffusionists maintained that there had been only one or, perhaps, a very few "genius" cultures in antiquity. The cultural precocity of such a group or groups was ascribed by some diffusionists to their superior genetic endowment and by others to their location in a privileged, exceptionally generous natural habitat.

For Smith, the single genius culture, the source of all human cultural development, was ancient Egypt. In his view, before 6,000 years ago, people all over the world were living in a natural, primitive, and more or less fixed state. At about this time, a group of humans settled along the Nile and, as the result of an incredibly rich subsistence base made possible by the fertile valley soil, were liberated from the time-consuming requirements of subsistence production that so dominated the human condition nearly everywhere else. Using that free time to their advantage, Smith believed, the ancient Egyptians single-handedly produced most, if not all, of the key inventions that made civilized life possible: agriculture, animal domestication, ceramic technology, writing, metallurgy, monumental construction, and urban settlements.

In the diffusionist view, these cultural inventions spread like ripples on a still pond, emanating from Egypt and moving across the face of the earth. For Smith, the Egyptians alone had independently evolved a complex civilization. In his view, a number of other societies—including some located across the Atlantic Ocean in the New World—only later developed complex civilizations, inspired by contact with Egypt and by adoption of advanced technologies that had "diffused" from that ancient source. The proverb may be correct when it states that "all roads lead *to* Rome," but in Smith's view, all intellectual roads in the ancient world led *from* the Nile valley.

Though Egypt was viewed as a cultural font by many diffusionists, not all embraced that land as the ultimate source of civilization. Some diffusionists supported the notion that, instead of Egypt, a civilization now lost in the clichéd "dim mists of antiquity" had been the source of all human progress. We have already encountered this view in Chapter 8 in the form of Ignatius Donnelly's vision of the Lost Continent of Atlantis as articulated in his book *Atlantis: The Antediluvian World* (1882). You will recall that Donnelly believed Egypt was not the source but, instead, was only one of the many recipients of the wisdom and technological prowess of a singularly advanced society, that of the Atlanteans.

We have seen in the previous chapter how, instead of pointing a finger toward Egypt or out to a spot in the middle of the Atlantic, Erich von Däniken points his finger up to the heavens, electing to find the ultimate source for human civilization and technological achievement in the cosmos. Ultimately, von Däniken's writings amount to a space-age application of the diffusionist view. If intrinsically dull, uninventive, and unimaginative human beings had, in deep time, exhibited remarkable technologies, marvelous architectural skills, and mathematical sophistication, these abilities must have come from somewhere else. No human source underpins von Däniken's diffusionist argument— not remarkably advanced Egyptians and not denizens of a lost continent. For von Däniken, instead, human societies had progressed technologically through the good works of what amounts to an extraterrestrial Peace Corps.

Ancient Egypt

Are the achievements of the ancient world the product of independent invention, or diffusion from a source unrecognized by traditional science? A good historical test case can be found in the story of Egyptian civilization.

Most people are at least passingly familiar with the Egypt of the great pharaohs: the awe-inspiring pyramids, the mysterious Sphinx (Figure 10.3), the fabulous treasures of Tutankhamun, and so on. How did such a remarkable civilization develop, culminating in the construction of the Great Pyramid at Giza more than 4,500 years ago?

The mystery is amplified and exploited by von Däniken when he claims, "If we meekly accept the neat package of knowledge that Egyptologists serve

Figure 10.3   The Sphinx, at Giza, emblematic of ancient Egypt, is the product of human ingenuity and hard work. It was not built or inspired by ancient astronauts. (© Glow Images/Alamy RF)

up to us, ancient Egypt appears suddenly, and without transition with a fantastic, ready-made civilization" (1970:74). Echoing this sentiment, writer Graham Hancock (1995:135) asserts, "The archaeological evidence suggested that rather than developing slowly and painfully, as is normal with human societies, the civilization of Ancient Egypt [like that of the Olmecs] emerged *all at once and fully formed. . . .* Technological skills that should have taken hundreds or even thousands of years to evolve were brought into use almost overnight—and with no apparent antecedents whatever" (emphasis in the original).

In a sense, von Däniken and Hancock are correct; if we hypothesize that Egypt or any other civilization was transplanted full-blown from somewhere else—whether that somewhere else is simply a neighboring society, Atlantis in whatever guise, or even aliens from outer space—we should expect that it appeared quickly, fully formed, and without evolutionary antecedents. An important point needs to be brought up, however. Any claim of the sudden appearance, fully formed, of Egyptian civilization is utterly false and reflects a complete lack of familiarity with its actual development. In fact, the evidence clearly shows precisely the long and painful process that von Däniken and Hancock deny (Brewer and Teeter 1999; Brier and Houdin 2008; Clayton 1994; Lehner 1997; Kemp 1991; Romer 2012; Shaw 2000). The roots of this "sudden" civilization can be traced back more than 12,000 years, to when nomadic hunters and gatherers began to settle down along the Nile (Butzer 1976).

There is archaeological evidence for small villages along the Nile where the people were living no longer on wild but on domesticated plants and animals fully 8,000 years ago. Cultivating crops and raising animals provided a more secure, more dependable, and much more productive food base for these people. The archaeological evidence indicates clearly that in response to this, both the number of villages and the population of individual villages grew (Lamberg-Karlovsky and Sabloff 1995). After 7,000 years, the shift to agriculture was complete. The inhabitants grew wheat and barley and raised cattle, goats, pigs, and sheep. Eventually these villages began competing with each other for good farmland along the Nile.

Seen from satellite photographs, the Nile is a thin ribbon of green and blue flowing through a huge yellow desert (Figure 10.4). Clearly, the Nile is the "giver of life" to the plants, animals, and people of Egypt. As the circumscribed, precious, fertile land along the Nile became filled up between 8,000 and 6,000 years ago, competition for this rich land intensified.

Some Nile villages were quite successful and grew at the expense of others. One example is *Hierakonpolis,* a town that grew from an area of a few

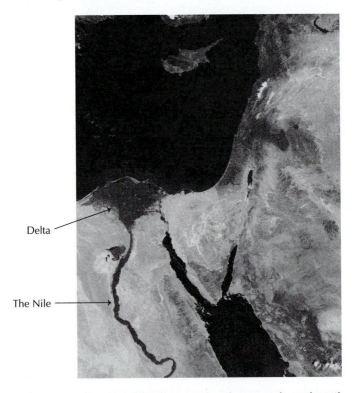

Figure 10.4   This stunning image from space makes the point clear: The Nile valley and Delta represent a clearly delineated fertile landscape surrounded by an enormous desert. (Jacques Descloitres, MODIS Land Rapid Response Team, NASA/GSFC)

acres in size to more than one hundred, and from a probable population of a few hundred to several thousand (Hoffman 1979, 1983). A local pottery industry also developed here.

Pottery manufactured in the kilns that archaeologists have discovered at Hierakonpolis can be found at sites all along the Nile. As the demand for the pottery of this successful town grew, so did the wealth of the people who owned the pottery kilns. It is here at Hierakonpolis that we first see large tombs where perhaps these wealthy pottery barons were laid to rest. Their tombs were sometimes carved out of bedrock and covered with mounds or small, crude pyramids of earth. Finely crafted goods were placed in the tombs of these men, perhaps to accompany them to the afterlife.

However, just as the small towns had previously competed for land, Hierakonpolis and other, larger villages began to compete for space and wealth. Again, based on the archaeological evidence for this period, we can conclude that power struggles leading to warfare were common after 5,200 years ago. One hundred years later, a ruler of Hierakonpolis, whose name has been passed down to us through later Egyptian writings as *Narmer,* was able through military conquest to subdue and then unify the competing villages along the Nile. Now with the wealth of not just one town but of every town along the Nile to call on, Narmer and his successors lived and were buried in increasingly sumptuous style.

Eventually, the old practice of burying a leader in a bedrock tomb with a small earthen pyramid on top was deemed insufficient for pharaohs. However, the pyramid did not appear "suddenly," as von Däniken would have us believe. The first generations of Egyptian pharaohs were buried in the royal cemetery complex located in the desert at a place call Abydos. Their tombs, called *mastabas,* are single-story square-block structures made of mud brick (O'Connor 2003). As the mastabas over the tombs got larger through time, pharaohs began to build stepped mastabas, with one block on top of another, culminating in a stepped pyramid for the pharaoh Djoser at Saqqara (Figure 10.5). Djoser ruled Egypt from 2668 to 2649 B.C. in what is referred to as the Third Dynasty of ancient Egypt.

Based on records kept by the ancient Egyptians themselves in their hieroglyphic language, we even know the name of the designer of Djoser's stepped pyramid: Imhotep. Imhotep was no mysterious intruder from Atlantis or outer space; he is a well-known historical figure in Egypt. Along with being a master architect, Imhotep became well known as a physician, priest, poet, and advisor to the pharaoh—a real "Renaissance man" 4,000 years before the Renaissance. Brier and Houdin (2008:23) call him "the Leonardo da Vinci of Egypt." Actually, it might be more appropriate to call Leonardo the Imhotep of Italy. Egyptologists have a pretty good idea who his parents were and have a short list of Egyptian towns in which he most likely was born. It should also be pointed out that statues depicting Imhotep show him as an ordinary Egyptian man dressed in plain attire; none portray him as a mysterious foreigner and, most assuredly, none show him as an alien from outer space (Figure 10.6).

Figure 10.5 Von Däniken's claims about the "sudden" appearance of the Egyptian pyramid are simply incorrect. The Egyptian pyramid was not introduced by aliens, extraterrestrial or otherwise, but evolved through several phases in Egypt itself. One of these phases is represented by the pharaoh Djoser's Step Pyramid in Saqqara, which had itself evolved from the single-tiered *mastabas*. (M. H. Feder)

Figure 10.6 This ancient Egyptian depiction of the brilliant architect, physician, priest, and poet Imhotep shows the designer of the pharaoh Djoser's pyramid, not as an Atlantean intruder or an extra-terrestrial from another star system, but as a typical Egyptian of his time. (© Erich Lessing/Art Resource, NY)

Djoser's Step Pyramid was built largely of stone, rising through six steps to a height of roughly 60 meters (197 feet—and, yes, that's taller than the Colosseum). Its base covers a rectangular footprint of more than 13,200 square meters (more than 142,000 square feet, or about 3.25 acres), and it is part of a mortuary complex of multiple structures built for the pharaoh.

The Step Pyramid literally was a monumental achievement, especially compared to the far smaller mastabas that predated it. At the same time, however, it actually was quite poorly built. The individual stone blocks that make up the bulk of the monument are small, barely 100 pounds each, crudely carved, and irregular. The individual steps of the Step Pyramid were inherently unstable and when Imhotep became aware of this, he was forced to devise a work-around in mid-build, angling the stones inward, toward the interior of the monument. The pyramid has been preserved as long as it has largely because, essentially, it leans in on itself (Brier and Houdin 2008).

Of course, the Step Pyramid's imperfection is exactly what you'd expect in the construction of what was, for the ancient Egyptians, a new kind of monument using a new raw material, stone (they previously utilized baked brick in most of their construction). It certainly isn't what you'd expect from an advanced ancient civilization, immigrants from the Lost Continent of Atlantis (Chapter 8), or technologically sophisticated extraterrestrial visitors to Earth (Chapter 9).

A number of pharaohs ruled for short periods after Djoser's death. Then, in 2613 B.C., the pharaoh Sneferu ascended to the throne. He initiated construction of his funerary monument to the south of Saqqara at a place called Meidum (Perez-Accino 2003b). Sneferu's monument was begun as another stepped pyramid, this time with seven distinct platforms. During construction, however, Sneferu decided to alter the form of the pyramid, first adding an eighth platform and then deciding to change the exterior to the shape we are more familiar with today, with flat, triangular faces leading to a common apex at the top, which was intended to rise to a height of 92 meters (302 feet). The work was only partially completed when the project was abandoned as a result of the king's decision to move his funerary monument to Dashur, north of Meidum and closer to Saqqara. The Meidum pyramid ultimately was stripped of much of its polished exterior casing stone for recycling in other construction projects. Today it looks like an abandoned and then cannibalized construction site—which is what it is (Figure 10.7, top). As Egyptologist Mark Lehner (1997) characterizes it, though never completed, Meidum marks the transition between stepped and true pyramids in Egypt.

At Dashur, Sneferu next commanded the construction of a geometrically true pyramid. The faces of individual platforms of Egyptian stepped pyramids were sloped at between 72 and 78 degrees. With the technology and raw materials utilized, this slope would have been too steep in a non-stepped pyramid, resulting in an inherently unstable structure. Construction of Sneferu's pyramid at Dashur was commenced with its surfaces sloped at only about 54.5 degrees. That was smart, but the builders did something not-so-smart in positioning the pyramid. Three of the monument's corners rested on bedrock, which provided a solid, immovable foundation for the massive weight of the structure. That was good. What wasn't good was the fact that the fourth corner was positioned over a gravel deposit. As construction proceeded, the gravel began to compact under the enormous weight of the stone courses above it. This resulted in instability and cracking as that one corner settled into the softer gravel beneath it while the other corners remained firm. To compound the problem, as the building continued to settle irregularly, the burial chamber built within the structure began to deform, its walls twisting awkwardly. In an inelegant attempt to salvage the room, the builders wedged in huge cedar logs at the top, hoping to keep the ceiling from collapsing. That worked only marginally well. Clearly the project was a mess, wholly unacceptable as the pharaoh's final resting place (Brier and Houdin 2008).

Rather than abandon the project altogether, the architects devised a quick and dirty way to finish and then walk away from it. They decreased the angle of the pyramid's faces in mid-build from 54.5 to 43.5 degrees, and less material was therefore needed to reach the now lowered apex. This strategy resulted in a monument that deserves its name: the Bent Pyramid for the bend produced by changing the angle of its faces in the middle of construction (Figure 10.7, bottom).

By diminishing the size, the builders diminished the possibility that the strain on the side built on gravel would lead to utter collapse which would have been even more embarrassing than a funny-looking pyramid. Like the Step Pyramid and the Collapsed Pyramid before it, the Bent Pyramid clearly reflects a process of trial and error (plenty of errors, in fact) that characterize the evolution of the Egyptian pyramids. It was an entirely human and entirely predictable process, again without any justification for the suggestion that Atlanteans or extraterrestrials were involved, unless they too were challenged by the learning curve for piling up big stones in a pyramidal form.

Finally, by about 2589 B.C., Sneferu's builders got it right, constructing an entire, true pyramid (Figure 10.8). They began construction of this monument at a 43-degree angle, and maintained that slope throughout. The Red, or North, Pyramid that resulted fits our conception of what an Egyptian pyramid should look like, with four flat, triangular faces joined at an apex, here rising to a stunning 105 meters (345 feet).

These pyramids are all remarkable achievements, wonderful examples of the architectural, mathematical, engineering, and organizational skills of ancient Egyptians. But, understand, the pyramids were not an abrupt or overnight accomplishment. The timeline of Egyptian pyramid building shows that it was only through what amounts to four generations of pyramid building and close to a century of trial and error, attempt and mistake, challenge and solution, that the architects and engineers of ancient Egypt were able to perfect their craft.

Figure 10.7 Errors and false starts in construction like those exhibited in the Collapsed Pyramid at Meidum (**top**); and shoddy construction and work-arounds like those seen in the Bent Pyramid at Dashur (**bottom**), reflect the very human process that characterizes the evolution of Egyptian pyramid-building technology. Problems like these contradict any assertion that pyramid building arrived fully formed in Egypt from an outside superhuman source like ancient astronauts. (M. H. Feder)

Figure 10.8   The Red Pyramid was constructed after the Collapsed and Bent Pyramids. Mistakes made in those projects and the lessons learned led to the more standard appearance—and greater durability—of the Red Pyramid. (M. H. Feder)

Consider the evolution of the pyramids as a function of their height, beginning with the oldest of the monuments. Djoser's Step Pyramid, finished in 2649 B.C., is about 60 meters (197 feet) high. The next pyramid in the chronology, Sneferu's first attempt—the Collapsed Pyramid—was designed to stand 92 meters (302 feet) tall, a 53 percent jump in height compared to Djoser's pyramid. As we have seen, it was a failure, too big a jump, perhaps, over the step pyramid, and never completed. Sneferu's next try, the Bent Pyramid, was another less-than-sterling success. It had a planned height of 128.5 meters (421.6 feet). This would have been a 40 percent rise in height over the Collapsed Pyramid. Its actual finished height was considerably less because, as noted, its architects were forced to decrease the angle of its rise midway through construction. The Bent Pyramid, nevertheless, is a still impressive 105 meters (344.5 feet) high, a jump of about 14 percent over the Collapsed Pyramid. Sneferu's final construction, the Red Pyramid, is about the same height as the Bent Pyramid, exhibiting no growth at all in pyramid size. By the way, pyramid workers sometimes left graffiti on pyramid blocks. Rather conveniently, they occasionally included dates in the written messages they left behind, unintentionally recording when they had moved the marked stones into place. Using a sequence of dates found on stone blocks in the Red Pyramid, it has been calculated that it took about eleven years to build the monument (Brier and Houdin 2008:61).

Figure 10.9   The three spectacular pyramids at Giza represent the pinnacle of Egyptian pyramid-building technology. They clearly reflect the end point along a continuum of technological refinement with the process of trial and error evident in the structures that preceded them. The pyramids at Giza are the only remaining monuments of the original "seven wonders of the world." (PhotoLink/Getty Images)

Perfection of the craft of pyramid building occurred subsequently in the burial monument of the pharaoh Khufu, whose pyramid can be found north of Dashur, at Giza (Figure 10.9; Perez-Accino 2003a). Finished in 2566 B.C., Khufu's pyramid is one of the Giza triad of monuments (the other two are the pyramids of Khufu's son Khafre and grandson Menkaure). Khufu's is the largest, a stupendous 146.6 meters (481 feet) high, a 40 percent jump in height compared to the previous successful monument, his father Sneferu's Red Pyramid. Khufu's was the tallest pyramid ever built in ancient Egypt and, rather remarkably, was the tallest human-made structure in the world until the construction of the Washington Monument and the Eiffel Tower in the 1880s (even so, it cannot be seen from the moon with the naked eye, as one urban legend would have you believe). Based on the eleven-year estimate for the Red Pyramid, it's calculated that Khufu's much larger burial monument likely took about twenty years to complete (Brier and Houdin 2008:60).

The pattern reflected in the timeline of pyramid construction in ancient Egypt is clearly evolutionary, showing the step-by-step development of the architectural form by Egyptians—as well as one-up-manship by each subsequent pharaoh as he tried to outdo his predecessor—over the course of more than eight decades, from Djoser's stepped pyramid in 2649 B.C. to Khufu's masterpiece completed in 2566 B.C. The progression shown in the archaeological and historical records is unlike anything that would be expected if

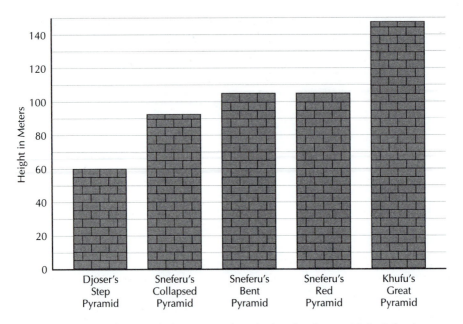

Figure 10.10   This histogram shows growth in the height of pyramids built by the ancient Egyptians from the construction of Djoser's Step Pyramid through Khufu's Great Pyramid more than eighty years later. The pattern shown here of slowly increasing height is a clear indication of the evolutionary development of pyramid-building technology within Egypt and contradicts any notion that pyramid building was introduced by a more advanced intelligence, whether terrestrial or extraterrestrial in origin.

pyramid building had been developed somewhere else and then introduced into Egypt in its perfected form (Figure 10.10). I might add that I would be quite reluctant to get into the spaceship of an extraterrestrial alien civilization that took eighty years to figure out how to pile up large stones in a gigantic pyramid shape. The evidence is unequivocal; pyramid construction was developed over time in Egypt by Egyptians. It was not introduced by anyone from Atlantis, outer space, or anywhere else.

Unfortunately, everybody in ancient Egypt knew that the pyramids contained great wealth, and most were broken into soon after the pharaoh was laid to rest. After building about 118 of them, the Egyptians gave up pyramid building completely and buried pharaohs underground, where their tombs might be better hidden and protected.

Remember, in science we propose a hypothesis to explain something, we deduce those things that must also be true if our hypothesis is true, and then we do further research to determine if our deduced implications can be verified. Only then can we say that our hypothesis is upheld. Here, our hypothesis is that the ancient Egyptians built the pyramids using their own skill, intelligence, ingenuity, and labor. We can deduce that if this were true, then we should find archaeological evidence for the slow development of these skills and abilities through time.

This is precisely what we have found. Egyptian civilization evolved not "suddenly" but after some 12,000 years of development marked by

- The adoption of agriculture
- Increasing village size
- Intervillage competition
- Village differentiation
- Concentration of wealth
- Increase in tomb size
- Consolidation under a single leader or pharaoh
- Obvious trials and errors in the development of the pyramids as monuments to their dead kings

The Egyptians kept accurate historical records of their kings. The so-called Royal Canon of Turin contains the names of about three hundred pharaohs (Kemp 1991:23). It is a detailed and virtually complete listing of Egyptian rulers for the first part of their history, providing the duration of their reigns, sometimes to the exact numbers of years, months, and even days. This list traces Egyptian kingship for 958 years, all the way back to Narmer. Not surprisingly, there's not a single Atlantean or extraterrestrial in the bunch; it is, instead, a clearly connected family lineage of descent from father to son, pharaoh to pharaoh.

Tutankhamun

I don't know particularly much about insurance, but I do know from experience that insurance companies set their rates at least in part on the basis of statistics. For example, we were charged an absurdly high premium for automobile insurance for our teenaged sons because they were members of a demographic category—teenage boys—statistically far more likely than other groups to take risks, drive fast, drive stupidly, and get into accidents.

It seems reasonable that insurance companies, who are, after all, not in business to lose money, base their rates on the statistical histories of the groups they insure. That being the case, one might assume that archaeologists are paying huge sums for their medical and life insurance premiums. After all, don't archaeologists, especially Egyptologists, regularly break into ancient tombs protected by deadly curses whereupon they (1) are driven insane, (2) spend the rest of their blighted lives on life support, or (3) immediately and mysteriously drop dead?

Guess what? Insurance companies charge archaeologists not a penny more than anybody else for medical or life insurance. Apparently, insurance adjusters do not believe that archaeologists are any more likely than other cohorts in the population to be afflicted by a pharaoh's—or anybody else's—curse.

Okay, I am lamely attempting to be cute here, but the fact is, insurance adjusters are not stupid. If there really were effective curses that killed archaeologists, it would be clear statistically and our insurance premiums would be astronomical. Medical and life insurance adjusters don't charge archaeologists any more to insure their health and their lives, because there are no such things as effective curses on the ancient tombs we discover, excavate, and investigate.

Where then does the notion of cursed tombs come from? The best known of these mythological curses was one supposedly placed on the tomb of Egyptian pharaoh Tutankhamun. It might seem an insurmountable problem to those who spread the tale of Tut's curse that, in actual fact, there was no such curse, effective or otherwise, on his tomb (Tyldesley 2012). We can argue about whether or not entering Tut's tomb was bad for your health, but in fact there was no curse—no dire hieroglyphic warning of the consequences of despoiling the pharaoh's final resting place etched into the tomb's portal; no threat of a horrible fate to those who dared to enter his burial chamber; not even a pitiful, plaintive plea to leave the dead at rest; nothing (Figure 10.11). Nevertheless, the myth of the terrible consequences of Tut's nonexistent curse is astonishingly popular.

The real story of Tutankhamun is remarkable, filled with palace intrigue, power struggles, even mysterious deaths, and is far more interesting than any mythological curse. Tut himself is one of those historical characters who fits the modern sarcastic remark; he is well known

Figure 10.11 An iconic scene in Egyptology—archaeologists gazing in wonder into the freshly opened tomb of pharaoh Tutankhamun. Howard Carter is shown crouching, his face barely visible in the center of the photograph. (© Hulton-Deutsch Collection/ Corbis)

because he is famous. Tut's father, the pharaoh Akhenaten, is a far more significant historical figure, having led a revolution against the powerful priests of ancient Egypt in the so-called Amarna Revolt. Akhenaten displaced the traditional Egyptian pantheon, perhaps because the priests who represented these gods on earth were getting too rich and too powerful. Akhenaten also replaced the traditionally important gods, instituting the worship of a single, previously minor deity, Aten, the god of the disk of the sun.

One can imagine that this did not make Akhenaten particularly popular among the priests of the other gods. In fact, his death in 1334 B.C. may have been the result of an assassination plot sponsored by these priests in their attempt to wrest power back from the pharaoh. When Akhenaten's son, then called Tutankhaten, ascended to the throne, he was only nine years old. Not long after the death of his father, Tutankhaten had his name changed to Tutankhamun, thereby eliminating reference to Aten and reestablishing his loyalty to Amun, one of the gods Akhenaten had replaced and the most powerful in the Egyptian pantheon.

Only a child, Tutankhamun served as little more than a figurehead ruler for ten years and then, in 1325 B.C., he too died. His death at so young an age has long raised the suspicion that, like his father, he was killed in a power struggle over the throne (King and Cooper 2004). In a project funded by the National Geographic Society, researchers conducted a high-tech postmortem on Tut's mummified body in 2005 in an attempt to verify the cause of his death. A CT scan (computed tomography; the same kind of scan used in modern hospitals to peek inside a living person's body in the search for illness) showed that he had been a healthy and well-fed young man and revealed nothing to suggest a violent death (Handwerk 2005). There was no evidence of foul play. Some of the researchers believe a broken left thigh bone seen in the scan (perhaps the result of a bad fall) may have pierced Tut's skin, and the open wound resulted in a massive infection that caused his death (Quilici 2005).

Tut was not an important pharaoh; he fought no great battles, negotiated no significant treaties, and undertook no impressive construction projects. He was, in the end, only a boy who got caught up in historical, religious, and political forces that he played no role in shaping and of which he may have been only vaguely aware. He died, tragically, a teenager and was buried in a tomb meant for someone of lesser rank; his demise was so sudden, there wasn't even time to build him a final resting place appropriate for a pharaoh (Figure 10.12). And, in the biggest insult of all to a pharaoh, he was essentially forgotten, a barely remembered "boy king" whose sad, short life was not to be exalted by history. Of course, the irony here is that precisely because he was unimportant and largely forgotten, his tomb remained unplundered, not subject to the depredations of those who regularly raided the tombs of important rulers. When Tut's tomb was discovered in 1924 by Egyptologist Howard Carter, it was largely intact, drew the attention of the

Figure 10.12   A view of Egyptian pharaoh Tutankhamun's sarcophagus. He was only nineteen years old when he died, the result, in all likelihood, of an accident and not murder. (© Royalty-Free/Corbis)

world, and inspired the public's fascination with ancient Egypt, a fascination that continues unabated to this day.

But the simple fact is that no curse had been written anywhere in or around Tut's tomb. The myth of not just a curse but an effective, working, deadly curse that actually killed people got started after the wealthy benefactor who funded the excavation, Lord Carnarvon, died four months after the tomb was opened. It was no great shock at the time; he was old and weak, and he was sick even before the tomb was discovered. As much as he wished to be there to share in the glory, a sickly Carnarvon had no business making an arduous trip to Egypt to witness the opening of the tomb that his money helped discover. Not surprisingly, he fell ill, and, after additionally suffering a serious insect bite that became infected, he died. Assertions about the lights going out in Cairo at the moment of his death mean little, as electrical service was entirely unpredictable there and failed regularly. Similarly, tales about Carnarvon's dog's death back in England simultaneous with the death of his master are irrelevant and unverifiable.

But, the curse purveyors maintain, a large number of people did die after the tomb was opened, and their deaths cannot be so easily dismissed. In actual fact, however, the allegation that the tomb was a death trap can be disproved with the kinds of statistics insurance adjusters regularly rely on. For example, the twenty-three people most intimately involved with the opening of the tomb, including Howard Carter (director of excavations), as well as other archaeologists, photographers, guards, and the like, lived an average of twenty-four years (yes, *years*) after the opening of the tomb, and their average age of death was seventy-three (all data from Hoggart and Hutchinson 1995). Carnarvon's daughter, who was with her father when the tomb was first entered, lived for another fifty-seven years, and Howard Carter, the man who discovered the tomb and who would have been the most obvious target of a curse, lived for sixteen more years after entering the tomb—during which time he analyzed and wrote about the splendid objects found there. For the best deconstruction of the ostensible curse, check out Joyce Tyldesley's wonderful book, *Tutankhamen: The Search for an Egyptian King* (2012). As Tyldesley points out, it was a novelist, Marie Corelli, who first claimed reading: "Death comes on wings to he who enters the tomb of the pharaoh," in an ancient book, but there was no such curse anywhere near or in Tut's tomb.

Recognizing that the longevity of the tomb's discoverer and chief excavator seems the clearest evidence against the existence of a curse, one especially silly television "documentary" went so far as to assert that, though he lived a long life, Howard Carter actually was the individual most sorely afflicted, having been "cursed" to spend the rest of his life examining the objects found in Tut's tomb. Imagine that: an archaeologist "cursed" to spend his life analyzing, discussing, and writing about the most spectacular archaeological discovery of the twentieth century. Poor Howard! Where do I sign up for a curse like that?

Pyramids in Bosnia?

The charismatic archaeologist, expedition leader, project director, fundraiser, and author, Semir Osmanagic (in his day job, he's a metalwork contractor in Houston, Texas), has labeled the features the "Pyramid of the Sun," the "Pyramid of the Moon," the "Pyramid of the Dragon," the "Pyramid of Love," and the "Temple of Earth" (Bohannon 2006; Kampschror 2006). These pyramids and temples are not exactly where you might expect them to be. They're not located in Egypt or Mesoamerica, for instance. They are, instead, in Bosnia, a small eastern European republic, until recently wracked by warfare and genocide, where an uncertain peace is still maintained by United Nations troops. The largest feature, the Pyramid of the Sun, is raised to a stupendous 360 meters—nearly 1,200 feet, or two-and-a-half times the height of Khufu's pyramid, presumed by conservative archaeologists to be the tallest pyramid in the ancient world (Figure 10.13). You will remember that Khufu's pyramid was built about 4,570 years ago, the culmination of nearly 100 years of pyramid construction. Well, it's a real youngster compared to its Bosnian counterparts, which Osmanagic asserts are 12,500 years old, predating the cream of Egyptian construction by nearly 8,000 years.

Figure 10.13 Located in Bosnia, about 30 kilometers (19 miles) from Sarajevo, these hills have spawned an entire alternative archaeology industry. Some of the features have been interpreted as being, not naturally configured, but enormous, artificial pyramids, more than two-and-a-half times the size of the largest Egyptian pyramid and more than twice as ancient. No actual archaeological or geological evidence has yet been presented that supports this remarkable interpretation. (© AP photo/Hidajet Delic)

Osmanagic has been nothing if not a good salesman concerning the Bosnian pyramids. Local geologists have long been aware of the hills overlooking the town of Visoko, about 30 kilometers (a little less than 19 miles) north of Sarajevo, the city that hosted the 1984 Winter Olympics. The so-called pyramids are, in fact, natural landscape features, angular eminences that appear pyramidal only from certain angles. The angular appearance of segments of the hills is the product of well-known geological processes and resulting features, described by Bosnian geologist Stjepan Coric as "fractured chunks of sediment called breccia, the remains of a 7-million-year-old lakebed that was thrust up by natural forces" (as cited in Bohannon 2006).

Remember the misidentification of a natural rock formation off the coast of Bimini as an Atlantean road or wall by Atlantis supporters (Chapter 8)? Well, here we go again. Many entirely natural geological features are patterned and might appear to the untrained eye to be artificial. Take a look at Figure 10.14. Compare it to the "pyramid" in Figure 10.13. Is this the Bosnian Pyramid of the Moon from another angle? Or another Bosnian pyramid altogether? Well, no, not unless they taught the natives of Utah to build pyramids. Figure 10.14 is a photograph I took of an entirely natural mountain

Figure 10.14 Looking every bit as pyramidal as the Bosnian "Pyramid of the Moon," this entirely natural mountain is located in Nine Mile Canyon, Utah. Geological processes commonly produce patterned, symmetrical features like these. Neither this mountain, nor the one depicted in Figure 10.13, were the result of human labor. (K. Feder)

located in Nine Mile Canyon in Utah. You can find mountains like it all over the world and they are the product of well-understood geological processes.

Though Osmanagic has been conducting excavations on the hills for about four years, it is telling that not a single tool dating to the ostensible construction of the ostensible pyramids has been found—no sleds, no mallets, no copper chisels, no measuring devices, none of the kinds of stuff found in ancient Egypt, for example, and already mentioned in this chapter. Neither have carbon samples been forthcoming that might be used to date the period of supposed pyramid construction.

There are two broader points to be made here about the Bosnian pyramids and the excitement they have generated specifically in Bosnia. First, it is important to point out that to prove that the Bosnian pyramids are not natural geological features but, instead, the product of human labor, there must be substantial archaeological evidence in the region for the infrastructure necessary for their construction. Pyramids don't build themselves. As pointed out in the FAQs in this chapter, Egyptologists have found the remnants of the dormitories in which pyramid builders were housed, the bakeries in which their bread was baked, food remains from their meals, and even the cemeteries in which they were buried. We should expect no less in Bosnia. It is not terribly surprising that Osmanagic, who asserts that the technology used to build the pyramids of the Maya was derived from ancient Atlantis and Lemuria, isn't aware of standard archaeological reasoning (Bohannon 2006).

The second point consists of a reminder of the discussion in the first chapter in this book about the motives for an archaeological hoax, along with the discussion in Chapter 3 of the rules for a successful one. Osmanagic's claim of a super-ancient, super-civilization in ancient Bosnia is restoring pride among a people who can use some good news for a change (Pruitt 2012). Along with creating a bit of a tourist industry with the Sun Pyramid Motel, pyramid T-shirts, pyramid slippers, and pyramid brandy (Kampschror 2006), "To believe in the pyramids has become synonymous with patriotism" (as stated by Zilka Kujundzic-Vejzagic, the Bosnian National Museum's expert on prehistoric archaeology, as quoted in Bohannon 2006:1718). Apparently, local archaeologists who have questioned the reality of the pyramids have been threatened, and a local official has proposed that these skeptics be prevented from conducting any archaeological research and even have their academic degrees revoked (Bohannon 2006)! "Give the people what they want" was one of the rules I enumerated for a successful archaeological hoax in Chapter 3. I fear that Osmanagic is doing precisely this.

Current Perspectives: How Did They Build the Pyramids?

Any building project, ancient or modern, no matter how large, difficult, impressive, or even seemingly impossible, ultimately involves the coordinated execution of a large number of smaller jobs that are individually achievable. The pyramids, including the largest, are, after all, just very impressive construction projects that, when broken down into their component tasks, certainly were within the capabilities of a large workforce laboring for long stretches of time.

Broken down most simply, pyramid construction involved several steps, including quarrying the rock, mostly soft limestone, that made up most of the structure; preparing the work site by producing a flat surface on which to construct the pyramid; moving the quarried stone to the work site; shaping the building materials (in the case of Khufu's pyramid, more than 2.3 million blocks of limestone) into their desired final form; moving the building materials into place (both horizontally and vertically) to produce the final form of the pyramid; and, finally, carving rooms, chambers, passageways, and tunnels from the artificial mountain of pyramid blocks.

Though we cannot travel back through time and actually watch as a pyramid project progresses, the Egyptians themselves left a substantial body of evidence indicating how the component steps in the undertaking were carried out. For example, the limestone quarry from which much of the material used in the construction of the Great Pyramid was extracted has been located and studied by Egyptologists. Just like abandoned quarries of a more recent vintage—for example, the nineteenth-century sandstone quarries of Connecticut that produced building materials for all of those "brownstone"

Figure 10.15   Photograph taken from inside the Giza limestone quarry from which most of the blocks making up the Great Pyramid were extracted. In the background can be seen the straight, flat wall of the quarry face. Seen in the foreground, the pattern of squares separated by a gridwork of channels reflects the manner of stone block extraction employed by the Egyptians. Using simple copper tools, channels were cut at right angles to isolate cubes of limestone that constituted much of the raw material of pyramid construction. (Courtesy Frank Roy)

buildings in New York City—the imprint of the quarriers in ancient Egyptian quarries is obvious in the form of channels, grooves, trenches, and other tool marks left in the face of the exposed rock (Figure 10.15).

Today, the Khufu quarry is a huge gash about 30 meters (almost 100 feet) deep from which, it has been estimated, the Egyptians extracted more than 2.75 million cubic meters (more than 97 million cubic feet) of limestone (Jackson and Stamp 2003:50). By no small coincidence, the volume of the Great Pyramid is about 2.6 million cubic meters (91 million cubic feet). The location of the pyramid project was selected, almost certainly, with the location of the source of building materials in mind; the Great Pyramid is positioned just 300 meters (1,000 feet) away from the quarry. Copper chisels used in quarrying and shaping stone as well as wooden mallets used to hammer on the chisels have been found, providing additional evidence of how the stone was extracted. Also, archaeologists have recovered a set of perfectly preserved measuring tools in the tomb of an architect at Deir el Medina; an examination of these tools indicates that Egyptians would have been perfectly capable of accurately measuring the quarried stones for their fit into the scheme of the pyramid.

The methods used by ancient Egyptians to move the pyramid stones are evidenced in a number of ways (Arnold 1991). The stones themselves sometimes exhibit "handling bosses"—extra ridges or knobs left on surfaces that wouldn't be visible on the finished structure—used to facilitate the attachment of a rope. Beyond this, some stones exhibit carved grooves and sockets to accommodate the positioning of a lever. Wooden pulley wheels and even some of the rope have been found, further indicating how Egyptians solved the problems presented by moving large, heavy stones.

Archaeologists have also found wooden sleds that were used to facilitate the transport of heavy blocks of stone and even finished sculptures. The sleds were moved along on flat surfaces, ramps, and maybe even trackways of "sleepers," flat slabs of wood laid in the ground perpendicular to the direction of sled movement. To reduce friction and ease movement, surfaces of the sleepers were lubricated with vegetable oil or even just water. We are fairly certain that this was at least one common way in which large, heavy blocks were moved because the Egyptians themselves recorded these activities in artistic form. For example, a nearly 3,900-year-old wall painting in the tomb of Djehutihotep depicts the movement of an enormous statue of this regional leader that, based on its size relative to the size of the men hauling it, is more than 20 feet (6 meters) tall (Figure 10.16). The statue, which we know weighed more than 52,000 kilograms (about 58 tons), is tied down to a sled; and 172 men set out in four rows of forty-two men each are pulling it (it is difficult to see in the artist's re-creation of the painting in Figure 10.16,

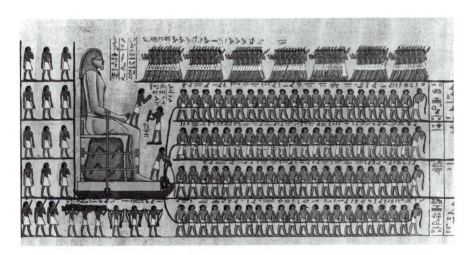

Figure 10.16   Von Däniken (Chapter 9) cannot conceive how the ancient Egyptians were able to build pyramids and move the enormous stone blocks and statues that are a part of the archaeological record of their civilization. But the ancient Egyptians themselves left records, like this image copied from a wall panel, of how they did it. Here, a crew of 172 men pull ropes attached to a sled on which sits a statue more than 20 feet (6 meters) tall. A worker on the sled pours a lubricant—perhaps an oil—onto the ground in front of the sled. (K. Feder)

but each man in the image has another man right behind him) (Arnold 1991:61). Along with other workers shown around the statue, one additional worker is shown standing on the sled, emptying the contents of a jar, clearly lubricating the ground in front of the statue.

Though the Egyptians did not leave behind texts detailing the methods used in their stonework, they did leave behind artistic depictions that are the equivalent of eyewitness accounts of the preparation of the surfaces of their pyramid-building stones through the use of wooden mallets, metal chisels, and a measuring tool called a boning rod to keep the chiseled surface flat (Figure 10.17a). Other artwork shows them using staging and small polishing stones to produce the finished surface of a large statue of a nobleman (Figure 10.17b). In other words, we know how the Egyptians accomplished some of their astonishing stonework because they told us in their artistic representations of that work.

So we have clear evidence of where and how the Egyptians quarried stone, how they moved the stone to the building site, and how they smoothed and polished the stone to give it its finished appearance. The greatest challenge awaited them at the site itself, in having to raise the stones, to place course upon course, reaching up to a height of 50, or 100, or even nearly 150 meters (almost 500 feet) in the case of the apex of Khufu's pyramid. How did the ancient Egyptians accomplish this remarkable feat? We know with certainty that they built ramps made of rubble, and in some cases tracked those ramps with sleepers, to ease the movement upward of large stones attached to sleds. In some cases the ramps may have climbed the pyramid directly as it was built; at Meidum, a large, broad depression is visible on the surface of a portion of what's left of the collapsed pyramid, most likely where a ramp had been attached before it was dismantled (Arnold 1991:83). In other cases, a ramp may have been built along one face of the pyramid in the form of a series of switchbacks or even as a continuous corkscrew along all four faces of the pyramid, spiraling its way to the top (Figure 10.18).

In a recent analysis, French architect Jean-Pierre Houdin, with the assistance of his engineering father Henri, suggests that the spiraling ramp was actually built on the inside of Khufu's pyramid (Brier and Houdin 2008). In Houdin's view, for the first 60 meters (200 feet) of pyramid height (that's about the height of Djoser's Step Pyramid), a straight-run ramp works well to raise the stone blocks (see Figure 10.18, left). Such a ramp would have been of reasonable size with a slope of about eight degrees at its steepest, gentle enough to facilitate hauling up the average 2.5-ton (2,300 kilogram) pyramid block. Once the pyramid base exceeded 200 feet (60 meters) in height, however, the angle of the existing ramp would have needed to be raised, making it too steep to easily haul up the blocks. One option would have been to increase the length of the ramp to keep the slope less than eight degrees, but by the time you reach the top of the pyramid, the ramp would have been more than a mile long to maintain that angle, a construction project at least as massive as the pyramid itself.

a

b

Figure 10.17 The methods and tools used by the ancient Egyptians to move and sculpt stone was sometimes revealed to us by the Egyptians themselves in the form of drawings and paintings depicting the process. Workers are shown here producing a smooth flat surface with a chisel and a leveling device called a boning rod (**a**) Perched on scaffolding; another group of workers is depicted using a brush, a polishing stone, and a small chisel, applying the finishing touches to the statue of a man (**b**). Both images are from the tomb of the Rekhmira, an Egyptian official. (© The Metropolitan Museum of Art/Art Resource, NY)

If Houdin is correct, the Egyptians devised a simple, elegant, and brilliant solution by internalizing the ramp, spiraling it up inside the pyramid during construction. In other words, rather than a separate, monumental construction project, the ramp, essentially, is built as part of the pyramid. By keeping the ramp inside the pyramid, the architects and engineers could

Figure 10.18   Three different conceptions of how ramps may have been built by ancient Egyptians to facilitate raising courses of pyramid blocks: a steeply inclined direct ramp; a series of switchbacks; a ramp that corkscrews around the four faces of the pyramid. There is direct evidence of such construction ramps having been built by ancient Egyptians.

keep a careful eye on the pyramid's corners as the building rose, maintaining their angles precisely, an impossible task had there been a separate ramp spiraling along the exterior of the pyramid.

While no one has yet been able to peer directly into Khufu's pyramid to look for remnants of an interior ramp, a microgravimetry survey—a form of remote sensing used to look into the interior of the Great Pyramid—conducted back in the 1980s showed a peculiar and then seemingly inexplicable pattern. The survey imaging clearly showed, a continuous spiral of lower density than in the surrounding pyramid stones. This pattern may now be explained by Houdin's hypothesis; the spiral of lower density represents the passageway that now is a remnant of the internal ramp (Figure 10.19).

Figure 10.19   A computer-generated, transparent image of the Great Pyramid, showing the construction by use of an internal ramp. Rather than being an additional structure that would need to be taken down when the pyramid was complete, the internal ramp is doubly efficient, providing a way in which pyramid blocks could be raised and then becoming a part of the internal structure of the pyramid. (Courtesy J-P Houdin/Dassault Systemes)

Houdin's internal ramp, derived just by using his imagination, remarkably ends up matching evidence separately found by researchers unaffiliated with Houdin through their application of microgravimetrics. The correspondence between Houdin's hypothesis and the microgravimetry survey images has been described in this way: "it was as if someone had photographed their theory" (Brier and Houdin 2008:133), years before the theory existed. It's spectacular when you achieve that kind of confirmation in the scientific process. Working with Houdin, Dassault Systemes has created an amazing three-dimensional simulation of the interior ramp hypothesis (Figure 10.20)

Figure 10.20 The microgravimetric image of the Great Pyramid, produced in 1986 by the French company EDF. Years before architect Jean-Pierre Houdin proposed his internal ramp hypothesis—and years before its existence became known to Houdin—the image showed lower density areas within the pyramid, spiraling up the interior. This image supported Houdin's hypothesis even before he came up with it. (Courtesy EDF)

(http://khufu.3ds.com/introduction/). It will choke a computer with a slow processor, but it's certainly worth a look.

An episode of the *Nova* science series on PBS (titled "This Old Pyramid") put many elements of ancient Egyptian pyramid construction to the test. Using traditional techniques to quarry, transport, and raise the stones, an archaeologist, a Massachusetts stonemason, a sculptor, and a crew of Egyptian laborers were able to reproduce a small-scale pyramid over the course of about three weeks. Though not perfect—and not without disagreements erupting among the participants about the best way to proceed—the mini-pyramid the team constructed was a successful test of many of the individual elements of pyramid construction.

Stuart Kirkman Weir (1996) has calculated that a workforce of about 10,000 people, laboring for the entirety of Khufu's twenty-eight-year reign, could have constructed his burial tomb, the largest pyramid in Egypt. That is an enormous workforce, and, to be sure, the pyramid of Khufu was built on such a gigantic scale that it is easy to lose track of the individual human in the construction equation. We need always to remind ourselves, however, that the pyramids were built by individual people working together in a coordinated way toward a common goal.

The best example of this was revealed when explorer Howard Vyse entered Khufu's pyramid in 1837. Vyse was fascinated by the ceiling of the so-called King's Chamber located in the heart of the monument's interior. The roof of the chamber consists of nine huge granite slabs, above which—Vyse knew from the work of previous investigators—was a mysterious chamber. From the interior of that chamber, Vyse detected even more open space above its ceiling. He smashed his way through and found a stack of four more small chambers built, one on top of the other, apparently to relieve the incredible stresses produced by the enormous weight of the overlying limestone. It was in the highest of those chambers that the human factor in the construction of the Great Pyramid was most poignantly exposed. There on the ceiling was a written message more than 4,500 years old left by the workers, the real people who actually built the pyramid: "We did this with pride in the name of our great King Khnum-Khuf," the formal name of the pharaoh Khufu (Jackson and Stamp 2003:78). In that short message, the utter humanness of the gigantic project is revealed: real people responding to the enormous challenges laid out before them, constructing an eternal resting place for the spirit of a real person who ruled over a real nation. The genuine discoveries of archaeology, like that small moment frozen in time when an exhausted but exultant worker left a message of pride and accomplishment in a sealed chamber he could not have imagined would ever be seen again, are more wonderful than any of those the purveyors of nonsense about the human past would like you to believe.

FREQUENTLY ASKED QUESTIONS

1. Were the pyramids built by slaves?

If you have read the book of Exodus in the Old Testament of the Bible or seen the Hollywood epic *The Ten Commandments* (with no less a figure than Charlton Heston playing Moses), you probably have the impression that the pyramids were built by a large population of mistreated, oppressed, and expendable slaves. It turns out that this common conception is incorrect. There are no written records in Egypt that support this notion: no mention of the use of slaves in pyramid building and no hieroglyphic "spreadsheets" keeping track of an enslaved workforce listing, for example, the number of slaves, where they came from, their skill levels, ages, or names (such listings were, in fact, standard operating procedure in the American South before the Civil War). Egyptologist Mark Lehner has directed the excavation of a pyramid-worker community located on the Giza Plateau near the pyramids of Khufu, Khafre, and Menkare (see Figure 10.9). The worker's community at Giza doesn't look like a slave compound, but, rather, a series of rather comfortable dormitories. Further, Lehner found food remains that indicate that pyramid-workers were eating better than nearly everybody else in Egypt; beef, sheep, and goat—all prime cuts taken from healthy animals—were on the workers' menus to a far greater extent than what has been found in most ancient Egyptian communities (Shaw 2003:49). Even nearby cemeteries, burial sites for the workers who died during their labors, reflect a level of respect and care in death that would be highly unlikely had they been slaves (Pérez-Accino 2003c; Shaw 2003). Apparently, it was considered by many a privilege to help build and maintain the eternal home of the dead pharaoh's spirit, and workers drafted into service could expect a better diet and an elevated social status for their work for the king's spirit.

2. Even if there wasn't one on Tut's tomb, weren't there real "curses" on some Egyptian tombs?

Yes, actually there were inscribed curses on some Egyptian tombs intended to scare away anyone who might defile the burial in an attempt to obtain precious grave goods. Some of the curses are actually very creative and dramatic. Here are a handful of actual curses threatening what would happen to whosoever might enter the tomb:

- He shall die from hunger and thirst (on a statue of Herihor, High Priest of Amun, Dyn. 20–21).
- He shall have no heir (inscription of Tuthmosis I, Dyn. 18).
- His years shall be diminished (on a statue of Monthuemhat, Dyn. 25–26).

- His estate shall belong to the fire, and his house shall belong to the consuming flame . . .

- His relatives shall detest him (tomb of Tefib, Dyn. 9–10).

- He shall be miserable and persecuted (tomb of Penniut, Dyn. 20).

- His face shall be spat at (El-Hasaia tomb, Dyn. 26).

- A donkey shall violate him, a donkey shall violate his wife (Deir el-Bahri Graffito No. 11, Dyn. 20).

I'll assume, like me, you find the final curse particularly disturbing. Shudder.

3. *Is it true that even with our modern technology, we could not build the Great Pyramid?*

This little piece of nonsense can be found repeated endlessly by those who know little about Egypt, ancient Egyptian technology and, perhaps especially, modern technology. Walk through any major, modern city where construction is ongoing. For example, consider the Freedom Tower now being built in the footprint of the downed Twin Towers at the lower end of Manhattan. A marvel of technology, the building itself measures in at 1,368 feet in height, with a planned antenna that will top off at a symbolic 1,776 feet. Looking at that project, is it conceivable that modern technology couldn't replicate the Great Pyramid? Nonsense.

   BEST OF THE WEB

http://guardians.net/egypt

About as all-inclusive as you can get in a website devoted to as broad a topic as ancient Egyptian culture. Great graphics, terrific discussion, links to everything from the official Egyptian Supreme Council of Antiquities to tour groups, online catalogs of Egyptian goods, and chat groups. If you visit one website on Egypt, this is the one.

http://www.pbs.org/wgbh/nova/pyramid/textindex.html

Website on ancient Egypt produced by PBS. Features an online interview with famed Egyptologist Mark Lehner and virtual tours of the pyramids at Giza.

http://www.catchpenny.org/

Larry Orcutt's entertaining site exploring some of the supposed mysteries of ancient Egypt. "Mysteries of the Sphinx," "Pyramid Enigmas," and pharaoh's curses are explored here, all within the context of the application of the scientific method to the investigation of the Egypt of the pharaohs. Lots of fun and enormously informative.

http://khufu.3ds.com/introduction/

You can find a terrific computer-generated animation of the internal ramp hypothesis produced by Dassault Systemes.

   CRITICAL THINKING EXERCISE

Test the following hypothesis: Pyramid building was introduced into Egypt by bearers of an alien, non-Egyptian culture. What should the archaeological record in Egypt look like if this hypothesis is an accurate description of Egyptian history? What does the archaeological record actually show regarding the history of pyramid construction in Egypt?

11

Good Vibrations:
Psychics and Archaeology

The Farmington River watershed encompasses more than 1,500 square kilometers (600 square miles or 384,000 acres) of north-central Connecticut with its thick deciduous forest and topographically varied landscape (Figure 11.1). The region is marked by distinct seasonality with long, cold winters; gloriously rich springs; humid, warm summers; and the most astonishingly pleasant and beautiful of autumns. An abundance of swiftly flowing freshwater streams feed the Farmington River and provide good, clean drinking water throughout the watershed (Figure 11.2).

Local geology provided several different durable rock types the inhabitants could use for making spearpoints, knives, scraping tools, and axes and adzes (Figure 11.3). Deer, beaver, coyote, raccoons, bobcats, all manner of waterfowl, and freshwater fish are abundant still and in the past provided a rich source of food and pelts for the ancient inhabitants of the valley (Figure 11.4). We have, since 1979, looked for the remnants of the settlements of those inhabitants in the Farmington River Archaeological Project (FRAP; Feder 1981a, 1990a, 2001).

Finding ancient, buried archaeological remains may seem like magic, but there is no magic to it. Archaeologists are guided, in part, by experience. We are practiced at identifying the kinds of environmental features that attracted ancient settlement: proximity to fresh water, relatively flat and dry land, and places where the surrounding territory would have supplied basic resources, including food, wood to fuel fires and build dwellings, stone for tools, and clay for pots.

Areas so identified represent hypotheses that need to be tested. The test is in the search for artifacts in those places, the physical objects people made and used, and then lost or discarded. Over the course of more than thirty years of research, we have investigated large swaths of the subsurface

Figure 11.1 Looking out onto the floodplain of the Farmington River. Providing fresh water, abundant plant, fish, and animal life, along with presenting inhabitants with a convenient route of transportation, the river has long attracted human settlement. It doesn't take psychic power, only common sense, to predict that archaeological sites will be found on the shores of a river. (K. Feder)

of the valley, but, of course, we have not stripped back all of the soil in our 600-square-mile research domain. To minimize disruption of the ecology of the valley and to use our time efficiently, we have employed a sampling strategy (Orton 2000; Shafer 1997). Since 1993, we have excavated a large number of individual, shovel-dug test pits, each 50 centimeters (close to 20 inches) on a side, 10 meters (about 33 feet) apart, along a series of widely dispersed transects, or lines. We have positioned these transects to pass through all of the various habitats and landforms in the valley. We don't want to sample only areas along streams or places near rock outcrops. Doing so would guarantee that we find sites only near streams or outcrops, but we do not know that these are the only kinds of places where the ancient inhabitants lived or worked. Our goal is representative coverage of all of the many different watershed habitats. No area is over-sampled and no place is underrepresented in our test pit sample. In this way, we increase the likelihood that the kinds of sites we have discovered are a representative subset of the kinds of sites present in the region. All of the soil we dug in these test excavations was passed through ⅛-inch-mesh hardware cloth (screen). Soil passes through the screen, but artifacts like stone flakes, sherds of pottery, burned bone, and charred nut fragments are caught and represent clear evidence of ancient habitation.

Figure 11.2   Dozens of small streams feed into the Farmington River, providing drinking water, fish habitat, and hydraulic power that supplied the energy for water-powered mills in the eighteenth and nineteenth centuries. Again, predicting that prehistoric and historical groups of people utilized stream habitats like the one pictured here and that the archaeological evidence of their presence will be found takes little more than an understanding of the settlement patterns of those groups. (K. Feder)

It's not magical, and it certainly is not easy. Much of the survey work is in pretty rough territory, far from the gentle, established trails. Our backpacks are laden with heavy equipment, and we carry shovels and screens that are awkward to negotiate through the dense growth. Mosquitoes (some carrying West Nile virus), ticks (some carrying Lyme disease), snakes (some poisonous), poison ivy, stifling heat, and thick humidity (we conduct fieldwork mainly in the summer) add to the mix. Certainly, for those dedicated few who devote themselves to this task, the rewards are great when an ancient site whose people lived thousands of years ago is revealed. When we are the first to encounter the remnants of the daily lives of people who lived and died so long ago, it is worth every mile, every mosquito bite, every sprained ankle.

For example, in the summer of 2011, my archaeology crew focused on the investigation of a location where the ancient native people of Connecticut quarried a resource called steatite. Also called "soapstone," for its slick, soapy feel, steatite is a soft, easily carved stone that is also relatively durable. Today, soapstone is sometimes used in the manufacture of wood stoves because of its heat retentive capabilities. Before ceramics were made and used by the people of my state—manufacturing clay pots began here around 3,000 years ago—they

Figure 11.3 Stone tools typical of those found at prehistoric sites in the Farmington Valley. Here are pictured spearpoints, knives, scraping tools, and, at the far right, a delicate flint drill, all recovered from a 3,000-year-old site in Barkhamsted, Connecticut. (K. Feder)

Figure 11.4 The Farmington Valley provided an abundance of food resources to its ancient inhabitants. Nut trees provided acorn, hickory, and chestnut; wild plants like goosefoot and amaranth provided nutritious seeds; animals like deer and birds like the geese shown here were valuable as sources for protein-rich meat. (K. Feder)

Figure 11.5 Two partially carved, "unharvested" soapstone bowls rest in place where ancient people had started, but never completed, their extraction from bedrock more than 3,000 years ago. Our careful excavation revealed this moment frozen in time. (K. Feder)

quarried soapstone, which they then carved into bowls, plates, platters, cups, and ladles. My crew of eighteen students meticulously excavated the spot where the quarry was located, digging six, 2-meter by 2-meter square units, painstakingly scraping back the soil in 5-centimeter layers. Recording every discovery, my students recovered literally thousands of spalls of steatite—debris from the quarrying process—and discovered two "unharvested bowls," which had been shaped in place as the soapstone was being quarried, but never finished or extracted (Figure 11.5). They also found several stone tools, including picks and scrapers used in the extraction and carving of the soapstone (Figure 11.6). I admit that it was exceptionally hard work, but this kind of fieldwork remains the only way that archaeologists can recover artifacts and investigate ancient sites in an attempt to reconstruct the lives of past people. The excavation of a site necessarily involves its destruction, so great care and thorough documentation are absolutely vital if we are to preserve the information about past lives that the site can provide (see Ashmore and Sharer 2006; Fagan 2006; Feder 2008; Thomas and Kelly 2010, for discussions of survey and excavation methodology).

Finally, we hope to be able to reconstruct as completely as possible an ancient way of life. To do so, archaeologists have had to devise methods to coax information out of the often meager remains we recover; the artifacts are mute, the bones silent. Detailed examination of stone tools under the

Figure 11.6   Four quartzite quarry picks recovered at the same site where we discovered the unharvested soapstone bowls shown in Figure 11.5. These were large, hand-held tools used by the quarriers to both initially shape and extract the bowls from their bedrock source. (K. Feder)

microscope can tell us how they were made and used. Chemical analysis of human bone can provide insight into ancient diets. Physicists can help us determine the age of sites. Nuclear reactors are used to trace raw materials to their prehistoric sources. Pollen, starch grains from plants, and even blood residue can survive for thousands of years on the interior surfaces of ancient pots, on the smoothed façades of grinding tools, and even on the cutting edges of sharp-edged stone knives; these organic remnants can be recovered and analyzed, providing a wealth of information about the tasks people performed with these artifacts. Powerful computers are needed to map the distributions of artifacts within sites and of sites within regions to help us illuminate the nature of human behavior. Archaeologists are like detectives of the human past. We try to reconstruct not a crime but a way of life from the fragmentary remains people accidentally and incidentally left behind.

But is there a better, easier way of going about our various tasks? Can we locate sites by simply looking at a map of an area and intuiting their existence? Can we know where to dig at a site simply by walking over the ancient habitation and "feeling" where artifacts are? Can we reconstruct, in exquisite detail, the lives not just of general "cultures," but also of specific, identifiable human beings simply by handling the objects they touched in their daily lives? Is there a methodology that could obviate the tedious and hard work of archaeology and get right at that which interests us most—ancient people and their cultures? Though virtually all archaeologists would wish the answer to this question were yes, most would realistically answer no.

Some new methodologies have been suggested, however—mostly by nonarchaeologists—that are alleged to do precisely this.

Psychic Archaeology

For example, some claim that "psychic power" is a tool that can be applied to the archaeological record (Goodman 1977; Jones 1979; Schwartz 1978, 1983).

Whatever one's preconceptions might be regarding the existence of psychic power, hypotheses regarding the reality of such phenomena and their utility in archaeological site survey, excavation, and analysis can be tested just as all hypotheses are tested—within a scientific, deductive framework. When a psychic predicts the location of a site, we must test the claim archaeologically. When a certain artifact or feature is predicted at a particular spot in a site, such a claim also must be tested by digging. Finally, when a psychic attempts to reconstruct the activities at a site or the behavior of the people at a site, those involved in testing the legitimacy of such an ability must devise a way to test such reconstructions with independent archaeological data.

In such testing, sources of information other than psychic must be controlled for. Here the application of Occam's razor (Chapter 2) should be clear. If the information reported by the psychic is correct but could have been obtained in some more pedestrian way (through such simple avenues as reading the available literature on a site or time period or the application of common sense), then Occam's razor would demand that we accept the simpler explanation before we accept the validity of a paranormal phenomenon. Unfortunately, as you shall see, such tests of psychic archaeology either are not conducted or are conducted so poorly as to render the results meaningless (Feder 1980b, 1995a).

Psychic Site Location

In reference to the claimed ability to locate archaeological sites through the application of psychic skills, it is most important to consider the fact that archaeologists regularly discover sites by employing some rather commonsense techniques. Human beings—prehistoric, ancient historic, and modern—do not locate their habitations randomly. Among the more important factors considered by a human group when deciding where to settle are distance to potable water, distance to a navigable waterway, topographic relief, defensibility, protection from the elements, soil type, food resources, and the availability of other resources such as stone, clay, or metal for tools.

Using such a list, even an untrained person can examine a map of an area and point out the most likely places where ancient people might have settled. In my own introductory course in archaeology, after lecturing on settlement location choice, I distribute United States Geological Survey maps (1:24,000 scale) of areas in Connecticut where we have conducted archaeological surveys. I ask students to peruse the maps and to suggest areas where sites might be located. It is quite common for students to come up with precise locations where, indeed, sites have already been discovered. Once an area deemed attractive for human settlement or use has been identified, the long and difficult process begins of testing the place for the material evidence of a past human presence (Figure 11.7). This is the "ground-truthing" part of an archaeological site survey where shovel test pits are excavated, soil is passed through hardware cloth, and, if our predictions are borne out, materials lost or discarded by past people are recovered. Even if a psychic could come up with an accurate prediction for the location of an unknown site, and artifacts were found in field testing, we would have to consider the simple explanation that, consciously or not, the psychic was merely relying

Figure 11.7   Archaeologists dig lots of holes in the search for subsurface remains of a once vibrant culture. Here, archaeology students have been arranged at 10-meter (about 32 feet) intervals along a transect, a straight line of test pits, where each is excavating a small sounding, exploring the subsoil in an attempt to locate archaeological remains. (K. Feder)

on commonsense cues rather than ESP to make the prediction. The lack of control of these variables renders such tests impossible to assess.

I guess I could claim to have psychic abilities as well when it comes to predicting the location of archaeological sites. Certainly, my field crew was mightily impressed by my seemingly paranormal abilities when I placed an X on the map we were using in our search for sites in Peoples State Forest in northwestern Connecticut, predicting that they would find a site in that very location (Feder 2008). Sure enough, when I next saw my crew chief later that same day, she expressed her amazement at my prescience. I assure you, as I assured her, no psychic skills were employed. I based my guess on the nearby presence of a permanent stream, a relatively flat surrounding area in an otherwise topographically rough and irregular part of the forest, and an abruptly rising slope to the west, offering a bit of protection from winds that usually come in from that direction. I wasn't psychic; I was merely aware of previous archaeological research that had already revealed the general pattern of settlement location among the prehistoric inhabitants of the region. And I was lucky. A little knowledge and a little luck may be all that is needed in many instances to accurately predict the location of a site.

Psychic Excavation

Jeffrey Goodman (1977, 1981) claims to have used psychic revelations to locate an outpost of immigrants from the Lost Continent of Atlantis in Arizona (see Chapter 8). Goodman's psychic predicted that excavators would find the following at the "site": "carvings, paintings, wooden ankhs, cured leather, and parchment scrolls with hieroglyphiclike writing" (1981:128). Also predicted among the finds were an underground tunnel system, domesticated horses and dogs, and corn and rye (p. 134). Goodman admits, "My beliefs may appear to outstrip the physical discoveries at Flagstaff so far" (p. 134), showing that he is nothing if not a master at understatement. *None* of the predicted items was, in fact, discovered at the site. The utility of psychic archaeology as a method for supplementing excavation has not been supported experimentally. The process of excavating an archaeological site, of, in essence, uncloaking the remains of a community where people once worked and lived—exposing the remnants of their homes, uncovering their hearths and trash pits, revealing the places now littered with their broken stone tools and potsherds, all now secreted beneath sometimes many feet of silt, sand, stone, and even volcanic ash— is another laborious process (Figure 11.8). If a psychic could tell us precisely what we will find and where, well, it certainly would save us a lot of time and energy. To date, unfortunately, they haven't shown that they can accomplish this task.

Figure 11.8   Once a site is found, the laborious process of excavation may commence. Though we would greatly appreciate the shortcut psychic excavation would provide, it turns out that the only way to actually determine what reposes beneath the surface is to excavate, carefully and slowly scraping away the soil with trowels and screening that soil through, in this case, ⅛-inch hardware cloth. (K. Feder)

Psychic Cultural Reconstruction

Archaeologist Marshall McKusick (1982, 1984) has produced useful summaries of the claims of the psychic archaeologists. Regarding the psychic reconstruction of prehistoric cultures, he has come up with the phrase "the captive-of-his-own-time principle" (1982:100). He uses this phrase to underscore the fact that when psychics have attempted to reconstruct past lifeways, invariably they have done so within the framework of popular notions of those lifeways with all their biases, inconsistencies, and errors. In other words, the "vibrations" psychics allegedly receive by walking over a site, studying a map, or "psychometrizing" an artifact (holding the object to link up in some way with the person who made and used it thousands of years ago) do not come from some other plane of reality but rather from more mundane sources like popular books, newspaper articles, and the like.

Psychic Archaeology: A Test

A little experiment I ran a few years ago provides a perfect example of this.

One of the excavators in my archaeology field school had a friend who claimed to have psychic powers. This friend was very interested in our archaeological fieldwork and, in what was a sincere effort to assist, offered his psychic skills. My student's friend truly believed he could help by making a direct, paranormal connection to the long-dead people who had lived at the 1,300-year-old site we were excavating. I tried, valiantly and as politely as I could, to dissuade him, not really wanting to engage in what I thought would be a waste of time, his and especially mine. My student kept bringing up the possibility of incorporating his psychic friend in our work, assuring me that he had manifested amazing abilities on many occasions, being eerily accurate in his psychic descriptions and predictions. I finally relented but, rather than get the psychic directly involved at my dig, I suggested a lab test of one of the abilities he purported to have. He claimed the ability to "psychometrize" an artifact—in other words, read the history of an individual simply by holding the object that had belonged to him or her. We agreed on a protocol; in a laboratory setting, I would hand the self-proclaimed psychic a series of stone artifacts. He would then apply his paranormal skills and describe in whatever detail he could, the life of the person who had made and used the tool.

As a test of psychic power, I knew this was an egregiously badly designed experiment. I mean, how could I test the accuracy of any of the psychic's claims when he described people gone for more than a thousand years? You might think, based on what I've just told you, that there was no way to test that accuracy, but as I'll reveal, that's not quite true.

During the test, the psychic went into great detail on each object. Remember, my fieldwork focuses on New England's native people (a fact the psychic knew), so it was no surprise when handling the first artifact, a stone spearpoint, that he described it as having been made by a tall man with tawny skin and long, thick black hair. Oh, and the man lived in a bark-covered wigwam and he hunted in the woodlands. In a word, "Duh!" Along with the obvious, he continued with wholly untestable assertions: The man who made the spearpoint had a beautiful wife and several children, was wounded in a battle with his neighbors, and died before he reached the age of 50.

Each of his psychic readings was much the same. The psychic provided descriptions, some of which were almost certainly true, but trivially so, based on common knowledge or assumptions about the native people of Connecticut. He also provided other, very specific details whose accuracy was impossible to verify. Or so you might have thought.

Now, you well might ask why I hadn't devised a protocol for testing the psychic that would have been more objectively testable, where we could assess his descriptions with an independent source of data. Well, there is one fact I haven't provided you and I certainly did not provide the psychic before the experiment. In fact, none of the stone tools I handed the psychic on which to perform a "reading" were genuine. None were tools *found* by me. Instead, all of the tools had been *made* by me. I teach a course in experimental archaeology where students attempt to replicate tools to gain an appreciation for ancient technologies. I've been dabbling in "lithic replication" since grad school and can do a passable job of making stone spearpoints, knives, and scraping tools. I had completely scammed the psychic. I am not a nice person.

Now, had the psychic, after handling the tools, described the maker as a short professor with curly white hair, I might have been impressed. As it played out, I wasn't so impressed. The psychic was rather disappointed that his abilities had deserted him in the test I had devised. He actually was very apologetic and not the least bit upset with my little bit of subterfuge. He went on to suggest that, perhaps, when I make tools, the vibrations of the genuine tools I have handled in my life had managed to rub off on my replicas. Seriously? After that rationalization, if I had been tempted to feel bad about my approach, well, that feeling dissipated in a hurry. No one can read the vibrations from an ancient artifact for the simple reason that there are no vibrations to feel.

Psychic Archaeology: The Verdict

As an archaeologist, I wish psychic archaeology worked. As an archaeologist committed to a scientific and skeptical approach, I can only say that wishing doesn't make it so. The verdict on psychic archaeology based on experiments under controlled conditions is decidedly negative.

Current Perspectives: Archaeology Without Digging

All over the world archaeologists are leaving many of their traditional tools—shovels, trowels, brushes, and screens—back in the lab and toolshed, at least in the initial phases of some projects. Deeply buried artifacts, the outlines of ancient farmers' fields, human burials, houses long since turned to dust, and enclosed sacred spaces are being found—all without moving a cubic centimeter of dirt (Burks 2010; Burks and Cook 2011; Conyers 2004, 2006; Kvamme 2003).

For example, in an archaeological survey conducted at Fort Benning, Georgia, at the historic Creek Indian village of Upatoi, Frederick Briuer, Janet Simms, and Lawson Smith (1997) used a proton magnetometer and *ground-penetrating radar (GPR)* to scan the subsurface to determine patterns of activity in the eighteenth-century native settlement. The proton magnetometer measures local changes in the earth's magnetic field that may be caused by metal artifacts, buried walls, or alterations in the soil caused by previous disturbance resulting from excavation of old irrigation canals or even the digging of human burials. In GPR, an electromagnetic pulse is transmitted into the ground. The nature of the return signal is a factor of the medium through which the pulse travels and can be interpreted as the result of some previous activity that involved disturbing the ground. In both instances, measurements are taken at regular intervals on the surface with no disturbance of the soil (Conyers 2004, 2006; Conyers and Goodman 1997).

It may sound like dowsing, but there are major differences: Proton magnetometry and GPR are based on known, understood natural phenomena—and they work. After taking a series of readings at fixed intervals by walking across the area where a part of the Upatoi village had already been located, these researchers located six probable human burials that can now be protected without any further disturbance.

In another example, it would simply not have been practical to pepper a popular Key West, Florida, beach with test pits looking for what amounted to a handful of needles in a very large haystack. Local authorities desired to pinpoint the locations of the unmarked burials of a small group of African slaves who had shipwrecked and died there just before the Civil War, but how could they do it without a major disturbance to the beach? University of Denver archaeologist Larry Conyers and his GPR team were called in to attempt to solve the problem and locate the graves (Conyers 2003).

The images on Conyers's GPR printouts from the beach are eerie and ghost-like (http://www.du.edu/~lconyer/grids1,3_annotated.jpg). Small, vaguely oval blobs of red and green float on an otherwise homogeneous blue background. The green and red do not appear to be randomly distributed on the sea of blue, but are neatly lined up and clustered. The red and green blobs represent the computer depictions of discontinuities in radar reflectivity beneath the surface sand and were the right size and a reasonable depth to have been the result of human burials. Excavation verified that these radar anomalies, indeed, were the graves of the African slaves.

From the aerial photograph taken in 1994, the agricultural field located in Ross County in south-central Ohio doesn't look all that interesting (Figure 11.9, top). There is a ghostly impression of a circular feature in the lower part of the field, the remnants of an ancient earthwork—called the Steel Group—recorded in 1848 by Ephraim Squier and Edwin Davis, the mound surveying team mentioned in Chapter 7. It is difficult, if not impossible, to see anything else of archaeological significance in the aerial photograph. However, when archaeologist Jarrod Burks (Burks and Scott 2011) applied proton magnetometry to the field, he was able to reveal a profusion of earthworks that, after two centuries of plowing and leveling, had become invisible to the naked eye (Figure 11.9, bottom). Burks was able to identify several additional earth-bank enclosures, most shaped like giant capital Cs—the largest is close to 30 meters (100 feet) across—and even one that was diamond-shaped. Like a hidden message on a sheet of paper revealed only by the application of the right chemical, these earthworks virtually pop out at you in the magnetometry readout, salvaging information about the past use of this spot that might otherwise have been lost.

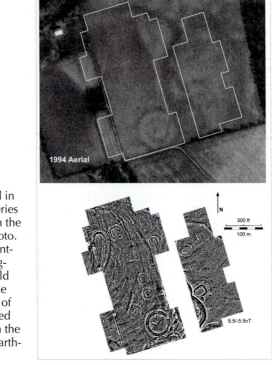

Figure 11.9   The top image is a 1994 aerial photograph of a field in Ohio, only vaguely showing a series of concentric, circular features in the soil toward the bottom of the photo. The image on the bottom is a print-out of the results of a proton magnetometry survey of the same field by archaeologist Jarrod Burks. The survey exhibits a complex series of soil features, invisible to the naked eye, but still detectable based on the magnetic signatures left by the earthworks. Courtesy, Jarrod Burks.

Psychic archaeology is lame. The work of Lawrence Conyers, Jarrod Burks, and a growing group of archaeologists employing remote sensing technology clearly shows that the real magic underpinning the discovery of archaeological remains is provided by science not psychics.

   FREQUENTLY ASKED QUESTION

Didn't the "prophet" Nostradamus accurately predict future events, including things that have happened in the twentieth century?

Though the allegedly accurate prognostications of sixteenth-century prophet Michel de Notredame (Nostradamus was his pen name) are beyond the scope of this book, I get this question so often in class that a brief answer is in order—no.

Specifically, Nostradamus was a physician and writer who became quite popular in France for his supposed prophetic abilities. Nostradamus made a name for himself with his book *Centuries*—a reference not to time but to the nine groupings of 100 predictions of four lines each (quatrains) contained in the book (the final edition published during his lifetime had 940 quatrains).

The vast majority of the quatrains are incredibly obscure, dense, vague, and incomprehensible. For example, you may read that Nostradamus accurately predicted the rise of Napoléon Bonaparte, actually naming the French emperor more than 200 years before he was born. You may also read that Nostradamus predicted World War II and even named the German leader Hitler nearly 400 years before the fact. Neither of these claims is true. In the former case, the Nostradamus quatrain in question states what seems like gibberish:

> PAU, NAY, OLORON will be more in fire than in blood.
> Swimming the Aude, the great one fleeing to the mountains.
> He refuses the magpies entrance.
> Pamplona, the Durance River holds them enclosed.

(Translations are taken from James Randi's book, *The Mask of Nostradamus* [1993], a terrific place to learn the truth behind the legend.) What this quatrain has to do with the ascendance of Napoléon is anybody's guess. PAU, NAY, and OLORON (uppercase in the original) are three towns located in southwestern France, near the Spanish border. The tortured attempts by Nostradamus boosters to coax Napoléon's name out of the letters of these town names is pretty lame.

The so-called Hitler quatrain is no better:

> Beasts mad with hunger will swim across rivers,
> Most of the army will be against the Hister.
> The great one shall be dragged in an iron cage
> When the child brother will observe nothing.

This is more meaningless prattle, but what about "Hister"? It is very close to "Hitler," and even though the meaning of the quatrain is completely obscure, does this hint that Nostradamus actually had prophetic abilities? No. On ancient Roman maps of Austria, the lower reaches of the Danube River were named the "Hister." Nostradamus certainly is referring to some unnamed army encamped or trapped against the Lower Danube River.

And while we are on the subject, despite what you may have heard, Nostradamus did not predict the September 11 terrorist attack on America. A quatrain circulated on the Internet soon after the attack seemed to show that he had done just that, with references to a "city of God" (New York), a "great thunder" (the sound made by the World Trade Center's towers collapsing), and "two brothers torn apart by chaos" (the two buildings falling). The delicious irony here is that this quatrain, in fact, was not written by Nostradamus, but by a college student, Neil Marshall, a few years before 9/11, in the style of the prophet. This fake quatrain was picked up by someone who, apparently, didn't realize it was a fake, and the next thing you know, everyone is speaking in hushed tones about the incredible abilities of Nostradamus.

I guess Marshall succeeded, in a way he could not possibly have imagined, in showing how Nostradamus-like quatrains could be interpreted in so many ways as to render them meaningless. Apparently, this made-up quatrain next morphed into something even spookier, with references to "two steel birds falling from the sky." This version, sounding even closer to the actual event, is akin to P. T. Barnum's fake of the Cardiff Giant; it is an intentionally faked version of the original fake Nostradamus quatrain, written, of course, after the 9/11 attack.

Even Nostradamus could not have predicted the extreme measures his twenty-first-century followers have taken to force his quatrains to match recent events. Unfortunately, it is all a sham. Nostradamus exploited the gullibility of a jaded nobility; he was the "psychic friends network" of his day. He predicted nothing.

BEST OF THE WEB

http://www.du.edu/~lconyer/

Check out the enormous utility of GPR in the search for buried archaeological remains without digging or ground disturbance at Lawrence B. Conyers's web page, *Ground Penetrating Radar in Archaeology.* Click on the link "G.P.R. examples from around the world." GPR and other remote sensing techniques present a distinct advantage over psychic archaeology and dowsing; they actually work and their ground truth can be verified.

CRITICAL THINKING EXERCISE

Design an experiment to test this claim.

- After a self-proclaimed psychic successfully locates a previously unknown archaeological site, the claim is made that archaeological sites can be discovered, excavated, and interpreted by the application of psychic power.

Old-Time Religion, New Age Visions, and Paranormal Predictions

The purpose of this book is certainly not to assess the veracity of anyone's religious beliefs or to judge anyone's faith. However, when individuals claim there is physical, archaeological evidence for underpinning a particular religious belief, the argument is removed from the field of theological discourse and placed squarely within the proper boundaries of scientific discussion. In other words, once a religious belief is supported with what is asserted to be scientific evidence or proof, its testing falls under the mantle of science and must obey the standard rules of evidence and reasoning applied to any other claim, assertion, or conclusion.

We can assess such claims as we have assessed all other claims made in the name of archaeology—within the context of the scientific method and deductive reasoning. This is precisely what I will attempt in this chapter.

Scientific Creationism and the Claim of Intelligent Design

You may have heard of the so-called Scopes Monkey Trial, which took place in Tennessee in 1925. That trial focused on a high school teacher, John T. Scopes, who broke Tennessee state law by teaching Darwin's theory of evolution in a public school classroom—a law that stayed on the books until 1967. The celebrated trial attracted international attention; famous defense lawyer Clarence Darrow served as counsel for Scopes, and thrice-failed presidential aspirant William Jennings Bryan served on the prosecutorial team (Figure 12.1). You can find excerpts from the trial transcript, plus a lot of interesting material related to the trial, at http://law2.umkc.edu/faculty/projects/ftrials/scopes/scopes.htm.

Figure 12.1 The so-called Scopes Monkey Trial of 1925 certainly called attention to issues related to the teaching of evolution in public schools. The trial resulted from a challenge of a state law enacted in Tennessee, making the teaching of evolution illegal in those public schools. Part of that attention was the result of the presence of two famous lawyers: defense attorney Clarence Darrow (on the left) and, on the side of the prosecutors, William Jennings Bryan (on the right).

Though Scopes was convicted and fined $100 (he never did have to pay the fine but only because of a technical error committed by the judge), most presume that the notoriety—and ridicule—that accrued to Tennessee as a result of the trial resulted in a victory for science and the teaching of evolution. As scientist Stephen Jay Gould (1981, 1982) points out, however, this was not the case. Emotions ran high both during and after the trial. To avoid controversy that might hurt sales, most publishers began a practice of regularly ignoring evolution in their high school textbooks. Generations of American students went unexposed to evolution—the most essential principle underlying the biological sciences.

This changed rather drastically in the 1950s after the Soviets successfully launched *Sputnik,* the first artificial satellite to orbit the earth. American complacency regarding our superiority in all fields was shaken, and among the results was a revamping of science curricula from elementary school on up. Evolution once again took its rightful place in the biology classroom.

Creationist Strategies in Education

Following the reintegration of evolution in high school biology curriculums, those opposed to teaching evolution in public schools altered their strategy. Dare I say it? Their approach to teaching evolution evolved. The Scopes trial reflects their initial tactic, which was simply to outlaw the teaching of evolution in the public school classroom. You can't get more direct than that. Imagine southern states decreeing it illegal to teach about the Civil War or, at least, to forbid teachers from teaching that the South lost that war, and you get an idea of how extraordinary that approach was. Nevertheless, as just pointed out, it worked until Sputnik and the reconfiguration of science education in America.

Following this, the anti-evolution strategy shifted toward an attempt to mandate the teaching of what was called "scientific creationism" as an alternative, often with the stipulation that creationism be afforded "equal time" to the teaching of evolution. Scientific creationism is the perspective that *scientific evidence* supports the hypothesis that the universe, the Earth, all life on Earth, and humanity itself was the work of an all-powerful creator.

I realize that most of us reflexively respond positively to a call for "equal time" or "equal consideration." I mean, it sounds fair, right? If there are a couple of different perspectives—Republican and Democrat, conservative and liberal, capitalist and socialist, Yankees and Red Sox—why not present both sides to students, expose them to the arguments, and let them decide? In fact, while that might work with political and social issues, and maybe even sports rivalries, does that make sense in the classroom when there is overwhelming consensus on an issue among professional scientists or historians? For example, should we afford equal time in a social studies classroom both to those who characterize slavery as an abomination and the lunatic fringe who present it as an overall positive experience for African captives (I'm not making up that attitude; it has been published). How about the Holocaust? Must every social studies and history teacher, when dealing with the genocidal regime of Nazi Germany, provide equal time to those who deny that the Nazis exterminated of millions of Jews, Gypsies, and Poles? Few would agree with that. So why should the perspective of equal time apply to a fringe perspective in biology?

Beyond this, don't make the mistake of thinking there are only two sides to this debate: evolution and a creationist view that sounds suspiciously like Genesis. Actually, there are lots of "creationist views," and in the spirit of fairness, wouldn't we have to cover all of them? Should we afford equal time in a biology or geology classroom for the view that the universe began as a giant, floating cosmic egg (a traditional story told in China) or that the Earth was once populated by a race of giants who were created from the sweat of Ymir, himself a giant born of ice (a Norse creation tale)? Don't forget the story about Sky-Woman falling through a hole in the heavens, caught by birds and then gently lowered onto the shell of a giant turtle (an Iroquois story). Remember, we're talking about a high school biology curriculum. Creation myths like these, as well as the tale told in Genesis about Adam and Eve and the Garden of Eden, are lovely stories, truly, that teach us how to live and how to treat other people; that inform us of our relationship to Earth, its plants, and animals; and that tell us of about the meaning of our existence. But these stories, including Genesis, have nothing to do with geology, biology, or archaeology.

In any event, the "equal time for creationism" mandate has been deemed unconstitutional by the courts in the United States in every instance in which it had been litigated, because judges have interpreted creationism as reflecting the beliefs of a particular religion or religions, and therefore in violation of the constitutional clause forbidding the establishment of a state religion (Scott 1987; Shermer 1997). In effect, lawyers representing school districts, counties, or states that put the equal time mandate into effect are placed in the unenviable position of having to argue an absurdity: that a school curriculum requiring teaching that the universe, the world, life, and humanity had been instantaneously created something on the order of 6,000 years ago (and that a great flood destroyed much of that creation sometime soon thereafter) was *not* mandating the inclusion of the Judeo-Christian Bible in biology class. But, of course, it was. Creationism is the Genesis story and should not—and legally cannot—be taught in a high school science classroom.

If you are a northerner and feel somehow superior to southerners on this issue (after all, the Scopes trial was the result of a Tennessee law; the state of Georgia mandated the placement of a disclaimer about evolution in high school biology textbooks), not so fast. One of the most significant court cases in the United States resulted from the introduction of creationism into the public schools in 2005 in Dover, Pennsylvania (*Kitzmiller et al. v. Dover Area School District*). In that school district, teachers were required to read a disclaimer about evolution to their students. They similarly had to include a statement about creationism, and students were directed to a supplemental, anti-evolution biology textbook (*Of Pandas and People*). The judge in the case came down hard on the school district's anti-evolution requirements and declared them unconstitutional. For a fascinating account of the cast of characters in this case, see science writer Gordy Slack's (2007) book, *The Battle Over the Meaning of Everything: Evolution, Intelligent Design, and a School Board in Dover, PA*.

Unfortunately, as a recent article (Berkman and Loutzer 2011) points out, winning in the courts has not guaranteed winning in the classroom. In a survey conducted among a group of 926 public school biology teachers, researchers found that less than one-third (28 percent) of them included a detailed and robust treatment of evolution in their classrooms. Despite its unconstitutionality, 13 percent of public school biology teachers actually teach creationism as a plausible alternative to evolution, and another 5 percent, while not explicitly including creationism in their curriculum, present it in a positive light if a student asks a specific question about it. In this sample of teachers, fully 60 percent essentially admitted that they are not personally invested in either evolution or creationism. They just want to teach biology and not get nasty letters from parents. The problem with that attitude is, as the vast majority of biologists will tell you, you can't effectively teach biology without emphasizing the evolutionary perspective and context of life on Earth.

And the beat goes on. State legislatures keep attempting to introduce bills that will require the teaching of creationism in public schools, hoping they will eventually come up with wording that will pass constitutional muster. In 2011 alone, at least eight bills in six states were seriously considered that would have required the teaching of creationism as an alternative to evolution. As I write this in February 2013, a bill has been proposed in the Missouri House of Representatives that, if passed, would require equal time for "biological intelligent design." In a response to a similar bill in Indiana, a State Senator (Vi Simpson) slyly proposed adding wording to the creationist bill that would require biology teachers to include, along with the standard creationist view that sounds an awful lot like Genesis, a Muslim, Buddhist, Hindu, as well as Scientologist view of creation (Ortega 2012). She was serious, but only in the sense of showing how foolish the bill was in the first place.

Intelligent Design

More recently, scientific creationists have presented a new underpinning to their view, labeling it *intelligent design* or ID (Dembski 1999). Intelligent design is, fundamentally, an old argument dressed up in some new clothing. The argument is essentially this: the universe we see around us, the mechanics of the solar system, the complexity of ecological communities, the incredible and amazing complexity of life, even fundamental elements like the individual cell, appears to be so consistent, so regular, so well synchronized, so unlikely, so, and I hesitate to use the term, *miraculous*, it could not be the result of natural processes. The universe, the solar system, our planet, and life and all its constituent elements appear to have been designed by an intelligence, so the argument goes. Thus, the name of this perspective: intelligent design.

But the entire notion that, for example, nature reflects the design of a perfect creator is unsupported by fact; either that or the designer has a wickedly nasty sense of humor. In fact, nature is filled with examples of decidedly bad "design," instances in which even a marginally intelligent designer would have made some very different choices.

For example, paleontologists usually calculate that more than 95 percent of all the plant and animal species that ever existed are now extinct. They must not have been designed very intelligently. Professor of ecology and evolution at the University of Chicago, Jeffrey Coyne (2009), enumerates examples of very unintelligent designs in his book, *Why Evolution Is True*. Just think of various maladies that plague humanity—hernias, prostate issues, back problems, hemorrhoids, the regularity with which people choke to death while eating. These are all the result of terrible "design" flaws in our bodies. No designer in his or her right mind would produce abdominal walls so weak that they regularly tear (hernias). No intelligent designer would run the male urethra through a gland (the prostate) that swells with age, cutting off urine flow and wreaking all sorts of havoc. No intelligent engineer would design the human spinal column. It's a mess, with one element, the sacrum, shaped like a wedge and positioned in a way that, if anything, seems designed to tear apart our pelvises. If it was designed that way on purpose, the designer had a terrible sense of humor. And what intelligent designer would produce a single tube through which people need both to breath air and swallow food? That's a recipe for disaster. Oh, and just ask a woman who has gone through twenty-four excrutiating hours—or more—of labor, how intelligently designed that whole process is. Yet, as Coyne (2009:81–85) points out, the configuration of all of these seemingly unintelligently designed parts of our anatomy are explained precisely by evolution. Human anatomy is jerry-rigged, the result of a series of evolutionary compromises, not the plan of an intelligent designer.

Recently, the Thomas B. Fordham Foundation (which in 2005 surveyed state high school biology programs regarding coverage of evolution) published its assessment of public school science programs in each of the fifty states and the District of Columbia (Lerner et al. 2012). The Foundation based its grades (from A to F) on a very thorough and detailed assessment based essentially on what each state expects students to know and understand at different grade levels. The conclusion, which this time included but was not limited to coverage of evolution, was that a lot of our states' science programs are pretty bad: only one state, California, and the District of Columbia were given A grades (there also were some A minuses). The Fordham Foundation assessors assigned Ds to sixteen states and Fs to ten (Table 12.1). That's horrible for a country that prides itself in its scientific strength. You can see the entire report and check out each state's assessment and grade online at http://www.edexcellencemedia.net/publications/2012/2012-State-of-State-Science-Standards/2012-State-of-State-Science-Standards-FINAL.pdf.

There are several fine books on the nature of creationism and intelligent design and the threat it poses to science education in America and elsewhere (McKown 1993; Strahler 1999). Writer Michael Shermer (1997) presents a point-by-point refutation of twenty-five creationist claims. For a detailed treatment of the way the intelligent design argument is being used

Table 12.1   *Fordham Foundation State-By-State Grading of Science Programs*

A	2	CA, DC
A−	4	IN, MA, SC, VA
B+	1	NY
B	6	AR, KS, LA, MD, OH, UT
C	12	CT, DE, FL, GA, MI, MN, MS, MO, NM, TX, VT, WA
D	16	AL, AZ, CO, HI, IL, IA, KY, ME, NV, NH, NJ, NC, PA, RI, TN, WV
F	10	AK, ID, MT, NE, ND, OK, OR, SD, WI, WY

in an attempt to include creationism in school curricula, see Barbara Carrol Forrest and Paul R. Gross's *Creationism's Trojan Horse* (2003). Also, take a look at Kenneth Miller's 2008 book, *Only a Theory: Evolution and the Battle for America's Soul.* Miller is a biologist, a textbook author, and has a unique perspective on the debate. These are all excellent sources on the topic of creationism. We needn't go into this issue in more depth here.

However, the purported existence of physical evidence supporting biblical literalism is often used to support the *scientific* underpinnings of creationism. Such physical evidence falls into the field of focus of this book. The two pieces of ostensible evidence I will assess here are (1) the existence of the "artifact" of Noah's Ark and (2) evidence of the recent creation of the earth in the form of proof of the contemporaneity of human beings and dinosaurs.

Noah's Ark

The biblical version of the Flood story was first written down between 500 and 450 B.C., and similar tales had been circulating in the Middle East since at least 1800 B.C. (Cohn 1996). In most versions, an angry and vengeful God decides to destroy his creation in an enormous flood. A single, righteous man (variously: Ziusudra, Atrahasis, Utnapishtim, or Noah) is warned of the impending deluge and is given specific instructions to build a boat with compartments, to coat it with pitch, and to fill it with plants and animals (Figure 12.2). Even the story of sending first a raven and then a dove out from the boat or ark to search for dry land after the rain ends is found in some of the older versions of the legend. This shows quite clearly that the biblical Flood story was not unadulterated history but was borrowed and adapted by the ancient Hebrews from other people in the Middle East.

With this in mind, using a deductive approach as applied elsewhere in this book to nonreligious claims about the past, we can ask the following questions: (1) Could the Ark as described in the Bible have actually been built? (2) Could the people involved have saved representatives of each animal species? (3) Is there any geological evidence of a universal Flood? (4) Is there archaeological evidence of the Flood? (5) Are there actual remains of the Ark itself resting where the Ark landed after the Flood? And, finally, (6) Is there evidence of a catastrophic flood not of global but of local proportions that might have served as the inspiration for the biblical story? Let's consider these questions individually.

1. *Could the Ark have been built?*

> Robert A. Moore (1983) and Mark Isaak (1998) have written point-by-point examinations of the Flood story. They conclude independently that building the Ark would have been impossible. According to the biblical account, the Ark measured 300 cubits in length and

Figure 12.2   An artist's rendition of the gathering of animals boarding Noah's Ark. Geological, biological, paleontological, and archaeological evidence indicates that Noah's Flood was not a historical event. (*Noah's Ark,* 1846, by Edward Hicks. Philadelphia Museum of Art. Bequest of Lisa Norris Elkins)

50 cubits in width. Remember from Chapter 3, in our comparison of the biblical giant Goliath to the Cardiff Giant archaeological hoax, that a cubit equals approximately 18 inches (45 centimeters). Using this measurement, Noah's Ark, built entirely with hand tools by a few people, would have been about 450 feet (137 meters) long and more than 75 feet (23 meters) wide! This was an enormous ship. Vessels this size did not become common in the U.S. Navy until the 1940s, and these ships were built by enormous contingents of experienced workers, not a handful of untrained people like Noah's family. The technology necessary for building a seaworthy vessel with anything approaching these dimensions did not even exist until the nineteenth century A.D. We do know what boats looked like 5,000 years ago when the Ark was supposed to have been built. Egyptologists have unearthed the oldest example of an engineered boat—something other than a hollowed

out log. It has been dated to between 3100 and 2890 B.C. Its substantial size—75 feet (23 meters) long and 7 feet (2 meters) wide—still makes it just a bit more than 1.5 percent of the claimed size of the Ark (Oldest boat 2000). There is no archaeological or historical evidence that anything bigger than this Egyptian boat was built during this period.

2. *Could the people involved have saved representatives of each and every animal species on earth?*

Noah and his family (his wife, three sons, and their wives) could not have gathered and accommodated all the animals allegedly saved on the Ark—some from as much as 12,000 miles (nearly 20,000 kilometers) away, from continents not even known to Noah. Beyond this, some of the landmasses that supplied animals to the Ark were separated from Noah's location by enormous expanses of open ocean. How exactly did llamas and alpacas (from South America) or even kangaroos and koalas (from Australia) manage to get to the Ark in the first place?

We can estimate that, had the Ark housed representatives of every animal species alive in the world before the Flood—as the Bible indicates was done—this would mean that 25,000 species of birds, 15,000 species of mammals, 6,000 species of reptiles, 2,500 species of amphibians, and more than 1,000,000 species of insects, all multiplied by two for each kind of the "beasts that are not clean" and by seven for each kind of the "clean beasts" (Genesis 7:2), were brought on board and taken care of for about a year (Schneour 1986:312). The small number of people on the Ark could not possibly have fed, watered, and tended this vast number of animals—and imagine cleaning out all those stalls!

Beyond this, even considering the enormous size of the Ark, there would have been less than 1 cubic meter (a stall a little more than 3 feet by 3 feet by 3 feet) for each vertebrate and its food supply—more than enough for small animals, but how about a rhinoceros, a giraffe, or an elephant (Schneour 1986:313)? And remember, as we will see in the next section, many creationists believe that dinosaurs lived during Noah's time and were among the animals saved on the Ark (Taylor 1985a). Obviously, a 30-ton, 40-foot-tall, 100-foot-long *Supersaurus* would have been more than a little cramped in its quarters.

Further, even in the twenty-first century, zoos have trouble keeping some species alive in captivity; their dietary and other living requirements are so finely adjusted in nature that they cannot be duplicated. How did Noah accomplish this?

Finally, though extinction technically occurs when the last member of a species dies, species extinction effectively occurs when numbers fall below a certain threshold. For example, the population of about

500 Siberian tigers left in their natural habitat may be too small a number to prevent eventual disappearance of the species in the wild. Yet, if the Flood story were true, we would have to believe that Siberian tigers and all of the other species we see today were able to successfully survive after their numbers had dwindled to either two or seven of each. Genetic variability is so small with such a limited population size that most species would have disappeared.

3. *Is there geological evidence for the Flood itself?*

Certainly such a catastrophic event occurring so recently in the historic past would have left clear evidence. In fact, worldwide geological evidence does not support the claim of a great Flood. The vast majority of the features of the earth's surface are the result of gradually acting, uniform processes of erosion repeated over vast stretches of time, not short-lived, great catastrophes (though occasional catastrophic events like asteroid impacts do occur and may have had significant effects—one large asteroid strike may have been the cause for dinosaur extinction about 65 million years ago).

For example, paleontologists have long recognized the *biostratigraphic* layering present in the earth. Biostratigraphy refers not just to the layering of geological strata but also to the occurrence of plant and animal fossils in these strata. These biological traces are not present in a hodgepodge; they are not randomly associated in the layers but tend to be neatly ordered. That ordering—older species are found in deeper layers, more recent species are found in higher strata—is a reflection of lengthy chronology, not a recent catastrophe.

If a recent, universal Flood simultaneously destroyed virtually all plants and animals, their remains would have been deposited together in the sediments laid down in that Flood. Dinosaurs and people, trilobites and opossums, giant ground sloths and house cats, *Australopithecus* and the Neandertals—all would have been living at the same time before the Flood and should have been killed together during the Flood. We should be able to find their fossils together in the same geological layers.

Of course, we find no such thing. Plant remains are found in layers older than those containing animals. Single-celled organisms are found in layers below those containing multicelled organisms. Reptiles are found in older strata than are mammals. Layers containing dinosaurs never show evidence of human activity and are always far older than layers containing human fossils. (See "Footprints in Time" later in this chapter.)

Creationists recognize this powerful contradiction to their view. They speculate that biostratigraphy, instead of representing an ancient chronological sequence, represents differences in animal buoyancy during the Flood. In other words, reptiles are found in lower strata than are mammals because they don't float as well. Not only is this rationalization weak, it is not even original. Here creationists are only recycling an explanation put forth by John Woodward (1695) in *An Essay Toward a Natural History of the Earth*. Of course, we can forgive Woodward—he suggested this more than 300 years ago.

4. *Is there archaeological evidence for the Flood?*

If a universal Flood occurred between five and six thousand years ago, killing all humans except the eight on board the Ark, it would be abundantly clear in the archaeological record. Human history would be marked by an absolute break. We would see the devastation wrought by the catastrophe in terms of the destroyed physical remains of pre-Flood human settlements. Above all else, we would see sharp discontinuity in human cultural evolution. All advances in technology, art, architecture, and science made up until the point of the catastrophe would have been destroyed. Human cultural evolution, as reflected in the archaeological record, would have necessarily started all over again after the Flood.

Imagine the results of a nuclear war that left just a handful of people alive. Consider the devastation such a war would visit upon human culture. Think about what the remains of the pre- and postwar societies would look like from an archaeological perspective. This is comparable to what the differences would have been between pre- and post-Flood societies and their archaeology.

Unfortunately for the Flood enthusiasts, the destruction of all but eight of the world's people had no discernible impact on ancient culture and left no mark whatsoever on the archaeological record. The cultural records of the ancient Egyptians, Mesopotamians, Chinese, and Native American civilizations show no gaps in development. Either cultural trajectories in these world areas were affected not at all by the destruction of their entire populations, or there simply was no universal Flood. Applying Occam's razor, we have to conclude that, based on the archaeological record, there could have been no universal Flood like that described in the Bible.

5. *Do remains of Noah's Ark still exist?*

Are there archaeological remains of a great ship located on the slopes of a mountain in Turkey? Are these, in fact, the actual physical remains of Noah's Ark? For years various groups associated with numerous fundamentalist organizations have searched for remains of the Ark on Mount Ararat in Turkey (LeHaye and Morris 1976). One of these groups included former astronaut James Irwin. They have, as yet, all been unsuccessful.

Local Kurdish tribesmen who claim to have visited the largely intact Ark on the 17,000-foot (5,200-meter) peak have been interviewed. Stories have been collected of the Russian discovery of the Ark in 1916. That legend maintains that when the communists took control in the Soviet Union all photographs of the Ark were destroyed, and eyewitnesses to the Ark were executed. Some have circulated stories of an American discovery of the Ark in the 1960s. Here, a joint, secret expedition of the Smithsonian Institution and the National Geographic Society supposedly discovered the Ark but suppressed the information "in order to preserve the dominance of Darwinian theory" (Sallee 1983:2). An obvious question that might have been asked is, naturally enough, Then why did they go looking for the Ark in the first place?

Eyewitnesses have invariably been unable to relocate the Ark and bring people to it. Other alleged evidence for the Ark has consisted of photographs and movies. These have always either mysteriously disappeared or turned out to be of images of misidentified rock formations.

In 1959, a French explorer, Fernand Navarra, claimed to have visited the Ark and even brought back wood samples. Unfortunately for the "arkeologists," radiocarbon dating applied to the wood indicated that it dated not to 5,000 years ago as it should have according to biblical chronology, but to between the sixth and ninth centuries A.D. (Taylor and Berger 1980).

The search for the Ark continues, and in 2006 a team announced that the Ark had not landed on Ararat at all: instead, its remains in the form of petrified wood had been found on the 13,000-foot (4,000-meter) peak of Mount Suleiman in Iran (Ravilous 2006). Geologists who examined photographs of the discovery have responded that the "petrified wood" was, in actuality, a deposit of entirely natural sedimentary rocks. As geologist Robert Spicer points out, there is no evidence, for instance, of the kinds of joinery Noah would have employed in putting the Ark together, no evidence of mortises and tenons or pegging, for example (Ravilous 2006). The oval shape of the formation, deemed by the discoverers to be the prow of the Ark, is, instead, a clear example of a geological fold, a feature this area of Iran is known for. Beyond this, according to scientist Martin Bridge, even if you were to melt the polar ice caps and mountain glaciers, you still wouldn't bring sea level up nearly high enough to raise a boat above the 13,000-foot (4,000-meter) level (Ravilous 2006). If they've found the Ark on Suleiman, it could not have floated to that elevation.

And the "discoveries" go on and on. In April 2010 the Ark was found yet again. Back on Ararat, a self-described evangelical

Christian filmmaker announced that he is "99 percent" certain that he has found remains of Noah's boat which, according to his testimony, includes intact chambers preserved in glacial ice at the top of the mountain. Surprisingly (not really), he has so far refused to show anyone where he found it, though he claims to have confirming radiocarbon evidence (though again, nothing has been presented to confirm any carbon date, much less one that conforms to a biblical time frame). Biblical scholar Eric Cline suggests that the recent discovery may actually be merely an old shepherd's hut, but he will reserve judgment until more evidence is forthcoming (Watt, Romano, and Netter 2010). Cline (2007) has written a terrific book on biblical claims and mysteries. In it, he sums up claims of evidence for the biblical Flood and Noah's Ark in this way: Other than the possibility that the flood reflects the memory of a disaster that was neither universal nor supernatural (such as the in-filling of the Black Sea at the end of the Ice Age to be discussed in just a bit), "there is no other good evidence for the existence of the biblical flood or for Noah and his ark, despite numerous claims to the contrary by amateur sleuths and scholars each year" (p. 28). The latest discovery is unlikely to be any different.

6. *Was the story in the Bible of a worldwide flood inspired by a local event?*

The newspaper headlines of early September 2000 were breathtaking in their implications. "New Evidence of Great Flood," read one. Another read, "Found: Possible Pre-Flood Artifacts."

In actuality, the hyperventilated headline writers were being a little disingenuous about an intensely interesting research project being directed by underwater explorer Bob Ballard, who was also responsible for discovering the remains of the *Titanic.* Ballard is testing the hypothesis of geologists William Ryan and Walter Pitman (1998).

The scenario these geologists lay out is based on the indisputable fact that as a result of lowered worldwide sea level during the Pleistocene, the waters of the Mediterranean Sea and Black Sea, today connected indirectly by way of the Bosporus Strait, the Sea of Marmara, and the Dardanelles Strait, were entirely distinct bodies of water, separated by a rocky plateau that is now entirely underwater.

When the Pleistocene ended and glacial ice melted off, sea level rose all over the world. The same process that inundated the Beringian land connection between the Old and New Worlds (see Chapter 5) caused the Mediterranean to rise, eventually surpassing the height of the plateau, allowing its water to pour into the basin of the Black Sea.

Ryan and Pitman suggest that this water spill occurred about 7,500 years ago and was sudden and catastrophic, a stupendous waterfall in-filling the Black Sea with the force of as many as 200 Niagaras. The water poured precipitously into the shallow, post-Pleistocene Black Sea, raising its level and reestablishing a connection between it and the Mediterranean over the course of only a very few years.

The consensus among geologists contradicts this (Kerr 2007; Yanko-Hombach et al. 2006). There is no archaeological evidence whatsoever for a catastrophic abandonment of the area of the kind that certainly would have happened had a flood of the proposed magnitude occurred. There's no archaeological evidence at all of massive whole-sale destruction of ancient communities along the inundated shores of the lake. Geological evidence supports a scenario, not of a stupendous waterfall suddenly breaching a natural barrier and gushing into the Black Sea basin but, instead, a steady, slow, and incremental rise in the level of the Black Sea spread out over millennia (Kerr 2007). The bottom line: though Ryan and Pitman's idea presents a neat scenario in providing a natural explanation for Noah's Flood, there simply isn't any good evidence to support it.

Footprints in Time

It is a little more than 65 million years since dinosaurs thundered across the landscape. Some fundamentalist Christians deny this dating of the extinction of the dinosaurs. In fact, it is their view that the universe, including our world and ourselves, is only about 6,000 years old. In 1650, Irish archbishop James Ussher determined that God had created the universe in 4004 B.C. Some fundamentalists still accept the validity of that date and so claim that human beings and dinosaurs walked the earth during the same period—that is, before Noah's Flood.

Such a remarkable scenario, although in agreement with some awful Hollywood movies and *The Flintstones* cartoon, stands in contradiction to the accumulated wisdom of the fields of biology, zoology, paleontology, geology, and anthropology. Basing conclusions on the seemingly indisputable evidence of stratigraphy, fossils, artifacts, and radiometric dating, these fields show quite clearly that the last of the dinosaurs died off about 60 million years before the appearance of the first upright walking hominids.

Many creationists reject all these data in favor of one bit of presumed evidence they claim shows the contemporaneity of dinosaurs and human beings—footprints from the Paluxy River bed in Glen Rose, Texas (Morris 1980).

Fossilized dinosaur footprints along the Paluxy River were first brought to the attention of scientists and the general public in 1939 when scientist Roland Bird (1939) mentioned their existence. In the same article, Bird noted that giant, *fake* human footprints were being made and sold by people who lived in the area of the genuine dinosaur prints (Figure 12.3).

Figure 12.3   These obviously carved human footprints were found by scientist R. T. Bird (1939) in a store in Arizona. He traced them back to Glen Rose, Texas, where he subsequently located a rich deposit of genuine, fossilized dinosaur footprints in the Paluxy River bed. (Neg. #2A17485. Photo by K. Perkins and T. Beckett. Courtesy Department of Library Services, American Museum of Natural History)

Thereafter, claims were published in a Seventh-day Adventist church periodical that there were *genuine* "mantracks" side by side with, in the same stratum with, and sometimes overlapping dinosaur prints in the Paluxy River bed (Burdick 1950). Similar claims were made in a major creationist publication purporting to prove the validity of the biblical Flood story (Whitcomb and Morris 1961). Throughout the 1960s, 1970s, and 1980s, creationists of various denominations and perspectives conducted "research" in the area, looking for trackways and other evidence that dinosaurs and humans lived during the same recent period of the past—in Texas, at least.

Certainly, the association of dinosaur and human footprints in the same geological stratum in Glen Rose would contradict the biostratigraphic record of the rest of the world and would seem to indicate that human beings and dinosaurs, indeed, were contemporaries.

The footprint data have been summarized from a creationist perspective by John Morris (1980) in his book *Tracking Those Incredible Dinosaurs and the People Who Knew Them*. It is clear from his descriptions that there are at least three distinct categories of features in the Paluxy River bed: (1) indisputable dinosaur footprints, (2) indisputably fraudulent, carved giant human footprints, and (3) long (some more than 50 cm; almost 20 inches), narrow, ambiguous fossilized imprints.

Little needs to be said of the first two categories. Physical anthropologist Laurie Godfrey (1985) has shown quite clearly that the fraudulent mantracks were known to have been carved and sold by at least one local resident during the Depression. Extant examples of these frauds (see Figure 12.2) bear no relationship to the anatomy of the human foot or the way human footprints are produced (their *ichnology*).

The third category has caused the greatest amount of confusion. Those impressions available for study are invariably amorphous imprints that, while exhibiting only in a very general sense the outline of huge human feet, bear no actual humanlike features (Cole, Godfrey, and Schafersman 1985; Edwords 1983; Godfrey 1985; Kuban 1989a). Interestingly, many of the creationists who discovered the prints admit that, as a result of erosion, the prints are now unimpressive, while maintaining they were clearly human when first discovered (Taylor 1985b).

Godfrey (1985) shows quite clearly that the elongate fossil impressions are a mixed lot of erosional features and weathered, bipedal dinosaur footprints (Figure 12.4). Most of the prints are vague—even creationists cannot agree on the length, the width, or even the left/right designation of the same prints. None of the so-called mantracks exhibit anatomical features of the human foot, nor do the tracks exhibit evidence of the biomechanics of human locomotion. As Godfrey points out, humans have a unique way of walking that gets translated into the unique characteristics of our footprints. When we walk, each foot contacts the ground in a rolling motion—the heel strikes the surface first, then the outer margin of the foot, next the ball of the foot,

Figure 12.4 Creationists have claimed there are fossilized footprints of giant human beings in the same layer with, and side by side with, the dinosaur prints in the Paluxy River bed. These turn out to be misinterpreted portions of genuine dinosaur footprints. Impressions left by three claws can be discerned at the front (left) of this print. (© 1985 Glen J. Kuban)

and finally the big toe, or *hallux*. Godfrey's analysis shows that the Paluxy mantracks do not exhibit these aspects of human locomotion.

In recent years, most creationists have changed their minds concerning at least the tracks discovered before 1986 (Morris 1986; Taylor 1985b). Kuban (1989b) discovered that the exposed tracks had weathered, revealing the claw impressions of the three-toed dinosaurs who had made the prints creationists claimed were made by humans. Though hopeful that earlier, now-destroyed discoveries might have been genuine human footprints or that future discoveries might be made of real mantracks, most creationists for a time accepted what evolutionists had been saying all along; there is no evidence for the contemporaneity of human beings and dinosaurs in the Paluxy River bed.

The Shroud of Turin

In discussing scientific epistemology in Chapter 2, I pointed out that science does not proceed through a simple process of elimination. We do not simply suggest a number of hypotheses, eliminate those we can, and then accept whichever one is left. Yet just such an approach is at the heart of much of the pseudoscience surrounding the so-called *Shroud of Turin*.

Some presume that this 14-foot by 3½-foot piece of cloth is the burial garment of Jesus Christ. It is further asserted by some that the image on the cloth of the front and back of a man, apparently killed by crucifixion (Figure 12.5), was rendered not by any ordinary human agency but by miraculous intervention at the moment of Christ's resurrection (Stevenson and Habermas 1981a, 1981b; Wilson 1979). Some of the scientists who participated in the Shroud of Turin Research Project (STURP) in 1978 reached such a conclusion (Weaver 1980).

Unfortunately, the approach of many of the STURP researchers was not consistent with scientific methodology. In essence, they considered a limited number of prosaic explanations for the image on the shroud (oil painting, watercolors, stains from oils used to anoint the dead body). They applied high-tech equipment in testing these hypotheses and found none of the explanations to their satisfaction. They ended up suggesting that the image was actually a scorch mark created by an inexplicable burst of radiation (Stevenson 1977). Though, officially, STURP did not conclude that the image had been miraculously wrought, Mueller (1982) points out that STURP's "burst of radiation" from a dead body would most certainly have been miraculous.

Some STURP members (in particular, Stevenson and Habermas 1981a) were forthcoming in explicitly concluding that the image must have been the result of a miracle. They further maintained that the image is that of a person bearing precisely the wounds of Christ as mentioned in the New Testament (scourge marks, crown of thorns, crucifixion nail holes, stab wound). They finally concluded that the image on the shroud is, in fact, a miraculously wrought picture of Jesus Christ.

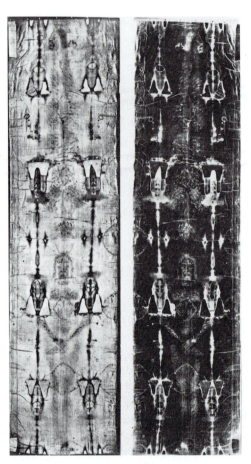

Figure 12.5   Positive (left) and negative (right) images of the Shroud of Turin. Some have claimed that the shroud was the actual burial garment of Jesus Christ and that the image on the shroud was miraculously wrought at the moment of resurrection. However, historical evidence, microscopic analysis, and a recently derived radiocarbon date show that it was the work of a fourteenth-century artist. (Photo by G. Enrie. Courtesy the Holy Shroud Guild)

Not all were convinced by STURP's official argument or the more religious claims of Stevenson and Habermas. One member of the original STURP team (he subsequently resigned) was the world-renowned microscopist Walter McCrone. McCrone and his associates examined more than eight thousand shroud fibers and collected data on thirty-two so-called sticky-tape lift samples—samples collected on a clear adhesive-coated tape that had been in direct contact with the shroud (1982). McCrone and his team used a number of techniques, including high-power (between 400× and 2500×) optical microscopy, to examine the physical characteristics of the image and ostensible bloodstains and used x-ray diffraction, polarized light microscopy, and electron microprobe analysis in determining their chemical makeup (McCrone 1990).

McCrone found that, far from being an enigmatic or inexplicable imprint on the cloth, the shroud body image and the supposed bloodstains contained evidence of two distinct artist's pigments made and used in the Middle Ages. The image itself showed the existence of red ochre, a common historical component of paint (McCrone 2000). The bloodstains showed the presence of a synthetic mercuric sulfide, a component of the artist's red pigment vermillion. The particular characteristics of the vermillion pigment found on the shroud are consistent with a type made in Europe beginning about A.D. 800. According to McCrone, the alleged bloodstains produced only negative results when a series of standard forensic blood tests were applied. From this he concluded that there was no blood on the shroud, only an artist's red pigment.

Joe Nickell (1987) has suggested a plausible artistic method for the production of the shroud. This involved daubing powdered pigment on cloth molded over a bas-relief of a human being. His method seemed to explain the curious fact that the image on the shroud appears more realistic in negative reproductions; that simply is a product of the technique of image manufacture (as in a grave rubbing). This technique has been used by European artists for 700 years, and his replica of the face on the shroud bears a strong resemblance to the original (Figure 12.6).

Walter McCrone's (1996) approach uses the simplest technique. He asked the artist Walter Sanford to paint on linen an image of the man on the shroud with a very dilute iron-oxide tempera paint, a formula McCrone produced based on his analysis of the paint residue he found on the shroud. The "negative imaging," the lack of absorption into the fibers of the linen, and the three-dimensional features of the Turin shroud were faithfully reproduced by Sanford and McCrone (see Figure 12.6). McCrone's painted shroud

Figure 12.6 Shroud enthusiasts claim that there is no natural explanation for the image on the shroud. However, using different prosaic and entirely natural methods, Joe Nickell (**left**, 1987); and Walter Sanford (**right**, cited in McCrone 1996) have produced reasonable facsimiles of the image on the shroud. (*Left:* Courtesy Joe Nickell; *right:* Courtesy Walter McCrone)

and the Turin shroud look virtually identical in a naked-eye comparison (compare Figures 12.5 and 12.6, right); in addition, McCrone (2000) has demonstrated that a microscopic comparison (between 400× and 1500×) of his painted shroud and the Turin shroud shows a very close match.

So, was the shroud daubed, brush-painted, or projected into existence? Ultimately, the answer to this question is not so important. Whatever process may have been used, it is clear that any assertion that the process that produced the image on the shroud is mysterious or miraculous and cannot be replicated using mundane artistic techniques is simply false.

Testing the Shroud

It must be admitted that if the image on the shroud is miraculous, it is, of course, beyond the capability of science to explain it. Nonetheless, we can apply scientific reasoning concerning the historical context of the shroud. In other words, if the shroud is the burial cloth of Jesus, and if the image appeared on the shroud through some inexplicable burst of divine energy at the moment of resurrection, then we might expect to find that

1. The shroud was a regular part of Jewish burial tradition.

2. The shroud image was described by early Christians and, as proof of Christ's divinity, used in proselytizing.

3. The Shroud of Turin can be historically traced to the burial garment of Christ mentioned in the New Testament.

4. The Shroud of Turin can be dated to the period of Jesus Christ.

We can test these implications of the hypothesis of the shroud's authenticity.

1. *Was the shroud a regular part of Jewish burial tradition?*

The story begins with the crucifixion of Jesus Christ. Whatever one's perspective concerning the divinity of Jesus, a few things are indisputable. Christ was a Jew and one among a handful of alleged messiahs about 2,000 years ago. As such, from the perspective of the Roman occupiers of Israel, Christ was one in a series of religious and political troublemakers. The Romans dealt harshly with those who directly or indirectly threatened their authority. Crucifixion—execution by nailing or tying the offender to a wooden cross in a public place— was a way of both eliminating the individual and reminding the populace of the cost of defying Roman rule.

As a Jew, Christ would have undergone a Jewish burial ceremony. In fact, the Gospel of John clearly states that Jesus was to be buried in the "manner of the Jews" (19:40). At the time, this would have involved scrupulously washing the body and anointing it with oils, shaving the face and head, and wrapping the body with a burial shroud of linen. According to *halacha* (Jewish law), burial ordinarily should occur within twenty-four hours of death or soon thereafter.

According to the New Testament, Christ was removed from the cross and placed in a cave whose entrance was sealed with a large rock. Christ is then supposed to have risen from the dead, and his body disappeared from the cave.

Taking an anthropological perspective, analysis of Jewish burial custom suggests that a burial sheet or shroud is to be expected in the case of the death and burial of Christ. But what should that shroud look like? Old Testament descriptions of shrouds seem to imply that the body was not wrapped in a single sheet (like the "winding sheets" used in burials in medieval Europe), but in linen strips, with a separate strip or veil placed over the face. In the Gospel of John, there is a description of the wrapping of Jesus' body in linen cloths and a separate face veil.

The image on the shroud has "blood" marks in various places. Shroud defenders have pointed to these supposed blood marks in an attempt to authenticate the shroud, comparing the wounds on the image to those of Christ as described in the New Testament. But there is a problem with this interpretation. If the image on the shroud is really that of Jesus produced through some supernatural agency, then the body of Christ could not have been ritually cleaned. Yet this would have been virtually unthinkable for the body of a Jew. Such ritual cleansing of a dead body is an absolute requirement for Jews, even on the Sabbath— Christ died on Friday around sundown when the Jewish Sabbath begins—when all other work would have been halted. The marks alleged to be Christ's actual blood, therefore, contradict the claim that the body of Jesus was wrapped in the shroud; he would already have been ritually cleaned for burial before being placed in his burial cloths.

Further, if the Turin shroud is authentic, then the cloth itself should be of a style consistent with other shrouds and other cloth manufactured 2,000 years ago in the Middle East. However, textile experts have stated that the herringbone pattern of the shroud weave is unique, never having been found in either Egypt or Palestine in the era of Jesus Christ (Gove 1996:243).

In sum, there are significant inconsistencies between what the burial garments of Jesus should look like and what the Gospel of John says it looked like on one hand and the actual appearance of the Shroud of Turin on the other.

2. *Was the shroud image mentioned in the Gospels?*

The Gospel of John states specifically, "took they the body of Jesus and wound it in linen cloths" (19:40). When the disciples entered the tomb, Jesus was gone but his burial garments were still there. Again, the Gospel of John provides a short but succinct description: "And the napkin, that was about his head, not lying with the linen cloths, but wrapped together in a place by itself" (20:7). This description matches Jewish burial custom—but not the Shroud of Turin.

Certainly the Gospels were not averse to proclaiming the miracles performed by Christ. A miraculous image of Jesus would have been noticed, recorded, and, in fact, shouted from the rooftops. But though the burial linens are seen and mentioned in John, there is no mention of an image on the cloth. In fact, there is no mention of an image on Jesus' burial garments anywhere in the New Testament. This is almost certainly because there was no image.

3. *Can the current shroud be traced to the burial of Jesus?*

With the preceding argument in mind, can we nevertheless trace the burial linens of Jesus mentioned in the New Testament to the shroud housed in the cathedral in Turin? The answer very simply is no.

The very earliest mention of the current shroud is A.D. 1353. Between the death of Jesus and A.D. 1353, there is no historical mention of the shroud and no evidence that it existed. It makes little or no sense, if indeed a shroud existed with a miraculous image of Christ on it, for it to have gone unnoticed and unmentioned for more than 1,300 years. Applying Occam's razor, a more reasonable explanation might be that the shroud with the image of Christ did not exist until the fourteenth century.

The history of the shroud after 1353 is quite a bit clearer. It has been described in an excellent book, *Inquest on the Shroud of Turin,* by science writer Joe Nickell (1987). A church named Our Lady of Lirey was established in 1353 to be a repository for the shroud, and it was first put on view there a few years later. It was advertised as "the true burial sheet of Christ," and admission was charged to the pilgrims who came to view it (Nickell 1987:11). Medallions were struck (and sold) to commemorate the first display of the shroud; existing medallions show an image of the shroud.

The Church in Rome took a skeptical approach to the shroud. As a result of the lack of reference to such a shroud in the Gospels, Bishop Henri de Poitiers initiated an investigation of the shroud, and a lengthy report was submitted to the Pope in 1359. The report pulls no punches; it concludes that the shroud was a fake produced to make money for the church at Lirey. It was even discovered that individuals had been paid to feign sickness or infirmity and to fake "miraculous" cures in the presence of the shroud. The report goes even further, mentioning the confession of the forger: "the truth being attested by the artist who had painted it, to wit, that it was a work of human skill and not miraculously wrought or bestowed" (as quoted in Nickell 1987:13).

As a result of the Church-sponsored report, Pope Clement VII declared that the shroud was a painted cloth and could be exhibited only if (1) no candles or incense were burned in its presence, (2) no honor guard accompanied it, and (3) the following disclaimer was announced during its exhibition: "It is not the True Shroud of Our Lord, but a painting or picture made in the semblance or representation of the Shroud" (as quoted in Nickell 1987:17).

Even with the disclaimer, the shroud attracted pilgrims and believers. The shroud became an article of commerce, being bartered for a palace in 1453. In 1578 it ended up in Turin, Italy, where it was exhibited in the sixteenth through twentieth centuries.

4. *What is the age of the shroud?*

Even if the Shroud of Turin turned out to be a 2,000-year-old piece of cloth, the shroud-as-miracle would not be established. It still could be a fraud rendered 2,000 years ago—or more recently on old cloth. However, a final blow would be struck to any hypotheses of authenticity if the cloth could be shown to be substantially younger than the time of Jesus. Recent analyses have shown just this.

The Church agreed to have three radiocarbon dating labs date the shroud. A postage-stamp-size sample was cut from the shroud. That is all that was needed for all three labs to date the cloth using accelerator mass spectrometry, a very precise form of carbon dating requiring very small samples (see Gove 1996 for a detailed description). A textile expert was on hand to make certain the sample was removed from the shroud itself and not patches added later to cover holes burned in a fire in A.D. 1532. Also, the entire process was videotaped to preserve a chain of evidence from the shroud to each of the labs. In this way, everyone would be certain that the labs actually received material cut from the shroud, and not material substituted for some nefarious purpose. Each lab was also provided with three control swatches: one small piece from each of three fabrics of known age that they also dated. This was done to determine the accuracy of the dates from each of the labs on known cloth, providing a measure of accuracy for a cloth of unknown age (the shroud). Furthermore, none of the labs knew which fabric sample was which; this was a blind test. In that way, no one could knowingly replace the actual shroud sample in an attempt to make it appear to be older (by replacing it with a sample known to be 2,000 years old) or younger (by replacing it with a sample known to be much more recent than 2,000 years old) than it actually is.

The shroud dates determined from all three labs indicate that the flax from which the shroud was woven was harvested sometime between A.D. 1260 and 1390 (Damon 1989; Nickell 1989; Vaughan 1988:229). These dates correspond not with the time of Jesus but with the first historical mention of the existence of the shroud.

How accurate is this date? In all certainty the date is very accurate. In dating the samples of known age, the labs were virtually perfect, and there is no reason to believe their shroud dates are any different (Table 12.2). Some have claimed that the shroud sample was contaminated, but Harry Gove, the physicist who is the "father" of the radiocarbon dating technique used, has determined that for a 2,000-year-old cloth to have enough contamination to make it appear to date to the fourteenth century A.D. the sample would have to be at least one-third pure contamination and only two-thirds cloth (1996:265)—an unlikely situation and one that would have been clearly visible to the naked eye. Though Raymond Rogers (2005) of Los Alamos National Laboratories suggests that the test revealing a medieval radiocarbon date was conducted, not on an original piece of the shroud linen, but on a much more recent patch used to fix the artifact after it had been damaged in a fire, his interpretation, though interesting, has not been verified; textile experts involved on site in the actual selection of material to radiocarbon-date were satisfied at the time that the piece extracted for analysis was part of the original cloth. Those involved with the original dating would be more than happy to redate the shroud using additional samples (Trivedi 2004), but whether that will occur is uncertain.

Writer John Frodsham (1989:329) maintains that although the shroud cannot have been the actual burial garment of Jesus, it may be a fourteenth-century miracle, the image appearing as a sign from God, "perhaps in response to fervent prayers, during an epoch noted for its mysticism, when the Black Death was raging throughout Europe." This is an interesting hypothesis, though perhaps European peasants dying in the tens of thousands might have better appreciated a more utilitarian miracle on God's part—say, elimination of the Black Plague—than an image on a piece of linen.

Table 12.2   *Results of Radiocarbon Dating for Historic Cloth Control Samples and Shroud of Turin*

	Known Date (historical records)	**Carbon Date** (three-lab average)
Thread from cloth cape	A.D. 1290 to 1310	A.D. 1273
Egyptian mummy wrapping	60 B.C.	A.D. 35
Nubian tomb linen	A.D. 1000 to 1300	A.D. 1093
Shroud of Turin	not known	A.D. 1325

Source: Gove 1996.

New Age Prehistory

Sedona, Arizona, is a red rock jewel of a place. Clean air contributes to a piercingly blue sky. The exposed bedrock, shading from deep brown through magenta to lipstick red all the way to pale pink, has been eroded into endless phantasmagoric shapes. It is no wonder that the area has attracted a wonderful mix of people, some of whom perceive a magic and power in their community, the source of which cannot be explained by science.

The Sedona New Agers believe that this magic and power emanate from the red rocks of their region and reside in the remnants left behind by the prehistoric inhabitants of northern Arizona. New Age Sedonans talk endlessly about vortexes, sacred places, and healing spots—which skeptics might suggest are merely particularly beautiful rock formations, architecturally impressive prehistoric ruins, or interesting ancient rock carvings (petroglyphs) and paintings (pictographs) (Figure 12.7).

Tourists can travel into Sedona's backcountry by taking any one of a number of jeep tours with companies called "Earth Wisdom Tours," "Mystic

Figure 12.7 Pictograph painted by the native inhabitants of Sedona, Arizona, likely more than 1,000 years ago. This intriguing image seems to depict a person beneath the full moon. (K. Feder)

Tours," or "Crossing Worlds Journeys." Archaeological sites often are important elements in these tours. One tour pamphlet suggests that "some will
sense the ancient resonance still present at these sites." Other tours promise
healing ceremonies, revelation of ancestral secrets of the "Medicine Wheel,"
and various other cosmic insights.

The two most important archaeological sites located in Sedona are
rather small cliff dwellings called Palatki and Honanki (Figure 12.8). The
Palatki dwellings were occupied from about A.D. 1150 to 1300, though many
of the nearby pictographs are much older. Honanki overlaps in time with the
end of the Palatki occupation. I have heard these sites described as "sacred"
or "mystical" places. One website author tells of "basking in the huge heart
energy" during a visit to the Palatki ruins (http://www.visionsofheaven.
com/journeys-sedonadocs/sedPalatki.html). That's fine; the archaeological
remnants of these ancient communities are fascinating and deserving of our
attention and respect. If people wish to read spiritual significance into the
ruins of ancient dwellings or artifacts tossed by the inhabitants onto their
trash heaps, so be it.

Figure 12.8   The cliff dwellings of the American Southwest reflect the architectural
sophistication and the construction skills of the Native Americans who built them. But
they were, after all, simply people's homes. Claims by New Agers that sites in Sedona
like the Palatki ruins shown here are "power vortexes" are devoid of any scientific
meaning. (K. Feder)

Crystal Skulls

If you've heard about the crystal skulls of ancient Mexico, odds are it's because of the latest Indiana Jones movie, *Indiana Jones and the Kingdom of the Crystal Skull*. That story was, of course, just Hollywood nonsense—I mean, come on: the skulls were made by extraterrestrial aliens or something. But there are plenty of stories about the actual crystal skulls that, while they are just as fictional as the Indian Jones story, are presented by their tellers as actual fact. The skulls are genuine artifacts made by the Native American people of Mesoamerica. Or the skulls reflect a technology beyond the capabilities of the native peoples of Central America. Those can't both be right, but both of those claims are made. The skulls possess mystical healing powers. Or, the skulls, or at least one of them, is a "skull of doom," either bringing a terrible fate down on its possessor or maybe even the entire world (Figure 12.9).

It's all nonsense, even, apparently, the claim that the skulls are simply very sophisticated and very cool genuine artifacts reflecting the amazing artistic abilities of the ancient Aztecs or Maya or whomever. You see, that's the first problem with the skulls: none of them, not one, has any sort of archaeological context. None of them has been found in place in an archaeological

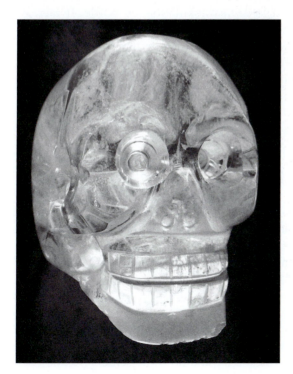

Figure 12.9 Not only do the crystal skulls not presage the end of the world, they're not even genuine Maya (or Aztec or Toltec or any other Mesoamerican civilization) artifacts. Close examination of the crystal skulls, like this one, located in the Musée du quai Branly, in Paris, indicates that they were made with the use of lapidary wheels and other modern tools. (© Corbis)

excavation and none has been documented by an archaeologist. The skulls—all of them—have just sort of appeared out of nowhere. Most often they've shown up, completely undocumented, on the antiquities market. In one bizarre case, a skull arrived in a package addressed to the Smithsonian Institution. No return address. No address on the enclosed note transferring ownership to the museum.

Archaeologist Jane MacLaren Walsh (2008) likely has conducted more actual research on the crystal skulls than anybody else. Her 2008 article in *Archaeology Magazine* thoroughly demystifies the artifacts. As she points out, none of them has any archaeological context. Many of the early ones—too many—are associated with the same nineteenth-century artifact dealer, Eugène Boban, who clearly played a role in their production. At the same time, the skulls don't match the style of any genuine Mesoamerican artifacts, they don't match the technical qualities of any genuine Mesoamerican artifact, and when subjected to an in-depth technical analysis, some show clear evidence of having been made with the use of modern lapidary wheels. The crystal skulls are all nineteenth- and twentieth-century fakes, produced to sell on the antiquities market. The stories told about them are about as factually reliable as the tale told in the movie.

Finally, I hesitate to point this out to you, but here goes; comedian, actor, and writer Dan Akroyd is so enamored of crystal skulls, he markets a vodka that is sold in a clear, skull-shaped bottle. If fact, he calls it Crystal Head Vodka. There's even a YouTube video (http://www.youtube.com/watch?v=SKqjIv91Zx8) in which he markets the product, extolling its purity and otherworldliness, bragging about the fact that the water used in its production is filtered through diamonds! Wow! I guess that's important, though the so-called Herkimer diamonds he mentions as being used in the filtration process aren't actually diamonds, but quartz crystals. Oh well.

Current Perspectives: Religions Old and New

Around 1885 a Paiute Indian named Wovoka had a vision in which God came to him and told of a new order that was to come. God instructed Wovoka to teach his people a new dance. If enough Indians from different tribes would only join in, this dance would lead to miracles. All sick or injured Indians would regain their health. All dead Indians from all the ages would come back to life and join in the dance. These countless Indians dancing together would float into the air, and a great flood would decimate the country, destroying in its wake all the white settlers. When the floodwaters subsided, the Indians would gently return to the ground to begin a paradisaical life of plenty, with lots of food, no sickness—and no white settlers (Kehoe 1989; Mooney 1892–93).

The *Ghost Dance,* as it came to be called, was what anthropologists label a *revitalistic movement.* Movements such as the Ghost Dance occur when a people sees its way of life threatened by a terrible, impending calamity. The old ways, including the old gods, seem to have no effect. A new, revolutionary belief system or sometimes simply a return to a previous, "purer" way is seized on as offering a solution.

One cannot help but be struck by the common thread running through this revitalistic movement of more than a century ago and the spiritual and religious upheavals in the modern world. Fundamentalist Christians and Moslems see all of the modern world's ills as spiritually based; if we could just return to the one true belief, all would be cured. At the same time, New Age beliefs seem to provide spiritual relief for those who perceive the precariousness of modern existence but who do not see the solution in old-time religion.

How comforting to believe that we can change all this simply by returning to a more fundamental belief in the Bible or that the solution to our problems is just a few years away in the guise of godlike extraterrestrial aliens who have been here before and who will save us, ultimately, from ourselves.

It is all the better, then, if the archaeological record can be interpreted as supporting such beliefs. In this perspective, both fundamentalism (of all sorts) and the New Age philosophy can be viewed as twenty-first-century revitalistic movements, offering hope to people desperate to believe there is a spiritual solution to our otherwise seemingly insoluble dilemmas.

◈ ◈ ◈ FREQUENTLY ASKED QUESTIONS ◈ ◈ ◈

1. Are all scientists atheists?

No, though it is true that a greater proportion of scientists are nonbelievers than is the case for the general public. A Gallup poll conducted in 1991 indicated that about 87 percent of Americans believe in God, 9 percent do not, and 3 percent say they do not know (Gallup and Newport 1991). A 1996 survey among American scientists revealed that close to 40 percent believe in God, about 45 percent do not, and about 15 percent are agnostics (Larson and Witham 1997). So, although belief in God measures at less than half the level it does among the general public, and a far greater proportion of scientists than nonscientists are atheists, a sizable minority of scientists do believe in a personal God.

2. Aren't religion and evolution irreconcilable?

Again, the answer is no. Two popes, including John Paul II, six major Protestant organizations, and the Conference of American Rabbis, among others, have all published statements accepting at least the possibility that evolution was the process by which God created life (Lieberman and Kirk 1996). They accept the scientific evidence for an ancient and changing earth and accept the evidence of change in plant and animal species.

BEST OF THE WEB

CREATIONISM

http://www.natcenscied.org/

Website of the National Center for Science Education, an organization devoted to defending the teaching of evolution in public schools. A good source for current events concerning the creation/evolution debate.

http://www.talkorigins.org/

Fantastic site devoted to the creation/evolution debate. A great place to find specific and detailed responses to creationist claims.

NOAH'S ARK

http://www.talkorigins.org/faqs/faq-noahs-ark.html

A web page at the talkorigins site providing an enormously detailed enumeration of the impossibility of the biblical Flood.

CLAIMED CO-OCCURRENCE OF DINOSAUR AND HUMAN FOOTPRINTS

http://paleo.cc/paluxy/paluxy.htm

The website of Glen J. Kuban, probably the most knowledgeable person concerning the actual dinosaur and misidentified giant human footprints at Paluxy. The claims of those few creationists who still maintain that the Paluxy mantracks are genuine are thoroughly debunked here.

THE SHROUD OF TURIN

http://www.mcri.org/home/section/63-64/the-shroud-of-turin

A brief, skeptical note regarding the shroud. Click on the link to the carbon-14 graph to see how unlikely it is that recent contamination has contributed to its late-thirteenth–early-fourteenth-century radiocarbon date.

CRITICAL THINKING EXERCISE

Using the deductive approach outlined in Chapter 2, how would you test these hypotheses? In each case, what archaeological and biological data must you find to conclude that the hypothetical statement is an accurate assertion, that it describes what actually happened in the ancient human past?

- The world was all but destroyed in a cataclysmic flood about 5,000 years ago. Only a small group of people and animals were saved.
- Human beings and dinosaurs lived at the same time a relatively short time ago (within the past 6,000–10,000 years).
- The Shroud of Turin was the actual burial shroud of Jesus Christ.
- The burial box found in Jerusalem and announced in 2007 contained the remains of Jesus Christ of Nazareth.

◈◈◈◈◈◈◈◈ **13** ◈◈◈◈◈◈◈◈

Real Mysteries
of a Veritable Past

Let's face it; I'm an archaeology nerd. Though I am a professional archaeologist with more than thirty years of experience excavating, analyzing, and
writing about the human past, I continue to be awestruck when I am in the
presence of the remnants of antiquity. I didn't expect it, for example, but I
was literally overwhelmed by emotion when I first walked into the broad
plaza—ancient, awesome, and somehow alien—at the Maya site of Chichén
Itzá; I could barely contain my excitement, my heart pounding, as I emerged
from the dark tunnel leading from the car park in the here and now up to
the surface of what seemed to be another time and another place, where the
mysterious gray sentinels of Stonehenge reposed in their great circle; I was as
giddy as a kid when the trail turned back in around on itself at Mesa Verde
and I gazed down into the pocket in the cliff where the ancient ones had
built the fairy-castle-like dwelling we today call Square Tower House (see
Figure 13.1).

I get it. These places and sites are spectacular and fascinating and
inspire wonder in us all. Perhaps this is what makes so many of us suscep-
tible to frauds, myths, and supposed mysteries like those detailed in this
book. Note that I have here repeated the book's title but inserted the word
supposed, because the mysteries of the Moundbuilders, Atlantis, ancient
aliens, and the rest have been shown to be not mysteries at all but simply
confusion resulting from misinterpretation or misrepresentation of human
antiquity.

Eliminating the false "mysteries" does not, however, leave us with a
dull or mundane human past. There are still plenty of mysteries and some
enormously interesting, open questions about what has gone before. Three
such examples of genuine mysteries of the past relate to the Paleolithic cave
paintings of Europe, the development—and fall—of the Maya Indian civilization, and the European megalithic site of Stonehenge.

Figure 13.1   Square Tower House at Mesa Verde, in Colorado. Like the pyramids, the Colosseum, and countless other "wonders of the ancient world," these cliff dwellings reflect the enormous intelligence of ancient people as well as their remarkable architectural and engineering abilities. Structures like this do not imply to the rational among us that extraterrestrial aliens must have been responsible for these magnificent works. (K. Feder)

The Cave Painters of Europe

Imagine this scene. In the dark, dim, and distant recesses of a cave's narrow passageway, a flickering oil lamp smears dancing shadows on a flat rock wall. A young woman, tall and lithe, her muscular arms coated with a thin layer of grime and sweat, carefully places a dark slurry in her mouth. With one hand she picks up a hollow reed and holds it to her lips. She places her other hand, palm down, on the rock face. Aiming the reed at the area around her hand, she begins puffing up her cheeks and blows, spraying a fine mist of pigment out of the end of the reed. Some of the paint thinly coats her hand, but much of it covers the cave wall immediately around the area hidden by her palm and fingers. After a few puffs through the reed, she removes her hand from the cave wall and we see in our mind's eye her remarkable artistic creation: a negative image of her own hand, a signature some 20,000 years old calling out across time (Figure 13.2).

By her side, a young man, tall and broad, with a deeply lined face belying his years, dips a frayed twig into a thick red paste. Using skills of observation and artistry developed during his short life, he conjures up a

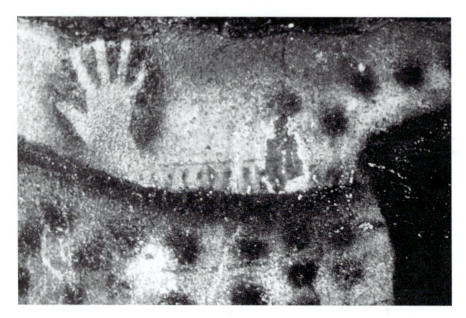

Figure 13.2   A 20,000-year-old "signature" left by a Paleolithic artist; a negative handprint produced by placing a hand flat on a cave wall and then blowing paint through a hollow reed all around the hand. From the cave of Peche-Merle in France. (© Musée de l'Homme)

vision held in a part of his memory as deep as where he now labors breathlessly in the cave.

The horse, wild and free, runs across his mind, her legs leaving the ground as she gallops in her desperate but doomed attempt to flee from the hunters. A deep, red gash on her belly where a stone-tipped spear pierced her hide leaks her life blood. Soon, he remembers, she falls, and his comrades are upon her, thrusting their spears deep into her. Then, at last, she is quiet and still. He shudders, thinking of her spirit now returned to the sky. Then he remembers the taste of her still warm flesh in his mouth—her life lost, the life of his people maintained. It is the way of life and death in the world that he knows.

Though long dead and no longer of this life but of another world, a world of stories and magic, the mare lives again in a creation of pigment, memory, sorcery, and awe. Once a creature of blood and bone, of sinew and muscle, she is now a creature of color and binder. No longer running across the ice-shrouded plains of western Europe, she now runs and bellows on a flat sheet of rock, straining against her fate and bleeding eternally in the deep recesses of a dark cave. In this incarnation she has lived for 20,000 years, and in this life of pigment and memory and magic, she will live forever (Figure 13.3).

Figure 13.3   The so-called Chinese Horse from the cave of Lascaux in France. The animal was depicted in full gallop by visitors to the cave nearly 20,000 years ago. (© Art Resource, NY)

Explaining the Cave Paintings

The imagined scene just described took place more than 20,000 years ago in the period called the Upper Paleolithic of prehistoric Europe. The individuals described are emblematic of the people who painted the fabulous and now famous depictions of their ancient and extinct world in the deep recesses of more than three hundred caves in western Europe (Chauvet, Deschamps and Hillaire, 1996; Clottes and Courtin 1996; Clottes and Lewis-Williams 1998; Ruspoli 1986; Saura Ramos 1998; White 1986).

A bestiary of ancient animals stands frozen in time on the walls of the caves of Altamira, Chauvet, Cosquer, Lascaux, and Niaux. Rendered in pigments of orange, yellow, red, and brown derived from iron oxides, along with black produced from manganese, many of these paintings are astonishingly lifelike, displaying a realism unexpected among a people so ancient and supposedly so primitive.

There are horses and elk, woolly mammoths and wild cattle, rhinoceroses and bison, all captured in exquisite detail by the ancient artists' skill and talent. Often, the animals are shown not in simple, static poses but in fluid motion. A red horse flees from spears on the cave wall at Lascaux. Two woolly mammoths confront each other, locked in a dance for dominance, on a wall in the cave of Rouffignac. Two spears hang from a dying bison at Lascaux. Four stiff-maned horses graze on the wall at Chauvet; frozen in eternal stillness, they nervously probe for the scent of a predator dead now for some thirty millennia. Dates derived directly from the charcoal used to produce black pigment in the paintings at Chauvet indicates an age of between 30,000 and 32,000 years (Balter 2008).

In some caves, there seems to be a clear relationship between the animals depicted on the walls and the actual remains of animals killed and eaten by the people who lived at the same time. Small, nonaggressive animals such as reindeer and red deer were important in the diet of the cave painters and were depicted on cave walls in a frequency proportional to their economic importance (Rice and Paterson 1985, 1986).

The ancient artists, however, did not depict only those animals that the archaeological record indicates were hunted for food. Bears, lions, and other carnivores also are rendered. These were often placed on walls far from the central parts of the caves, down long, sinuous, rock-strewn passageways. At Chauvet Cave in southeastern France, paintings of cave bears, cave lions, and an astonishing count of fifty rhinoceroses are among the perhaps more than three hundred images found there that also include wild horses, cattle, and elephants (Chauvet, Deschamps, and Hillaire 1996; Hughes 1995).

And there is more. Animals were not the only objects commanding the attention of Paleolithic artists. Abstract designs, geometric patterns, human handprints, and mythical beasts also adorn the cave walls. Rarely, we even find depictions of the humans themselves. Intriguingly, such "self-portraits" are often vague and indistinct—quite unlike the realistic depictions of the animals with whom our ancestors shared their ancient world.

The artists of the Upper Paleolithic did not confine themselves to two-dimensional depictions of their world; they produced sculptures as well, in bone, antler, and ivory. Among the oldest are carvings of a water bird in flight and the head of a horse, found in excavations in Hohle Fels Cave in southwestern Germany and dated to between 33,000 and 30,000 years ago (Conrad 2003). A tiny ivory carving of a woolly mammoth found in Germany has been dated to about 30,000 years ago (Holden 2007).

Beyond sculpting creatures of their physical world, the ancient artists of the Paleolithic also produced depictions of creatures that inhabited their spiritual world, including beasts that are a curious amalgam of human and animal. For example, in Hohlenstein-Stadel cave in Germany, excavators recovered an upright figure with a human's body and a lion's head (a "lion man"; Figure 13.4). The meaning of carvings of part-human/part-animal creatures like these is uncertain. Perhaps they reflect aspects of the spiritual world of the ancient people who produced them, a world in which beasts hosted the spirits of both people and the animals whose courage and ferocity those people hoped to emulate.

Figure 13.4   Called "Der Löwenmensch" (the Lion Man), this artifact was found in Hohlenstein-Stadel cave in Germany and depicts what appears to be a lion's head and face atop the body of a human being. We cannot determine precisely what the sculptor intended in creating this fanciful creature, but almost certainly it reflects the work of an artist with a fully human intellectual capacity. (Photo by Thomas Stephan, © Ulmer Museum)

Handprints like those described in the imaginary word picture I presented at the beginning of this section are found in about thirty different Upper Paleolithic caves in Europe. Interestingly, it now seems that most of these remarkable tags left by ancient people were made by teenagers. Comparison of the measurements of a large sample (201) of these handprints to those of modern human beings led researcher R. Dale Guthrie (2006) to a fascinating conclusion; the sizes of the cave wall handprints suggest that most were made by kids between 13 and 16 years of age. Perhaps like modern kids who leave graffiti signatures announcing their existence to anyone who glances at the wall, building, or subway car they marked, Upper Paleolithic teenagers left their indelibel mark, similarly announcing to the denizens of the underworld deep in a dark cavern: "I was here!"

In the cave paintings and sculptures rests a mystery. What prompted our ancient ancestors to produce these works on the cave walls? Was it simply "art" done for the sake of beauty (Halverson 1987)? Were the painted caves the equivalent of today's art galleries or museums where great artists exhibited their finest work? We can recognize the beauty in the work and today can appreciate it as art, but was that the intention of those who produced it (Conkey 1987)?

Was there some more complex reason for painting the images on the cave walls or carving sculptures of animals or spirits beyond simply a "delight in appearance" (Halverson 1987:68)? Were the cave paintings of food animals sympathetic magic—an attempt to capture the spirit of animals and thereby ensure their capture in the hunt (Breuil 1952)? Were the paintings the equivalent of our modern trophy heads—in effect, historically recording the successes of actual hunts (Eaton 1978)? Were the paintings part of a symbolic system that revolved around male and female imagery (Leroi-Gourhan 1968)? Or were the animal paintings part of a system of marking territory by different human groups during periods of environmental stress (Conkey 1980; Jochim 1983)?

And how about the geometric designs—the dots, squares, wavy lines, and the rest? An intriguing suggestion has been made by researchers J. D. Lewis-Williams and T. A. Dowson (1988). They propose that these images are visual artifacts of the human nervous system during altered states of consciousness. These "visions" result from the structure of the optic system itself and are therefore universal. You can even see some of these visual patterns simply by rubbing your eyes. Perhaps through sleep deprivation, fasting, gazing for hours at a flickering fire, or even ingestion of hallucinogenic drugs, Upper Paleolithic shamans or priests induced these images in their own optic systems and then translated these images to cave walls as part of religious rituals.

Several prehistorians are focusing on the meaning of the cave art; see the book *The Shamans of Prehistory: Trance and Magic in the Painted Caves*, by Jean Clottes and David Lewis-Williams (1998), for a detailed and innovative analysis of the paintings. There are as yet no definitive answers; there may never be. In that sense, the art of the Paleolithic—though certainly recognizable as the work of ancient human beings and not attributable to refugees from Atlantis or extraterrestrial visitors—is a fascinating legacy of our past and can, indeed, be labeled an unsolved mystery of human antiquity.

The Civilization of the Maya

Chichén Itzá, Uxmal, Tikal, Copán, Sayil, Palenque—the names resound with mystery. These were all cities of the ancient Maya civilization that flourished more than ten centuries ago in the lowlands of Guatemala, Honduras, El Salvador, Belize, and the Yucatán Peninsula of Mexico (Figure 13.5). Archaeological research in the past few decades has brought to light some of the remarkable accomplishments of this indigenous American Indian civilization (Sabloff 1989, 1994).

The architectural achievements of the Maya match those of any of the world's ancient cultures. The imposing, elliptical Pyramid of the Magician

Figure 13.5   Map of eastern Mexico (including the Yucatán Peninsula), Belize, Guatemala, Honduras, and El Salvador showing the location of some of the most important villages, ceremonial centers, and cities of the Maya civilization.

at Uxmal is a stunning piece of architecture and engineering (Figure 13.6). The ninety-four-room palace at Sayil, with its columned façade and imposing stone staircase, is similarly impressive. The Temple of Inscriptions at Palenque, El Castillo at Chichén Itzá, and the Temple of the Jaguar at Tikal all provide mute testimony to the splendid architecture of the Maya world.

Beyond their ability at construction, the Maya also developed their own hieroglyphic writing system and left a fascinating legacy of written work in the form of relief carvings, paintings, and books called *codices*. Recent advances in translating the written language of the Maya have enabled researchers to begin studying Maya history from a Maya perspective, much in the way we can study European history (Coe 1992; Montgomery 2002; Schele and Freidel 1990).

Explaining the Maya

Von Dänikenesque extraterrestrials and Giorgio Tsoukalos's ancient aliens are silly, superfluous, and completely unnecessary for explaining the Maya. Though the story of the Maya is still being written, there is no great enigma

Figure 13.6   The elliptical Pyramid of the Magician at the Maya site of Uxmal, located in the Yucatán Peninsula of Mexico. Unlike Egyptian pyramids, Maya pyramids have steps leading to temples placed at their apexes. (K. Feder)

or mystery to their origins or history. Maya roots can be traced back more than 2,800 years. Initially the Maya lived in small hamlets; by 2,300 years ago some settlements, including Nakbe, El Mirador, Lamanai, Cerros, Cival, and Tikal in the south and Dzibichaltún and Komchén in the north, had become larger with evidence of public architecture in the form of large stone platforms. Settlements like Cerros, located on a bay by the mouth of a river, became trading centers where raw obsidian and jade, as well as finely crafted goods from these raw materials, were concentrated, adding to the power of the developing elite class of people (Sabloff 1994).

Some of these Maya villages evolved into true urban settlements that became the capitals of a series of independent kingdoms that shared a common religious iconography and economic system. A highly productive agricultural system focusing on maize provided food for a growing population. A developing class of Maya leaders had the power to command the construction of monuments like pyramids and temples.

Dense settlements marked by monumental architecture, as well as magnificent artwork produced by specialists, are diagnostic of early civilizations. Recent discoveries indicate that such urbanization, monument building, and specialist art began as much as 2,300 years ago among the Maya. Dating to this time, the recently excavated Cival is one of the largest of the earliest Maya cities (Skidmore 2004). Cival had an estimated population of 10,000 people, and the main part of the settlement was encircled by a defensive wall of earth. The 800-meter- (half-mile-) long ceremonial center of this teeming ancient metropolis was marked by three major plazas demarcated by five flat-topped pyramids. In the middle of this ceremonial heart of the city, archaeologist Francisco Estrada-Belli has found the remains of two enormous carved terra-cotta masks, each one approximately 3 meters (9.8 feet) tall and 5 meters (16.4 feet) wide. When the city was occupied, these huge masks dramatically flanked a stairway leading to the top of a pyramid 33 meters (108 feet) high (Lovgren 2004). Estrada-Belli describes the masks as having faces part human and part jaguar; one is adorned with carved corn husks over its eyes, the other has snake fangs. In the center of the main city plaza, archaeologists found a cluster of 120 finely polished green and blue jade cobbles; nearby, five polished jade axe heads were also found. Jade was a stone sacred to the Maya and associated with their main crop, maize.

From here, the development of Maya civilization accelerated, and its essential, "classic" character was established by about 1,750 years ago (about A.D. 250), including the following elements as enumerated by archaeologist David Webster (2002:79–80): a stratified society with an elite class led by a powerful royal family and a great king; imposing pyramids, temples, and palaces; decorated stone altars; an art style featuring depictions of death, human sacrifice, and mutilation; a hieroglyphic written language; screenfold, bark paper books in that written language; stelae—erect stone slabs—with messages in that written language; a written number system characterized by bars and dots; a double calendar of 365 and 260 days, respectively; a ritualized ball game played on a dedicated court; a veneration of jade; and the use of chocolate in preparing a ceremonial beverage.

At the height of the Classic Maya period there may have been as many as forty to fifty "regal-ritual cities," as defined by Webster (2002:151). These were more or less autonomous city-states, each ruled by royal dynasties that commanded the construction of the pyramids, temples, and palaces that draw the rapt attention of archaeologists and tourists alike (Figure 13.7).

Farming, focused in part on the production of maize, provided a major portion of Maya subsistence. Webster (2002:86) estimates that maize comprised about 60 percent of the Maya diet and the production of food was the major task of as much as 90 percent of the Maya population. In many regions the Maya practiced slash-and-burn agriculture, cutting and burning forest land to produce fields that were abandoned after only a short period of use and allowed to grow over, to be used again after a period of dormancy. This is the primary agricultural technique used by the modern Maya. To this, as archaeologists have documented, the ancient Maya added a number of other, more intensive techniques, including terracing hill slopes, building raised fields in swampy areas (as indicated by radar imaging), planting kitchen gardens, and tree-cropping, the specialized use of tree crops in rain forests and within settlements (McKillop 1994; Turner and Harrison 1983). Of necessity, the Maya relied on a number of techniques, both extensive and intensive, to feed the large and dense populations in their cities.

Figure 13.7 The 35-meter-(115-feet-) tall Temple of the Great Jaguar at the Maya site Tikal. At its peak around 1,300 years ago, Tikal was a Maya city with a population estimated by some to have been as much as 60,000 people. (© Brand X Pictures/PunchStock RF)

The Mysterious "Collapse" of the Maya?

When the Spanish arrived in the sixteenth century, the Maya world was vastly different than it had been just a few centuries previously. The large urban centers of the south had been abandoned, and the focus of Maya civilization had shifted to the north, into the Yucatán Peninsula. The difference between Classic Maya cities and those encountered by the Spanish in the early 1500s has long been a great historical mystery. Indeed, what happened to the Maya to cause such a great "collapse" of their civilization?

Archaeologist Arthur Demarest (2004) makes an interesting point about this "collapse." In his view, it involved just one element of the Maya tradition, the construction of large cities in the lowlands with impressive pyramids and palaces. When those lowland centers were abandoned between A.D. 800 and A.D. 900, however, other elements of the Maya civilization continued to thrive and even expand and elaborate, especially in the northern Yucatán Peninsula. Cities there like Uxmal and Chichén Itzá did not experience any such collapse, nor did they mysteriously disappear; just the opposite, they grew in size and power to fill the power vacuum created by the disintegration of the political and social structure in the south.

In David Webster's view, lowland Maya civilization always represented a delicate balance between nature, a growing population, and the land-hungry system of slash-and-burn agriculture. That balance, in fact, was upset several times during Maya history, leading to a series of dislocations. Slash-and-burn agriculture was an effective subsistence strategy in this tropical lowland habitat; but as population grew in Maya communities, the need for more intensive use of the land to produce crops grew as well. However, slash-and-burn agriculture requires an enormous amount of land (perhaps as much as 20 acres for each family) and quickly depletes the soil of nutrients, requiring a long rest or fallow period to allow the soil to regain its productivity. When the Maya agricultural fields, previously allowed to rest and regain nutrients, were pressed back into service more quickly in order to produce more food, ultimately and ironically productivity declined even more rapidly.

Adding other, more intensive agricultural techniques—terraced hill slopes, raised fields in swamps, kitchen gardens, and tree-cropping—certainly helped feed more mouths. For example, by artificially mounding up fields in wetlands, the Maya were able to exploit rich floodplains previously too wet to farm and were able to farm the same plots every year. At the Pulltrouser Swamp site in Belize, for instance, the Maya essentially reclaimed part of the swamp by building fields into the wetlands, producing extremely rich agricultural plots that could have yielded multiple crops each year (Turner and Harrison 1983).

Ultimately, however, the more intensive use of farmland like that evidenced at Pulltrouser Swamp was not enough to solve the Maya's food production problems. Another strategy employed by individual Maya cities was to expand their land base by aggressively appropriating the agricultural fields of their neighbors. Warfare for land capture may have been a short-term solution by growing a community's farmland base; but, as population continued to grow and productivity to decline, the need accelerated for ever more land, and warfare became endemic, an everyday, unpleasant fact of life for the Maya peasants who may have made up 80 to 90 percent of the population (Webster 2002:140). As foot soldiers, these peasants bore the major burden of these wars. Webster suggests that as agricultural productivity declined further and as the need to fight wars to capture land increased, the peasants, whose labor and lives were required for the system to work, lost faith in the ability of their kings to solve the problems plaguing them, to ease their increasing burden either materially or spiritually. As Webster points out, a civilization is no longer viable when farmers/foot soldiers/workers simply walk away; Webster calls it "voting with their feet." In his view, many peasants, disaffected by the inability of those kings to improve their lot, simply moved away from those lands controlled by their rulers. When this happened, Maya kings lost their most important resource: people. This is clearly reflected in the almost complete cessation of temple construction at many Maya cities after A.D. 950.

The series of crises experienced by the Maya, including the most dramatic of them in A.D. 950, may be explained, at least in part, as a result of a subsistence system inadequate to meet the needs of a growing population, accompanying soil depletion, and, finally, bloody conflicts. In previous collapses, the Maya had been able to recover; new cities cropped up, ruled by new kingly lineages who directed new bursts of pyramid and temple construction. Had the Spanish not arrived in the early sixteenth century, it is entirely possible that the Maya would have experienced yet another resurgence with an attendant explosion of new cities, spectacular temples, and graceful pyramids. We will, of course, never know.

Finally, maybe the entire notion of the "collapse" of the Maya is misguided. After all, as Arthur Demarest (2004:242) points out, modern historians do not refer to the fall of Rome after the fourth century A.D. as the "collapse" of Western civilization. The fall of Rome marked a significant change in the course of the history of the Western world, to be sure, but it certainly did not mark its termination. So too, the fall of the southern lowland Classic Maya city-states more than a thousand years ago did not mean that the Maya became extinct: they merely evolved. Even after the invasion of the Spanish in the sixteenth century, Maya culture continued and has survived, certainly in a different form, into the present where, as Demarest (2004:242) points out, it is experiencing a "cultural and political resurgence." In that way, Maya civilization is no different from Western civilization; it hasn't collapsed in a broad or all-encompassing sense. Instead, it has shifted, evolved, and adapted as circumstances have changed. This leaves us without any great mystery but, instead, a fascinating challenge to better understand the rise and endurance of the Maya people and culture.

If You're Alive and Reading This, Then I Guess the World Didn't End on December 21, 2012

Imagine returning home sometime during the last week of December to find a member of your family cowering in the basement, clutching a copy of the calendar.

"What's wrong," you ask him. "Why are you crouched down here?" Terrified, he holds up to the dim light of the basement the calendar, its pages turned to December. He points to the day labeled "31" and in hushed, trembling tones, says, "Look here. December 31. Now turn the page. What do you see?"

Of course, you see nothing. "Well, there's nothing there," you say.

"Exactly! There's nothing more," he responds. "December 31 is the final day on the calendar. Nothing follows it. That's the end. It's all over. We're doomed!"

Fearing that your family member has gone totally bonkers, you assure him that if he would only drive down to the local Barnes & Noble, he would find racks of calendars for the new year, variously festooned with photographs of kittens, puppies, clouds, vampires, and all other manner of amusing, awe-inspiring, or uplifting images.

That scenario is pretty silly. After all, who would be foolish enough to believe that merely because one cycle of a calendar—in this case, one year—ends, that the earth would end too? I mean, you'd have to be a bit of a dope to believe that, wouldn't you? Well, that's pretty much what all the 2012 hoopla was based on, the end of a cycle in the Maya calendar and, in fact, not one that the Maya believed would be all that momentous.

The Maya people of Guatemala, Mexico, Belize, and Honduras produced a remarkable Native American civilization replete with great cities, imposing pyramids, and a sophisticated series of calendars. Like ours, the Maya calendar had days (Figure 13.8), months (of 20 days each; Figure 13.9), and years (made up of 18 Maya months of 20 days and one of 5, adding up to 365 days). And, just as we recognize longer time periods (10 years for a

Figure 13.8 The twenty Maya day names or *kin* and their corresponding glyphs. (Jennifer Davis)

Figure 13.9 The names and glyphs representing the eighteen Maya "months" or *uinals*. Each *uinal* consisted of one cycle of the twenty named days depicted in Figure 13.8. The nineteenth and final glyph shown here is the *Wayeb*, a "short month" period of just five days. Eighteen months of twenty days each plus a *Wayeb* brings the Maya year or *tun* up to 365 days, very close to a full solar year. (Jennifer Davis)

decade, 100 years for a century, and 1,000 years for a millennium) the Maya did too. With their base-20 number system, the Maya had periods of 20 years (they called them *katuns*) and periods of about 400 years (a Maya *baktun*). Now here's where the confusion comes into play. While our calendar is linear, with the year numbers getting ever bigger as time proceeds, the Maya measured time as cyclical. For them, after 13 *baktuns* (in the current cycle which, the Maya believed, began about 5,125 years ago) the calendar simply goes back to zero, and—this is the important part—*it starts all over again.* Just like a year ends on December 31 and a new year begins again at the beginning, January 1, the Maya believed the same was true for periods of time longer than a year. No muss, no fuss, and no apocalyptic conflagrations.

The Maya never said that all of time or the earth or life on the planet will end after the thirteenth *baktun,* on the day that calculates on our calendar to December 21, 2012. The recent discovery of an astronomical calender painted on the wall of what appears to be the room of a Maya scribe at the Xultun site in Guatemala should put such nonsense to rest (Saturno et al. 2012). The calendar the scribe artfully painted onto the wall and that may have been used in the calculation of lunar eclipses doesn't end at the end of our calendar date of December 21, 2012, and, in fact, continues past that for more than a thousand years, including a date that corresponds on our calendar to A.D. 3500!

That's not the only example of a post-2012 date in the Maya calendar. Remember the burial chamber of the Maya ruler Pacal, discussed back in Chapter 9? Von Däniken thought Pacal's sarcophagus lid depicted a spaceman piloting a rocket. I deconstructed that bit of silliness there, but there is something very interesting written in Pacal's burial monument that you ought to know. The Maya scribes listed a date there for an important anniversary and celebration of Pacal's accession to the throne. The date they inscribed corresponds in our calendar to October 15, 4772 (Schele and Freidel 1990:82)! It makes no sense for the Maya to have planned an important celebration for a date *after* they thought the world was going to end. Clearly, the Maya did not believe that 2012 was to be the Apocalypse. The only thing supposed to happen on December 21, 2012, is that time's odometer will turn over to zero.

Surviving the Apocalypse

Flipping the dial recently, I found a documentary about 2012. The producers interviewed survivalist Patrick Geryl who believed that on December 21, 2012, the earth's rotation would reverse and most people on earth would die in a cataclysm of earthquakes and volcanoes. His grasp of physics isn't that strong, is it? Anyway, Geryl worked to convince people that they could survive this reversal if they sailed out into the middle of the ocean. Sure. That would have worked. But when asked if he planned to take his own advice, he sheepishly admitted on camera that, no, he wouldn't do that. The interviewer seemed genuinely surprised and asked him why. His answer: He would opt out of the surviving-the-Maya-apocalypse tactic of going out into the ocean on a boat to save his life because, drumroll, he gets seasick.

Do any of these people listen to themselves? The world is coming to an end—or so they think—the direction of rotation of the planet is going to reverse, the continents will crumble, great mountain chains will go sailing off into space, all of our cities will disintegrate, and Patrick has a plan for survival but can't do it because his tummy would feel icky. OMG.

Now, I wish I could tell you that the Maya never predicted the end of everything, but that would be giving you a false sense of security. In fact, on a monument located at the Maya site of Coba, in Mexico, there is a Mayan date that marks the day they believed the end of the earth would come. That predicted date is quite a bit further out than December 21, 2012. It's actually 41,341,050,000,000,000,000,000,000,000 years in the future, which is about 32 billion times longer than the universe has existed (Schele and Freidel 1990:430). That would be cumbersome on a movie marque, but, it's pretty good news.

About the Maya Calendar

In his book *Fingerprints of the Gods,* author Graham Hancock refers to the great sophistication of the calendar used by the ancient Maya of Mesoamerica and maintains that we should be greatly skeptical of their ability to have come up with it by themselves. He proposes that, in fact, they didn't develop it, but "inherited it" from a much older, super-sophisticated, lost civilization. This ancient civilization is the functional equivalent of Donnelly's Atlantis: a technologically sophisticated society that existed thousands of years before those recognized by archaeologists and historians and from whose shores diffused the advanced technologies found in the much more recent societies of ancient Egypt, Mesopotamia, and the Maya. To support his thesis that a lost civilization must have been responsible, however, Hancock must show that the Mesoamerican calendar is inexplicably, even shockingly, out of character with the rest of Mesoamerican culture; otherwise, no hypothesis of an outside source for the calendar is warranted. Here, Hancock has painted himself into a methodological corner and has no choice but to characterize the noncalendrical achievements of the Maya—as I've just shown, an impressive and awe-inspiring ancient civilization—as "generally unremarkable" (Hancock 1995:158) and to portray their way of life as being only "semi-civilized" (Hancock 1995:161). He must maintain this nonsense because an objective analysis of the remarkable achievements of the Maya in architecture, agriculture, artwork, and mathematics indicates that their calendar is not out of character at all, but was just one marvelous achievement in a long list. Let's ignore for a moment the fact that there is no evidence whatsoever for nonsense like ancient aliens or lost civilizations. The history of the Maya people shows that no such intervention is necessary to explain the development of their spectacular and sophisticated civilization. They were fully capable of developing it on their own.

Stonehenge

In the summer of 1996 I made a pilgrimage, of sorts, returning as an adult to a place that had amazed and inspired me as a teenager. My wife, our two kids, and I spent two weeks in Great Britain, and we made it a point to make the trip from London to Stonehenge.

My family and I were part of a gaggle of tourists from the United States and all over Europe as well who were visiting the ancient monument that day. Reflecting the "world" culture that permeates much of the planet, we were all dressed pretty much alike; most of Stonehenge's visitors were wearing sneakers, jeans, and T-shirts emblazoned with the logos of assorted rock bands, cartoon characters, and software companies. But there alone, amidst the Smashing Pumpkins and Beavis and Butt-head shirts, was a rather striking-looking individual, a woman dressed from head to toe in black. She had on black boots, loosely fitting black pants, a black shirt, and finally was enveloped in a long, rather dramatic, black velvet, hooded cape.

At first she stood still in her solitude. Then, as I watched she, almost imperceptibly, began to rock back and forth to some internal, inaudible rhythm, her eyes shut and her lips mouthing a silent mantra. I wondered, in a whisper to no one in particular, who she was. Someone answered: "Oh, she fancies herself the reincarnation of a Druid princess." Of course. It was a peculiar sight, indeed, but we were to see many peculiar sights on our trip.

We visited other "stone circles." Stonehenge is an extreme example of an ancient circle laid out in monumental stone or "megalithic" sentinels, but there are hundreds in Great Britain, so many, in fact, that there is an atlas/ tourist guide of them (Burl 1995) and a truly beautiful "gazetteer" of 300 of the most impressive of the sites (Cope 1998). In some we found people meditating in their geometric centers, hoping to focus the ancient and mysterious energy supposedly contained within them. At Avebury, a town encircled by an ancient monument of standing stones, the shelves of the tourist shops were filled with healing crystals, pyramid pendants, and even dowsing rods (pairs of bent brass rods going for five pounds, about $7.50, each) for channeling the "ancient energies" ostensibly focused in the prehistoric monument.

The ancient past of Great Britain has been invaded, or so it seems, by people espousing New Age beliefs (see Chapter 12). Seeking salvation and redemption in the fabric of antiquity, they congregate at the stone circles of Great Britain. In late June on the summer solstice they descend on Stonehenge to practice so-called ancient, pagan rites. Traditionally, a riot ensues as the local police attempt to protect the site from the scores of ecstatic, sometimes naked, latter-day Druids who have, in the past, climbed the ancient stones of the monument. Too often, the modern, reconstructed Druids revert to the historical behavior of the people they base their worldview on and rain violence down on the local constabulary.

What is Stonehenge, really? Is it some great archaeological mystery? Does it vibrate with some ancient and mystical energy? My then 10-year-old son Josh found "awesome" to be the most appropriate word to describe Stonehenge—and who could argue with his use of that term? In describing an ancient city on Mars, science fiction author Ray Bradbury (2006:110) described it this way: "Perfect, I (faultless), in ruins, yes, but perfect, nonetheless." I think that's a spot-on characterization of the modern manifestation of Stonehenge. About 5,000 years ago an otherwise simple farming people first excavated an almost perfectly circular ditch about 100 meters (300 feet) in diameter. At first, this is all that Stonehenge was. Then, 4,600 years ago, the Stonehenge people transported dozens of volcanic stones (called bluestones for their slightly blue hue) to Stonehenge from the Preseli Mountains in southwest Wales, a distance of about 385 kilometers (240 miles). Each of the bluestones weighed up to 4,000 kilograms (almost 9,000 pounds), and they were arranged in a double half-circle in the center of the circle demarcated by the ditch. Moving these heavy stones across that great a distance and then erecting them was no mean feat for a people with no mechanical contrivances or draught animals. But even this impressive, early incarnation of Stonehenge was a pale premonition of what it was to become (Darvill, Marshall, Pearson, and Wainwright 2012).

New radiocarbon dating of organic material found in the sockets the builders dug for the next set of large upright stones shows that about the same time they were transporting and erecting the bluestone semicircle, in other words, by about 4,600 years ago, they also were quarrying, transporting, shaping, and erecting the largest stones in the monument. These were the five separate sets of three stones each called the trilithons (Darvill, Marshall, Pearson, and Wainwright 2012). Each of the trilithons was composed of two massive uprights joined by a capstone (Figure 13.10 and 13.11). The five trilithons were arranged in the shape of a horseshoe and each stone was made of a rock type called "sarsen"—an ancient variety of sandstone found at Avebury about 40 kilometers (25 miles) to the north of Stonehenge. Each trilithon upright stands about 8 meters (26 feet) above the surface, with an additional 2 meters (6 feet) of stone buried in the chalky ground underlying the monument. The largest of the trilithon uprights weighs 50,000 kilograms (55 tons), and the associated lintel or cross-piece positioned on top weighs 9,000 kilograms (10 tons). Remember, each of these 10-ton blocks had to be raised up to the top of its 26-foot-high trilithon upright pair (for the facts and figures behind Stonehenge see Chippindale 2004; Hudson 2008; and Wernick et al. 1973).

Very soon thereafter, the builders of Stonehenge began shaping and transporting thirty additional sarsen stones. Though smaller than the trilithon uprights, these sarsens nevertheless were massive, with each more than 3 meters (10 feet) tall and weighing 25,000 kilograms (55,000 pounds). These thirty sarsens were erected in a complete circle 30 meters (98 feet) across, surrounding the trilithon horseshoe and inside of and concentric with the older ditch, (Figure 13.10, 13.11 and Table 13.1; Ruggles 1996). Thirty lintels, each weighing about 5,500 kilograms (6 tons), were perched in a continuous ring atop the sarsens. Adjacent sarsens were linked via the lintels using mortise-and-tenon joinery. Applying this method, the tops of the sarsens were shaped to produce two nobs (tenons), and two hollows (mortises) were sculpted on the bottom of each lintel. The lintels and sarsen circle were then connected almost like a giant Lego set. Further, each lintel was shaped precisely, curved on the

Figure 13.10   Even in ruin, Stonehenge is an evocative monument, reflecting the remarkable abilities of its ancient builders. (K. Feder)

Table 13.1

	Bluestones	Sarsens	Lintels	Trilithon Uprights	Trilithon Lintels	Heelstone
Number	50–80	30	30	10	5	1
Length	6.5 feet	13 feet	7 feet	22–32 feet	10 feet	20 feet
Weight	9,000 pounds	50,000 pounds	12,000 pounds	100,000 pounds	20,000 pounds	70,000 pounds
Distance from source	240 miles	25 miles	25 miles	25 miles	25 miles	25 miles

Figure 13.11 Depiction of an intact Stonehenge upon completion 4,000 years ago. Note the precision with which the enormous sarsens and trilithon uprights were connected to each other by their associated lintels.

exterior and interior to match the arc of the circle of the sarsens. What resulted was a smooth circle of stones, precisely positioned and joined together.

"Awesome" truly is the only word to describe it (see Figure 13.11). Other concentric rings of smaller stones were at one time contained within the sarsen circle. Other uprights were placed outside the sarsens, including the so-called heelstone—a 73,000-kilogram (80-ton) stone located about 80 meters (260 feet) northeast of the center of the sarsen circle.

Explaining Stonehenge

Stonehenge has justifiably generated a prodigious amount of interest. How did an ancient and presumably simple farming people construct the monument? How did they quarry the stones? How did they move them? How could they have planned and designed the monument? How did they erect the huge stones? And finally, perhaps the greatest mystery, why did they do it?

Some of the mystery of Stonehenge is a result of our own temporal bias. We find it hard to conceive of ancient people as being inventive, ingenious, or clever. Certainly, it took ingenuity and not just a little hard work to produce Stonehenge and the thousands of other megalithic monuments that are found in Europe (Figure 13.12). If we can leave behind our temporal preconceptions, we can clearly see that the archaeological record of the human

a

b

Figure 13.12   Four examples of the megalithic monuments of Great Britain: the Swinside circle (**a**) and Long Meg (**b**), a large upright stone, both in England; the Stones of Stenness (**c**) in the Orkney Islands, Scotland; and the Castlerigg (**d**) stone circle in England. Swinside consists of more than fifty stones and Castlerigg has thirty-eight stones, set in circles nearly 100 feet (30 meters) across. Long Meg is part of an enormous set of originally about seventy stones called "her daughters." The tallest of the Stenness stones looms more than 30 feet (9 meters) above the surrounding surface. (K. Feder)

c

d

Figure 13.12 *(continued)*

past shows that people, including those from 5,000 years ago, are capable of ingenuity and hard work. We need not fall back on lost continents or ancient astronauts to explain the accomplishments of the megalith builders or any other ancient human group.

How was Stonehenge built? The stone likely was quarried by taking advantage of natural breaks in the bedrock and using fire, cold water, and persistent hammering to split the stones into the desired shapes. The stones could have been moved on wooden sledges pulled by rope, perhaps using log rollers to quicken the pace. In an episode of the science series *Nova* (Secrets of Lost Empires 1997), replicative experiments were conducted in an attempt to discover how Stonehenge might have been built. Two parallel sets of squared-off log beams were placed in the ground, producing a wooden track.

Figure 13.13   Artist's conception of the raising of the lintels at Stonehenge. Through construction of a series of wooden platforms, the heavy stone lintels could have been levered up to their places atop the sarsens and trilithons. (From C. Chippindale, *Stonehenge Complete,* London: Routledge)

An upright trilithon-size cement block weighing 50 tons (45,000 kilograms) was attached to a wooden sled that fit onto the long trackway. The crew of fewer than two hundred volunteers certainly pulled some muscles and worked up a sweat, but once the trackway was greased, they were able to move the enormously heavy replica relatively easily.

The upright stones were likely erected using levers, and the lintels raised by a combination of levering and the construction of wooden staging around the uprights (Figure 13.13). The accomplishment was—and is—truly remarkable but, echoing a theme presented previously in this book (Chapter 10, for example), certainly within the capabilities of a large number of dedicated people working diligently toward a desired goal.

The people who built Stonehenge weren't from Atlantis or outer space; in fact, they lived practically next door. A large habitation and festival site dating to the period of Stonehenge's most significant construction has been found just 3 kilometers (about 2 miles) away. The site, called Durrington Walls, is characterized by the remains of an impressive circle, not of stones but of timbers, numerous square house foundations, dozens of hearths, and tens of thousands of animal bones, the apparent remains of great feasts (Olding-Smee 2007a). The timber circle is oriented toward the midwinter sunrise—the winter solstice, or December 21, the shortest day of the year in terms of number of hours of daylight (Schmid 2008). This is the precise opposite of the orientation of Stonehenge itself which, as we'll see, was oriented toward the midsummer solstice or June 21—the longest day of the year in terms of the number of hours of daylight.

Researchers estimate that between 300 and 1,000 residences were built at Durrington Walls, the homes of, perhaps, the pilgrims to the site. Seasonal indicators suggest that the structures at Durrington Walls were occupied during midwinter and midsummer, which fits nicely with the idea that Stonehenge was a monumental, ceremonial calendar, marking the location of the sun on the horizon (Schmid 2008). A broad stone road leads from the village to the nearby River Avon; if you travel that river upstream you encounter a similar stone road that leads directly to Stonehenge itself. Stonehenge was not an isolated, intrusive, inexplicable artifact; it was part of a broad cultural context that archaeologists are continuing to study and reveal.

The first major archaeological excavation conducted at Stonehenge in forty years took place in 2008, and lots of new information was retrieved (Morgan 2008). The new dig revealed that Stonehenge was a cemetery throughout its existence; the excavators estimated that the cremated remains of about 240 people were interred at Stonehenge. Because Stonehenge was so obviously a place of enormous ceremonial significance, researchers believe that those buried there were members of a ruling elite, perhaps the members of the same noble family.

Along with the cremation burials of people thought to be members of an elite class, researchers also point out that there are a large number of burials outside the monument proper. The remains of many of these people show signs of physical injury or sickness that likely contributed to their deaths, and a large portion, about half, display chemical signatures in their bones indicating that they did not live in the area near the monument. The chemical signature of one of the skeletons found near Stonehenge suggests he lived somewhere in the Alps (Morgan 2008). Based on this, researchers suggest that Stonehenge may have been, among other things, a place where people across a broad geographic area may have come for a "center of healing," a place where the sick and injured congregated in the hope of a cure for whatever ailed them (Morgan 2008).

An Ancient Astronomy?

Perhaps the most interesting theory presented to explain Stonehenge has been that proposed by astronomer Gerald Hawkins (1965) suggesting that Stonehenge was, in effect, an astronomical computer designed to keep track of the sun's position on the horizon at sunrise and sunset, as well as the moon's position on the horizon at "moonrise" and "moonset." He went on to suggest that Stonehenge was even used as an eclipse predictor.

In essence, Hawkins sees Stonehenge as an enormous sighting device. From the center, one's view of the surrounding horizon is limited; one is not afforded a 360-degree vista, because much of the horizon is blocked by sarsens or trilithons. Hawkins hypothesized that those points on the horizon that one can see from the center of Stonehenge and that appear to be marked by additional stones outside of the sarsen circle are all significant astronomically. Most obvious is the sighting from the center of Stonehenge to the northeast. Hawkins related this orientation to the rising of the sun.

The sun does not "rise in the east and set in the west" as many think. In fact, the sun's position on the horizon at sunrise and sunset moves slightly from day to day during the course of a year. In the Northern Hemisphere, the sun's position at sunrise moves a little bit north along the horizon each day in the spring until it reaches its northernmost point on the first day of summer—the specific *azimuth*, or angle, differs depending on one's latitude.

After its northernmost rising, the sun appears to rise a little farther south each day. On the first day of fall, the *autumnal equinox*, it rises due east. It then continues to rise farther south until it rises at its southernmost position on the first day of winter, the *winter solstice*. The sun then appears to change direction and rise a little farther north each day, rising due east again on the first day of spring, the *vernal equinox*. Continuing its apparent motion north, it again reaches its northernmost rising point exactly one year since it previously rose in that spot (Figure 13.14).

At any given location in the Northern Hemisphere, the sun rises at its farthest northern point on the horizon on the longest day of the year, the *summer solstice*. For the latitude of Stonehenge, the compass direction of that farthest northern point is 51 degrees (remember, of course, that north is located at 0 degrees and due east would be 90 degrees). Standing in the center of Stonehenge, the compass direction of the heelstone is that very same 51 degrees. In other words, upon sunrise on the summer solstice at the precise latitude of Stonehenge, one can look toward the compass direction of 51 degrees and see the sun rise directly over the heelstone.

Is this coincidental? As long ago as the early eighteenth century, Stonehenge investigator William Stukeley recognized the orientation of Stonehenge toward the summer sunrise. Hawkins maintains that this orientation of Stonehenge is no coincidence and that many of the possible solar and lunar sighting points at Stonehenge relate to significant points like the sunrise at the solstice.

Hawkins proposed that Stonehenge began as a simple, though large-scale, calendar for keeping track of the seasons—a valuable thing for people dependent on farming for their subsistence—and evolved over some 2,000 years into the impressive monument we see today.

Circular Reasoning About Stonehenge

Among the more bizarre hypotheses proposed for Stonehenge is one that explains its appearance as a Neolithic artistic representation of a *crop circle*. The modern crop circle phenomenon peaked in the 1980s and was centered in England, though circles and myriad other, sometimes quite beautiful and complex patterns of flattened wheat and other crops were reported in Canada,

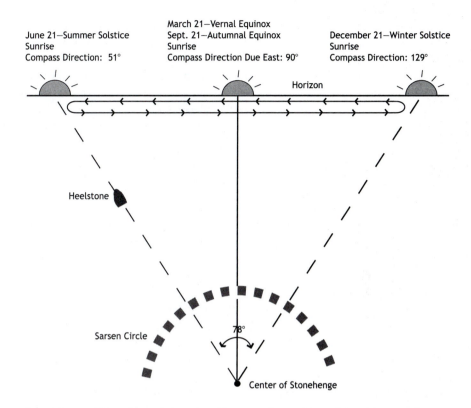

Figure 13.14 This schematic drawing illustrates the position of the rising sun during a year at Stonehenge. The observer standing in the center of Stonehenge can look out onto the horizon encircling the Salisbury Plain and see the rising sun through the upright sarsen stones. On December 21, the winter solstice, the sun appears to rise at a compass direction of 129°, the furthest south that sunrise appears at the latitude of Stonehenge. Each day following the winter solstice, the sun appear to rise a little to the north and by March 21, the first day of spring or the vernal equinox, the sun rises at due east (90°). The sun continues its apparent daily march to the north until, on June 21, the summer solstice, it rises at a compass direction of 51°. From the observer's position at the center of the monument, the disc of the sun appears to rise directly over the heelstone. After the solstice the sun appears to change direction, rising a little further to the south each day, reaching due east again on the first day of fall (the autumnal equinox), eventually returning to 129° a full year later, back on the first day of winter, only to shift to the north again, in an endless astronomical cycle.

the United States, Australia, and elsewhere (Figure 13.15; see Jim Schnabel's 1994 book, *Round in Circles*, for an in-depth look at the phenomenon).

The mysterious patterns of flattened crops were ascribed to whirlwinds, little understood earth energy vortexes, and even the mating patterns of oversexed hedgehogs. It was even suggested that the circular impressions that constituted so many of the crop circles were made when UFOs actually landed on earth. Because Stonehenge was built in a pattern of concentric circles, some of the crop circle afficionados saw a connection and suggested

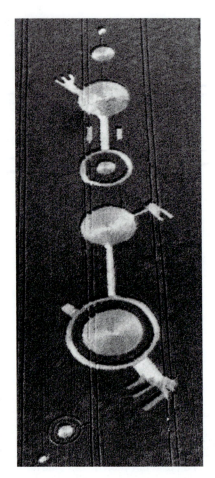

Figure 13.15   An enormous, beautiful, and elaborate pattern made by flattening a crop in a cornfield in Wiltshire, England, in July 1990. As the "crop circles" became more intricate through time, it became increasingly obvious to many that they were the result of pranksters (some of whom later confessed) and not extra-terrestrial aliens. (© Fortean Picture Library)

that ancient British farmers found crop circles in their own fields, realized they were caused by mysterious flying objects, and then proceeded to repli-cate the phenomenon in stone by constructing Stonehenge and other circular megalithic monuments.

Just as there is no Santa Claus, there turns out to be no mysterious crop-crushing vortexes or UFO landing fields in the UK or anywhere else. The crop circle mystery was solved in 1991 when two British men, Doug Chorley and Dave Bower, confessed to starting the phenomenon as a sim-ple prank (Irving and Lundberg 2006). The two best friends were initially inspired by UFO sightings. Apparently, in 1976, during one of their conver-sations about UFOs—and while hoisting a few pints at the local pub they frequented—Doug suggested to Dave that it would be great fun to traipse out into a nearby field in the middle of the night and make a circle of pressed-down plant growth, just to have a laugh at how the locals might react. Within a week, the merry and slightly tipsy pranksters grabbed a metal bar from

Doug's framing shop and singlehandedly started the crop circle craze (Irving and Lundberg 2006:63). It should be pointed out that the two men used a technique to flatten crops similar to one used by clandestine lovers in southern England from time immemorial. Without any nearby motels, such lovers were known to head out into a private field late at night and create a bed of flattened wheat on which to comfortably consummate their relationship.

Chorley and Bower explained how they had produced the circles to anyone who would listen. They would first set one end of the metal bar into the ground, and then by swinging it around they flattened a circular path, whose radius was the length of the bar, in the wheat (or whatever the crop). Next, they moved out to the edge of the circle, following its circumference and using the bar to flatten an additional ring around the original circle. Continuing this process, Chorley and Bower estimated that they could flatten a 30-foot-diameter circle in about thirty minutes (Schnabel 1994:268).

Later, they used an approach that employed 4-foot wooden planks. They threaded rope through the ends of the boards. Holding onto the ropes with both hands, they then balanced one foot on the board and, while applying a bit of pressure by pulling on the board, simply walked over the crop, leaving flattened patterns in their wake. For a time, they even used a sighting device attached to a baseball cap to ensure that their lines were straight, their circles round, and their other patterns geometrically accurate.

The biggest blow to those who hypothesized that the entire phenomenon was related to UFOs or mysterious earth energies occurred when Chorley and Bower, in cahoots with a television producer, secretly made a flattened crop pattern in front of television cameras. A number of crop circle experts, unaware of the conspiracy, were invited to examine the circle. They declared it genuine, beyond the capabilities of any mere human hoaxer. Needless to say, their credibility, along with the credibility of their esoteric explanations for the crop patterns, suffered tremendously.

Doug and Dave and those who followed freely admitted that they kept trying to one-up other circlemakers and, especially, to stay one step ahead of the people who kept trying to explain the circles as paranormal, supernatural, or extraterrestrial phenomena. They were so good at it that even today, nearly twenty years after they admitted it was all a prank and even though groups of circlemakers talk about their work openly—you can even purchase a book (Irving and Lundberg 2006) that provides a primer on how to make crop circles—some still inexplicably cling to the belief—and hope—that crop circles are an unexplained mystery.

Why Was Stonehenge Built?

Most writers about Stonehenge recognize that there is no great mystery surrounding how the monument was built. We have a pretty good idea of how the megalith builders moved the stones, how they shaped them, how they erected the uprights, and even how they raised the lintels to the top of the sarsens and trilithons. But *why* did the builders of Stonehenge go to such an incredible amount of trouble? To many writers, this is the great unsolved mystery of Stonehenge.

The construction of Stonehenge is no mystery at all, however, if we but look at ourselves. As human beings we revel in the construction of great public edifices. The builders of Stonehenge were no different. Generation after generation, they contributed to a monument whose destiny lay deep in a distant future. There is no mystery in that but only surprise born of an intellectual and temporal conceit on our part. We look back four or five thousand years and see nothing but primitive and alien strangers—this is our fundamental mistake—and from this we contrive a mystery. When we look back at the builders of Stonehenge and the painters of Paleolithic masterpieces and the creators of the civilization of the Maya, what is it that surprises us? Their familiarity! We recognize ourselves in the care, effort, time, and skill reflected in these ancient accomplishments.

We continue to be awed by the monument today, even building replicas—from the reverential full-size models in poured concrete located in Maryhill, Washington, and Stonehenge Aotearoa on the north island of New Zealand to the hilarious Carhenge in Alliance, Nebraska, a model faithful to the appearance of the real ruin, except that instead of being constructed of large stone monoliths, it is made entirely of old automobiles!

Stonehenge is a great cathedral, a colosseum, an impressive temple, a skyscraper. It is a reflection of what humans are capable of. It is a manifestation of our unique understanding that though we are individually ephemeral, our works can be eternal. In this, the builders of Stonehenge were remarkably successful. Stonehenge commands our attention. Millions of tourists, scholars, myth-makers, and fools alike are drawn to this monument. The builders of Stonehenge have attained that which they could have secured in no other way—they have achieved immortality. There is no mystery to this quest, only a remarkable continuity between the past and the present.

Conclusion: A Past We Deserve

Obviously, the past no longer exists. It is gone, whether we are contemplating human evolution, the earliest settlement of the Americas, the origins of civilization, the veracity of biblical stories, or any of the past times and events discussed in this book. In this sense, all of us are forced always to invent or construct an image of the past in the present.

Nevertheless, scientists and historians hope to construct a past that is veritable, that is accurate in terms of actual past events. We believe we can do this because, though the past is gone, it has left its mark in the present. But the data of antiquity are often vague, ambiguous, and difficult to interpret. Therefore, many different possible pasts can be constructed. All scientists, in whatever field, who consider the past history of the universe, the planet, life, or humanity recognize this. The message of this book has been that, although there are many different possibilities, not all of these constructed pasts—not all of the possibilities—are equally plausible.

Ultimately, then, we get the past we deserve. In every generation, thinkers, writers, scholars, charlatans, and kooks (these are not necessarily mutually exclusive categories) attempt to cast the past in an image either they or the public desire or find comforting. Biblical giants—some, apparently, walking their pet dinosaurs—large-brained, ape-jawed ancestors, lost tribes, lost continents, mysterious races, and ancient astronauts have all been a part of their concocted fantasies.

But I believe, and have tried to show in this book, that we deserve better—and we can do better. We deserve a veritable past, a real past constructed from the sturdy fabric of geology, paleontology, archaeology, and history, woven on the loom of science. We deserve better and can do better than weave a past from the whole cloth of fantasy and fiction. Finally, I hope I have shown in this book that the veritable past is every bit as interesting as those pasts constructed by the fantasy weavers of frauds, myths, and mysteries.

 FREQUENTLY ASKED QUESTION

1. *When the questions raised about the cave painters of Europe, the Maya, and Stonehenge are answered, does archaeology run out of mysteries?*

Of course not. Human antiquity is a dynamic field of study. We learn more about the history of our species every day. As old questions are answered, new ones are raised: What is the significance of the recently recovered Neandertal mitochondrial DNA? What is the meaning of newly discovered evidence of widespread warfare and cannibalism in the American Southwest? How far back can we trace the first Native Americans—and how did they come to the New World? There will always be questions; there will always be mysteries. With the use of new methods of analysis and the application of new perspectives, we will continue our largely successful attempt to answer and solve them.

 BEST OF THE WEB

CAVE PAINTERS

http://www.culture.gouv.fr/culture/arcnat/chauvet/en/
Official web page of the French Ministry of Culture focusing on Chauvet Cave. The site includes a photo album, map, history, and links to websites devoted to other Upper Paleolithic painted caves.

http://www.culture.gouv.fr/culture/arcnat/lascaux/en/

Splendid website devoted to Lascaux Cave. Take a virtual walk through the cave and gaze upon most of the major works of art.

MAYA

http://www.d.umn.edu/cla/faculty/troufs/anth3618/mamaya.html

Website with many links to web pages that discuss the culture of the Maya people, both ancient and modern.

http://www.mesoweb.com/

A website focusing on all things Mesoamerican. Links to articles, websites, news, excavations, and just about anything else you might want to know about Mesoamerica.

STONEHENGE/STONE CIRCLES

http://www.stonepages.com/home.html

If you want a virtual visit to almost any megalithic site in England, Scotland, Ireland, Wales, France, or Italy, go to this website. Lots of photographs and detailed information.

http://www.stonehenge.co.uk/

A comprehensive guide to Stonehenge, including information about visiting the ancient site.

CRITICAL THINKING EXERCISE

Using the deductive approach outlined in Chapter 2, how would you test these hypotheses? In each case, what archaeological data must you find to conclude that the hypothetical statement is an accurate assertion, that it describes what actually happened in the ancient human past?

- The cave paintings of the Upper Paleolithic in Europe served a magical function. Rendering the animals on cave walls represented a spiritual "capturing" of food animals that the ancient artists hoped literally to capture in the hunt.
- The collapse of the ancient Maya civilization was caused by an invasion of outsiders from the Valley of Mexico.
- The function of Stonehenge was as a giant solar calendar.

References

Achenbach, J. 1999. *Captured by Aliens: The Search for Life and Truth in a Very Large Universe.* New York: Simon and Schuster.

Adovasio, J. M., J. Donahue, and R. Stuckenrath. 1990. The Meadowcroft Rockshelter carbon chronology—1975–1990. *American Antiquity* 55:348–353.

Albers, A. 1999. Mystical journeys: Sedona special places, Palatki ruins. http://www.visionsofheaven.com/journeys-sedonadocs/sedPalatki.html.

Allen, J. M. 1999. *Atlantis: The Andes Solution.* New York: St. Martin's Press.

Allen, S. 1989. *Meeting of Minds.* Buffalo: Prometheus.

Applebaum, E. 1996. Holy stones. *Jewish News.* August 23:47–51.

Arnold, B. 1992. The past as propaganda. *Archaeology* 45(4):30–37.

Arnold, D. 1991. *Building in Egypt: Pharaonic Stone Masonry.* Oxford: Oxford University Press.

Arthur, J. 1996. Creationism: Bad science or immoral pseudoscience. *Skeptic* 4(4):88–93.

Ashe, G. 1971. Analysis of the legends. In *Quest for America,* ed. G. Ash, pp. 15–52. New York: Praeger.

Ashmore, W., and R. J. Sharer. 2006. *Discovering Our Past: A Brief Introduction to Archaelogy.* 4th ed. New York: McGraw-Hill.

Atwater, C. 1820. *Description of the Antiquities Discovered in the State of Ohio and Other Western States.* Transactions and Collections of the American Antiquarian Society. New York: AMS Press (reprinted in 1973 for the Peabody Museum of Ethnology and Archaeology, Harvard University).

Bakeless, J. 1964. *The Journals of Lewis and Clark.* New York: Mentor Books.

Ball, G. 2011. Finding Atlantis. *National Geographic Channel.* First broadcast March 13, 2011.

Balter, M. 2008. Going deeper into the grotte chauvet. *Science* 321:904–905.

Barton, B. S. 1787. *Observations on Some Parts of Natural History.* London.

Bartram, W. 1791. *The Travels of William Bartram.* 1928 reprint. New York: Dover.

BBC News. Russians seek Atlantis off Cornwall. 1997. http://news.bbc.co.uk/2/hi/uk_news/43172.stm.

Bellantoni, N. 2002. The Pachaug Forest artifact hoax. *Connecticut Preservation News* 25(5):3.

Berkman, M. B., and E. Plutzer, 2011. Defeating creationism in the courtroom, but not in the classroom. *Science* 331:404–405.

Berlitz, C. 1984. *Atlantis: The Eighth Continent.* New York: Fawcett Crest.

Bermúdez de Castro, J. M., J. L. Arsuaga, E. Carboneli, A. Rosas, I. Matinez, and M. Mosquera. 1997. A hominid from the Lower Pleistocene of Atapuerca, Spain: Possible ancestor to Neandertals and modern humans. *Science* 276: 1392–1395.

Bhattacharjee, V. 2009. Authors scramble to make textbooks conform to Texas science standards. *Science* 324:1385.

Bird, R. T. 1939. Thunder in his footsteps. *Natural History* 43(5):254–261, 302.

Bird, S. E. 1992. *For Enquiring Minds: A Cultural Study of Supermarket Tabloids.* Knoxville: University of Kentucky Press.

Blinderman, C. 1986. *The Piltdown Inquest*. Buffalo: Prometheus Books.

Bohannon, J. 2006. Mad about pyramids. *Science* 313:1718–1720.

Bolnick, D. A., D. I. Bolnick, and D. G. Smith. 2006. Asymmetric male and female genetic histories among Native Americans from Eastern North America. *Molecular Biological Evolution* 23(11):2161–2174.

Bolnick, D. A., K. L. Feder, B. T. Lepper, and T. A. Barnhart. 2012. Civilizations lost and found: Fabricating history. Part Three: Real messages in DNA. *Skeptical Inquirer* 36(1):48–51.

Bolnick, D. A., and D. G. Smith, 2007. Migration and social structure among the Hopewell: Evidence from ancient DNA. *American Antiquity* 72:627–644.

Bortolini, M.-C., et al. 2003. Y-chromosome evidence for differing ancient demographic histories in the Americas. *American Journal of Human Genetics* 73:524–539.

Bradbury, R., 2006. *The Martian Chronicles*. New York: William Morrow.

Breuil, H. 1952. *Four Hundred Years of Cave Art*. Montignac, France: Centre d'Études et de Documentation Prehistorique.

Brewer, D. J., and E. Teeter. 1999. *Egypt and the Egyptians*. Cambridge: Cambridge University Press.

Brier, B. 2007. How to build a pyramid. *Archaeology* 60(3):22–27.

Brier, B., and J.-P. Houdin. 2008. *The Secret of the Great Pyramid*. New York: Harper.

Briggs, A. W., et al. 2009. Targeted retrieval and analysis of five Neandertal mtDNA genomes. *Science* 325:318–321.

Briuer, F., J. Simms, and L. Smith. 1997. Site Mapping, Geophysical Investigation, and Geomorphic Reconnaissance at Site 9 ME 395 Upatio Town, Fort Benning, Georgia. *U.S. Army Corps of Engineers, Miscellaneous Paper* EL-97-3.

Brown, D. 1970. *Bury My Heart at Wounded Knee*. New York: Bantam.

Bruhns, K. O. 1994. *Ancient South America*. Cambridge World Archaeology. Cambridge: Cambridge University Press.

Buckley, T. 1976. The discovery of Tutankhamun's tomb. In *The Treasures of Tutankhamun*, ed. K. S. Gilbert, J. K. Holt, and S. Hudson, pp. 9–18. New York: The Metropolitan Museum of Art.

Burdick, C. 1950. When GIANTS roamed the earth: Their fossil footprints still visible. *Signs of the Times*, July 25:6, 9.

Burl, A. 1995. *A Guide to the Stone Circles of Britain, Ireland, and Brittany*. New Haven: Yale University Press.

Butzer, K. 1976. *Early Hydraulic Civilization of Egypt: A Study in Cultural Ecology*. Chicago: University of Chicago Press.

Byrne, M. St. Clere (ed.). 1979. *The Elizabethan Zoo: A Book of Beasts Fabulous and Authentic* (selected from Philemon Holland's 1601 translation of Pliny and Edward Topsell's 1607 *Historie of Foure-Footed Beastes* and his 1608 *Historie of Serpents*). Boston: Nonpareil Press.

Campbell, S. (1995). *The Loch Ness Monster: The Evidence*. Amherst, New York, Prometheus Books.

Cardiff Giant, The. 1869. *Harper's Weekly*, p. 776.

Cardiff Giant, The. 1898. *Ithaca Daily Journal*, Jan. 4. Ithaca, N.Y.

Carlin, G. 1997. *Brain Droppings*. New York: Hyperion.

Case of the Ancient Astronauts (television program). 1978. *Nova*. Boston: WGBH.

Chang, K. C. 2002. *The Formation of Chinese Civilization: An Archaeological Perspective*. New Haven: Yale University Press.

Chateaubriand, F. R. V. de. 1801. Historical discussion of the ruins found at the border of Ohio in North America and which is spoken about in the voyage in Pennsylvania by M. Creveceur.

Chatters, J. C. 2002. *Ancient Encounters: Kennewick Man and the First Americans.* New York: Touchstone.

Chauvet, J.-M., É. B. Deschamps, and C. Hillaire. 1996. *Dawn of Art: The Chauvet Cave.* New York: Abrams.

Chippindale, C. 1983. *Stonehenge Complete.* Ithaca: Cornell University Press.

———. 1990. Piltdown: Whodunit? Who cares? *Science* 250:1162–1163.

———. 2004. *Stonehenge Complete.* New York: Thames and Hudson.

Clayton, P. A. 1994. *Chronicle of the Pharaohs: The Reign-by-Reign Record of the Rulers and Dynasties of Ancient Egypt.* London: Thames and Hudson.

Cline, E. 2007. *From Eden to Exile: Unraveling Mysteries of the Bible.* National Geographic, Washington, D.C.

Clottes, J., and D. Lewis-Williams. 1998. *The Shamans of Prehistory: Trance and Magic in the Painted Caves.* New York: Abrams.

Clottes, J., and J. Courtin. 1996. *The Cave Beneath the Sea: Paleolithic Images at Cosquer.* New York: Abrams.

Coe, M. D. 1992. *Breaking the Maya Code.* London: Thames and Hudson.

———. 1993. *The Maya.* New York: Thames and Hudson.

Cohen, D. 1969. *Mysterious Places.* New York: Dodd, Mead.

Cohn, N. 1996. *Noah's Flood: The Genesis Story in Western Thought.* New Haven: Yale University Press.

Cole, J. R. 1979. Inscriptionmania, hyperdiffusionism, and the public: Fallout from a 1977 meeting. *Man in the Northeast* 17:27–53.

———. 1982. Western Massachusetts "Monk's caves": 1979 University of Massachusetts field research. *Man in the Northeast* 24:37–70.

Cole, J. R., L. Godfrey, and S. Schafersman. 1985. Mantracks: The fossils say no! *Creation/Evolution* 5(1):37–45.

Collina-Girard, J. 2001. L'Atlantide devant le detroit de Gibralter? Myth et geologie. *Comptes Rendus de l'Academie des Sciences (2a)* 333:233–240.

Collins, A. 2002. *Gateway to Atlantis.* New York: Carroll and Graff.

Conkey, M. 1980. The identification of prehistoric hunter-gatherer aggregation sites: The case of Altamira. *Current Anthropology* 21(5):609–639.

———. 1987. New approaches in the search for meaning? A review of research in "Paleolithic art." *Journal of Field Archaeology* 14:413–430.

Conrad, N. J. 2003. Paleolithic ivory sculptures from southwestern Germany and the origins of figurative art. *Nature* 426:830–832.

Conyers, L. B. 2003. Ground penetrating radar in archaeology. http://www.du.edu/~lconyer/graves.htm.

———. 2004. *Ground Penetrating Radar for Archaeology.* Walnut Creek, Calif.: AltaMira Press.

———. 2006. Innovative ground-penetrating radar methods for archaeological mapping. *Archaeological Prospection* 13:137–139.

Conyers, L. B., and D. Goodman. 1997. *Ground Penetrating Radar: An Introduction for Archaeologists.* Walnut Creek, Calif.: AltaMira Press.

Cope, J. 1998. *The Modern Antiquarian: A Pre-Millennial Odyssey Through Megalithic Great Britain.* London: Thorsons.

Cowen, R. 1995. After the fall. *Science News* 148:248–249.

Coyne, J. A. 2009. *Why Evolution Is True.* New York: Viking.

Crawford, G. W. 1992. Prehistoric plant domestication in East Asia. In *The Origins of Agriculture: An International Perspective,* ed. C. W. Cowan and P. J. Watson, pp. 7–38. Washington, D.C.: Smithsonian Institution Press.

———. 1994. *The Hidden History of the Human Race.* San Diego: Govardhan Hill.

Curry, A. 2007. Digging into a desert mystery. *Science* 317:446–447.

Dall, W. H. 1877. On succession of shell heaps of the Aleutian Islands. In *Contributions to American Ethnology*, vol. 1, pp. 41–91. Washington, D.C.: U.S. Department of the Interior.

Damon, P. E. 1989. Radiocarbon dating of the Shroud of Turin. *Nature* 337:611–615.

Daniel, G. 1977. Review of *America B.C.* by Barry Fell. *New York Times Book Review Section*, March 13:8ff.

Darvill, T., P. Marshall, M.P. Pearson, and G. Wainwright. 2012. Stonehenge remodelled. *Antiquity* 86: 1021–1040.

Darwin, C. 1859. *On the Origin of Species by Means of Natural Selection*. 1898 reprint. New York: Appleton.

———. 1871. *The Descent of Man*. 1930 reprint. London: C. C. Watts.

Darwin theory is proved true. 1912. *New York Times*, Dec. 22.

David, A. 2009. Italian group claims to debunk shroud of Turin. http://news.yahoo.com/s/ap/20091006/ap_on_re_eu/eu_italy_shroud_of_turin_10.

———. 2009. Researcher says text proves Shroud of Turin real. Associated Press, November 20. http://www.breitbart.com/article.php?id=D9C3C4A00&show_article=1.

Dawkins, R. 2011. *The Magic of Reality*. New York, Free Press.

Dawson, C., and A. S. Woodward. 1913. On the discovery of a Paleolithic human skull and mandible in a flint bearing gravel overlying the Wealden (Hastings Beds) at Piltdown, Fletching (Sussex). *Quarterly Journal of the Geological Society* LXIX:117–151.

Deacon, R. 1966. *Madoc and the Discovery of America*. New York: Braziller.

Deagan, K., and J. M. Cruxent. 1997. Medieval foothold in the Americas. *Archaeology* 50(4):54–59.

de Camp, L. S. 1970. *Lost Continents: The Atlantis Theme in History, Science, and Literature*. New York: Dover.

de la Vega, G. 1988. *The Florida of the Inca*. 1605 ed. Translated by J. G. Varner and J. J. Varner. Austin: University of Texas Press.

Demarest, A. 2004. *Ancient Maya: The Rise and Fall of a Rainforest Civilization*. Cambridge: Cambridge University Press.

Dembski, W. A. 1999. *Intelligent Design: The Bridge Between Science and Theology*. Downer's Grove, Ill.: Intrauniversity Press.

Derenko, M. V., T. Grzybowski, B. A. Malyarchuk, J. Czarny, D. Miscicka-Sliwka, and I. A. Zakharov. 2001. The presence of mitochondrial haplogroup X in Altatians from south Siberia. *American Journal of Human Genetics* 69:237–241.

de Tapia, E. M. 1992. The origins of agriculture in Mesoamerica and South America. In *The Origins of Agriculture: An International Perspective*, ed. C. W. Cowan and P. J. Watson, pp. 143–171. Washington, D.C.: Smithsonian Institution Press.

DiBlasio, N. 2012. A third of Earthlings believe in UFOs, would befriend aliens. *USA Today*. http://www.usatoday.com/news/nation/story/2012-06-26/ufo-survey/55843742/1.

Diehl, R. A. 2004. *The Olmecs: America's First Civilization*. London: Thames and Hudson.

Dillehay, T. D., C. Ramirez, M. Pino, M. B. Collins, J. Rossen, and J. D. Pino-Navarro. 2008. Monte Verde: Seaweed, food, medicine, and the peopling of South America. *Science* 320:784–786.

Dillehay, T. D. 1989. *Monte Verde: A Late Pleistocene Settlement in Chile*, vol. 1, *Paleoenvironment and Site Context*. Washington, D.C.: Smithsonian Institution Press.

———. 1997. The Battle of Monte Verde. *Sciences*. Jan./Feb.: 28–33.

————. 2000. *The Settlement of the Americas: A New Prehistory.* New York: Basic Books.

Dillehay, T. D., and M. B. Collins. 1988. Early cultural evidence from Monte Verde in Chile. *Nature* 332:150–152.

Dincauze, D. 1982. Monk's caves and short memories. *Quarterly Review of Archaeology* 3(4):1, 10–11.

DiPietro, V., and G. Molenaar. 1982. *Unusual Martian Surface Features.* Glen Dale, Md.: Mars Research.

Dirty-digger scandal spreads to 42 sites nationwide. 2001. *Mainichi Shimbun,* October 7, 2001.

Donnelly, I. 1882. *Atlantis, the Antediluvian World.* 1971 reprint. New York: Harper.

Donohue, D. J., J. S. Olin, and G. Harbottle. 2002. Determination of the radiocarbon age of parchment of the Vinland Map. *Radiocarbon* 44(1):45–52.

dos Santos, A. N. 1997. Atlantis: The Lost Continent finally found. http://www.atlan.org/.

Downey, R. 2000. *Riddle of the Bones: Politics, Science, Race, and the Story of Kennewick Man.* New York: Springer-Verlag.

Doyle, A. C. 1891–1902. *The Celebrated Cases of Sherlock Holmes.* 1981 reprint. London: Octopus Books.

Drake, F. 2003. The Drake equation revisited. http://www.astrobio.net/index .php?option=com_retrospection&task=detail&id=610.

Du Pratz, L. P. 1774. *History of Louisiana.* London: Printed for T. Becket.

Eaton, R. 1978. The evolution of trophy hunting. *Carnivore* 1(1):110–121.

Edwords, F. 1983. Creation/evolution update: Footprints in the mind. *Humanist* 43(2):31.

Eggert, G. 1996. The enigmatic "Battery of Baghdad." *Skeptical Inquirer* 20(3):31–34.

Elvas, Gentleman of. 1611. *The Discovery and Conquest of Terra Florida by Don Ferdinando de Soto and Six Hundred Spaniards, His Followers.* The Hakluyt Society. 1907 reprint. New York: Burt Franklin.

Erlandson, J. M., T. C. Rick, T. J. Braje, M. Casperson, B. Culleton, B. Fulfrost, T. Garcia, D. A. Guthrie, N. Jew, D. J. Kenett, M. L. Moss, L. Reeder, C. Skinner, J. Watts, and L. Willis, 2011. Paleoindian seafaring, maritime technologies, and coastal foraging on California's Channel Islands. *Science* 331:1181–1184.

Ewen, C. R. 1989. Anhaica: Discovery of Hernando de Soto's 1539–1540 winter camp. In *First Encounters: Spanish Exploration in the Caribbean and the United States, 1492–1570,* ed. J. T. Milanich and S. Milbrath, pp. 110–118. Gainesville: University Press of Florida.

Fagan, B. M. 2006. *Archaeology: A Brief Introduction.* 9th ed. Upper Saddle River, N.J.: Prentice-Hall.

Fash, W. L. 2001. *Scribes, Warriors and Kings: The City of Copan and the Ancient Maya.* New York: Thames and Hudson.

Faulkner, C. 1971. *The Old Stone Fort.* Knoxville: University of Tennessee Press.

Fears, J. Rufus. 1978. Atlantis and the Minoan Thalassocracy: A study in modern mythopoeism. In *Atlantis: Fact or Fiction,* ed. E. S. Ramage, pp. 103–134. Bloomington: Indiana University Press.

Feder, K. L. 1980a. Foolsgold of the gods. *The Humanist,* Jan./Feb.:20–23.

————. 1980b. Psychic archaeology: The anatomy of irrationalist prehistoric studies. *Skeptical Inquirer* 4(4):32–43.

————. 1981a. The Farmington River Archaeological Project: Focus on a small river valley. *Man in the Northeast* 22:131–146.

————. 1981b. Waste not, want not: Differential lithic utilization and efficiency of use. *North American Archaeologist* 2(3):193–205.

———. 1984. Irrationality and archaeology. *American Antiquity* 49(3):525–541.

———. 1987. Cult archaeology and creationism: A coordinated research project. In *Cult Archaeology and Creationism: Understanding Pseudoscientific Beliefs About the Past,* ed. F. Harrold and R. Eve, pp. 34–48. Iowa City: University of Iowa Press.

———. 1990a. Late Woodland occupation of the uplands of northwestern Connecticut. *Bulletin of the Massachusetts Archaeological Society* 51(2):61–68.

———. 1990b. Piltdown, paradigms, and the paranormal. *Skeptical Inquirer* 14(4):397–402.

———. 1994. The Spanish *entrada:* A model for assessing claims of pre-Columbian contact between the Old and New Worlds. *North American Archaeologist* 15:147–166.

———. 1995a. Archaeology and the paranormal. In *Encyclopedia of the Paranormal,* ed. G. Steiner. Buffalo: Prometheus Books.

———. 1995b. Ten years after: Surveying misconceptions about the human past. *CRM (Cultural Resource Management)* 18(3):10–14.

———. 1998. Perceptions of the past: Survey results—how students perceive the past. *General Anthropology* 4(2):1, 8–12.

———. 1998–99. Archaeology and Afrocentrism: An attempt to set the record straight. *A Current Bibliography on African Affairs* 29(3):199–210.

———. 2001. Prehistoric land-use patterns in north-central Connecticut: A matter of scale. In *Archaeology of the Appalachian Highlands,* ed. L. Sullivan and S. Prezzanno, pp. 19–30. Knoxville: University of Tennessee Press.

———. 2004. *Linking to the Past: A Brief Introduction to Archaeology.* New York: Oxford University Press.

———. 2006. Skeptics, fence-sitters, and true believers: Student acceptance of an improbable prehistory. In *Archaeological Fantasies: How Pseudoarchaeology Misrepresents the Past and Misleads the Public,* ed. G. Fagan. Oxford: Routledge.

———. 2006. Hoaxes in anthropology. In *Encyclopedia of Anthropology,* ed. H. J. Birx, vol. 3, pp. 1169–1176. Thousand Oaks: Sage.

Feder, K. L. 2008. *Linking to the Past: A Brief Introduction to Archaeology.* New York: Oxford University Press.

Fell, B. 1976. *America B.C.: Ancient Settlers in the New World.* New York: Demeter Press.

———. 1980. *Saga America.* New York: Times Books.

———. 1982. *Bronze Age America.* New York: Times Books.

Fernandez-Armesto, F. 1974. *Columbus and the Conquest of the Impossible.* New York: Saturday Review Press.

Fitzhugh, W. 1972. *Environmental Archaeology and Cultural Systems in Hamilton Inlet, Labrador: A Survey of the Central Labrador Coast from 3000 B.C. to the Present.* Smithsonian Contributions to Anthropology, No. 16. Washington, D.C.: Smithsonian Institution Press.

Flem-Ath, R., and R. Flem-Ath. 1995. *When the Sky Fell: In Search of Atlantis.* New York: St. Martin's Press.

Flynn, S. 2006. Touro Park dig comes up empty. In *Newport Daily News.* http://www.newportdailynews.com/ee/newportdailynews/default.php?pSetup=newportdailynews_archive.

Forrest, B. C., and P. R. Gross. 2003. *Creationism's Trojan Horse: The Wedge of Intelligent Design.* New York: Oxford University Press.

Foster, J. W. 1873. *Prehistoric Races of the United States of America.* Chicago: S. C. Griggs.

Fowler, M. 1974. *Cahokia: Ancient Capital of the Midwest.* Addison-Wesley Module No. 48. Menlo Park, Calif.: Cummings.

———.1975. A Precolumbian urban center on the Mississippi. *Scientific American* 233(2):92–101.

———.1989. *The Cahokia Atlas: A Historical Atlas of Cahokia Archaeology.* Studies in Illinois Archaeology 6. Springfield: Illinois Historic Preservation Agency.

Franco, B. 1969. *The Cardiff Giant: A Hundred Year Old Hoax.* Cooperstown: New York State Historical Association.

Frayling, C. 2005. *Mad, Bad and Dangerous? The Scientist and the Cinema.* London: Reaktion.

Friedlander, P. 1969. *Plato: The Dialogues,* vol. 3. Princeton: Princeton University Press.

Friedrich, W. L., B. Kromer, M. Friedrich, J. Heinemeier, T. Pfeiffer, and S. Talamo. 2006. Santorini eruption radiocarbon dated to 6127–1600 B.C. *Science* 312:548.

Frodsham, J. D. 1989. The enigmatic shroud. *The World & I,* June:320–329.

Frost, F. 1982. The Palos Verdes Chinese anchor mystery. *Archaeology,* Jan./Feb.:23–27.

Fuson, R. 1987. *The Log of Christopher Columbus.* Camden, Maine: International Marine.

Gallup, C. H. Jr., and F. Newport. 1991. Belief in paranormal phenomena among adult Americans. *Skeptical Inquirer* 15:137–146.

Gardner, M. 1985. Notes of a psi-watcher: The great stone face and other nonmysteries. *Skeptical Inquirer* 10(1):14–18.

Garvin, J. 2001. The "Face on Mars" trail map. http://science.nasa.gov/headlines/y2001/ast24may_1.htm?list540155.

Gee, H. 1996. Box of bones "clinches" identity of Piltdown paleontology hoaxer. *Nature* 381:261–262.

Gibson, J. 2000. *The Ancient Mounds of Poverty Point.* Gainesville: University of Florida Press.

Gifford-Gonzalez, D. 1993. You can hide, but you can't run: Representation of women's work in illustrations of Paleolithic life. *Visual Anthropology Review* 9(1):23–41.

Gilbert, M. T. P., et al., 2008. DNA from pre-Clovis human coprolites in Oregon, North America. *Science* 320:786–789.

Godfrey, L. 1985. Footnotes of an anatomist. *Creation/Evolution* 5(1):16–36.

Godfrey, W. 1951. The archaeology of the Old Stone Mill in Newport, Rhode Island. *American Antiquity* 17:120–129.

Goebel, T., M. R. Waters, and D. H. O'Rourke. 2008. The late Pleistocene dispersal of modern humans in the Americas. *Science* 319:1497–1502.

Goodman, J. 1977. *Psychic Archaeology: Time Machine to the Past.* New York: Berkley.

———.1981. *American Genesis.* New York: Berkley.

Goodwin, W. 1946. *The Ruins of Great Ireland in New England.* Boston: Meader.

Gottfried, K., and K. G. Wilson. 1997. Science as a cultural construct. *Nature* 386:545–547.

Gould, S. J. 1980. The Piltdown conspiracy. *Natural History,* Aug.:8–28.

———.1981. A visit to Dayton. *Natural History,* Nov.:8ff.

———.1982. Moon, Mann, and Otto. *Natural History,* Jan.:4–10.

Gove, H. E. 1996. *Relic, Icon or Hoax? Carbon Dating the Turin Shroud.* Philadelphia: Institute of Physics.

Gradie, R. F. 1981. Irish immigration to 18th century New England and the stone chamber controversy. *Bulletin of the Archaeological Society of Connecticut* 44:30–39.

Green, R. E., et al. 2010. A draft sequence of the Neanderthal genome. *Science* 328:710–722.

Greene, J. 1959. *The Death of Adam: Evolution and Its Impact on Western Thought.* Ames: Iowa State University Press.

Gross, P. R., and N. Levitt. 1994. *Higher Superstition: The Academic Left and Its Quarrel with Science.* Baltimore: Johns Hopkins.

Grothe, D. J. 2009. A skeptic's guide to podcasts. *Skeptical Inquirer* 33(6):30–31.

Guthrie, R. D. 2006. *The Nature of Paleolithic Art.* Chicago: University of Chicago Press.

Halsey, J. R. 2009. The "Michigan Relics": America's longest running archaeological fraud. In *Midwest Archaeological Conference,* Iowa City, Iowa.

Halverson, J. 1987. Art for art's sake in the Paleolithic. *Current Anthropology* 28:63–71.

Hamilton, R. A. 2004. CGA instructor believes Atlantis is no longer lost. *New London Day* (Connecticut), Nov. 19.

Hancock, G. 1995. *Fingerprints of the Gods.* New York: Three Rivers Press.

———. 2003. *Underworld: The Mysterious Origins of Civilization.* New York: Three Rivers Press.

Handwerk, B. 2005. King Tut not murdered violently, CT scans show. http://national geographic.com/news/2005/03/0308_050308_kingtutmurder.html.

Harlan, J. 1992. Indigenous African agriculture. In *The Origins of Agriculture: An International Perspective,* ed. C. W. Cowan and P. J. Watson, pp. 59–70. Washington, D.C.: Smithsonian Institution Press.

Harris, M. 1968. *The Rise of Anthropological Theory.* New York: Crowell.

Hattendorf, I. 1997. From the collection: William S. Godfrey's Old Stone Mill archaeological collection. *Newport History* 68(2):109–111.

Hawkins, G. 1965. *Stonehenge Decoded.* New York: Dell.

Headrick, A. 2007. *The Teotihuacan Trinity.* Austin: University of Texas Press.

Hearn, Lafcadio. 1876. The Mound Builders. In *The Commercial,* Cincinnati, Ohio.

Henry, D. O. 1989. *From Foraging to Agriculture: The Levant at the End of the Ice Age.* Philadelphia: University of Pennsylvania Press.

Hertz, J. 1997. Round church or windmill? New light on the Newport Tower. *Newport History* 68(2):55–91.

Hoffman, C. 1987. The Long Bay Site, San Salvador. *American Archaeology* 6(2):96–101.

Hoffman, M. 1979. *Egypt Before the Pharaohs.* New York: Knopf.

———. 1983. Where nations began. *Science 83* 4(8):42–51.

Hoggart, S., and M. Hutchinson. 1995. *Bizarre Beliefs.* London: Richard Cohen Books.

Holden, C. 2000. Random samples. *Science* 290:1083.

———. 2006. Earliest America. *Science* 316:809.

Holden, C. 2007. The mammoth and the modern mind. *Science* 316:1821.

Hole, F. 1981. *Saga America:* Book review. *Bulletin of the Archaeological Society of Connecticut* 44:81–83.

Hole, F., K. Flannery, and J. A. Neely. 1969. *Prehistory and Human Ecology of the Deh Luran Plain: An Early Village Sequence from Khuzistan, Iran.* Ann Arbor: University of Michigan Press.

Hopkin, M. 2004. Return of the mummy: An ancient Egyptian has a virtual life at London's British Museum. *Nature* 430:406.

Howard, R. W. 1975. *The Dawn Seekers.* New York: Harcourt Brace Jovanovich.

Huddleston, L. 1967. *Origins of the American Indians: European Concepts, 1492–1729.* Austin: University of Texas Press.

Hughes, R. 1995. Behold the Stone Age. *Time* 145(6):52ff.

Hutchins, R. M. (ed.). 1952. *The Dialogues of Plato,* trans. B. Jowett. Chicago: William Benton/Encyclopaedia Britannica.

Incredible Discovery of Noah's Ark, The. 1993. Sun International Pictures.

Ingstad, A. S. 1977. *The Discovery of a Norse Settlement in America.* Oslo, Norway: Universitetsforlaget.

———. 1982. The Norse settlement of L'Anse aux Meadows, Newfoundland. In *Vikings in the West,* ed. E. Guralnick, pp. 31–37. Chicago: Archaeological Institute of America.

Ingstad, H. 1964. Viking ruins prove Vikings found the New World. *National Geographic* 126(5):708–734.

———. 1971. Norse site at L'Anse aux Meadows. In *The Quest for America,* ed. G. Ashe, pp. 175–198. New York: Praeger.

———. 1982. The discovery of a Norse settlement in America: In *Vikings in the West,* ed. E. Guralnick, pp. 24–30. Chicago: Archaeological Institute of America.

Ingstad, H., and A. S. Ingstad. 2000. *The Viking Discovery of America: The Excavation of a Norse Settlement in L'Anse aux Meadows, Newfoundland.* St. John's, Newfoundland: Breakwater Books.

Irving, R., and J. Lundberg. 2006. *The Field Guide: The Art, History, and Philosophy of Crop Circle Making.* London: Strange Attractor Press.

Isaak, M. 1998. Problems with a global flood. http://www.talkorigins.org/faqs/faq-noahs-ark.html.

Iseminger, W. R. 1996. Mighty Cahokia. *Archaeology* 49(3):30–37.

Ives, R. 1956. An early speculation concerning the Asiatic origin of the American Indians. *American Antiquity* 21:420–421.

Jackson, K., and J. Stamp. 2003. *Building the Great Pyramid.* Buffalo: Firefly Books.

Jacobsen, T. W. 1976. 17,000 years of Greek prehistory. *Scientific American* 234(6):76–87.

James, P. 1998. *The Sunken Kingdom: The Atlantis Mystery Solved.* London: Ramboro Books.

Jaroff, L. 1993. Phony arkaeology. *Time,* July 5, p. 51.

Jesus, Magdalene & son in Talpiot tomb. 2007. *Jerusalem Post,* Jerusalem. February 26, 2007. http://www.jpost.com/servlet/Satellite?pagename=JPost%2FJPArticle%2FShowFull&cid=1171894518254.

Jochim, M. 1983. Paleolithic cave art in ecological perspective. In *Hunter-Gatherer Economy in Prehistory: A European Perspective,* ed. G. Bailey, pp. 211–219. Cambridge: Cambridge University Press.

Johanson, D., and M. Edey. 1982. *Lucy: The Beginnings of Humankind.* New York: Warner Books.

Johnson, E. B. 1994. Not all tabloids are created equal, but they sure sell. *National Forum* 74(4):26–29.

Johnson, T. 2008. *Solving Stonehenge: The New Key to an Ancient Enigma.* London: Thames and Hudson.

Jones, D. 1979. *Visions of Time: Experiments in Psychic Archaeology.* Wheaton, Ill.: Theosophical Publishing House.

Jones, G. 1982. Historical evidence for Viking voyages to the New World. In *Vikings in the West,* ed. E. Guralnick, pp. 1–12. Chicago: Archaeological Institute of America.

———. 1986. *The Norse Atlantic Saga.* New York: Oxford University Press.

Josenhans, H., D. Fedje, R. Pienitz, and J. Southon. 1997. Early humans and rapidly changing Holocene sea levels in the Queen Charlotte Islands–Hectate Strait, British Columbia, Canada. *Science* 277:71–74.

Josselyn, J. 1674. *An Account of Two Voyages to New England Made During the Years 1638, 1663.* 1865 reprint. Boston: W. Veazie.

Kampschror, B. 2006. Pyramid scheme: Has a Houston contractor discovered the world's oldest pyramids in Bosnia? *Archaeology* 59(4):22–28.

Kehoe, A. B. 1989. *The Ghost Dance: Ethnohistory and Revitalization.* New York: Holt, Rinehart and Winston.

———. 2005. *The Kensington Runestone: Approaching a Research Question Holistically.* Long Grove, Ill.: Waveland Press.

Keith, A. 1913. The Piltdown skull and brain cast. *Nature* 92:197–199.

Kemp, B. J. 1991. *Ancient Egypt: Anatomy of a Civilization.* New York: Routledge.

Kennedy, D. 2005. Twilight for the enlightenment. *Science* 308:165.

Kennedy, K. A. R. 1975. *Neanderthal Man.* Minneapolis: Burgess Press.

Kerr, R. A. 2007. Support is drying up for Noah's Flood filling the Black Sea. *Science* 317:886.

King, M. R., and G. M. Cooper. 2004. *Who Killed King Tut? Using Modern Forensics to Solve a 3,300-Year-Old Mystery.* Buffalo: Prometheus Books.

Kopper, P. 1986. *The Smithsonian Book of North American Indians Before the Coming of the Europeans.* Washington, D.C.: Smithsonian Books.

Kosok, P., and M. Reiche. 1949. Ancient drawings on the desert of Peru. *Archaeology* 2(4):206–215.

Krause, J., et al. 2007. Neanderthals in Central Asia and Siberia. *Nature* 449:902–904.

Kuban, G. 1989a. Retracking those incredible mantracks. *National Center for Science Education Reports* 94(4):13–16.

———. 1989b. Elongate dinosaur tracks. In *Dinosaur Tracks and Traces,* ed. D. D. Gillette and M. G. Lockley, pp. 57–72. New York: Cambridge University Press.

Kühne, R. W. 2004. A location for "Atlantis"? *Antiquity* 78(300).

Künzle, A. 2006. Closure of Mystery Park is no enigma. *SwissInfo.* http://www.swissinfo.org/eng/top_news/detail/Closure_of_Mystery_Park_is_no_enigma.html?siteSect=106&sid=7266028&cKey=1163955688000.

Kusche, L. 1995. *The Bermuda Triangle Mystery Solved.* Buffalo: Prometheus Books.

Kvamme, K. L. 2003. Geophysical surveys as landscape archaeology. *American Antiquity* 68:435–457.

Lafayette wonder, The. 1869. *Syracuse Daily Journal,* Oct. 20. Syracuse, N.Y.

Lamberg-Karlovsky, C. C., and J. A. Sabloff. 1995. *Ancient Civilizations: The Near East and Mesoamerica.* Prospect Heights, Ill.: Waveland Press.

Larson, E. J., and L. Witham. 1997. Scientists are still keeping the faith. *Nature* 386:435–436.

Lawler, A. 2011. America's lost city. *Science* 334:1618–1623.

Lee, D. 1965. Appendix on Atlantis. In *Plato,* pp. 146–167. New York: Penguin.

LeHaye, T., and J. Morris. 1976. *The Ark on Ararat.* San Diego: Creation Life.

Lehner, M. 1997. *The Complete Pyramids: Solving the Ancient Mysteries.* London: Thames and Hudson.

Lepper, B. T. 1995a. Hidden history, hidden agenda. *Skeptic* 4(1):98–100.

———. 1995b. *People of the Mounds: Ohio's Hopewell Culture.* Hopewell, Ohio: Hopewell Culture National Historical Park.

———. 1995c. Tracking Ohio's Great Hopewell Road. *Archaeology* 48(6):52–56.

———. 1998a. Ancient astronomers of the Ohio Valley. *Timeline* 15(1):2–11.

———. 1998b. Great Serpent. *Timeline* 15(5):30–45.

———. 2001. Paleolithic archaeological frauds. *Current Research in the Pleistocene* 18:vii–ix.

———. 2002. *The Newark Earthworks: A Wonder of the Ancient World.* Columbus: Ohio Historical Society.

————. 2005. *Ohio Archaeology: An Illustrated Chronicle of Ohio's Ancient American Indian.* Wilmington, Ohio: Orange Frazer Press.

Lepper, B. T. 2009. New light shone on "Old Relics." *Columbus Dispatch.* July 12. http://www.dispatch.com/live/content/science/stories/2009/07/12/light .html?sid=101.

Lepper, B. T., and J. Gill. 2000. The Newark Holy Stones. *Timeline* 17(3):16–25.

Lerner, L. S., U. Goodenough, J. Lynch, M. Schwartz, and R. Schwartz. 2012. *The State of State Science Standards.* Thomas B. Fordham Institute. http://www .edexcellence.net/.

Leroi-Gourhan, A. 1968. The evolution of Paleolithic art. *Scientific American* 209(2):58–74.

Lewis-Williams, J. D., and T. A. Dowson. 1988. The signs of all times. *Current Anthropology* 29(2):201–217.

Lieberman, L., and R. C. Kirk. 1996. The trial is over: Religious voices for evolution and the "fairness" doctrine. *Creation/Evolution* 16(2):1–9.

Lipo, C. P., and S. Sakai. 2009. *Luminescence Results—Clay Tablet Sample (IIRMES-0041).*

Lippard, J. 1994. Sun goes down in flames: The Jammal ark hoax. *Skeptic* 2(3):22–33.

Lippert, D. 1997. In front of the mirror: Native Americans and academic archaeology. In *Native Americans and Archaeologists: Stepping Stones to Common Ground,* ed. N. Swindler, K. E. Dongoske, R. Anyon, and A. S. Downer, pp. 120–127. Walnut Creek, Calif.: AltaMira Press.

Lovgren, S. 2004. Masks, other finds suggest early Maya flourished. National Geographic News. http://news.nationalgeographic.com/news/2004/05/0504_040 505_mayamasks.html.

Luce, J. V. 1969. *Lost Atlantis: New Light on an Old Legend.* New York: McGraw-Hill.

MacCurdy, G. 1914. The man of Piltdown. *Science* 40:158–160.

MacNeish, R. S. 1967. An interdisciplinary approach to an archaeological problem. In *The Prehistory of the Tehuacan Valley,* vol. 1, *Environment and Subsistence,* ed. D. Byers, pp. 14–23. Austin: University of Texas Press.

Magnusson, M., and H. Paulsson (trans.). 1965. *The Vinland Sagas.* New York: Penguin.

Malin, M. 1995. The "Face on Mars." http://barsoom.msss.com/education/facepage/ face.html.

Manifort, R. C. Jr., and M. L. Kwas. 2004. The Bat Creek Stone revisited. *American Antiquity* 69:761–769.

Manning, S. W., C. B. Ramsey, W. Kutschera, T. Higham, B. Kromer, P. Steier, and W. M. Wild. 2006. Chronology for the Aegean Late Bronze Age 1700–1400 B.C. *Science* 312:565–569.

Marden, L. 1986. The first land fall of Columbus. *National Geographic* 170(5):572–577.

Marshack, A. 1972. *The Roots of Civilization.* New York: McGraw-Hill.

Mayor, A. 2005. *Fossil Legends of the First Americans.* Princeton: Princeton University Press.

Martin, S. 2008. *Chronicle of the Maya Kings and Queens: Deciphering the Dynasties of the Ancient Maya.* London: Thames and Hudson.

Martinson, B. C., M. S. Anderson, and R. de Vries. 2005. Scientists behaving badly. *Nature* 435:737–738.

Mayor, A. 2000. *The First Fossil Hunters: Paleontology in Greek and Roman Times.* Princeton: Princeton University Press.

McCarthy, C. 2009. OMG! Did Google Earth find Atlantis? February 20. http://news .cnet.com/omg-did-google-earth-find-atlantis/.

McCrone, W. C. 1982. Shroud image is the work of an artist. *Skeptical Inquirer* 6(3):35–36.

———. 1990. The Shroud of Turin: Blood or artist's pigment? *Accounts of Chemical Research* 23:77–83.

———. 1996. *Judgement Day for the Turin Shroud.* Chelsea, Mich.: McCrone Research Institute.

———. 2000. The shroud image. *Microscope* 48(2):79–85.

McDougall, I., F. H. Brown, and J. G. Fleagle. 2005. Stratigraphic placement and age of modern humans from Kibish, Ethiopia. *Nature* 433:733–736.

McGhee, R. 1984. Contact between native North Americans and the medieval Norse: A review of the evidence. *American Antiquity* 49:4–26.

McGovern, T. 1980–81. The Vinland adventure: A North Atlantic perspective. *North American Archaeologist* 2(4):285–308.

———. 1982. The lost Norse colony of Greenland. In *Vikings in the West,* ed. E. Guralnick, pp. 13–23. Chicago: Archaeological Institute of America.

McIntyre, I. 1975. Mystery of the ancient Nazca lines. *National Geographic* 147(5):716–728.

McKillop, H. 1994. Ancient Maya tree-cropping. *Ancient Mesoamerica* 5:129–140.

McKown, D. B. 1993. *The Mythmakers Magic: Behind the Illusion of "Creation Science."* Amherst, N.Y.: Prometheus Books.

McKusick, M. 1976. Contemporary American folklore about antiquity. *Bulletin of the Philadelphia Anthropological Society* 28:1–23.

———. 1982. Psychic archaeology: Theory, method, and mythology. *Journal of Field Archaeology* 9:99–118.

———. 1984. Psychic archaeology from Atlantis to Oz. *Archaeology* Sept./Oct.:48–52.

———. 1991. *The Davenport Conspiracy Revisited.* Ames: Iowa State University Press.

McNaughton, D. 2000. A world in transition: Early cartography of the North Atlantic. In *Vikings: The North Atlantic Saga,* ed. W. W. Fitzhugh and E. I. Ward, pp. 257–269. Washington, D.C.: Smithsonian Institution Press.

Meltzer, D. J. 1997. Monte Verde and the Pleistocene peopling of the Americas. *Science* 276:754–755.

Meltzer, D. J. 2009. *First Peoples in a New World: Colonizing Ice Age America.* Berkeley: University of California Press.

Menzies, G. 2002. *1421: The Year China Discovered America.* New York: Perennial.

Merriwether, D. A., G. S. Cabana, and D. M. Reed. 2000. Kennewick Man ancient DNA analysis: Final report submitted to the Department of the Interior, National Park Service. http://www.cr.nps.gov/archeology/kennewick/merriwether_cabana.htm.

Michigan Historical Museum. 2004. Digging up controversy: The Michigan Relics. http://www.sos.state.mi.us/history/michrelics/index.html.

Millar, R. 1972. *The Piltdown Men.* New York: Ballantine Books.

Miller, G. S. Jr. 1915. The jaw of Piltdown man. *Smithsonian Miscellaneous Collections* 65:1–31.

Miller, K. R. 2008. *Only a Theory: Evolution and the Battle for America's Soul.* New York: Viking.

Milner, G. R. 2004. *The Moundbuilders: Ancient Peoples of Eastern North America.* London: Thames and Hudson.

Montague, A. 1960. Artificial thickening of bone and the Piltdown skull. *Nature* 187:174.

Montgomery, J. 2002. *How to Read Maya Hieroglyphs.* New York: Hippocrene Books.

Mooney, J. 1892–93. *The Ghost-Dance Religion and the Sioux Outbreak of 1890.* 1965 reprint. Chicago: University of Chicago Press.

Moore, C. 1860. Editorial note. *Masonic Review* 23(6):379.

Moore, R. A. 1983. The impossible voyage of Noah's ark. *Creation/Evolution* XI:1–43.

Morgan, J. 2008. Dig pinpoints Stonehenge origins. http://news.bbc.co.uk/2/hi/science/nature/7625145.stm.

Morris, H. 1986. The Paluxy River Mystery. *Impact* No. 151. El Cajon, Calif.: Creation Research Institute.

Morris, J. 1980. *Tracking Those Incredible Dinosaurs and the People Who Knew Them.* San Diego: Creation Life.

Mueller, M. 1982. The Shroud of Turin: A critical approach. *Skeptical Inquirer* 6(3):15–34.

NASA. 2001. Unmasking the "Face on Mars." http://science.nasa.gov/headlines/y2001/ast24may_1.htm?list540155.

Neudorfer, G. 1980. *Vermont Stone Chambers: An Inquiry into Their Past.* Montpelier: Vermont Historical Society.

News. 1912. *Nature* 92:390.

Nickell, J. 1983. The Nazca drawings revisited. *Skeptical Inquirer* 7(3):36–44.

———. 1987. *Inquest on the Shroud of Turin.* 2nd ed. Buffalo: Prometheus Books.

———. 1989. Unshrouding a mystery: Science, pseudoscience and the cloth of Turin. *Skeptical Inquirer* 13(3):296–299.

Noonan, J. P., et al. 2006. Sequencing and analysis of Neanderthal genomic DNA. *Science* 314:1113–1118.

Normile, D. 2001a. Japanese fraud highlights media-driven research ethic. *Science* 291:34–35.

———. 2001b. Questions arise over second Japanese site. *Science* 294:1634.

Nuland, S. B. 2003. *The Doctors' Plague: Genes, Childbed Fever, and the Strange Story of Ignac Semmelweis.* New York: Norton.

Oakley, K. P. 1976. The Piltdown problem reconsidered. *Antiquity* 50 (March):9–13.

Oakley, K. P., and J. S. Weiner. 1955. Piltdown Man. *American Scientist* 43:573–583.

O'Connor, D. 2003. Origins of the pyramids. In *The Seventy Great Mysteries of Ancient Egypt,* ed. B. Manley, pp. 45–49. London: Thames and Hudson.

Oestreicher, D. 2008. *Grave Creek Stone.* Unpublished ms.

Officer, L. H., and S. H. Williamson. 2007. Purchasing power of money in the United States from 1774 to 2006. MeasuringWorth. http://measuringworth.com/ppowerus/.

Oldest boat of pharaohs found. October 31, 2000. http://www.discovery.com/news/briefs/20001031/hi_royalboat.html.

Olding-Smee, L. 2007. Dig links Stonehenge to circle of life. *Nature* 445:574.

Omohundro, J. T. 1976. Von Däniken's chariots: A primer in the art of crooked science. *Zetetic* 1(1):58–67.

One-third believe in ghosts, UFOs. 2007. Poll. http://www.usatoday.com/news/offbeat/2007-10-25-ghosts-poll_N.htm.

Ortega, T. 2012. Vi Simpson: The woman who punked the radical Republicans in the Indiana State Senate and their creationist bill. http://blogs.villagevoice.com/runninscared/2012/02/vi_simpson_the.php.

Ortiz de Montellano, B. 1991. Multicultural pseudoscience: Spreading scientific illiteracy among minorities: Part I. *Skeptical Inquirer* 16(1):46–50.

———. 1992. Magic melanin: Spreading scientific illiteracy among minorities: Part II. *Skeptical Inquirer* 16(2):162–166.

Ortiz de Montellano, B., G. Haslip-Viera, and Warren Barbour. 1997a. Robbing Native American cultures: Van Sertima and the Olmecs. *Current Anthropology* 38:419–441.

———. 1997b. They were not here before Columbus: Afrocentric diffusionism in the 1990s. *Ethnohistory* 44:199–234.

Orton, C. 2000. *Sampling in Archaeology.* Cambridge: Cambridge University Press.

Osborn, H. F. 1921. The Dawn Man of Piltdown, Sussex. *Natural History* 21:577–590.

Packard, M. 2006. *MythBusters: Don't Try This at Home.* San Francisco: Jossey-Bass.

Paleolithic Man. 1912. *Nature* 92:438.

Paleolithic skull is missing link. 1912. *New York Times*, Dec. 19.

Park, M. P. 2012. *Exploring Evolution.* London: Vivays.

Pauketat, T. R. 1994. *The Ascent of Chiefs: Cahokia and Mississippian Politics in Native America.* Tuscaloosa: University of Alabama Press.

———. 2009. *Cahokia: Ancient America's Great City on the Mississippi.* New York: Viking.

Pauwels, L., and J. Bergier. 1960. *The Morning of the Magicians.* 1964 reprint. New York: Stein and Day.

Pearsall, D. 1992. The origins of plant cultivation in South America. In *The Origins of Agriculture: An International Perspective*, ed. C. W. Cowan and P. J. Watson, pp. 173–205. Washington, D.C.: Smithsonian Institution Press.

Pellegrino, C. 1991. *Unearthing Atlantis: An Archaeological Odyssey.* New York: Random House.

Perez-Accino, J.-R. 2003a. The Great Pyramid. In *The Seventy Great Mysteries of Ancient Egypt*, ed. B. Manley, pp. 61–66. London: Thames and Hudson.

———. 2003b. The multiple pyramids of Snofru. In *The Seventy Great Mysteries of Ancient Egypt*, ed. B. Manley, pp. 57–60. London: Thames and Hudson.

———. 2003c. Were the pyramids built by slaves? In *The Seventy Great Mysteries of Ancient Egypt*, ed. B. Manley, pp. 54–56. London: Thames and Hudson.

Phillipson, D. W. 1993. *African Archaeology.* 2nd ed. Cambridge: Cambridge University Press.

Pigliucci, M. 2010. *Nonsense on Stilts: How to Tell Science from Bunk.* Chicago: University of Chicago Press.

Poole, B. 2007. *Madonna of the Toast.* New York: Mark Batty Publisher.

Poundstone, W. 1999. *Carl Sagan: A Life in the Cosmos.* New York: Henry Holt.

Powell, E. 2004. Theme park of the gods? *Archaeology* 57(1):62–67.

Powell, J. F., and J. C. Rose. 1999. Report on the osteological assessment of the "Kennewick Man" skeleton. National Park Service. http://www.nps.gov/archeology/Kennewick/powell_rose.html.

Pringle, H. 1997. Death in Norse Greenland. *Science* 275:924–926.

Pruit, T. 2012. The politics and performance of pseudo-pyramids. Paper presented at the annual meeting of the *Society for American Archaeology*. Memphis Tennessee. April 9.

Putnam, C. E. 1886. The Davenport Tablets. *Science* 7(157):119–120.

Quilici, B. 2005. *King Tut's Final Secrets.* Video; National Geographic.

Quinion, M. B. 2008. *Cidermaking.* Oxford: Shire Publications.

Quinn, D. B. (ed.). 1979. *New American World: A Documentary History of North America to 1612.* New York: Arno Press.

Ramenofsky, A. F. 1987. *Vectors of Death.* Albuquerque: University of New Mexico Press.

Randi, J. 1975. *The Magic of Uri Geller.* New York: Ballantine Books.

———. 1979. A controlled test of dowsing abilities. *Skeptical Inquirer* 4(1):16–20.

———. 1981. Atlantean road: The Bimini beach-rock. *Skeptical Inquirer* 5(3):42–43.

———. 1984. The great $110,000 dowsing challenge. *Skeptical Inquirer* 8(4):329–333.

———. 1993. *The Mask of Nostradamus.* Buffalo: Prometheus Books.

Ravilous, K. 2006. Noah's ark discovered in Iran? *National Geographic News.* http://news.nationalgeographic.com/news/2006/07/060705-noahs-ark.html.

Reiche, M. 1978. *Mystery on the Desert.* Stuttgart: Heinrich Fink.

Rice, P., and A. Paterson. 1985. Cave art and bones: Exploring the interrelationships. *American Anthropologist* 87:94–100.

———. 1986. Validating the cave art-archaeofaunal relationship in Cantabrian Spain. *American Anthropologist* 88:658–667.

Richardson, S. 2000. Vanished Vikings. *Discover* 21(3):64–69.

Roach, J. 1999. Everest climbs to new heights. National Geographic Society. http://www.ngnews.com/news/1999/11/111299/everest_7303.asp.

Robertson, M. G. 1974. *Primera Mesa Redonda de Palenque.* Pebble Beach, Calif.: Robert Louis Stevenson School.

Rogers, R. N. 2005. Studies on the radiocarbon sample from the Shroud of Turin. *Thermochimica Acta* 425:189–194.

Romer, J. 2012. *A History of Ancient Egypt: From the First Farmers to the Great Pyramid.* New York: Penguin Global.

Rose, C., and G. Wright. 2004. Inscribed matter as an energy-efficient means of communication with an extraterrestrial civilization. *Nature* 431:47–49.

Ross, A., and P. Reynolds. 1978. "Ancient Vermont." *Antiquity* 52:100–107.

Rowe, J. H. 1966. Diffusionism and archaeology. *American Antiquity* 31:334–337.

Rowland, I. D. 2004. *The Scarith of Scornello: A Tale of Renaissance Forgery.* Chicago: University of Chicago Press.

Ruggles, C. 1996. Stonehenge for the 1990s. *Nature* 381:278–279.

Ruspoli, M. 1986. *The Cave of Lascaux: The Final Photographs.* New York: Abrams.

Russell, M. 2003. *Piltdown Man: The Secret Life of Charles Dawson & the World's Greatest Archaeological Hoax.* Gloucestershire: Tempus.

Ryan, W., and W. Pitman. 1998. *Noah's Flood: The New Scientific Discoveries About the Event That Changed History.* New York: Touchstone.

Sabloff, J. 1989. *The Cities of Ancient Mexico: Reconstructing a Lost World.* New York: Thames and Hudson.

———. 1994. *The New Archaeology and the Ancient Maya.* New York: Scientific American Library.

Sagan, C. 1963. Direct contact among galactic civilizations by relativistic interstellar spaceflight. *Planetary Space Science* 11:485–498.

———. 1996. *The Demon-Haunted World: Science as a Candle in the Dark.* New York: Random House.

Saturno, W. A., D. Stuart, A. F. Aveni, and F. Rossi. 2012. Ancient Maya astronomical tables from Xultun, Guatemala. *Science* 336:714–717.

Saunders, J. W., R. D. Mandel, R. T. Saucier, E. T. Allen, C. T. Hallmark, J. K. Johnson, E. H. Jackson, C. M. Allen, G. L. Stringer, D. S. Frink, J. K. Feathers, S. Williams, K. J. Gremillion, M. F. Vidrine, and R. Jones. 1997. A mound complex in Louisiana at 5400–5000 years before the present. *Science* 277:1796–1799.

Saura Ramos, P. A. 1998. *The Cave of Altamira.* New York: Abrams.

Schele, L., and D. Freidel. 1990. *A Forest of Kings.* New York: William Morrow.

Schick, T., and L. Vaughn. 2010. *How to Think About Weird Things: Critical Thinking for a New Age.* New York: Prometheus Books.

Schledermann, P. 1981. Eskimo and Viking finds in the High Arctic. *National Geographic* 159(5):575–601.

———. 2000. Ellesmere: Vikings in the far north. In *Vikings: The North Atlantic Saga*, ed. W. W. Fitzhugh and E. I. Ward, pp. 248–256. Washington, D.C.: Smithsonian Institution Press.

Schmid, R. E. 2008. Study: Stonehenge was a burial site for centuries. http://news .yahoo.com/s/ap/20080529/ap_on_sc/sci_stonehenge_8.

Schnabel, J. 1994. *Round in Circles: Poltergeists, Pranksters, and the Secret History of Crop Watchers*. Buffalo: Prometheus Books.

Schneour, E. 1986. Occam's razor. *Skeptical Inquirer* 10(4):310–313.

Schoolcraft, H. R. 1854. *Historical and Statistical Information Regarding the History, Condition, and Prospects of the Indian Tribes of the United States*. Part IV. Philadelphia: Grambo.

Schwartz, S. 1978. *The Secret Vaults of Time: Psychic Archaeology and the Quest for Man's Beginnings*. New York: Grosset and Dunlap.

———. 1983. *The Alexandria Project*. New York: Delacorte Press.

Seaver, K. A. 2004. *Maps, Myths, and Men: The Story of the Vinland Map*. Stanford: Stanford University Press.

Secrets of Lost Empires: Stonehenge (television program). 1997. *Nova*. Boston: WGBH.

Selling it: Monkey business. 2000. *Consumer Reports* 65(9):67.

Severin, T. 1977. The voyages of "Brendan." *National Geographic* 152(6):770–797.

Shafer, H. J. 1997. Research design and sampling technique. In *Field Methods in Archaeology*, ed. T. R. Hester, H. Shafer, and K. L. Feder, pp. 21–40. Mountain View, Calif.: Mayfield Publishing.

Shapiro, H. 1974. *Peking Man: The Discovery, Disappearance, and Mystery of a Priceless Scientific Treasure*. New York: Simon and Schuster.

Shaw, I. (ed.) 2000. *The Oxford History of Ancient Egypt*. London: Oxford University Press.

Shaw, J. 2003. Who built the pyramids? *Harvard Magazine*, July/August: 43–49, 99.

Shermer, M. 1997. *Why People Believe Weird Things*. New York: W. H. Freeman.

Shermer, M., and A. Grobman. 2000. *Denying History: Who Says the Holocaust Never Happened and Why Do They Say It?* Berkeley: University of California Press.

Silverberg, R. 1989. *The Moundbuilders*. Athens: Ohio University Press.

Skelton, R. A., T. Marston, and G. O. Painter. 1995. *The Vinland Map and the Tartar Relation*. New Haven: Yale University Press.

Skidmore, J. 2004. Cival: A Preclassic Maya site in the news. *MesoWeb*. http://www .mesoweb.com/reports/cival.html#.

Slack, G. 2007. *The Battle Over the Meaning of Everything: Evolution, Intelligent Design, and a School Board in Dover, PA*. New York: Jossey-Bass.

Smith, B. D. 1995. *The Emergence of Agriculture*. New York: Scientific American Library.

Smith, C. B. 2004. *How the Great Pyramid Was Built*. New York: Smithsonian Books.

Smith, G. E. 1927. *Essays on the Evolution of Man*. London: Oxford University Press.

So big: The all time mass market best sellers. 1989. *Publishers Weekly*, May 26:531.

Solheim, W. 1972. An earlier agricultural revolution. *Scientific American* 226(4):34–41.

Spanuth, J. 1979. *Atlantis of the North*. London: Sidgwick and Jackson.

Spencer, F. 1984. The Neandertals and their evolutionary significance: A brief history and historical survey. In *The Origins of Modern Humans: A World Survey of the Fossil Evidence*, ed. F. Smith and F. Spencer, pp. 1–50. New York: Alan R. Liss.

———. 1990. *Piltdown: A Scientific Forgery*. Oxford: Oxford University Press.

Spencer, F., and C. Stringer. 1989. Piltdown. In Radiocarbon dates from the Oxford AMS system: Archaeometry Datelist 9, ed. R. E. M. Hedgtes, R. A. Housley, I. A. Law, and C. R. Bronk. *Archaeometry* 31:207–234.

Squier, E. G., and E. H. Davis. 1848. *Ancient Monuments of the Mississippi Valley: Comprising the Results of Extensive Original Surveys and Explorations.* Smithsonian Contributions to Knowledge, vol. 1. New York: AMS Press (reprinted in 1973 for the Peabody Museum of Archaeology and Ethnology, Harvard University).

Stanford, D., and B. Bradley. 2000. The Solutrean solution: Did some ancient Americans come from Europe? *Discovering Archaeology* 2(1):54–55.

Stanford, D. J., and B. Bradley. 2012. *Across the Atlantic Ice: The Origin of America's Clovis Culture.* Berkeley: University of California Press.

Stevenson, K. (ed.). 1977. *Proceedings of the 1977 United States Conference of Research on the Shroud of Turin, March 23–24, 1977,* Albuquerque, New Mexico. New York: Holy Shroud Guild, Bronx.

Stevenson, K. E., and G. R. Habermas. 1981a. *Verdict on the Shroud.* Ann Arbor, Mich.: Servant Publications.

———. 1981b. We tested the shroud. *Catholic Digest,* Nov.:74–78.

Steward, T. D. 1973. *The People of America.* New York: Scribner's.

Stiebing, W. 1984. *Ancient Astronauts, Cosmic Collisions, and Other Popular Theories About Man's Past.* Buffalo: Prometheus Books.

Stone Giant, The. 1869. *Syracuse Standard,* Nov. 1. Syracuse, N.Y.

Stowe, S. 2001. Archaeological hoax raises query: Why? *New York Times,* March 4, Section 14CN, p. 3.

Strahler, A. N. 1999. *Science and Earth History: The Evolution/Creation Controversy.* Amherst, N.Y.: Prometheus Books.

Straus, L. G. 2000. Solutrean settlement of North America? A review of reality. *American Antiquity* 65:219–226.

Stuart, G. 1993. New light on the Olmec. *National Geographic* 184(5):88–115.

Stukeley, W. 1752. Memoirs of Sir Isaac Newton. In *The Newton Project* (2010), edited by R. Iliffe. University of Sussex, East Sussex. http://www.newtonproject.sussex.ac.uk/view/texts/normalized/OTHE00001.

Sullivan, W. T. III. 2004. Message in a bottle. *Nature* 431:27–28.

Sutherland, P. D. 2000a. The Norse and Native North Americans. In *Vikings: The North Atlantic Saga,* ed. W. W. Fitzhugh and E. I. Ward, pp. 238–247. Washington, D.C.: Smithsonian Institution Press.

———. 2000b. *Scattered Signs: The Evidence for Native/Norse Contact in North America.* Paper presented at Vikings, The North Atlantic Saga, Washington, D.C.

Swanton, J. R. 1985. *Final Report of the United States De Soto Expedition Commission [1939].* 1939 ed. Classics of Smithsonian Anthropology. Washington D.C.: Smithsonian Institution Press.

Swauger, J. L. 1980. Petroglyphs, tar burner rocks, and lye leaching stones. *Pennsylvania Archaeologist* 51(1–2):1–7.

Tattersall, I., and J. Schwartz. 2000. *Extinct Humans.* New York: Westview Press.

Taylor, P. 1985a. *Young People's Guide to the Bible and the Great Dinosaur Mystery.* Mesa, Ariz.: Films for Christ Association.

———. 1985b. *Notice Regarding the Motion Picture "Footprints in Stone."* Mesa, Ariz.: Films for Christ Association.

Taylor, R. E., and R. Berger. 1980. The date of Noah's Ark. *Antiquity* 44:34–36.

This Old Pyramid (television program). 1993. *Nova.* Boston: WGBH.

Thomas, C. 1894. *Report on the Mound Explorations of the Bureau of Ethnology.* Washington, D.C.: BAE (reprinted 1985 by Smithsonian Institution Press).

Thomas, D. H. 2000. *Skull Wars: Kennewick Man, Archaeology, and the Battle for Native American Identity.* New York: Basic Books.

Thomas, D. H., and R. L. Kelly. 2010. *Archaelogy: Down to Earth.* 4th ed. Belmont, Calif.: Wadsworth.

Tobias, P. V. 1992. Piltdown: An appraisal of the case against Sir Arthur Keith. *Current Anthropology* 33(3):243–260.

Toner, M. 2006. Impossibly old America? New sites and controversial theories fuel the debate over the origins of America's first people. *Archaeology* 59(3):40–45.

Tribble, S. 2009. *A Colossal Hoax: The Giant From Cardiff That Fooled America.* New York: Rowman and Littlefield.

Trivedi, B. P. 2004. Jesus shroud? Recent findings renew authenticity debate. *National Geographic News.* http://www.nationalgeographic.com/news/2004/04/0409_040 409_TVJesusshroud.html.

Turner, B. L., and P. Harrison (eds.). 1983. *Pulltrouser Swamp: Ancient Maya Habitat, Agriculture, and Settlement in Northern Belize.* Austin: University of Texas Press.

Turner, C. G. 1987. Telltale teeth. *Natural History,* Jan.:6–10.

UFOs and extraterrestrial life: Americans' beliefs and personal experiences. 2002. http://www.scifi.com/ufo/roper/.

Updates. 2010. *Reports of the National Center for Science Education* 30(1–2):4–11.

van Kampen, H. 1979. The case of the lost panda. *Skeptical Inquirer* 4(1):48–50.

Van Sertima, I. 1976. *They Came Before Columbus.* New York: Random House.

Van Tilburg, J. A. 1994. *Easter Island: Archaeology, Ecology, and Culture.* Washington, D.C.: Smithsonian Institution Press.

Vaughan, C. 1988. Shroud of Turin is a fake, official confirms. *Science News* 134(15):229.

Vescelius, G. 1956. Excavations at Pattee's Caves. *Bulletin of the Eastern States Archaeological Federation* 15:13–14.

Vespucci, A. 1904. *The Letters of Amerigo Vespucci and Other Documents Illustrative of His Career.* The Hakluyt Society. New York: Burt Franklin.

von Däniken, E. 1970. *Chariots of the Gods?* New York: Bantam Books.

———. 1971. *Gods from Outer Space.* New York: Bantam Books.

———. 1973. *Gold of the Gods.* New York: Bantam Books.

———. 1975. *Miracles of the Gods.* New York: Bantam Books.

———. 1982. *Pathways to the Gods.* New York: G. P. Putnam's Sons.

———. 1989. *In Search of the Gods.* New York: Avenel.

———. 1996. *The Eyes of the Sphinx: The Newest Evidence of Extraterrestrial Contact in Ancient Egypt.* New York: Berkley Books.

———. 1997a. *Chariots of the Gods? The Mysteries Continue.* Stamford, Conn.: Capital Cities/ABC Video.

———. 1997b. *The Return of the Gods.* Boston: Element Books.

———. 1998. *Arrival of the Gods: Revealing the Alien Landing Sites of Nazca.* Boston: Element Books.

———. 2000. *Odyssey of the Gods: The Alien History of Ancient Greece.* Boston: Element Books.

———. 2003. *The Gods Were Astronauts: Evidence of the True Identities of the Old "Gods."* New York: Sterling.

———. 2009. *History Is Wrong.* Pompton Plains, N.J.: New Page Books.

———. 2010. *Twilight of the Gods.* Pompton Plains, N.J.: New Page Books.

Walker, A., and R. Leakey (eds.). 1993. *The Nariokotome* Homo erectus *Skeleton.* Cambridge, Mass.: Harvard University Press.

Wallace, B. 2000. The Viking settlement at L'Anse aux Meadows. In *Vikings: The North Atlantic Saga,* ed. W. W. Fitzhugh and E. I. Ward, pp. 208–215. Washington, D.C.: Smithsonian Institution Press.

Wallbridge, T. C. 1861. Notes upon the mound structures of southern Illinois and Ohio, in the vicinity of St. Louis, Cincinnati, and Newark. *The Canadian Institute;* conference, February 23, 1861.

Walsh, J. E. 1996. *Unraveling Piltdown: The Science Fraud of the Century and Its Solution.* New York: Random House.

Walsh, J. M. 2008. Legend of the crystal skulls. *Archaeology* 61(3).

Ward, C. V., W. H. Kimbel, and D. C. Johanson. 2011. Complete fourth metatarsal and arches in the foot of *Australopithecus afarensis. Science* 331:750–753.

Warner, F. 1981. Stone structures at Gungywamp. *Bulletin of the Archaeological Society of Connecticut* 44:4–19.

Waters, M. R., S. L. Forman, T. A. Jennings, L. C. Nordt, S. G. Driese, J. M. Feinberg, J. L. Keene, J. Halligan, A. Lindquist, J. Pierson, C. T. Hallmark, M. B. Collins, and J. E. Wiederhold. 2011a. The Buttermilk Creek complex and the origins of Clovis at the Debra L. Friedkin site, Texas. *Science* 331:1599–1603.

———.M. R., T. W. Stafford Jr., H. G. McDonald, C. Gustafson, M. Rasmussen, E. Cappellini, J. V. Olsen, D. Szklarczyk, L. J. Jensen, M. T. P. Gilbert, and E. Willerslev. 2011b. Pre-Clovis mastodon hunting 13,800 years ago at the Manis Site, Washington. *Science* 334:351–353.

———.M. R., C. D. Pevny, and D. L. Carlson. 2011. *Clovis Lithic Technology: Investigation of a Stratified Workshop at the Gault Site, Texas.* College Station: Texas A&M University Press.

Waterston, D. 1913. The Piltdown mandible. *Nature* 92:319.

Watt, N., C. Romano, and S. Netter. 2010. Finding Noah's Ark: Hong Kong film-maker claims to have found biblical treasure. http://abcnews.go.com/GMA/finding-noahs-ark-filmmaker-found-pieces-biblical-treasure/story?id=10495740.

Weaver, K. 1980. Science seeks to solve the mystery of the shroud. *National Geographic* 157(4): 730–751.

Webster, D. 2002. *The Fall of the Ancient Maya: Solving the Mystery of the Maya Collapse.* London: Thames and Hudson.

Weidenreich, F. 1943. Piltdown Man. *Paleontologica Sinica* 129:273.

Weiner, J. S. 1955. *The Piltdown Forgery.* London: Oxford University Press.

Weir, S. K. 1996. Insight from geometry and physics into the construction of Egyptian Old Kingdom pyramids. *Cambridge Archaeological Journal* 6:150–163.

Wernick, R., and the editors of Time-Life Books. 1973. *The Monument Builders.* New York: Time-Life Books.

Whitcomb, J. C., and H. Morris. 1961. *The Genesis Flood.* Nutley, N.J.: Presbyterian and Reformed Publishing.

White, R. 1986. *Dark Caves, Bright Visions: Life in Ice Age Europe.* New York: Norton.

White, T. D., B. Asfaw, Y. Beyene, Y. Haile-Selassie, O. C. Lovejoy, G. Suwa, and G. WoldeGabriel. 2009. *Ardipithecus ramidus* and the paleobiology of early homi-nids. *Science* 326:64–86.

White, T. D., and G. Suwa. 1987. Hominid footprints at Laetoli: Facts and interpreta-tions. *American Journal of Physical Anthropology* 72:485–514.

Willey, G., and J. Sabloff. 1993. *A History of American Archaeology.* London: Thames and Hudson.

Wilson, D. 1988. Desert ground drawings in the lower Santa Valley, north coast of Peru. *American Antiquity* 53(4):794–803.

Wilson, I. 1979. *The Shroud of Turin: The Burial Cloth of Jesus Christ?* New York: Image Books.

Wilson, N. D. 2005. Father Brown fakes the shroud. *Book and Culture.* http://www .ctlibrary.com/bc/2005/marapr/3.22.html.

Woodward, J. 1695. *An Essay Toward a Natural History of the Earth.* London.

Wynn, T. and F. L. Cooldige 2012. *How to Think Like a Neandertal.* New York: Oxford University Press.

Yamada, S. 2002. Politics and personality: Japan's worst archaeology scandal. *Harvard Asia Quarterly* 6(3):48–54.

Yanko-Hombach, V., A. S. Gilbert, N. Panin, and P. M. Dolukhanov (eds). 2006. *The Black Sea Flood Question.* New York: Springer.

Yokoyama, Y., K. Lambeck, P. De Deckker, P. Johnsston, and L. K. Fifield. 2000. Timing of the last glacial maximum from observed sea-level minima. *Nature* 406:713–716.

Index

Note: Page numbers in *italic* indicate illustrations, tables, and figures.